"The events of 9/11 brought Christians a new ...... about the pervasive divine violence found in the .... can a God of love be involved with and, even worse, bring harm against his human creatures? Webb and Oeste have thought long and hard with great biblical insight about this question. Everyone who struggles with the ethics of divine warfare needs to read *Bloody, Brutal, and Barbaric?* in order to gain a biblical perspective on this difficult subject."

Tremper Longman III, Distinguished Scholar and Professor Emeritus of Biblical Studies, author of *Confronting Old Testament Controversies*

"William Webb and Gordon Oeste have written a courageous book dealing with some of the most challenging ethical questions about war, rape, and violence in the Old Testament. They approach it with ethical sensitivity and a high regard for biblical authority, explaining ancient war practices, and advocating what I regard as a convincing thesis about an incremental redemptive ethic. A landmark publication on a perplexing subject!"

Michael F. Bird, lecturer in theology at Ridley College, Melbourne, Australia

"Webb and Oeste have undertaken a daunting task. They have tackled a host of moral and theological questions related to the challenging, emotionally charged topic of Old Testament warfare. They have digested a large and ever-growing literature on the subject as they articulate their redemptive-movement approach. Their book not only offers a comprehensive assessment of the issues. It also adds important layers to the discussion—for example, the contrast between Israel's more humane, far-less cruel warfare practices compared to the rape and dehumanizing atrocities of other ancient Near Eastern nations. And in contrast to the work of some recent 'functional Marcionite' scholars, Webb and Oeste's judicious, nuanced, and insightful treatment of this subject recognizes the inescapable reality of *divinely* commanded warfare. They are to be congratulated on significantly advancing the discussion."

Paul Copan, Pledger Family Chair of Philosophy and Ethics, Palm Beach Atlantic University, author of *Is God a Moral Monster?*

"The authors provide an important survey of the theological implications of this, the most difficult of biblical and theological issues in our world, and move the question beyond what books such as this often do. Read this work for a better understanding of the different views. Read it even more to benefit from the fruitful connections between the God of reluctant violence in the Old Testament and the sacrifice of Jesus Christ in the New Testament."

Richard S. Hess, distinguished professor of Old Testament, Denver Seminary

"Reading the Bible well involves asking questions of the text. In probing some of the ethically troubling passages of the Old Testament, Oeste and Webb show that we not only need good questions, we must also learn to ask the right questions. Doing this helps us to place the text more carefully in its own time, while also helping us to understand more clearly how it speaks to ours. Anyone who has struggled with the issue of violence in the Bible will therefore find this volume to be a helpful and constructive guide that shows how to ask the right questions and so understand the Bible better."

David G. Firth, Old Testament tutor, Trinity College Bristol

"First you have to face and admit there's a moral problem in the Bible about God's relationship to war and violence. Then you have to believe in the Bible enough to think the Bible ought somehow to provide light at the end of this moral problem's tunnel. But how does one resolve some of those violence texts? This problem is for me a career-long vexation, and among the many studies that have brought me at least some relief, this new book by William J. Webb and Gordon K. Oeste is one of the finest because it cares about the Bible and method and results. Webb is well-known for his redemptive movement hermeneutic, and he applies it in this book with finesse and sensitivity and provides, at least for me, more relief than I've felt in a long time."

Scot McKnight, professor of New Testament at Northern Seminary

"A welcome addition to the discussion of holy war texts, Webb and Oeste's 'realigned traditional view' affirms biblical authority while asking a fresh set of questions. With thorough scholarship and pastoral sensitivity, their redemptive-movement hermeneutic suggests a way forward that acknowledges the ethical challenge of these texts without rejecting them as irredeemable. The book's measured and irenic tone invites the reader to consider its carefully-argued thesis. This is a must-read for those working with or troubled by these texts."

Lissa M. Wray Beal, professor of Old Testament, Providence Theological Seminary

"The well-chosen book title, *Bloody, Brutal, and Barbaric?*, draws readers into the violent world of the Old Testament that offends so many postmodern readers. Webb and Oeste present the pros and cons of traditional approaches to genocide and war rape before making a strong case for 'a theological reading of the biblical text with an eye to hermeneutical, ethical, canonical, and ancient-cultural contexts.' Thoughtful readers of Scripture will treasure this book because it answers their own questions and responds to those for whom the troubling texts of the Old Testament present a barrier to faith."

Marion Ann Taylor, professor of Old Testament, Wycliffe College at the University of Toronto

"The Old Testament is filled with acts of violence that offend our ethical sensibilities. Webb and Oeste have spent fourteen years wrestling with the ethical problem of these biblical texts. They are to be commended for honestly grappling with the biblical evidence rather than merely parroting shallow traditional answers or escaping to a neo-Marcionite approach that fails to respect the authority of inspired Scripture. Their analysis is grounded, as it should be, in the historical and cultural context of the Old Testament. This allows the authors to detect the presence of an 'incremental redemptive-movement ethic.' They admit that this does not completely solve the problem of the Bible's war ethic, yet it does soften the pain of reading such texts. It also points us toward a final resolution of the problem of war—a resolution that the text itself presents as an ideal and as an eschatological certainty. Webb and Oeste are careful thinkers who have thoroughly researched a scary, intimidating topic and have given us a sophisticated hermeneutical model to consider. Their courage and persistence deserve a fair hearing from both the academy and the church."

Robert B. Chisholm Jr., chair and senior professor of Old Testament Studies, Dallas Theological Seminary

"After reading through this book—the fruit of fourteen years of research—I find myself echoing the authors themselves in their concluding chapter: 'Our hearts are not nearly as heavy nor our minds as perplexed as when we first started this project.' This is the most biblically comprehensive, ethically nuanced, and persuasively argued case that I have yet encountered on one of the most troubling parts of the Bible. Writing out of profound theological reflection and deep personal suffering, the authors neither dismiss the problem ('God just commanded it; there is no problem') nor weaponize it ('We must reject a "God" who could command such things'). Instead they offer, in great detail but with constant clarity and summation of each stage of their argument, a thoroughly fresh way of addressing the issue in the light of both the Ancient Near Eastern context of Old Testament Israel and the whole canonical narrative, including the death, resurrection, and ascension of Christ, and the eschatological hope of perfect rectifying justice in the new creation. A magnificent gift for all of us who, as lovers of God and his Word, still struggle with texts that match the book's title."

Christopher J. H. Wright, Langham Partnership, author of *Knowing God Through the Old Testament* and *Old Testament Ethics for the People of God*

"Almost as confusing as the barbaric war texts themselves is the diverse array of possible 'solutions' for understanding these troubling texts. Webb and Oeste helpfully examine these brutal passages in depth, insightfully clarify when traditional answers work (or don't), and wisely provide a fresh interpretation that not only takes seriously both the Old Testament and its context but also brings clarity out of confusion."

David T. Lamb, Allan A. MacRae Professor of Old Testament at Missio Seminary, author of *God Behaving Badly* and *Prostitutes and Polygamists*

"People of faith often stumble when they trip over the 'bloody, brutal, and barbaric' texts of the Bible that seem to portray God as associated with holy war, violence, and genocide. While no one book can resolve all the complex ethical and theological issues involved, Webb and Oeste reexamine the details of these troubling texts in the context of the ancient world and the larger witness of Scripture. They attempt to shine a light on 'incrementally redemptive' elements hidden within these war texts that lessen or counteract their seeming barbarity. In the end, they argue that at the deepest core, the one God of the Old and New Testaments is a God of peace, not of war."

Dennis Olson, professor of Old Testament theology, Princeton Theological Seminary

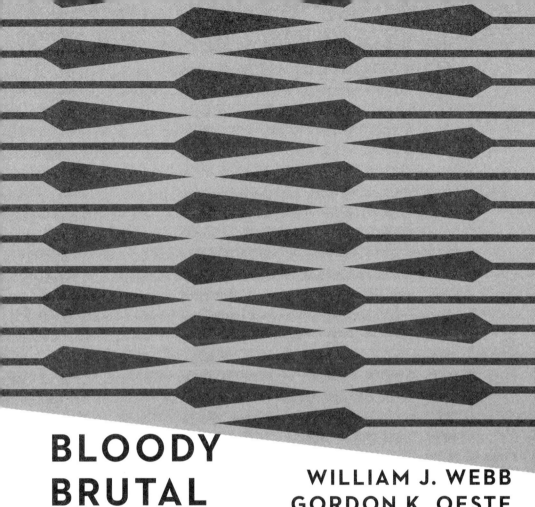

BLOODY
BRUTAL
AND
BARBARIC?

WILLIAM J. WEBB
GORDON K. OESTE

Wrestling with Troubling War Texts

ivp
Academic
An imprint of InterVarsity Press
Downers Grove, Illinois

InterVarsity Press
P.O. Box 1400, Downers Grove, IL 60515-1426
ivpress.com
email@ivpress.com

InterVarsity Press˚ is the book-publishing division of InterVarsity Christian Fellowship/USA˚, a movement of students and faculty active on campus at hundreds of universities, colleges, and schools of nursing in the United States of America, and a member movement of the International Fellowship of Evangelical Students. For information about local and regional activities, visit intervarsity.org.

Cover design and image composite: David Fassett
Interior design: Jeanna Wiggins
Images: black marble texture: © yokeetod / iStock / Getty Images Plus

ISBN 978-0-8308-5249-9 (print)
ISBN 978-0-8308-7073-8 (digital)

Printed in the United States of America ∞

InterVarsity Press is committed to ecological stewardship and to the conservation of natural resources in all our operations. This book was printed using sustainably sourced paper.

Library of Congress Cataloging-in-Publication Data
Names: Webb, William J., 1957- author. | Oeste, Gordon K., author.
Title: Bloody, brutal, and barbaric? : wrestling with troubling war texts / William J. Webb, Gordon K. Oeste.
Description: Downers Grove, Illinois: IVP Academic, an imprint of InterVarsity Press, [2019] |
  Includes bibliographical references and index.
Identifiers: LCCN 2019029417 (print) | LCCN 2019029418 (ebook) | ISBN 9780830852499 (paperback) |
  ISBN 9780830870738 (ebook)
Subjects: LCSH: War—Biblical teaching. | War—Religious aspects—Christianity.
Classification: LCC BS680.W2 W43 2019 (print) | LCC BS680.W2 (ebook) | DDC 220.8/35502—dc23
LC record available at https://lccn.loc.gov/2019029417
LC ebook record available at https://lccn.loc.gov/2019029418

| P | 22 | 21 | 20 | 19 | 18 | 17 | 16 | 15 | 14 | 13 | 12 | 11 | 10 | 9 | 8 | 7 | 6 | 5 | 4 | 3 | 2 | 1 |
| Y | 37 | 36 | 35 | 34 | 33 | 32 | 31 | 30 | 29 | 28 | 27 | 26 | 25 | 24 | 23 | 22 | 21 | 20 | 19 |

TO JAMES,

a friend whose war ethic captures

the spirit of Amos.

CONTENTS

PREFACE

The Story Behind the Book

BLOODY, BRUTAL, AND BARBARIC? Quite the question for any book. Admittedly so. Yet the title fits because this book wrestles with the ethics of holy war in Scripture. To be clear, our answer is unabashedly "yes." Yes, the biblical war texts are bloody, brutal, and barbaric. There are good reasons why these war texts are so deeply troubling. But *that daunting reality is not the whole story.* There is a powerfully intriguing side that is often missed. This book presents a search for better answers to the troubling war texts—answers that legitimately reduce their ethical challenge by noting what is often (wrongly) understood and by highlighting redemptive aspects of these difficult texts. Welcome to a fascinating journey.

It has taken fourteen years to write this book. Its reputation as long overdue has become a standing joke. I (Bill) have often laughed with various InterVarsity Press staff (particularly with Andy Le Peau) at my exceedingly prolonged efforts. In my defense, however, those years were hardly wasted. Along the way several key events shaped my thinking on the war texts. First, during these war-text years our older son, Jon, slowly slid downhill with a degenerative brain disease; from being a healthy, normal young man he gradually became a quadriplegic with the cognitive ability of a preschooler. He passed away on Saturday, June 8, 2013. That parental, crushed-love journey broke me over and over and over again. It was so intensely painful (still is at times) that I cannot describe it. But a surprising thing happened during these years. The pain—almost debilitating at times—allowed me to see the extent of my own brokenness and the brokenness of the world around me. Even more important, it allowed me to see with new eyes the connection between our brokenness and the intense grief and greater pain felt by God himself, and I wrote one small piece of theological reflection that helped me wrestle with the agonizingly slow, month-by-month, grindingly gradual loss of Jon. It is a sermon titled "Tears in Heaven: Four Portraits of the Suffering/Crying God."[1]

That tiny sermon opened large windows through which I could look and then think about God differently within the war texts. On the one hand, understanding Yahweh as a tearful, crying God affected this book when I began to see passages of Scripture that describe Yahweh weeping about war destruction. Yahweh cries for his own people when he brings war against them, *and* he cries a river of tears even over the war destruction that he brings against his and Israel's enemies (this concern for enemies is nothing short of amazing—quite unlike the behavior of ANE gods). On the other hand, this discovery prompted me to search for a whole range of what one might call subversive war texts—ones that, like the crying texts, in some manner subvert or undermine the standard war texts. (Important note: I am using the terms *subvert* and *undermine* in a *positive sense* because these alternative-to-the-norm war portraits help us realign our thinking with a fuller and more complete understanding of *all* the war material in the Bible.) Biblical texts such as the ones describing David's bloody hands and numerous others (see chapter fourteen and appendix H) caused me to rethink my understanding of the better-known portraits of Yahweh as a warrior God. This collection of subversive/antithetical (in a good sense) war texts was crucial for relating Yahweh of the Old Testament to Jesus of the Gospels, resulting in a Yahweh-and-Jesus portrait that makes sense.

Second, I stepped away from writing the war book for a few years and worked on other projects that unexpectedly helped me better understand the war material. I had started having nightmares—waking in a cold sweat—from researching the larger ANE war context and especially the gruesome war atrocities that were part of the ancient world. So I transferred my efforts for a while into writing *Corporal Punishment in the Bible:*

---

[1]I first preached the "Tears in Heaven" sermon twelve or more years ago. I have since delivered it numerous times but only on request, since, as you might imagine, it takes me several days to recover.

A Redemptive-Movement Hermeneutic for Troubling Texts.[2] The break was healthy. To my surprise, however, the corporal-punishment book gave me a new set of tools for understanding the biblical war texts. As with a previous book on hermeneutics, it strengthened my conviction that much of Scripture is written using an incremental ethic, or, better, an incrementally redemptive ethic.[3] This of course will be a major contribution of the war book. The greatest "Oh my goodness!" moment came when, in writing the chapter on ancient-world war atrocities, I realized how the corporal-punishment book had prepared me for seeing a profoundly redemptive element that I might otherwise have missed (I have sensed in this provision the quiet hand of God). The lights came on in my mind: There is an entire parallel or mirror image in the ANE world between court-based punishments and war-based punishments. This insight verified that, despite all their ugliness, something strangely redemptive was happening in the biblical war texts, and this redemptive evidence is not simply the creation of wishful Christian thinking. I hope you sense that aha moment (chapter thirteen) and find it compelling and encouraging—like discovering a cluster of beautiful, fragrant flowers growing from a dung pile in the desert.

Third, Gord Oeste joined me about halfway through the fourteen-year journey of writing this book, and I thank God for Gord and for our seven years of working together. On three occasions we taught a course on holy war ethics at Tyndale Seminary, which provided a great laboratory for testing ideas.[4] Gord eats and breathes the biblical and ANE war texts. He published his dissertation on Judges in a renowned series and has taught Joshua and Judges for many years.[5] He works relentlessly at seeing the war texts first through the lens of an ancient Israelite and ANE world and then adding other helpful lenses. What makes me especially humbled and honored to work

---

[2]William J. Webb, *Corporal Punishment in the Bible: A Redemptive-Movement Hermeneutic for Troubling Texts* (Downers Grove, IL: InterVarsity Press, 2011).

[3]William J. Webb, *Slaves, Women and Homosexuals: Exploring the Hermeneutics of Cultural Analysis* (Downers Grove, IL: InterVarsity Press, 2001).

[4]Throughout this book we use the term "holy war" as a label for any war within Scripture (not just the conquest battles) where Yahweh is portrayed by the biblical authors as fighting in conjunction with (or through) some human version of war.

[5]Gordon K. Oeste, *Legitimacy, Illegitimacy, and the Right to Rule: Windows on Abimelech's Rise and Demise in Judges 9*, LHBOTS 546 (New York: T&T Clark, 2011).

with Gord is that I know something of what it cost him to write this book with me. In short, it cost him his job. When faced with the alternative, he made the painful but deliberate decision to keep writing. That choice speaks volumes about the rigors and perils of rethinking traditional views. Some choices are difficult but worth making.

The chapters that lie ahead have been transformative for us. They have enabled us to think differently about Yahweh and Jesus in ways that have renewed and deepened our faith. The journey has led us to new and sacred places in our thinking—beautiful landscapes with open horizons and fresh air that restore feeling after spiritual numbness and rejuvenate the troubled soul. We hope that readers who share our struggle with the war texts of Scripture—the utter ugliness of genocide and war rape—will find a new sense of joy in thinking more deeply and accurately about Yahweh as holy warrior and Jesus as apocalyptic warrior.

ACKNOWLEDGMENTS

ANY BOOK THAT TAKES FOURTEEN YEARS to write and one more (fifteenth) year of editorial input requires the generous support of many people. Our wives, Carolyn (Gord) and Marilyn (Bill), deserve an Oscar, Tony, Emmy, and Olympic gold medals for their unending love and support; they have graciously endured late nights, preoccupied thoughts, and even occupational journeys that have come as a part of writing this work.

Our thanks go to Dorian Coover-Cox (and her husband, Chuck), whose editorial input has touched every page of this manuscript. Her Old Testament expertise and years of professional editing at Dallas Theological Seminary have added wonderful clarity and insight to the final product. At the Society of Biblical Literature meeting in Denver we pulled off an epic surprise to thank Dorian for her incredible labor of love, not only in this manuscript but also in other miserably written items of mine (Bill) that she has taken to new levels.

An unusual type of thanks must go to InterVarsity Press, since this manuscript was notoriously late in fulfilling even the most elastic of contractual definitions. As noted earlier in the preface, Andy Le Peau and Gary Deddo used to joke with me (Bill) about getting IVP's "_____Award [the blank represents the name of a well-known author whose identity I will leave unstated]." (Aside: This award was not exactly a compliment, as I found out, since apparently—whether fact or fiction I do not know—this particular author had the longest outstanding contract in the history of IVP.) It was a wonderful honor to have this work edited by Dan Reid as his intentional (according to him) "last manuscript read." His comments and input were most encouraging. Then, after Dan retired in December 2017, Jon Boyd read the manuscript along with an anonymous reader outside IVP, whom we dubbed "Dr. Anon." Our special thanks to Jon Boyd for shepherding the manuscript along through its final stages. From these three sources (and Dorian's input) we had a wealth of ideas that made our time of integrating editorial insights a tremendous developmental (stretching?) experience for both of us. At the polish stage we thank Claire Brubaker and Rebecca Carhart for taking this book across the finish line. We owe the entire IVP team a great debt of thanks for their protracted patience and, when it did finally appear, for bringing a much-improved book to press.

Our final word of thanks goes to a community of friends and academic colleagues who have supported us. Numerous friends have read early versions of these pages with great benefit to our own thinking. If we start mentioning names, we are going to miss some. We do wish to acknowledge the generous support of Tyndale Seminary (Toronto, Canada)—a wonderful community of learners—for offering our holy war course during several summers. The collaborative involvement of students, faculty, and administrators/board leadership contributed in various ways to bringing this book across the finish line.

Our many thanks!

ABBREVIATIONS

AB	Anchor Bible
ABD	*Anchor Bible Dictionary*. Edited by D. N. Freedman. 6 vols. New York: Doubleday, 1992
ABRL	Anchor Bible Reference Library
AEL	*Ancient Egyptian Literature*. Miriam Lichtheim. 3 vols. Berkeley: University of California Press, 1973
AIL	Ancient Israel and Its Literature
ANE	Ancient Near East
ANET	*Ancient Near Eastern Texts Relating to the Old Testament* Edited by James Bennett Pritchard. 3rd ed. with supplement Princeton, NJ: Princeton University Press, 1969
AOTC	Apollos Old Testament Commentary
ARAB	*Ancient Records of Asssyria and Babylonia*. Daniel David Luckenbill. 2 vols. Chicago: University of Chicago Press, 1926–1927. Reprint, New York: Greenwood, 1968
ARE	*Ancient Records of Egypt*. Edited by James Henry Breasted. 5 vols. Chicago: University of Chicago Press, 1906
ASOR	American Schools of Oriental Research
BARev	*Biblical Archaeology Review*
BASOR	*Bulletin of the American Schools of Oriental Research*
BBR	*Bulletin for Biblical Research*
BBRSup	Bulletin for Biblical Research Supplement
BECNT	Baker Evangelical Commentary on the New Testament
BETL	Bibliotheca Ephemeridum Theologicarum Lovaniensium
Bib	*Biblica*
BibSac	*Bibliotheca Sacra*
BJS	Brown Judaic Studies
BNTC	Black's New Testament Commentaries
BO	Berit Olam Studies in Hebrew Narrative and Poetry
BRS	The Biblical Resource Series
BT	*The Bible Translator*

BZAW	Beihefte zur Zeitschrift für die alttestamentliche Wissenschaft
CANE	*Civilizations of the Ancient Near East*. Edited by J. Sasson. 4 vols. Peabody, MA: Hendrickson, 1995
CBQ	*Catholic Biblical Quarterly*
CBQMS	Catholic Biblical Quarterly Monograph Series
CHANE	Culture and History of the Ancient Near East
COS	*The Context of Scripture*. 3 vols. Edited by William W. Hallo and K. Lawson Younger. Leiden: Brill, 1997–2003
CSHB	Critical Studies in Hebrew Bible
CSHJ	Chicago Studies in the History of Judaism
DH	Deuteronomistic History
Dtn	Deuteronomic, or the Deuteronomic editor
Dtr	Deuteronomistic, or the Deuteronomist
EQ	*Evangelical Quarterly*
FAT	Forschungen zum Alten Testament
FCI	Foundations of Contemporary Interpretation
HACL	History, Archaeology, and the Culture of the Levant
HALOT	*The Hebrew and Aramaic Lexicon of the Old Testament*. Study ed. 2 vols. L. Koehler and W. Baumgartner. Edited by M. E. J. Richardson. Leiden, Boston: Brill, 2001
HDB	*Harvard Divinity Bulletin*
HSM	Harvard Semitic Monographs
HSS	Harvard Semitic Studies
HTR	*Harvard Theological Review*
IEJ	*Israel Exploration Journal*
JAOS	*Journal of the American Oriental Society*
JBL	*Journal of Biblical Literature*
JBQ	*Jewish Bible Quarterly*
JETS	*Journal of the Evangelical Theological Society*
JNES	*Journal of Near Eastern Studies*
JQR	*Jewish Quarterly Review*
JSNTSup	Journal for the Study of the New Testament Supplement Series
JSOT	*Journal for the Study of the Old Testament*
JSOTSup	Journal for the Study of the Old Testament Supplement Series
LAI	Library of Ancient Israel
LH	Laws of Hammurabi
LHBOTS	Library of Hebrew Bible Old Testament Studies
LNTS	Library of New Testament Studies
LXX	Septuagint
MAL	Middle Assyrian Laws

MSAW	Münchner Studien zur Alten Welt
MT	Masoretic Text
NAC	New American Commentary
NCBC	New Cambridge Bible Commentary
NEA	*Near Eastern Archaeology*
NICOT	New International Commentary on the Old Testament
NIDB	*New Interpreter's Dictionary of the Bible.* 5 vols. Edited by Katherine Doob Sakenfeld. Nashville: Abingdon, 2005
NIDOTTE	*New International Dictionary of Old Testament Theology and Exegesis.* Edited by Willem VanGemeren. Grand Rapids: Zondervan, 1997
NIGTC	New International Greek Testament Commentary
NIVAC	NIV Application Commentary
NSBT	New Studies in Biblical Theology
NTL	New Testament Library
NTT	New Testament Theology
OBT	Overtures to Biblical Theology
OIS	Oriental Institute Seminars
OTE	*Old Testament Essays*
OTL	Old Testament Library
PEQ	*Palestine Exploration Quarterly*
RevExp	*Review and Expositor*
RIM.EP	The Royal Inscriptions of Mesopotamia: Early Periods
SAA	State Archives of Assyria
SAAS	State Archives of Assyria Studies
SAHL	Studies in the Archaeology and History of the Levant
SANER	Studies in Ancient Near Eastern Records
SBLABS	Society of Biblical Literature Archaeology and Biblical Studies
SBLMS	Society of Biblical Literature Monograph Series
SBLWAW	Society of Biblical Literature Writings from the Ancient World
SJOT	*Scandinavian Journal of the Old Testament*
SOTBT	Studies in Old Testament Biblical Theology
SWBA	Social World of Biblical Antiquity
TDOT	*Theological Dictionary of the Old Testament.* Edited by G. J. Botterweck, H. Ringgren, et al. Translated by J. T. Willis, G. W. Bromiley, and D. E. Green. 15 vols. Grand Rapids: Eerdmans, 1974–2006
THAT	*Theologisches Handwörterbuch Zum Alten Testament.* 2 vols. Edited by E. Jenni and Claus Westermann. München: Chr. Kaiser Verlag, 1971–1976

TOTC   Tyndale Old Testament Commentary
TynBul   *Tyndale Bulletin*
UF   *Ugarit Forschungen*
VT   *Vetus Testamentum*
VTSup   Vetus Testamentum Supplements
WBC   Word Biblical Commentary
WTJ   *Westminster Theological Journal*
WMANT   Wissenschaftliche Monographien zum Alten und Neuen
              Testament
WUNT   Wissenschaftliche Untersuchungen zum Neuen Testament
ZAW   *Zeitschrift für die alttestamentliche Wissenschaft*

INTRODUCTION

Rethinking Holy War Texts

A POST-9/11 WORLD THINKS DIFFERENTLY about war texts in the
Bible. The decades ahead will chronicle the profound impact on Christian
theological reflection resulting from the events of September 11, 2001, and a
stream of religiously inspired violence—today's version of holy war. One can
no longer ignore the intersection of religion and violence and, more specifically, the biblical war texts that seemingly approve of genocidal killings and
war rape—forcibly taking attractive female captives for wives. This monumental shift, while posing a dilemma for people of faith, ironically offers Christians an opportunity and a new horizon from which to reflect on war texts and
our understanding of them: Have we missed something in our traditional
readings of Scripture? Is there any evidence that should cause us to rethink the
Bible's war texts?

Here is how this book began. I (Bill here) started writing the early stages
of this book when a small group of biblical scholars in the Toronto area
gathered to study the biblical war texts.[1] We dubbed our group "the genocide
fraternity"—a label that conveyed something of a twisted attempt at humor
among academics (we do not get out much). More importantly, the label
expressed the exact *opposite* of what we felt about the subject matter. We
were all deeply disturbed by genocide and contemporary occurrences of holy
war around us and, as a result, experienced growing dissonance between our
faith in God and the war traditions of the biblical text. We were all looking
for answers.

---

[1]In this book the singular "I" refers to myself, William (Bill) Webb. The collective "we" or
"us" refers to Gord Oeste and me or, as on this page, to groups mentioned in the context.

An exceptionally bright young man named James joined our group. James was in his mid-twenties, a nonacademic and unabashedly vocal in his raging disdain for the holy war texts of Scripture. While James grew up in an evangelical home and had once embraced the Christian faith, in his early twenties he dropped his church connections and struggled with his belief in the God of the Bible. Several factors led to this disconnection. But one of the core issues was that James could no longer stomach the portrait of Yahweh as a "genocidal baby killer." I crossed paths with James just before starting our study and asked him to join our group. I thought he could keep us academics honest.

Over the summer of 2004 we met four times. We were all reading the recently released *Show Them No Mercy: Four Views on God and Canaanite Genocide*, along with a foot-high stack of more academic material on ANE warfare.[2] At one point of intense frustration with the genocidal passages in the Bible, James blurted out, "These texts are bloody, brutal, and barbaric!" I still hear his impassioned voice. To fully capture how his words—*bloody, brutal, and barbaric*—sounded, try adding James's British accent, his eyes wide open, and both hands (fingers spread) shaking back and forth around his head. The visual version said, "Aah!?! Why can't people see this?" That was and is James—a delightful and most welcome addition to a comparatively sedate group of scholar types. As you surely have guessed by now, I must thank James for providing the title of this book. If you check the front pages, this volume is dedicated "To James, a friend whose war ethic captures the spirit of Amos."[3]

As I began writing the early pages of this book the words "bloody, brutal, and barbaric" haunted me. At first I did not want to admit this assessment of the war traditions of Scripture. I was raised in a church tradition that said these war stories were right and just, without ethical blemish. But the longer I worked with the biblical war texts, the more I came to realize that what James said was true in the sense that it accurately describes *one* part of the story.[4]

---

[2]C. S. Cowles, Eugene H. Merrill, Daniel L. Gard, and Tremper Longman III, *Show Them No Mercy: Four Views on God and Canaanite Genocide*, ed. Stanley N. Gundry (Grand Rapids: Zondervan, 2003).

[3]James contributed a present-day expression and spirit of Amos in our ethical discussions of the biblical war passages.

[4]In addition to fully acknowledging the ugly side of the war texts, this book will equally endeavor to celebrate features of an incremental ethic that move in a strikingly redemptive

AN OVERVIEW: WHERE WE ARE HEADED

Open disclosure of where we are headed may be less intriguing than a suspenseful, inductive approach (one that lets the mystery unfold bit by bit). Yet, we have observed when teaching this material that the breadth of the war texts (Genesis to Revelation) and the complexity of the ethical, hermeneutical, and theological issues call for as much clarity up front as possible. This war book contains not just *one* thesis but *six* theses, woven together to form the argument as a whole. Here are the key ideas that we present in the pages ahead.

Thesis one: Square pegs, round holes. Our "square pegs, round holes" description is a way of saying that, unfortunately, many Christians are trying to plug *traditional answers* (divine commands ["God said it"], God's holiness, Canaanite evil, etc.) like square pegs into the round holes of *contemporary questions* about the ethical issues of genocide and war rape. This does not work for several reasons. First, the pairing of traditional answers with genocide and war rape fails the test of logical, hermeneutical, and ethical reasoning (chapter two). Furthermore, a museum-like walk through the gruesome world of ancient war atrocities (chapter thirteen) should convince any reader that the type of genocide and war rape in the biblical text, when understood correctly, would not have been on the ethical radar of the original audience (not even close).[5] In addition, the degree of divine accommodation in a collection of subversive war texts (chapter fourteen)—a perspective often missed by readers—places Yahweh in a dramatically different light as the highly reluctant warrior God. They tell us about a large gap between what happened in Israel's own backyard and what God would have preferred. Meanwhile, the genocide and war rape that one encounters in Scripture do not square well with the best possible war practices in a fallen world.[6]

---

direction. Our journey includes both ethically troubling aspects of the text and its redemptive spirit in the context of the war ethic of its day.

[5]The accommodation gap helps us understand what would have been and what would not have been on the original audience's ethical radar. Since Israel settled for (was happy with) a war ethic that fell well *below* what Yahweh truly wanted, there is little chance that Israelite warriors (or the original readers) would have been troubled by the type of genocide or war rape described in the text. At numerous places throughout the book we develop evidence for how horizons (both ancient and contemporary) shape what we might call our ethical radar regarding war actions.

[6]As one wrestles with the biblical war texts, it becomes apparent that many instances of plans B, C, or D found their way into the war domain. Very little of the war material, if any, should

Genocide and war rape in the biblical texts connect far better with Yahweh's accommodating attempts to move his faith-fumbling, idolatry-loving people along in the mired-down, fallen world around them. Sometimes God enters our world in hip waders (mediated actions), sloshing through the sewer water in order to bring about instances of incremental redemption. But these redemptive acts—small and large—in the ugly world of war are a beautiful thing, for they shout loudly about hope for complete redemption one day.

That said, we should not abandon the traditional answers. No. They are still excellent answers. They simply must be connected with the right question(s), namely, the biblical *story-line questions* that were on the mind of the original readers. We will unpack what the original readers' broader, big-picture war questions most likely were (hint: they relate to the land and a new Eden) and how they differ from our contemporary, more narrowly focused investigation into the ethics of specific war actions, namely, genocide and war rape (chapter three). This realignment within our square-pegs-in-round-holes thesis provides a venue for discovering exactly where the traditional answers *do* work and, indeed, fit extremely well. It pulls together an amazing canonical story from Genesis to Revelation in terms of God's active presence, sacred space, and the anticipation of a restored Eden. The story line, then, and its ethical questions (not ours) are where the traditional answers make sense.

Thesis two: Total-kill rhetoric as hyperbole. A second major thesis might in short form be called the hyperbole thesis. In five chapters (eight through twelve) and three appendixes (A through C) we develop evidence that the language related to total-kill or genocide statements in the biblical war texts is best understood as hyperbolic. That does not mean such events never occurred. They happened, but with significantly reduced killing and without requiring the death of the entire enemy population, as seemingly instructed (and reported). If total kill did not happen, then how many people were actually killed? Here we begin to talk in terms of probabilities. The *most probable* (and strategic) enemy killed in biblical holy war would have been

---

be connected to plan A—i.e., how Yahweh ideally wants his people to act. The cascading effect of Israel's lack of faith and its yearning for this-world war methods is clearly reflected in their insistence on a king, horses, chariots, and the like. These issues and dramatic examples of subversive war texts will be developed in chapters fourteen and sixteen.

the king or his general and in all likelihood the males (in some cases also the females) of the royal family. Next in terms of probability would be the slaughter of the army—but generally this would include those who continued to resist. The killing of large numbers of the nonmilitary, general population was *least likely*.

Much biblical war language is hyperbolic, never intended to be taken literally. When the text of Joshua 11:4 describes the invading enemy troops, horses, and chariots being "as numerous as the sand on the seashore," it is not intending to report a literal result of counting—that the enemy forces included more soldiers than the number of every person birthed in human history. Rather, the text is vividly saying something that would have been readily understood by its audience: "Their forces were significantly larger [and weapons stronger] than ours." The figurative, sand-on-the-seashore way of describing the situation also spoke on an emotive level: "The opposing army was huge compared to ours, and *we were scared out of our skins!*"

Most war hyperbole was used to communicate to the ancient readers an *emotive* force within the battle record (afterwards) or as part of the earlier instructions (beforehand). In the ancient world, overstating war reality in terms of total destruction was usually meant to convey that (1) the battle was decisively won, (2) the enemy as a people group no longer existed as a threat because the king and his family had fallen (collective identity in the ancient culture meant that killing the king, some of his family, and resisting armed forces was equivalent to or represented the total destruction of that city or people group), and (3) resistant armed forces had surrendered or fled. In the case of biblical rhetoric, Scripture co-opts this exaggerated war language of the ANE world for its own purposes of accentuating an eschatological hope of someday eliminating idolatry from the land *entirely* and enjoying the worship of Yahweh *exclusively*. The underlying objective in biblical holy war is *not* the killing of people or the killing of *all* the enemy; rather, it is about the hoped-for creation of idolatry-free sacred space in the formation of a new Eden.

Thesis three: Accommodation. A third thesis, to which we have already alluded, is the accommodation of Yahweh in holy war to the ethical war practices of Israel. Yahweh stoops down when he plays in the sandbox of this fallen world; there is often a Grand Canyon–like gap between what God truly wants and what he actually enacts in war with his people. Many times throughout Scripture we see God giving commands or instructions to his people, and though the instructions come from an untainted, pristine, holy God, they reflect justice or love at a concrete-specific level in a limited way and not its best ethical expression. In order to appreciate this accommodation thesis, we will turn to a collection of subversive war texts: portraits of Yahweh as a weeping war God, the unwillingness of Yahweh to have his name/reputation tarnished by David's bloody warrior hands (the "I am not David!" portrait of Yahweh screams as a counter pattern to the norms of temple building in the ANE world), finding a dwelling place for his name under the label of shalom instead, including only flowers, pomegranates, and animals in the temple carvings (no war scenes, which were common to ANE temples), hamstringing captive horses and burning chariots, not really wanting a king in the first place—an action *explicitly* tied to war issues—and so forth.

Antiwar and subversive war texts provide crucial evidence that Yahweh's involvement in Israel's warfare required that he leave his lofty, untainted world and at times stoop low, very low, when working with his people. Could killing babies (traditional position) or even the rhetoric of total kill (our view) within biblical holy war contain *real* ethical deficiencies? Do Yahweh's instructions to Israelite male warriors about taking good-looking virgins similarly contain *real* ethical deficiencies? We will argue yes in both cases, namely, that these very real ethical deficiencies reflect God's accommodation to Israel and its ancient-world context. Much of what occurs in the biblical text represents Israel's war practices, seduced by the war ideology of other nations, and not truly Yahweh's preferred war (or peace) practices. Simply put: Yahweh accommodates himself to another/Israel's level of ethic. The breadth of accommodation evidence (chapter fourteen) in the war domain makes this case more than just plausible.

Thesis four: Incremental, redemptive-movement ethic. A fourth thesis in this book—an incrementally redemptive ethic—is the happier flip side of the previous one. Accommodation looks at the sad reality of a huge gap between what Israel does in war and what God truly wants. Its happier side is twofold, namely, that (1) God cares about his people Israel and about bringing redemption to all humanity to the extent that he is willing to humble himself and stoop low in our fallen world, and (2) God gently tugs his people toward something better, even if that redemptive better is measured in incremental terms. An incremental redemptive-movement ethic means that God often brings his people along in at least *incremental* steps relative to the world around them (foreign movement) or relative to earlier stages in the redemptive story line (canonical movement).

We will explore and celebrate God's quietly redemptive hand even in the ugliness of biblical holy war. Believe it or not, there exists a redemptive side to the highly disturbing war rape passages in the Bible (chapter six) when they are read in light of the war practices of an ancient world. Also, if the total-kill language of Scripture amounts to rhetorical overstatement, as we will argue (chapters eight through twelve and appendixes A, B, and C), then biblical war practices are hugely redemptive—at least in an incremental sense—relative to the horrific war atrocities of the day (chapter thirteen). Finally, Jesus' version of apocalyptic holy war sets a new canonical standard as the final battle forges a pathway into a new-creation world, where all stand at the judgment. The traditionalist holy war view in its literal understanding of Revelation (woefully problematic) contradicts the peaceful Jesus of the Gospels, his teachings, and his mode of discipleship. As followers of Jesus, those more disposed toward violence—Simon the Zealot, Peter, and Paul— were taught to lay down their swords and put away their violent inclinations. We will develop seven differences between Israel's practice of holy war in the Old Testament and Jesus' final holy war battle, where each difference demonstrates ethical development. The final battle ought to be understood as something real and powerful, not in a literal sense but as Jesus' spoken word. That is all. One spoken word. No more is needed or intended. The final battle is fought by Christ alone (see chapter sixteen) and is the purest of all battles, for it is won (contra traditional holy war positions) through the *earlier* death of Christ and through one *final* spoken word.

Thesis five: Converging God portraits—bringing Yahweh and Jesus together. A fifth thesis considers the best way to unite the portraits of God within a canonical development of Scripture. The variance in what God looks like over the pages of Scripture is particularly problematic when trying to relate three elements: (1) Yahweh as warrior in the Old Testament, (2) Jesus of the Gospels and in Paul, and (3) Jesus as the apocalyptic warrior in the book of Revelation. In brief, there are three pieces to a large jigsaw puzzle. (Aside: Keep one finger here and flip ahead a few pages to the figure near the end of this introduction, if needed, to understand the labels.) The *traditional* view dislocates the central puzzle piece (2) from the other two. The *antitraditional* view detaches the first piece (1) from the other two. We will propose that the *realigned-traditional* view best links together all three pieces—(1), (2), and (3)—of the puzzle without dislocation.

Let's consider the portraits of God as puzzle pieces a little further. First, the core of the Christian story is found in the Gospels and in Paul's letters. Jesus in the Gospels and the Spirit in Paul are powerful figures, but they do *not* seem to be engaged in violence or encourage a discipleship of violent ideology. In the Gospels Jesus teaches his followers to turn the cheek, put down the sword (do not take it up, Peter!), and love one's enemies. Similarly, in Paul's epistles, the presence of Jesus in our midst—the Spirit—functions in ways antithetical to violence. Just look at the fruits of the Spirit (versus the deeds of the flesh), and you will discover Jesus-like characteristics that strive for peace and harmony rather than violence. Also, Paul himself and at least one of Jesus' disciples (Simon the zealot) converted *out of* a violence-and-religion tradition in order to follow Jesus. Like Peter, they too put the sword away. Finally, the heart of Christian theology in the Gospels is that the cross is the place where Jesus' violent death absorbed the violence of our world. That is the center of the canonical puzzle.

Here's the connection issue. The core of Christian theology contained in the middle piece—Jesus of the Gospels and Paul—does not connect easily with what comes before or after: (1) Yahweh as Israel's warrior God and (3) Jesus as apocalyptic warrior. Both the traditional holy war view (that it exemplified *an untainted, pristine-good ethic*) and the antitraditional holy war view (*a dark-evil ethic*) leave Christians with a difficult, bumpy ride across the canon. Whether aware of the tension or not, traditional-view Christians typically distance themselves from Jesus of the Gospels, and most antitraditional-view Christians equally distance themselves from the Yahweh of the Old Testament.

Our position on biblical holy war texts (*an incrementally redemptive ethic*) brings a better convergence to the portraits of God in Scripture. We will argue that Yahweh as warrior, when understood through the lens of the subversive war texts (an often-missed scriptural voice for viewing the Yahweh portrait), merges well with the Jesus of the Gospels and Paul. In turn, these two pieces of the God portrait fit well with a "one word [not sword] will fell them" view of Jesus as apocalyptic warrior. If the evidence for this more unified holy war perspective is convincing (and we think it is), then readers should sense a burst of fresh air and much greater enjoyment in reading the whole of the Bible from cover to cover. This is solace for the troubled soul.

Thesis six: The unfinished justice story. A sixth thesis (see our conclusion) taps into the eschaton and how it functions within biblical ethics. We will briefly develop an argument of eschatological reversal as bringing closure to outstanding or unfinished elements of injustice in the enactment of justice in Scripture. If God is *absolutely* righteous, holy, and loving (and we believe he is), it would seem logical that his justice in the last day will right the wrongs of all injustice within this fallen world, even the experience of unjust elements within the messy actions of Old Testament holy war (appendix D).

WHERE THIS BOOK FITS: SOMEWHERE IN THE MIDDLE

This book addresses the *ethics* of reading the biblical holy war texts today on the issues of genocide and war rape. Obviously, a range of views are developing. For newcomers to the discussion, it might be helpful to get a feel for the spectrum of ethical views and where this book fits within that range. While hardly exhaustive in terms of the authors or views cited, this visual spectrum may help at least as an initial grid for sorting through the options. Clear labels for the *differing assessments of biblical holy war ethics* have not yet been developed, since the discussion between views is hardly at a mature stage. The figure that follows (figure 0.1) uses functional labels that are easy to understand. You will see that our view (Webb/Oeste) lies somewhere in the middle.[7] That does *not* make our position right; it just provides a sense

---

[7]Other authors exploring middle-ground approaches are Paul Copan/Matthew Flannagan. Greg Boyd's approach, though distinct from the antitraditional view, is much closer along the middle range of the spectrum to that view.

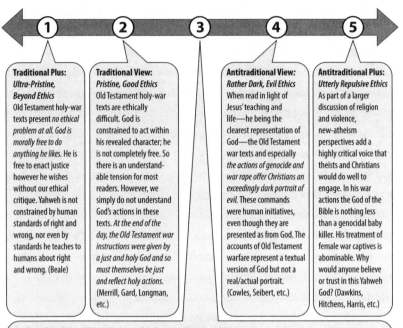

Figure 0.1. Spectrum of ethical views

of where it falls along a spectrum. It should be obvious that we are attempting to take what we consider the best of the traditional and antitraditional views and forge a middle position. The spectrum of labels is constructed around the traditional position (number two) since most readers will be familiar to some extent with that view. Also, labels that correspond to the traditional view provided the easiest way to communicate the alternatives.

We are embarrassed by at least four components in this figure. First, it fails to include another twenty or so scholars with finely nuanced distinctions that would fill in a three-page figure. At best the spectrum above is representative and intended for entry-level readers who need an initial footing within the discussion. Second, our own view gets the longest summary. There is a reason (other than it's our view). Since it sits next to the traditional view, we wanted not only to articulate the view but also to summarize how a realigned-traditional view differs from the traditional view. Third, we do not develop the differences between our view and the antitraditional view. That omission reflects our intention that this book primarily addresses readers who either hold or have been raised within the traditional view (or traditional-plus view). No book can do everything. Fourth and yet another grand omission, the figure and this book as a whole do not address approaches to the biblical war texts that stress dating texts, authorship, and/or archeology. Such is a helpful discussion but well beyond the scope of this book. Instead we are attempting to do a theological reading of the biblical text with an eye to hermeneutical, ethical, canonical, and ancient-cultural contexts.

We trust that readers find as much enjoyment in reading this book as we have had in writing it. Granted, our change-of-mind journeys tell of some intensely painful moments along the way.[8] But the comparatively greater delight of discovering even a handful of more seaworthy answers for the journey of faith . . . well, that was (and is) joy unspeakable.

---

[8]For these painful elements see the preface.

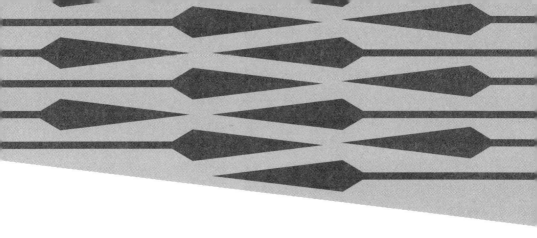

PART 1

HARD QUESTIONS: GENOCIDE AND WAR RAPE

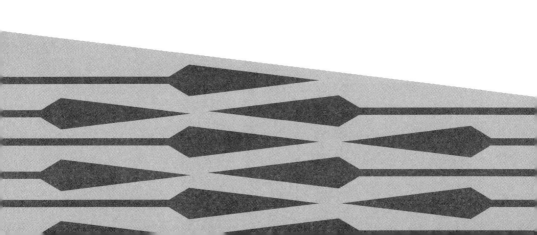

1

SLAUGHTERING CHILDREN?
GRABBING VIRGINS?

THIS BOOK EXPLORES THE ETHICS of two war actions within the biblical accounts: *genocide* and *war rape*.[1] Why these two? In short, they are the most ethically troubling components of holy war that readers encounter in the Bible. Genocide and war rape raise hard questions about the ethics of Scripture and about the character of the Yahweh God of the Old Testament. Today's religion-and-violence theorists and new-atheism proponents make their ethical assessment clear by labeling Yahweh as a "genocidal baby killer" and a "divine rapist."[2] Their viewpoint, of course, leaves little room for ethical virtue in either the text or the God of Scripture. We will argue that new atheism's assessment misreads the biblical text and terribly distorts the God of Scripture; the evidence for this counterassessment will unfold as we journey through the pages of this book. For now, however, those evocative labels capture the ethical problem and provide a starting point from which to untangle the hermeneutics, ethics, ancient setting, and story line of the biblical text. But, fair warning—it is a messy job because the pictures of war are muddled for many of us.

Let's begin the untangling process by talking about pictures—images in our minds. What comes to mind when reading the terms *genocide* and *war rape*?

---

[1]On genocide, see Josh 6:21; 1 Sam 15:3; Num 21:2-3; Deut 2:34; 3:6; 7:2; 13:15; 20:16-17, etc. On war rape, see Num 31:17-18, 35; Deut 21:10-14.

[2]For a helpful introduction to a range of new atheists/religion-and-violence theorists and a critique of the view that secularism (no religion) is the solution, see William T. Cavanaugh, "Does Religion Cause Violence?," *HDB* 35, nos. 2-3 (2007): 1-14.

THE MIXED-UP WAR PICTURES IN OUR MINDS

When we read literature—recent or ancient—our brains automatically supply mental pictures that correspond to the words we have just read. This imaging by the brain as it reads *war* literature is especially vivid because the imagination is highly attentive to imaging matters that contain an emotive impact. When we read biblical war passages, graphic war images automatically emerge in our brains. The crucial question is this: *From where within its massive storage system does the human brain pull to create war images that correspond to the words of Scripture?* Well, the images in our minds when reading biblical war material will predominantly come from an already-banked collection of war images from our own world of present-day war.

We cannot help it. It simply happens. Graphic pictures of *present-day* war violence fill our minds when reading *ancient* Scripture, especially when we bump into the biblical accounts that seem to describe genocide and war rape. Our brains almost automatically (without our making conscious decisions) produce images of genocide and war rape from picture files closer to home. In other words, we simply cannot read about ancient genocide in the Bible and escape the revolting images of Rwanda's mass graves—many containing the bodies of women and children who were hacked to death—in what has become a touchstone genocide image for us. Our minds inevitably jump between Rwanda (1994) pictures—whether printed photography, online sites, or movies we have seen—and other genocidal images that we cannot erase from our minds: the murder and deportation of Armenians (1915–1923), Nazi concentration camps (1933–1945), the killing fields of Cambodia (1975–1979), the brutal campaign of ethnic cleansing in Bosnia (1992–1995), or Sudan's ongoing genocidal murders of Darfuri civilians (2003–). Our minds do not lack for contemporary images of genocide as we read ancient war literature.

The same picture phenomenon occurs when reading of war rape. Should we encounter war rape within *ancient* literature, we are likely to have our mental images already shaped by *recent* war events. Our pictures come from images of Congo war rape with its staggering numbers—over eleven hundred rapes each day (conservative estimates by various health organizations[3])—

---

[3]See Jeffrey Gettleman, "Congo Study Sets Estimate for Rapes Much Higher," *The New York Times*, May 11, 2011, www.nytimes.com/2011/05/12/world/africa/12congo.html (accessed

or from images of heavily armed Boko Haram soldiers capturing young girls for wives and/or sex slaves; a parade of mothers crying in the streets, "Bring back our girls!" These war-rape images from the experiences of others are now etched into our collective psyche, along with experiences of our own or of people we know personally.

Modern war pictures, for better or worse, become slotted as stock images. This present-day filling in of war images could be good or bad *depending on the degree to which the images accurately reflect what was going on in the biblical war texts.* One of the most helpful steps in starting to make sense of the biblical war passages is to consciously disconnect—just a temporary move—from our contemporary war pictures and begin placing our collection of war images in different picture piles.

This book will help readers sift through a range of war pictures and put them in three or four distinctly different groups:

▶ Stack one: *Modern-day war pictures*—described above

▶ Stack two: *ANE war pictures*—developed throughout the book (especially chapter thirteen)

▶ Stack three: *Biblical war pictures, group one*—what Israel actually practiced in war

▶ Stack four: *Biblical war pictures, group two*—what Yahweh wanted Israel to do in war

While we cannot control the modern-day war pictures that presently exist in our minds, we can choose to keep them separate from the other three groups, not wrongly superimpose them onto ancient texts, and we can work at figuring out how these four photo stacks are similar or different.

By the end of the book, readers should be able to enter a conversation about how our modern pictures of genocide and war rape (stack one) look similar to or different from the biblical text (stacks three and four) and, in turn, how biblical pictures compare with ANE warfare pictures (stack two).

April 4, 2019). For the study that estimated over 407,000 to 430,00 war-related rapes in a 12-month period (roughly 1100 rapes per day) see Amber Peterman, Tia Palermo, Carn Bredenkamp, "Estimates and Determinants of Sexual Violence Against Women in the Democratic Republic of Congo," American Public Health Association, August 30, 2011, https://ajph.aphapublications.org/doi/10.2105/AJPH.2010.300070 (accessed April 4, 2019).

The importance of conscious image sorting cannot be overstated. We begin our journey by turning to the *traditional* understanding of the biblical war texts. Note well its set of images. As we will see, the traditional view pictures what happened in biblical holy war as literal mass killings—*all* Canaanite men, women, children, old and young killed by the sword. Obviously, the traditional perspective on biblical holy war overlaps closely with our modern-day scenes of genocide.

SQUARE PEGS, ROUND HOLES: FINDING ANSWERS THAT FIT

Probably all of us have seen children playing with toys that have some variation of the "square pegs, round holes" game. Their faces reveal puzzled frustration when trying to push an object into a hole that does not match. No matter how hard they try, it simply does not work. Conversely, their faces light up with delight and joy when they get all the pieces into the matching holes.

This square-pegs, round-holes idiom has become for Gord and me a short-form way of talking about one of six major theses of this book (see the introduction). In the next two chapters we maintain that what might be called the traditional explanation of war in the Bible has aligned its answers with the wrong questions. It is not that the traditional answers are bad. They are actually good answers, but they need to be connected or aligned with a set of story-line, ethics, and justice questions that relate to the original audience particularly. The traditional answers simply do *not* work with our contemporary questions about genocide and war rape. Investigating where traditional answers work and do not work is task of the next two chapters. These two chapters function as an invitation to the discussion in later chapters of answers that fit better with current questions.

Evidence for the square-pegs, round-holes thesis does not stop or end with the next two chapters. They simply begin the conversation. They show (negatively) in chapter two why the traditional answers do not fit. The arguments here derive from hermeneutics, ethics, and logic. Then (positively) in chapter three we will introduce where the traditional answers do make sense. Our arguments in that chapter derive from biblical theology and canonical themes at the level of the story line. But that is only the beginning.

The evidence for the square-pegs, round-holes thesis goes much deeper, as later chapters will show.

Finally, the square-pegs, round-holes thesis is also a way of describing where our position, called "realigned traditional view," derives its name. The realignment idea functions in two ways. First, the traditional answers need to be *realigned* with the right set of questions. Second, our modern ethical questions about genocide and war rape need to be *realigned* with a different set of answers from those proposed by the traditional view. We call this different set "better answers" (chapters four through twelve, appendixes A through C). We are not using the word *better* to talk about the intrinsic value of the answers or to disparage the traditional answers. Rather, the word *better* simply describes the fit. The answers in chapters four through twelve and appendixes A through C fit better with our contemporary questions about war rape and genocide.

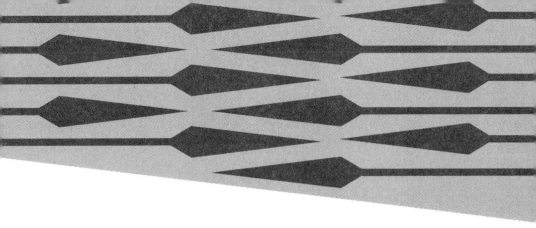

PART 2

TRADITIONAL ANSWERS: GOOD FOR BIG-PICTURE, STORY-LINE QUESTIONS

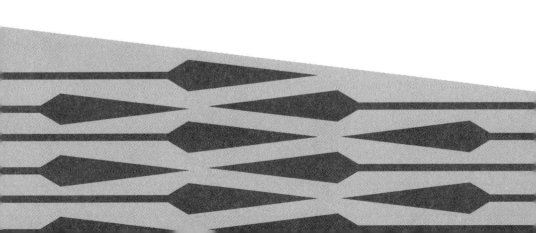

2

WHERE TRADITIONAL ANSWERS DO NOT WORK

IN WHAT BECAME KNOWN by our reading group as the "War Summer," we read the four-views book *Show Them No Mercy: Four Views on God and Canaanite Genocide.*[1] As mentioned earlier, my reflections on the biblical war texts began when some professors around the Toronto region gathered for an informal study group. The book was an easy read and a great introduction to the biblical war texts. To my surprise, however, I could not identify with any of the four views offered. I had fully expected to find *one* of the four options persuasive, but that did not happen.

From an *ethical* perspective our study group soon realized that the book really amounted to two views, not four. The ethical lines of debate are drawn between two polarized perspectives: biblical holy war as either a darkest evil (*one* author) or a pristine good (*three* authors). On the one hand, C. S. Cowles argues that biblical holy war reflects an evil of an exceedingly dark sort. Genocide and war rape within holy war actions are morally reprehensible, a blight within the Bible and sourced perhaps in Satanic origins or, more likely, in Moses' corrupted thinking; the genocide instructions were surely not revealed directives from God. Cowles's *antitraditional* view, as we have labeled it (see figure 0.1 in the introduction), has in more recent years been expanded and developed by Eric A. Seibert.[2]

---

[1]C. S. Cowles, Eugene H. Merrill, Daniel L. Gard, and Tremper Longman III, *Show Them No Mercy: Four Views on God and Canaanite Genocide*, ed. Stanley N. Gundry (Grand Rapids: Zondervan, 2003).

[2]Eric A. Seibert, *Disturbing Divine Behavior: Troubling Old Testament Images of God* (Minneapolis: Fortress, 2009); Seibert, *The Violence of Scripture: Overcoming the Old Testament's Troubling Legacy* (Minneapolis: Fortress, 2012).

On the other hand, Eugene Merrill, Daniel Gard, and Tremper Longman III represent the *traditional* view (again, see figure 0.1 in the introduction).[3] These three authors each contend that the holy war commands are from God and thus represent perfect/pristine (no ethical imperfections) righteousness and justice, albeit within a particular time period and circumstance. While Christians may struggle with the holy war texts, any ethical difficulty is really a matter of our own inability to understand God's justice. The book generates four views by subdividing the traditional, pristine-ethic position into three scenarios on how holy war plays out across the epochs of Scripture, that is, along dispensational and covenant lines.[4]

Before critiquing the traditional view, however, let us resurface the two most ethically gut-wrenching problems that contemporary readers encounter in the biblical accounts of holy war: (1) the genocidal slaughter of noncombatant men, women, and children, and (2) the keeping of choice females by Israelite warriors for sexual and reproductive purposes. Unlike what we argue later (chapters four through sixteen, appendixes A through C), the traditional view understands today's war portraits of genocide (mass killings of defenseless men, women, and children) as roughly equivalent to what was happening in the biblical text.[5]

THE TRADITIONAL ANSWERS

Merrill, Gard, and Longman—representatives of the traditional Christian view—respond to the difficult aspects of holy war by saying this: the problem is only a *perceived* ethical problem (not a real one); modern readers simply do not understand God's actions. The traditional, pristine-ethic "answers" to

---

[3]For a more recent development of the traditional view see M. Daniel Carroll R. and J. Blair Wilgus, eds., *Wrestling with the Violence of God: Soundings in the Old Testament*, BBRSup 10 (Winona Lake, IN: Eisenbrauns, 2015). While reluctantly taking the traditional view, Christopher J. H. Wright begins (tentatively) nudging toward some of our better answers: war rhetoric (88), hardness of heart (89), nonethnicity (92), etc., in *The God I Don't Understand: Reflections on Tough Questions of Faith* (Grand Rapids: Zondervan, 2008), 73-108.

[4]The threefold split of the traditional position based on continuity and discontinuity issues (as helpful as it is) seems somewhat parallel to rearranging chairs on the *Titanic*. The *ethical* issue of genocide (and war rape) is monumentally more important (and difficult) to wrestle through than tweaking issues of continuity and discontinuity in biblical theology. That said, I enjoyed the continuity/discontinuity discussion and particularly like the "spiritual continuity" development by Tremper Longman III.

[5]The traditional view is often silent about the war-rape texts.

genocide in the Bible can be summarized as including the following: (1) God as source of the holy war commands, (2) the lofty and good purposes of biblical holy war, (3) the noninnocent or evil status of the Canaanites, and (4) an understanding of holy war as foreshadowing eschatological judgment. But how viable are these four traditional pillars?

God as source of the holy war commands. For many Christians, ourselves included, the fact that God commands something in Scripture generates an almost automatic assumption about its inherent goodness, righteousness, and ethical virtue. Along these lines, Eugene Merrill states: "The issue then cannot be whether or not genocide is intrinsically good or evil—its sanction by a holy God settles that question."[6] The inference from Merrill's statement is that biblical genocide must be ethically good (pristine, without blemish) because it is instructed by a good God. Merrill similarly concludes his essay by saying, "Thus, the moral and ethical dilemma of Yahweh war must remain without satisfying explanation. At the risk of cliché, all that can be said is that if God is all the Bible says he is, all that he does must be good—and that includes his authorization of genocide." Gard and Longman likewise view the holy war texts as ultimate or pristine (without blemish) war ethic within a certain historical period and setting because a holy God sanctions such actions; any ethical tensions are due to distortions or limitations in human understanding.[7]

At many points within a biblical ethic, however, the treatment of human beings *as directed by God in Scripture* simply does *not* display an ultimate ethic at the level of its most concrete-specific expression. For instance, the slavery texts provide many examples where the social ethic of Scripture establishes a better treatment of human beings relative to its ancient social setting. Yet it does not achieve an ultimate ethic in a fully realized sense. The treatment of slaves within Scripture has *real* ethical problems (not just perceived ones) and is best described as making moderate or *incremental*

---

[6]Eugene H. Merrill, "The Case for Moderate Discontinuity," in *Show Them No Mercy: Four Views*, 93.

[7]Tremper Longman III, "The Case for Radical Discontinuity: Responses," in *Show Them No Mercy: Four Views*, 58; Daniel L. Gard, "The Case for Eschatological Continuity," in *Show Them No Mercy: Four Views*, 139-40. For similar perspectives on the morality of holy war based on divine command, see Walter C. Kaiser Jr., *Toward Old Testament Ethics* (Grand Rapids: Zondervan, 1983), 267.

redemptive moves in its ancient setting. For example, Exodus 21:20-21 enshrines the right of slave masters to beat their slaves, which permits a latitude of punishment that could well have included very bloody and brutal beatings, and does so by positively invoking (instead of rejecting) the notion of people as property.[8] While the slavery texts were redemptive in an *incremental* sense, their ethic hardly reflected the best possible treatment of human beings.[9]

Corporal-punishment texts offer other examples. Deuteronomy 25:11-12 describes a fight between two men, and the wife of one intervenes in an attempt to save her husband by grabbing (and presumably injuring) the genitals of her husband's opponent.[10] As a penalty, the wife is subject to corporal mutilation: "You shall cut off her hand." Please note that these instructions (1) would have been considered to be from Moses and, equally so, from God; (2) are stated in *command* form (like the genocide instructions); and (3) have the added reinforcement "show her no pity [mercy]" (the same phrase found alongside genocide commands).[11] I have elsewhere written a chapter on the ethics of Deuteronomy 25:11-12 in the context of ANE corporal punishment and mutilation texts.[12] Suffice it to say, one cannot escape the *real* (not simply apparent) ethical problems that are part of this text. These verses and the broader collection of corporal-punishment texts are redemptive in an *incremental* sense (very much so), but, once again, their ethic hardly reflects the best possible treatment of human beings.

---

[8]"Anyone who beats their male or female slave with a rod must be punished if the slave dies as a direct result, but they are not to be punished if the slave recovers after a day or two, since the slave is their property" (Ex 21:20-21).

[9]The abolition (freedom) of all slaves and thus the elimination of any notion of human beings as property would obviously be a good move toward a better treatment of human beings. In today's context even more improvements can and should be carried forward into better treatment of humans within contemporary labor law, etc. However, even without the abolition of slavery one could argue that (1) a greater curtailment of beatings (limiting strokes and/or specifying more constructive punishments) and (2) establishing a range of penalties for slave owners who abused their slaves would show an extension of the redemptive spirit within the biblical text toward a better treatment of these (enslaved) human beings.

[10]"If two men are fighting and the wife of one of them comes to rescue her husband from his assailant, and she reaches out and seizes him by his private parts, you shall cut off her hand. Show her no pity" (Deut 25:11-12).

[11]This mutilation text is important for understanding ANE holy war because, as will be developed later (chapter thirteen), ancient warfare functioned as a way of punishing crimes and thus mirrored the corporal-punishment texts.

[12]William J. Webb, *Corporal Punishment in the Bible: A Redemptive-Movement Hermeneutic for Troubling Texts* (Downers Grove, IL: InterVarsity Press, 2011), 97-118.

In a similar manner the treatment of women within Scripture provides many examples of *real* ethical problems (not just perceived ones). Often biblical instructions depict a less-than-ultimate ethic in their dealings with women in areas of sexuality, marriage, divorce, and reproduction.[13] Such examples are particularly important to the topic of holy war since one of the more disturbing aspects of biblical holy war is the treatment of female prisoners of war for sexual and reproductive use (chapters five and six). We will argue that God takes the existing cultural norms of ancient warfare and, to invoke a sports metaphor, moves the ethical scrimmage markers downfield (*incremental* redemptive movement) but not all the way to the ultimate-ethic or pristine-ethic goal line. To describe the treatment of women within Scripture as "sexist" or to speak of the biblical treatment of slaves as "abusive" is anachronistic and a highly one-sided evaluation. Such declarations neglect reading the biblical text within its ancient-world context. Similarly, to label the Bible's war texts as "a darkest evil" or as "texts of terror," as Cowles and others do, forgets to first read these war texts within their existing social environment.[14] More importantly, it misses out on a crucial and wonderful element of redemptive movement within these texts. Only after we have situated texts within their original context can we begin asking how to bring them into dialogue with our modern context. The antitraditional approach captures certain ethical issues but misses what is incrementally redemptive in the biblical text.

However, the traditional position fares little better than Cowles's antitraditional stance. The ethical problems in these biblical texts—slavery, women, corporal punishment, and so on—are *not* simply apparent ethical problems. They are very real ethical problems, which are best addressed by understanding that God uses an *incremental ethic* within a fallen world. We cannot

---

[13]William J. Webb, *Slaves, Women and Homosexuals: Exploring the Hermeneutics of Cultural Analysis* (Downers Grove, IL: InterVarsity Press, 2001), 164-67; Webb, "A Redemptive-Movement Hermeneutic: The Slavery Analogy," in *Discovering Biblical Equality: Complementarity Without Hierarchy*, ed. Gordon D. Fee, Rebecca M. Groothuis, and Ronald Pierce (Downers Grove, IL: InterVarsity Press, 2004), 385-87; Webb, "A Redemptive-Movement Model," in *Four Views on Moving Beyond the Bible to Theology*, ed. Gary T. Meadors (Grand Rapids: Zondervan, 2009), 215-48.

[14]C. S. Cowles, "The Case for Radical Discontinuity," in *Show Them No Mercy: Four Views*, 14, 18; compare Phyllis Trible, *Texts of Terror* (Philadelphia: Fortress, 1984); John Shelby Spong, *The Sins of Scripture: Exposing the Bible's Texts of Hate to Reveal the God of Love* (New York: HarperSanFrancisco, 2006), 18.

assume that because something is in the Bible and sanctioned by a good God it necessarily reflects absolute goodness in all of its particulars. Biblical ethics more broadly teaches us that lesson. Why should we expect the holy war texts to reveal the best possible ethical treatment of human beings in the realm of warfare, when the ethics of Scripture in general simply do not work that way? We are not persuaded.

Let us be clear. Like the traditional view, *we do see God's goodness revealed in Scripture but in an incrementally redemptive sense* (not always in an ultimate or fully realized ethical sense), especially if we are talking about the immediacy of this fallen world. The incremental moves in a redemptive direction even within the ugly war texts serve as harbingers of God's ultimate redemption in the eschaton.

The good purposes of holy war. There should be no doubt that the holy war texts contain some good and lofty purposes. Figure 2.1 below distinguishes between certain *abstracted purposes* found up the ladder of abstraction from the *concrete pragmatics* or methodology for accomplishing such purposes found down the ladder of abstraction.

Figure 2.1. Ladder of abstraction: Holy war

The traditional position frequently appeals to these good purposes of holy war for justifying the war actions of genocide against the Canaanites.[15] Unfortunately, the hermeneutical and ethical reasoning involved fails to make a convincing case. Let us unpack the fallacies.

Hermeneutical fallacy. An oft-repeated hermeneutical blunder occurs when Christians use "up the ladder" (abstract) components of meaning to validate "down the ladder" (more concrete) components of meaning in the biblical text. The use of such abstract components as the sole or exclusive rationale for the concrete components of meaning in Scripture wanders perilously into hermeneutical quicksand. I have argued within *Slaves, Women and Homosexuals* and elsewhere that abstracted values/principles in Scripture often take on unstated pragmatic or culture-based components of rationale that reflect a less-than-ultimate ethic as those principles are applied in the more concrete (down the ladder) expression of the biblical text.[16] Any sort of upper-validates-lower argument can work only if the pristine values reflected in the abstracted principles are the *only* components of rationale affecting the concrete articulation of the text. But this is often a faulty assumption. If there exist unstated pragmatic and cultural components affecting the lower part of the ladder (as we will argue in chapters four through sixteen), then such "upper blesses lower" approaches falter in their hermeneutical assumptions.

For example, we could go back to Exodus 21:20-21 (beating slaves) and Deuteronomy 25:11-12 (cutting off a wife's hand) to illustrate the upper-blesses-lower fallacy. The *upper-level*, abstracted principle of "justice," when fleshed out in its *lower-level*, concrete meaning and how-to development, often includes within it *customs and pragmatics of the ancient world that are far from ethically neutral*—the ownership of slaves, the beating of adult human beings, the legal limits of extremely severe beatings, the cutting off a

---

[15]For the use of up-the-ladder noble purposes to justify the concrete military actions taken in biblical holy war, see Merrill, Gard, and Longman in *Show Them No Mercy: Four Views*, 80-88, 120-29, 139-40, 164-74. The fourth view, by C. S. Cowles, while not making this particular ethical mistake, creates a host of other ensuing problems in terms of God's participation in revelation that are no less problematic.

[16]See Webb, *Slaves, Women and Homosexuals*, 209-16. See also Webb, "Redemptive-Movement Hermeneutic," 398-99; Webb, "Gender Equality and Homosexuality," in *Discovering Biblical Equality*, 410-12.

wife's hand as part of a much larger ancient-justice world of bodily mutilations. These are the justice practices that "worked" in an ancient world, and yet they contained within them elements of considerable injustice. In a few pages we will discuss corporate or collective (in)justice texts. In a similar manner, these biblical texts reflect an enculturated ethic with ancient-world components and pragmatics informing the development of what "justice" (now with various embedded ethical problems) looked like in its most concrete expression down the hermeneutical ladder. Any upper-validates-lower arguments simply do not work because they ignore the cultural and pragmatic shaping of the biblical text.[17]

Ethical fallacy. Even more problematic is the ethical fallacy. The notion that up-the-ladder purposes within Scripture morally validate the lower or down-the-ladder concrete means (the specific methodology of genocide and war rape) commits a type of ethical suicide. One crucial question that pervades all ethical thought and must especially engage any reflection about military ethics is, Does the end or one's larger purpose justify the means?[18] The answer to this utilitarian approach to ethics should be a resounding "No," regardless of how wonderful or lofty the purposes or goals.[19] A utilitarian approach to ethics (the end justifies the means) is almost universally rejected by Christians and viewed as faulty or problematic by most secular ethicists.[20]

---

[17]One might posit "punishment of the Canaanites for idolatry" as an abstracted principle. Yet, when one heads down the ladder of abstraction to concrete how-to specifics that include the slaughter of babies who have not yet had a chance to choose for or against idolatry and the taking of beautiful virgins for sexual purposes, the cultural specifics and ancient-world pragmatics that *flesh out* the principle become problematic.

[18]Interestingly, a group of Islamic leaders denounced current terrorist activities on this very basis: "If some have disregarded a long and well-established tradition in favor of utopian dreams where *the end justifies the means*, they have done so of their own accord and without the sanction of God, His Prophet, or the learned tradition" (italics added). See Muslim Leaders, "Open Letter to His Holiness Pope Benedict XVI," www.catholicculture.org/culture/library/view.cfm?recnum=7910 (accessed March 7, 2019). The fallacy of the end justifying the means has always plagued sloppy ethical reflection and especially in military ethics, where tensions run high.

[19]Furthermore, the answer is especially negative if other more just and more humane means are available to achieve the same end.

[20]For both Christian and secular ethicists who have argued against an "end justifies the means" approach, see Stanley J. Grenz, *The Moral Quest: Foundations of Christian Ethics* (Downers Grove, IL: InterVarsity Press, 1997), 33-44; William F. May, "Virtues in a Professional Setting," in *Readings in Christian Ethics*, vol. 1, *Theory and Method*, ed. David K. Clark and Robert V. Rakestraw (Grand Rapids: Baker, 1994), 270-72; Norman L. Geisler, *Christian Ethics: Options and Issues* (Grand Rapids: Baker, 1989), 37-38, 76-77; Arthur F.

Ironically, the attempt by Merrill, Gard, and Longman to justify the concrete means of warfare in Scripture unwittingly uses a logically deficient, non-Christian approach to ethics.

Let us illustrate with God's instructions to masters in the slave-beating text of Exodus 21:20-21—a text that involves very *real* (not just perceived) ethical problems. In this text slave owners are permitted to beat their slaves within an inch of their lives with no penalty, provided the slaves get up after a day or two. Now, most readers would recognize an aspect of abstracted meaning (i.e., the right of disciplinary action) within this text that can be readily applied at the *abstracted level* in our contemporary context. We might put it like this: Employers have the right to take disciplinary action against employees who are negligent in fulfilling the terms of their contracts. This implicit or embedded meaning (the right of disciplinary action) reflects a good abstracted principle and larger purpose within the words of Scripture. Thus the text can be viewed as good at the level of abstracted expression. However, such abstracted virtue hardly validates the concrete methodology of brutal physical beatings and treating people as property, as explicitly invoked by the Exodus text. The virtue of up-the-ladder principles or purposes never rescues down-the-ladder methodology. Such upper-blesses-lower arguments violate sound ethical and hermeneutical reasoning.

The noninnocent or evil status of the Canaanites. The rather brutal practices of biblical holy war—the seemingly indiscriminate slaughter of women and children, the use of female prisoners for sexual and reproductive purposes by Israelite warriors—are frequently justified by observing that the Canaanites were not innocent victims.[21] In an attempt to support their

---

Holmes, *Ethics: Approaching Moral Decisions* (Downers Grove, IL: InterVarsity Press, 1984), 40-47; Philip E. Hughes, *Christian Ethics in Secular Society* (Grand Rapids: Baker, 1983), 74-79; Erwin W. Lutzer, *The Morality Gap: An Evangelical Response to Situation Ethics* (Chicago: Moody, 1972), 31-36; Harry J. Gensler, *Ethics: A Contemporary Introduction* (New York: Routledge, 1998), 138-56; Philip Pettit, "Consequentialism," in *A Companion to Ethics*, ed. Peter Singer (Cambridge, MA: Basil Blackwell, 1993), 230-40; Bernard Williams, "A Critique of Utilitarianism," in *Vice and Virtue in Everyday Life: Introductory Readings in Ethics*, 3rd ed., ed. Christina Sommers and Fred Sommers (New York: Harcourt Brace College, 1993), 123-32; John Martin Fischer and Mark Ravizza, *Ethics: Problems and Principles* (New York: Harcourt Brace Jovanovich, 1992), 31-32.

[21]As mentioned once before, within this book we use the term "holy war" of any war within biblical texts (not just the Joshua conquest battles) where Yahweh is seen as fighting in conjunction with, on behalf of, or through some human version of war.

pristine-ethic approach, Merrill, Gard, and Longman each try to resolve or at least lessen the severity of the ethical problem by suggesting that there were "no innocent victims," not even among slaughtered babies, in the practice of biblical holy war.[22] Accordingly, they make much of certain evil Canaanite practices in order to justify Israel's brutal military actions against them.

No one would debate that many Canaanite practices were evil. Their sacrifice of children to Molech was a hideous evil. But that is not the issue for our reasoning here. The issue is *not* whether the Canaanites were evil. They were. Rather, the real question is whether evil actions by any person or people group provide ethical justification for *any and every sort of retaliatory action* taken against them. Within the Toronto region most Canadians are familiar with gruesome details of the trials of various rapists who held captive, repeatedly raped, tortured, and after several weeks killed their young female victims. One could argue that justice for such criminals could be found through treating them in like manner: incarcerate them, rape them many times, torture them, and slowly and painfully kill them. One might *feel* like doing so. But to *actually* do so would mean sinking to an extremely debased ethical level. Invoking such *ethically debased justice* against evil crimes never justifies the injustice component within such justice.

The evil nature of any crime, no matter how insidiously evil it is, does not legitimize *any and every sort of punishment action* taken against the perpetrator. We wish to make the point here that Canaanite evil practices do not (and did not) justify any and every form of action taken against them.

Unfortunately, Merrill, Gard, and Longman cloud the issue further by an unwitting equivocation on terms in their appeal to "no innocent victims." The equivocation revolves around usage of the word *innocents* within a discussion of war ethics. The classic understanding of *innocents* in the context of any contemporary discussion of war ethics is *noncombatants who are helpless against armed forces,* namely, unarmed civilians such as women,

---

[22]Merrill, "Case for Moderate Discontinuity," 82-84; Tremper Longman III, "The Case for Spiritual Continuity," in *Show Them No Mercy: Four Views,* 173-74; Daniel L. Gard, "Spiritual Continuity: Responses," in *Show Them No Mercy: Four Views,* 201. See also Christopher J. H. Wright, "Ethics," in *Dictionary of the Old Testament Historical Books,* ed. Bill T. Arnold and H. G. M. Williamson (Downers Grove, IL: InterVarsity Press, 2005), 266.

children, babies, the elderly, the insane, the crippled, and so on.[23] When the discussion quickly switches from (1) no *military innocents*, that is, noncombatants in warfare as a standard part of discussions about war ethics to (2) some kind of no *theological innocents*, then the writers have unwittingly used a semantic shift in order to avoid or mask the ethical issue. The shift may well not have been a conscious or intentional one, but it has happened.

Of course, all of us share a measure of theological noninnocence from birth within a fallen world. All of us to the degree that we violate God's commands increase the level of our theological noninnocence. Nevertheless, that one's enemy lacks "theological innocence" (to some degree or another) does not remove the need to treat one's enemies with dignity and respect, even in war. Here we encounter the real ethical issue. In other words, those who are not *theologically* innocent may well still be *militarily* innocent—that is, unarmed and helpless noncombatant people. Some war actions are simply more just and humane than other actions, regardless of how "bad" the behavior shown by the opponents.[24] The treatment today of military noncombatants with torture, rape, death, ritualistic mutilations, permanent imprisonment, and so on—any of these actions—is nothing short of grotesque brutality. These are and should be considered war crimes. This sort of horrific treatment of noncombatants falls woefully short in the pursuit of a "best possible" war ethic. Who would want to incorporate these actions as acceptable within an updated version of Geneva or Hague conventions?[25]

One must also address the ethics of intergenerational or corporate (in) justice within Scripture—biblical texts where babies, children, and wives are punished for the sins of their husband/father due to corporate and household identity. We will address this issue more fully at a later point (see appendix D), but a brief summary here will demonstrate its relevance to holy war. On the one hand, Scripture at times describes and accepts a highly indiscriminate corporate-identity approach to justice, where unfortunately children suffer

---

[23]See the excellent chapter "The Killing of Innocent Persons in Wartime," by Robert L. Holmes in *On War and Morality* (Princeton, NJ: Princeton University Press, 1989), 183-213.
[24]Perhaps the demented enemy behavior even led to/instigated the war actions.
[25]For the Geneva War Convention and other treaties governing conduct of war, see "The Avalon Project at Yale Law School: The Laws of War," http://avalon.law.yale.edu/subject _menus/lawwar.asp (accessed March 7, 2019).

for the sins or crimes of their parents. Such indiscriminate justice patterns are understandable within the collectivism and dominant patriarchy of the culture of the ancient world. It happened a lot. Nevertheless, its usage within Scripture creates a certain form of unjust justice. On the other hand, the biblical text itself seems to be moving *against* this prevailing ancient cultural trend when at times biblical authors cry out against indiscriminate corporate-identity justice, where innocent people suffer for the wrongful actions of others. This countercultural voice starts out small (a few verses in the Pentateuch) but finds greater canonical realization along the way and ultimate fulfillment within the New Testament's highly individualized justice at the final judgment.

If this description of canonical development has merit, then it demonstrates by the voice of Scripture itself the lack of complete or best-possible justice within those earlier justice actions. Here is the point. The theological noninnocence that all share at birth and that increases due to later wrongful acts does not justify killing the babies and children of really bad people. Labeling all infants and children as theological noninnocents is fine. However, to transfer the *increased* individual noninnocence from those who committed certain evils acts to those who did not commit the evil acts is highly problematic. This assumed cultural or pragmatic component (along with other unstated pragmatics; see appendix D) within biblical holy war texts ought to be recognized and assessed as such. Biblical justice takes place in a real, tangible social world with many time-locked components of ancient culture affecting concrete articulations of pristine abstracted purposes.

So let us ponder our earlier question about legitimizing penal/justice actions that are the same as the crime itself against the perpetrators of an evil crime. What about the specific punitive actions of biblical holy war? We must ask, What exactly was the specific crime for which slaughtered babies were guilty and being punished within the holy war texts? The answer is "None." What exactly was the crime of the virgins who were forced by Israelite warriors to fulfill their sexual and procreative desires? Their crime was certainly not the same as the general Canaanite populace or leaders within that group; these were probably teenage girls. Surely, questions about any and every action ought to haunt Christians as they reflect on these two specific acts of holy war justice. The evil nature of any crime, no matter how insidiously evil it is, does not legitimize *every sort of action* (such as inflicting punishment that exactly replicates the evil crime) becoming a best-justice punishment taken against the perpetrator, *let alone against those who are peripherally related to the perpetrator of the crime.*[26] Unfortunately, one cannot switch between *theological* innocence and *military* innocence to avoid such problems within a biblical war ethic.

Holy war as a foreshadowing of eschatological judgment. Finally, the traditional or pristine-ethic view attempts to justify biblical holy war as devoid of any (real) ethical problems by appealing to its foreshadowing of eschatological judgment. All three scholars—Longman, Merrill, and Gard—draw on Meredith Kline's concept of intrusion ethics, which argues that the actions of biblical holy war are justified because the total destruction of the Canaanites functions as a preview of the final judgment.[27] Accordingly, Gard suggests that seeing "the destruction of the Canaanites as the *final judgment foreshadowed* is extraordinarily helpful in coming to grips with what is for many an ethical quandary."[28] Longman summarizes Kline's understanding of holy war ethic as follows:

> Kline reminds us that the punishment for sin is death. The lesson that rebellion—and all sin is rebellion—leads to death is made clear in the Garden of Eden (Gen. 2:17). It is only because of God's extraordinary grace that Adam and Eve were not killed on the spot when they ate the fruit of the tree. Indeed, it is because of that grace that *any of us* breathe. The period of God's extraordinary grace, often called common grace, is a special circumstance. In this light, we

---

[26]All ethical discussion must engage the question of reasonable force. The most appropriate force is generally that which uses the least destructive means necessary to accomplish its purposes, and when the force is in war or personal self-defense (as opposed to punishment of individuals for crimes within a society), reasonable force is also the most highly discriminate, causing the least collateral damage to noncombatants or nonparticipants to the act of crime.

[27]Meredith G. Kline, *The Structure of Biblical Authority* (Grand Rapids: Eerdmans, 1972; repr., Eugene, OR: Wipf & Stock, 1997). Kline views the total-destruction component of holy war (*ḥerem*) as an intrusion of end-times ethics into an earlier biblical period; it is as if the final judgment of Revelation appears proleptically in the war stories of the Old Testament. Kline's intrusion ethics or "foreshadowing of eschatological judgment" is introduced by Longman ("Case for Spiritual Continuity," 185) but also strongly endorsed within the responses by Merrill and Gard ("Response to Tremper Longman III," in *Show Them No Mercy: Four Views*, 199, 202). See also Wright, "Ethics," 267.

[28]Gard, "Response to Tremper Longman III," 202 (italics added).

should not be amazed that God ordered the death of the Canaanites, but rather we should stand in amazement *that he lets anyone live.* The Conquest, according to Kline, involves the intrusion of the ethics of the end times, the consummation, into the period of common grace. In a sense, the destruction of the Canaanites is a preview of the final judgment.[29]

One can understand why the idea of eschatological judgment helps some Christians handle the difficulties of biblical holy war. By invoking the category of "final judgment" it leaves little room for debate about ethics. We also would affirm that God's final, eschatological justice is absolutely pure, pristine, and untainted. His final white-throne judgment at the end of salvation history surely does not succumb to any of this world's fallen enactments of justice. Furthermore, all Christians would agree that within our cursed world sin does bring about death—this is a dominant biblical concept. And of course God could, should he choose, enact a precursor of eschatological judgment at any time before the actual close of salvation history. Moreover, we would readily agree that biblical holy war *is* thematically linked to the eschatological battle in Revelation and to its portrait of final judgment.[30] Perhaps Christians should, therefore, view biblical holy war in some kind of unusual "outside time" or "superimposed time" occurrence that brings forward the categories of eschatological judgment and thus suspends the typical norms of military ethics.

While brought-forward eschatological judgment might seem like a nice solution, that answer does not make logical or ethical sense. First, are the *specific actions* of Old Testament holy war an accurate ethical reflection of eschatological judgment? While broad thematic connections exist between Old Testament holy war and eschatological judgment, this does not ethically validate the specific Old Testament war actions themselves. The argument works only if one can take those war actions along a time continuum and drop them—like drag-and-drop on a digital screen—into the future judgment scene without raising any ethical problems. In order to ponder this construct one might ask several questions about the future expression of justice: Could Christians rightly imagine Jesus taking his sword and physically slaying babies

---

[29]Longman III, "Case for Spiritual Continuity," 185 (italics original).
[30]See the thematic connections in chapter sixteen.

or children with Down Syndrome in an eschatological battle simply because they are related by birth to the enemy, namely, people who oppose God or who have not accepted Christ as Savior?[31] This repulsive portrait is not a Christian vision of God's pristine eschatological justice, let alone a good depiction of his revealed character, since he displays a restrained focus on justice and an infinitely greater and more lavish emphasis on love, forgiveness, and grace. So if the specifics of past holy war are not ethically compatible with the future framework, one might be wise to refrain from reading the absolute righteousness of eschatological judgment back into fallen-world enactments of judgment. Yes, there are clear thematic connections, and these are important at a story-line level (see chapters three and sixteen). But that is where the connective impact ends; eschatological justice does not magically erase all elements of ethical injustice found within the justice of an earlier world.[32]

Second, does the idea of placing future judgment into the past say anything about the ethics of specific military practices in "reverse" Old Testament holy war? At times God enacts holy war *against* Israel through foreign nations (e.g., Deut 28:7, 25; see appendix C). The war invasions by Assyria against the northern kingdom and by Babylon against the southern kingdom are cases in point. In this reversal setting the concept of holy war in the Bible is uniquely dissimilar to our contemporary understanding of genocide because Yahweh fights against Israel as much as he fights against its enemies, the Canaanites. The essence of war judgment in biblical holy war is not strictly ethnic (see appendix B). Both Longman and Gard provide a helpful discussion of reverse holy war, wherein God uses foreign nations to bring Israel to military defeat; Yahweh is even seen as leading these foreign armies into battle to fight against Israel (e.g., Jer 21:3-7; Dan 1:1-3; Is 45:1-7).[33]

---

[31]Also, what about the saints who ride with Christ into the eschatological battle? Could we imagine them being given good-looking virgins from among the captives?

[32]In the final battle *only* Jesus fights through a spoken word. See chapter sixteen. Saying that killing Canaanites is an eschatological precursor (and thus untainted) has additional problems: (1) using human agents makes the war actions susceptible to excess and enculturated/ accommodated ethic, and (2) it incurs the psychological trauma foisted on Israelite warriors of taking human lives. On psychological damage resulting from war killings see Dave Grossman, *On Killing: The Psychological Cost of Learning to Kill in War and Society*, rev. ed. (New York: Back Bay Books, 2009), 31, 53, 193-94, 273.

[33]Gard, "Case for Eschatological Continuity," 122-23; Longman, "Case for Spiritual Continuity," 176-77.

Accordingly, we should ask, Is this not *also* a harbinger of eschatological judgment? Are we to infer that a foreshadowing of the eschatological judgment in holy war takes place *only* where Yahweh fights on behalf of Israel (but not in holy war against Israel)? Surely the thematic connections and foreshadowing are part of both Yahweh scenes—holy war and reverse holy war. However, connections to the final eschatological judgment do not at all validate the ethics of particular war practices of the past, whether we are talking about the war practices of Israel against foreign nations or about the war practices of foreign nations against Israel. For surely, if anything can be settled with certainty (see chapter thirteen), the specific war practices of Assyria and Babylon were "ethically challenged" to the extreme! So, yes, a thematic connection exists between the final eschatological judgment and Old Testament holy war, even carrying through to reverse holy war. But that connection does not perform any magical cleansing of the horrendous war actions performed by the Assyrian and Babylonian armies.

Here is the rub. If we now have to argue that a flash foreshadowing earlier in time of the final eschatological judgment applies in *only* certain cases of holy warfare against foreign countries but not in Yahweh war against Israel, then the persuasion of such constructs begins to weaken considerably. This is to say nothing of the fact that intrusion ethics as a construct is entirely hypothetical and conjectural to begin with—it is never explicitly taught within Scripture.

Third, one could argue that *all* biblical justice connects as a foreshadowing or harbinger of the ultimate judgment day. In a sense all the justice passages of Scripture find their culmination in the last day. For instance, since the kings of Israel functioned as arbitrators in their earthly administration of justice, their justice foreshadowed the final judgment by the ultimate Davidic King and Messiah. For that matter, even a slave-beating text such as Exodus 21:20-21 connects thematically with the concept of eschatological justice. The temporal judgment administered by an Israelite slave owner in punishing his slave anticipates the final judgment day, since within biblical theology (1) slave owners are called on to remember that they have a master in heaven (Eph 6:9; Col 4:1) and (2) the eschatological day of judgment is depicted as a divine master administering beatings to unfaithful slaves (Lk 12:47-48). However, one simply cannot read backward from the eschatological portrait with its related imagery in order to bless all earlier precursors with ethical absolution. Thematic connections to pristine eschatological justice and judgment, although they clearly exist, hardly validate the less-than-ultimate ethic that is expressed in a text such as Exodus 21:20-21, used by Israelite masters.[34]

Fourth, the final eschatological battle fought by our Lord Jesus will not share the same ethical pitfalls of Israel's holy war battles. Yes, the holy war battles of the past and future have thematic continuity. No question. But there are significant differences. For instance, unlike Israel's holy war practices, the final eschatological battle (1) will not use literal swords—only the spoken word, (2) starts and finishes within an instant, (3) guards against the slaughter of any noncombatants, and (4) places proper weight on individual justice and is not encumbered by corporate, ethnic, or parental affiliations, and so on. For a development of the evidence see chapter sixteen. These are important differences that highlight canonical movement at an ethical level within the battlefield themes of Scripture—an unfolding or developing holy war ethic that culminates in the book of Revelation.

Now, we must make a confession. We also (like Merrill, Gard, and Longman) use a theology of the final eschatological judgment to "rescue us" in part from the ethical dilemmas of Old Testament holy war. However, there is a huge difference between our invocation of eschatological judgment and that of the traditional view. Instead of using the eschatological judgment to validate the ethics of particular holy war practices back in the days of ancient

---

[34]Such reasoning fails to appreciate the relationship between ethics and theological analogy. That a connection exists in biblical theology between what goes on *upstairs* (a biblical portrait of God) and what takes place down here on the *ground level* (human activity on earth) does not automatically validate the social ethics of particular human structures, customs, or actions even if they are directed by God and part of biblical instruction. For instance, just because Scripture (1) explicitly teaches the virtue of leaving marks or bruises as a part of corporal punishment and (2) contains theological portraits of Yahweh using the rod in beatings that leave such physical wounds, this does not mean that Christians today who affirm an "absolutely no marks" Dobson-style corporal punishment should change and begin to leave marks when spanking children. For a redemptive-movement approach to the corporal-punishment texts, see Webb, *Corporal Punishment in the Bible*. For an extended discussion of theological analogy, see Webb, *Slaves, Women and Homosexuals*, 185-92. Whether one jumps upstairs in present time or in future time (as Kline does with the war texts), these sorts of arguments from theological analogy are tenuous at best.

Israel (Merrill, Gard, and Longman), we appeal to eschatological judgment as the place where God will finally and perfectly provide a counterbalancing correction to the injustices of holy war justice and, for that matter, to any other elements of unjust justice within the incremental ethic of the biblical text. When it comes to the specifics of Old Testament holy war practices and their real (not just perceived) injustices, Christians need to embrace the theme of eschatological reversal within the ultimate justice story, namely, that God will someday right all wrongs. Our final better answer will emphasize the unfinished justice story.

CONCLUSION

This chapter explains why the traditional answers do not fit our contemporary ethical questions concerning genocide and war rape. Other chapters will provide further support for this square-pegs, round-holes thesis. By the end of the book it should be obvious that the ethics of these specific war actions—genocide and war rape—were not on the original readers' ethical radar. We will argue for placing the traditional answers where they fit best, namely, in relationship to the story-line questions of the ancient audience (chapter three).

Within this chapter, however, we have begun the discussion about alignment of the traditional answers based on logical, ethical, and hermeneutical reasoning. The appeal to God as source of the holy war commands, to their lofty and good purposes, and to the evil character of enemies, much as we might like it to, hardly makes a convincing case that the concrete-specific war methodology of Israel's holy war actions (genocide and war rape) reflects a pristine, untainted ethic. In short, these traditional answers do not connect very well with questions about genocide and war rape.

Nor does invoking the connection in biblical theology between the final eschatological judgment and past occasions of Old Testament holy war alleviate the ethical problems of specific war actions (genocide and war rape) within the biblical text. While the eschatology/foreshadowing solution sounds reasonable because of overarching themes that tie these events together, it fails to account for the differences in particular methodologies between the past and the future portraits, let alone the ethical incompatibility of placing the past elements into the final expression of justice. The actions would have to fit ethically at either end of the holy war continuum for the argument to work. Rather than saying that eschatological judgment makes it ethically okay for Israel to slaughter babies and grab pretty-looking women in holy war, it may be better to invoke eschatological judgment as the place where all deficiencies within Scripture's *incrementally redemptive ethic* (i.e., a partly but not fully redemptive ethic) will be resolved in a final sense, including these troublesome ones.

3

WHERE TRADITIONAL
ANSWERS DO WORK

THIS CHAPTER LOOKS AT where the traditional answers *do* work. It is the positive side of what we began in the last chapter as part of our square-pegs, round-holes thesis. Based on logical, hermeneutical, and ethical factors, chapter two argued that the traditional answers—*a holy God, removing idolatry, the evil of the Canaanites, and ties to eschatological judgment*—do not work well in answering our contemporary ethical questions about genocide and war rape. So where do the traditional answers fit? What questions do they answer?

This chapter argues that the traditional answers align well with the ethical questions of the *original* readers. These questions involve the land promised to Israel, sacred space, and formation of a new Eden—questions tied to the overarching story line of the Bible as a whole. The biblical authors were wrestling with the "Is God Just?" question in relation to a number of "Canaanite" events throughout their history and current life setting. (While perhaps confusing at first, we will soon unpack the difference between *ethnic* Canaanites and *literary* Canaanites.) Here is how the "Is God Just?" question unfolds in the canonical story of God's sacred space:

The Sacred Space Story [C = Canaanites]

1. Is God just in removing Adam and Eve [C1] from the garden?

2. Is God just in driving the Canaanites [C2] out of the Promised Land?

3. Is God just in removing the northern-kingdom Israelites [C3] from the land?

4. Is God just in taking the southern-kingdom Israelites [C4] from the land?

5. Is God/Jesus just in expanding the land promise to the entire earth and bringing "outsiders" into the kingdom while placing "insiders" [C5] outside?

6. Is God/Jesus just in taking the sins of idolaters [C6] on himself?[1]

7. Is God/Jesus just in creating a new heavens and earth (a final Eden) where unrepentant sinners/idolaters [C7] are not permitted to enter?

We will see that the biblical story about holy war starts in the early chapters of Genesis and ends in Revelation. It is a broad-based canonical story about the development of *sacred space*—a place for God to dwell with humans. This core issue ties together the function of holy war at each stage of the story line from Genesis to Revelation. Events in each section implicitly raised pressing questions of divine justice for the authors and original readers that we need to consider.

As chapters four through twelve and appendixes A through C show, the Bible's original readers were *not* asking the specific questions about military ethics that we do because of recent developments in war ethics (Hague/Geneva and beyond) and a greater sensitivity to issues of religion and violence (post-9/11). Today we are asking about genocide and war rape in the biblical narratives.[2] The original readers did not. Frankly, from their point of view within the ancient world, Israelite military practices looked rather gentle and tame. While from our contemporary war horizon we see Israelite war actions as horrific, and they were, early readers would have seen them as less violent than contemporary nations, and they were. Of concern for original readers was a different question:

---

[1]Perhaps this is a separate phase, or perhaps it should be included within the previous question. Also, one could easily add another stage in relation to Paul and the work of the Spirit. The layout and questions are by no means exhaustive.

[2]Contemporary readers should not make anachronistic judgments that eviscerate the ancient context as a mitigating factor in the ethically problematic war actions. On the other hand, the context, whether ancient or modern, never justifies the elements of ethical failings in any action no matter how contextually ubiquitous and thus to some extent "understandable." The *development* of ethics in any domain pushes us to evaluate the ethics of the present and the past in a critical and reasoned manner. While the context of ancient war surely ought to temper our assessment, it makes certain war actions/crimes (genocide and war rape) no less morally wrong or repugnant.

*In the creation of sacred space (an Eden-like place for dwelling with humans),
is God just in driving out the "Canaanite" idolaters of any generation (even his
own people) or not permitting them to enter that space?*

THE QUESTION ON THEIR MINDS

Why was this sacred-space/drive-out question on the minds of the original
readers? Here is the reason. The shaping of the Hebrew Bible over time was
heavily affected by the issues of a preexilic, exilic, and postexilic audience. As
effective communicators of all sorts have observed, if you feel the pain of
your audience, you know the felt needs that a writer or speaker must address.
The pain for much of the original audience and biblical writers was linked to
their experience of being driven out of the land (as the Canaanites once were).
In order for them to trust God—their Yahweh God—they needed to know
that God's actions in the broad story line (their being driven out of the land)—
were just and that God intended, one day, to fulfill his new-Eden promises.

As with Adam and Eve being driven out of Eden and the Canaanites under
Joshua being driven out of the land (a new Eden), the exile-horizon readers
were asking their *own* Eden-exile questions about their *own* day. We can see
this in how they framed their exilic experience in terms that connected it with
that of Canaanites previously driven out of the land. Many exilic and postexilic
Israelites at the culmination of the formation of the story line in the Hebrew
Bible were reading/hearing the biblical story through the lenses of their *own*
Canaanite experience. Even the later Ezra-Nehemiah audience and intertes-
tamental audiences, while back in the land, were struggling with the diminished conditions in their day due to the profound impact of the exile. To put
the exile question bluntly: *Why were we kicked out of the Promised Land?*
Their grief was tied to the land they had lost and their hopes for a final Eden.[3]

That driving-out/sacred-space question—on the minds of the original
audience—fits extremely well with the answers of a traditional view: God's

---

[3] The Israelite experience of being expelled from the land during exile (under Assyria and
Babylon) would have been far worse (in terms of war ethics) than the actions of Joshua's
generation against the original Canaanites. See chapter thirteen and appendix C. They
simply did not have our contemporary lenses of Geneva and Hague conventions. They had
their experience of being driven out (by the Assyrians and Babylonians) through which to
read the Canaanites' being driven out (by Joshua). That is the level at which most original
readers wrestled with God's justice.

holiness, removal of idolatry, sin of the "Canaanites" (the quotation marks mean every Canaanite-*like* generation, even the Israelites themselves), and future judgment that will bring about a final Eden-*like* experience. By seeing a canonical enlargement of the traditional answers (e.g., Eden-*like* hopes, Canaanite-*like* generations), one can capture in new and fresh ways how these traditional answers fit in terms of the original audience. Shortly, after raising a couple of other matters, we will spend the rest of the chapter walking through drive-out/sacred-space episodes in Scripture that carry forward the holy war story line in its canonical unfolding.

THEIR STORY-LINE QUESTION IS NOT OUR MILITARY-ETHICS QUESTION

At the risk of being repetitive, we need to say that *their* (Israel's) drive-out/sacred-space, broad story-line question is not the same as *our* contemporary ethical questions. For the purpose of comparison, let us restate the original readers' justice question:

> *In the creation of sacred space (an Eden-like place for dwelling with humans), is God just in driving out the "Canaanite" idolaters of any generation (even his own people) or not permitting them to enter that space?*

The original audience of the Hebrew Bible during the preexilic (driving out is coming), exilic (driving out is here), and postexile times (aftermath of being driven out) were reading/hearing the earlier Joshua war texts and even the original Eden account about Adam and Eve through their own experience of being driven out of sacred space. Earlier audiences during the time of the monarchy would have reflected on a similar question with a view to the successes and failures of their *own* Davidic king to rid their generation of idols, fight their war battles, restore the temple (Eden in miniature), and secure the land (a slightly larger new Eden).[4]

---

[4]For an excellent and accessible development of temple/land themes as a new Eden within biblical theology, see G. K. Beale and Mitchell Kim, *God Dwells Among Us: Expanding Eden to the Ends of the Earth* (Downers Grove, IL: InterVarsity Press, 2014). Two earlier works laid the foundation for this recent temple/land reflection: G. K. Beale, *The Temple and the Church's Mission: A Biblical Theology of the Dwelling Place of God*, NSBT 17 (Downers Grove, IL: InterVarsity Press, 2008); Beale, *We Become What We Worship: A Biblical Theology of Idolatry* (Downers Grove, IL: InterVarsity Press, 2004). See also Beale, "Eden, the Temple, and the Church's Mission in the New Creation," *JETS* 48, no. 1 (2005): 5-31;

By way of comparison, our questions are part of a conversation about present-day military ethics and the specific actions of genocide and war rape. Our ethical question was not theirs, whether voiced in the accusatory style of new atheism or the agonizing inquiry of a troubled Christian:

How can Christians believe in a God who encourages genocidal baby killing and virgin rape? In a post-9/11 world of wanton "holy war" actions, how can we possibly justify the cruel acts of genocide against the Canaanites and Israelite warriors grabbing young virgins?

Hopefully, the difference is becoming clearer. Our ethical questions are not at the broader level of the story line. Genocide and war rape, while at the top of our minds, reside in the ancient biblical text and for the original Israelite audience several floors below the level of the story line, with certain details of how warfare took place in an ancient world. Our questions zero in on a particular phase of the broader story line and the descriptions of particular war actions against the Canaanites. Our contemporary ethical questions are not about God *driving out* Adam and Eve from the garden, or about Israel's northern and southern kingdoms *being driven out* of the land, or about Jesus *placing/driving the religious elite* (those who thought they were insiders) outside the kingdom, and so forth. No, our questions are about particular war actions as they relate to the Canaanites and the norms of ancient warfare. We hope this differentiation helps. By the end of this book one should be convinced (more evidence is coming) that our contemporary questions about a biblical war ethic were not on the minds of the original readers. They were troubled by other matters and, given their ancient-war horizons, would not have seen certain ethical injustices in war practices that we see. More about this later.

We can now approach the main subject matter of this chapter—showing how the traditional answers fit nicely with the story-line questions of the original audience. The first thing we need to highlight is a proper understanding of the most holy God. We develop this topic first because it is central to understanding the need for sacred space.

John H. Walton and J. Harvey Walton, *The Lost World of the Israelite Conquest* (Downers Grove, IL: InterVarsity Press, 2017).

GOD MOST HOLY: MOUNTAIN, HOUSE, AND SACRIFICES

Many Christians live with a deficient, puny concept of God. Unless we expand our thinking to include the difference between our fallen, sinful world and an untainted, pristine God and the extent to which he goes on our behalf, we will never comprehend the interface between God and our world. *A cosmic-sized understanding of God's powerful holiness allows us to see the acute need for sacred space within the story line of Scripture.* Exodus and Leviticus present a portrait of God that, if caught in its fullness, is unforgettable and clearly seen in Israel's threefold encounter with Yahweh (1) on the mountain, (2) in the house/temple, and (3) through the sacrifice rituals inside the house.

The mountain. The mountain portrait in Exodus 19–24 captures a spine-shivering sense of God's powerful holiness in several ways. Only Moses, Aaron, Nadab, Abihu, and seventy elders were invited to go up the mountain; the people stayed at a distance. They all experienced darkness, thick smoke, thunder, and lightning. Yet, the leaders who climbed the mountain gazed also at a dramatically different reality. Under the feet of Yahweh, they saw a smooth, still surface—something like a crystal-clear lake. To our Canadian minds come images of a beautiful, tranquil, glacier-fed mountain lake in the Rocky Mountains—Louise or Moraine (similar to Tahoe or Crater Lake). Stunning beauty, peacefulness on the grandest scale, hypnotically inviting. As in a *symphony of peace* Yahweh eats and drinks a shalom meal with his people. (Note: Save this majestic image of the *peace-loving* God as defining the core of Yahweh's being for putting together the subversive war texts and especially the "I am not David!" portrait developed later [chapter fourteen].) Another element of profound holiness is found in the rituals that began this incredible mountain experience. All of the people had to prepare themselves with three days of ritual purification that included bathing, washing clothes, and, interestingly, not participating in sexual relationships. (Another note: Tuck this "no sex on the mountain" tidbit away for a powerfully redemptive feature in the war-rape chapters [chapters five and six].)

The house. At the bottom of the mountain God's people build his house—a temple. In the desert it was a moving temple known as a tabernacle/tent of meeting. Yahweh's temple communicated holy distance and yet provision for fellowship in a number of ways. For instance, the innermost room (holy of holies) was constructed with gold, and construction materials decreased in value as one progressed outward. Also, the persons and times of access moved from more restricted to less restricted as one moved away from the holy of holies. These differences marked the different levels of *graded holiness.*[5] With movement outward from the holy of holies, the level of holiness changed in a descending pattern. (1) Yahweh's cube-shaped room, where he would meet and speak with Moses, is known as the holy of holies—the most holy place. Then came two further descending levels of holiness within the temple: (2) the holy place and (3) the sacred courts. Beyond the gate of the temple, graded holiness kept descending with (4) the camp of the people; (5) outside the camp, where people with certain diseases had to live; and eventually (6) the vast desert. In biblical thinking the desert was the place where little grows, the haunt and abode of demons, the theological opposite to lush Eden and God's most concentrated presence. Once a year the sins of the people on Yom Kippur (including even the high-handed sins) were sent out on the Azazel-goat to the desert (Lev 16). Sacred space meant that sin remained as far away from God as possible.

Get ready for the next part. Here is where the sense of holy distance and personal involvement takes on cosmic proportions.[6] Within God's cube-shaped, boxlike room is another box—a rectangular box known as the ark of the covenant. Biblical authors refer to the ark of the covenant (the box within a box) as the footstool of God (1 Chron 28:2; see also Ps 99:5; 132:7). The footstool image helps complete the picture of God most holy. God does not live in the cube room. That is a faulty conception. Rather, he is enthroned in the heavens, and the ark is his footstool on earth. The mind-blowing image is this: *God is enthroned far off in the heavens so cosmically distant in his purity and being that it takes all of these layers or levels of graded holiness just for his toes to touch our earth.*

---

[5]Philip Peter Jenson, *Graded Holiness: A Key to the Priestly Conception of the World*, JSOT-Sup 106 (Sheffield: Sheffield Academic Press, 1992); see also Allen P. Ross, *Recalling the Hope of Glory: Biblical Worship from the Garden to the New Creation* (Grand Rapids: Kregel, 2006), 173-96.
[6]Even academics like us get shivers (literally) when we think of this portrait of God. The sensation of holiness and sacred space is overwhelming.

The mountain and temple share the image of God's feet. Moses and the leaders of Israel eat and drink a shalom meal before a *peaceful*, tranquil lake (a smooth, crystal-clear sea) that appears under God's feet. This mountain image carries over into the temple with its in-house version of a crystal sea (the lavers) and a place for God's feet (the ark of the covenant). Even so, the psalmist invites the worshiper to draw near to God's feet: "Exalt the LORD our God and worship at his footstool [the ark]; he is holy" (Ps 99:5; see also 1 Chron 28:2; Ps 132:7).

The sacrifices. At the bottom of the mountain, God built a house. Within the house Yahweh prescribed certain rituals known as sacrifices. The rabbis tell us that God gave us five fingers so that we would never forget the five sacrifices. If you use your fingers to number them (kinesthetic learning), they are easier to remember: reparation, purification, burnt, grain, peace.[7] The sacrifices capture holy distance and the recognition of sacred space in a number of ways that are different from yet complement the mountain and house. For starters, one can quickly grasp a theology of approach to a holy God (drawing near to his footstool) using three English prepositions—*from/ to/with*—in order to gain a sense of the holy distance of transformation a worshiper must travel. With reparation and purification sacrifices, the worshiper moves away *from* sin that displeases God and finds forgiveness. With burnt and grain sacrifices, the smell becomes a pleasing aroma, and the worshiper moves in dedication and consecration *to/toward* God. Finally, as a climax to the drawing-near ritual, the worshiper eats and drinks a shalom meal in the presence of God with the mountain backdrop of crystal-clear serenity (a peaceful, pure lake), celebrating being at peace *with* God.[8]

When we talk about God most holy, the multiple elements in these pictures— the mountain, house, and sacrifices—indicate what holiness and sacred space

---

[7]We have purposefully chosen the *drawing-near* order of sacrifices found in the passages of Scripture where worshipers in a live setting are approaching God's footstool in worship. There are at least five different orders of sacrifice that we find in the Bible; each serves a certain function. The procedural or drawing-near order teaches the worshiper a theology of approach to the holy God and thus converges with the mountain and temple portraits.

[8]The shalom meal celebrated being at peace *with*, in communion *with*, and in covenant *with* one another and God. See Ross, *Recalling the Hope of Glory*, 197-208. I (Bill) am highly indebted to Ross for having shaped my thinking through four Hebrew exegesis courses on the Pentateuch in addition to my ThM thesis, which I completed under Ross and Burns on the subject of Levitical sacrifice.

mean. That image of holiness and sacred space is crucial to putting together the drive-out war passages of the Bible. As we put it earlier: *a cosmic-sized understanding of God's holiness allows us to see the acute need for sacred space within the story line of Scripture.* God's character is so pure, untainted, and pristine that it takes many layers of graded holiness just for his toes to touch our world; at the same time, worshipers must journey to the footstool (and shalom lake) via five sacrifices. Without the creation of sacred space there is no meeting place for a most holy God and sinful human beings.

Here is the unfolding story of sacred space within Scripture—or at least a short version of it—as it relates to holy war, Canaanites, the land, and a new Eden.[9] Our overview here is at best a selective sampling. Nevertheless, it should provide the gist of how sacred space—temple, land, Eden—connects to the biblical war texts.

In the survey below we will designate *ethnic* Canaanites[E] with a raised letter *E* and *literary* Canaanites[L] with a raised *L*. In the story of sacred space, biblical authors sometimes use *ethnic* Canaanites to shape readers' understanding of *literary* Canaanites. A similar interplay exists between the *literary* new Eden at the time of the conquest or exile and the original Eden/garden in the opening chapters of Genesis, and the *literary* temple that was Eden itself and Moses'/David's later tabernacle/temple. A raised *L* at the end of Eden[L] or temple[L] will refer to the *literary* counterpart of these pairings.

FIRST [LITERARY] CANAANITES[L] DRIVEN OUT: ADAM AND EVE

The biblical story line of holy war begins not in Deuteronomy or Joshua but in Genesis. As we will see, Genesis 3:23-24 is the first occasion where the drive-out language of holy war is connected with sacred space and Eden themes:[10] "So the LORD God *banished him* [cast him out, *šālaḥ*] from the Garden of Eden to work the ground from which he had been taken. After *he drove the man out* [*gāraš*], he placed on the east side of the Garden of Eden cherubim and a flaming sword flashing back and forth to guard the way to the tree of life."

---

[9]G. K. Beale and Mitchell Kim have provided an excellent and far more complete biblical-theological development of temple, Eden, and sacred-space themes in *God Dwells Among Us*. See also Beale, *Temple and the Church's Mission; We Become What We Worship.*
[10]The drive-out language of holy war will be more fully developed below.

For readers with ears to hear, Yahweh *drives out* Adam and Eve from their *lush land of milk and honey* . . . from their *sacred space* . . . from their *temple-like* setting. It is hardly a coincidence that the author adds *angels* and a *sword* to complete the holy war picture. Think about it for a moment. If you are wearing exile-oriented glasses, what would you understand this text to be describing at a pattern-meaning level?[11] Who are Adam and Eve in a literary sense? Adam and Eve are the first *literary* Canaanites[(L)], who have been driven out of their land (like later exiles), who have had to leave their temple-meeting place behind (like the exiles), who have experienced dispossession and estrangement because of their sin (like the exiles), and so on. As we will see, the northern- and southern-kingdom exiles in a literary self-portrait paint themselves as the Canaanites[(L)] of their day. At this later stage of the Hebrew Bible these literary connections become pronounced: the Eden land and the Promised Land of Canaan, the Eden temple and the later Moses/David temples, the shared experience of being driven out of sacred space, and Canaanite sin and the sin of the exiles.

For even the earliest readers/hearers of the Pentateuch the connection between Genesis 3:23-24 and holy war would have been available. For example, in Exodus 33:1-3 Yahweh assures his people that he will send an *angel* before them to *drive out* the Canaanites from the Promised Land:

> Then the LORD said to Moses, "Leave this place, you and the people you brought up out of Egypt, and go up to the land I promised on oath to Abraham, Isaac and Jacob, saying, 'I will give it to your descendants.' I will send an angel before you and *drive out* [*gāraš*] the Canaanites, Amorites, Hittites, Perizzites, Hivites and Jebusites. Go up to the land flowing with milk and honey" (compare Num 22:31).

So let us read Genesis 3:24 with a Pentateuchal lens. Already the Pentateuch itself has joined together three ideas: (1) Eden's garden and the Promised Land of Canaan, (2) Eden's sanctuary/temple and Moses' tabernacle, and (3) sin as why Adam and Eve lost their garden, why the Canaanites lost/will lose their land, and why various Israelites lost their chance to enter the land.

---

[11]Pattern-level meaning is where one component (A) in the biblical text gets an overlay with meaning from similarities to another (B) event, person, place, etc., so that a reader/hearer is forced to look at the two together and think about the correlation.

Within the Pentateuch itself, the author and original audience would naturally have brought Genesis 3:24 and Exodus 33:1-3 together. The texts share angels who fight in holy war and residents who get driven out of their Eden-like land. They share recognition of the importance of sacred space. They share the story-line emphasis on a God of cosmic holiness who desires to touch our world and establish intimacy with human beings.

Astute contemporary readers of Genesis 3:23-24 will pick up on tacit implications from this first occurrence of holy war language in Scripture. This text foreshadows some of this book's central arguments (see the introduction for a quick overview). Even though the contribution of Genesis 3:23-24 is at a similar *pattern* level and we are talking about *literary* Canaanites, it is interesting to note at this pattern level that biblical holy war does not have to kill everyone involved in order to create or protect sacred space. The duration of life is limited, but no one physically dies. Driving out live human beings is quite sufficient. The issue is the formation of sacred space, not killing the people who live there. Nor is biblical holy war strictly, or even predominantly, about *ethnic*-kill objectives. Here in the domain of parallel patterns we discover that the ancestors to all ethnic races—Adam and Eve—experienced actions similar to holy war. The objective was the creation and/or preservation of divine space, not the ethnically motivated removal of these literary Canaanites. Such insights should begin to chip away at our misinformed modern ethnic genocide notions in the reading of Scripture.

But now back to the question of the original audience, concerning the broader story line and justice/ethics: *Is God just in driving Adam and Eve— the first Canaanites[L]—from their land?* The answer of the original Pentateuch readers and certainly the later, suffering exilic readers would have been a resounding "Yes!"

SECOND CANAANITES[E] DRIVEN OUT: ETHNIC CANAANITES AND THEIR ALLIES

Within the holy war story line of Scripture, the next group to be driven out of their land in the formation of sacred space are the ethnic Canaanites[E]. Joshua's conquest readily brings to mind the ethnic group of people dwelling in Canaan known as the Canaanites[E]. However, taking the land of Canaan included driving out (or enfolding within Israel) at least fifteen other groups who were ethnically distinct from the Canaanites[E]: Phoenicians, Hittites, Jebusites, Amorites, Girgashites, Hivites, Sinites, Arkites, Arvadites, Zemarites, Hamathites, Kenites, Kenezzites, Kadmonites, and Perizzites. The word *Canaanite* in the Hebrew text sometimes meant a distinct ethnic group of Canaanites[E] *different from* the other fourteen groups living in Canaan, and sometimes it meant the ethnic Canaanites[E] *plus* the fourteen other groups in a comprehensive term for all the Canaanite-like people living in Canaan (for a fuller development see appendix B). The people-group diversity under this umbrella or catchall usage of the term *Canaanite* further erodes any strict ethnic focus. It hints at *the land* (and creating sacred space) being the issue, not the ethnicity of the people on the land.

As with Adam and Eve being driven out of Eden, the primary language of the conquest is that of the Canaanites being driven out of the land. For the moment let us set aside the language of total kill or complete destruction (saving that topic for chapters eight through twelve and appendixes A through C). The point here is that the broad story-line understanding of holy war is that Israel drives out the Canaanite people groups little by little as their own Israelite population enlarges. As with the initial drive-out conquest under Joshua to gain a foothold, the long-term objective was a gradual driving out of idolatrous people from the land (Ex 23:30-31). The biblical authors describe the conquest with a range of *drive-out* language regarding the Canaanites: drive out, expel (*gāraš*); take possession of land by driving out and dispossessing (*yāraš*); clear away, remove (*nāšal*); thrust out, push out (*hādap*); cast out, send away (*šālaḥ*); and vomit out (*qîʾ*).[12] This drive-out

---

[12]*Gāraš*: Ex 23:28-30; 23:31; 33:2; 34:11; Deut 33:27; Josh 24:12, 18; Judg 2:3; 6:9; see also 1 Chron 17:21; Ps 78:55; 80:8. *Yāraš*: Gen 22:17; 24:60; 28:4; Ex 34:24; Lev 20:24; Num 13:30; 14:24; 21:24, 32, 35; 32:21, 39; 33:52, 53, 55; Deut 1:8, 21, 39; 2:12, 21-22, 24, 31; 3:12, 18, 20; 4:1, 5, 14, 22, 26, 38, 47; 5:31, 33; 6:1, 18; 7:1, 17; 8:1; 9:1, 3-5, 6, 23; 10:11; 11:8, 10-11, 23, 29, 31; 12:1-2, 29; 15:4; 16:20; 17:14; 18:12, 14; 19:1-2, 14; 21:1; 23:21; 25:19; 26:1; 28:21, 63; 30:5, 16, 18; 31:3, 13; 32:47; 33:23; Josh 1:11, 15; 3:10; 8:7; 12:1; 13:1, 6, 12-13; 14:12; 15:14, 63; 16:10; 17:12-13, 18; 18:3; 19:47; 21:43; 23:5, 9, 13; 24:4, 8; Judg 1:19-21, 27-33; 2:6, 21, 23; 3:13; 11:21-24; 1 Kings 14:24; 21:26; 2 Kings 16:3; 17:8, 24; 21:2; 1 Chron 28:8; 2 Chron 20:7; 28:3; 33:2; Ezra 9:11-12; Neh 9:15, 22-25; Ps 44:2-3; 69:36; 105:44; Jer 30:3; 32:23; Amos 2:10; see also Jer 49:2; Ezek 33:25-26; Amos 9:12; Obad 17, 19-20. *Nāšal*: Deut 7:1, 22; Josh 5:15; see also the removal of (dirty) sandals because one is standing on holy ground—Ex 3:5 and Josh 5:15. *Hādap*: Deut 6:19; 9:4; Josh 23:5. *Šālaḥ*: Lev 18:24; 20:23. *Qîʾ*: Lev 18:25, 28; 20:22.

language carries the weight of the holy war story line. The biblical authors use this drive-out language to connect the biggest pieces of the holy war story in terms of exile: the exile anticipated (Pentateuch) and the exile realized (Kings and Chronicles). That exile link clinches its central role within the biblical story line.

The reason or divine justification for people—any people—being driven out of sacred space within the biblical story line is quite simple: *sin, wickedness, and disobedience*. For instance, Adam and Eve are driven out of Eden because of their flagrant disobedience (Gen 3:24). Cain is driven from the land and hidden from God's presence—distance from God most holy—because of murdering his brother (Gen 4:14). Jonah is driven away from God's sight and the holy temple because of his disobedience (Jon 2:4). We could multiply examples.[13]

Likewise, the theological justification for removing Canaanites from the Promised Land was because of their sin.[14] Meanwhile, even within the Pentateuch, the reason for God removing the Canaanites is clearly stated—be sure to catch this—with an eye to the potential removal of the Israelites themselves from the land (exile anticipated):[15]

> I am the LORD your God. You must not do as they do in Egypt, where you used to live, and you must not do as they do in the land of Canaan, where I am bringing you. Do not follow their practices. (Lev 18:2-3)

> Do not defile yourselves in any of these ways, because this is how the nations that I am going to *drive out* [*šālaḥ*] before you became defiled. Even the land was defiled; so I punished it for its sin, and the land *vomited out* [*qîʾ*] its inhabitants. . . . And if you [Israel] defile the land, *it will vomit you out* [*qîʾ*] as it *vomited out* [*qîʾ*] the nations that were before you. (Lev 18:24-25, 28 [explicitly anticipated exile])

> Keep all my decrees and laws and follow them, so that the land where I am bringing you to live *may not vomit you out* [*qîʾ*]. You must not live according to the customs of the nations *I am going to drive out* [*šālaḥ*] before you. Because

---

[13]See the numerous exile-related texts below.
[14]See Gen 15:16 for the first intimation of sin as the basis for removing Canaanites/Amorites from the land.
[15]The drive-out story line is joined to the exile right from the start.

they did all these things, I abhorred them. But I said to you, "You will possess their land; I will give it to you as an inheritance, a land flowing with milk and honey." I am the LORD your God, who has set you apart from the nations. (Lev 20:22-24 [tacitly anticipated exile])

When you enter the land the LORD your God is giving you, do not learn to imitate the detestable ways of the nations there. Let no one be found among you who sacrifices their son or daughter in the fire, who practices divination or sorcery, interprets omens, engages in witchcraft, or casts spells, or who is a medium or spiritist or who consults the dead. Anyone who does these things is detestable to the LORD; because of these same detestable practices the LORD your God will drive out those nations before you. (Deut 18:9-12 [tacitly anticipated exile])

These texts emphasize the sin and wickedness of the *immediate* Canaanite[E] people of the time of Joshua living in the land of Canaan during the time of the conquest. We have cited these only (and not texts about the sins of past generations) for a reason that becomes evident after reading appendix D on corporate (in)justice and intergenerational (in)justice.[16] While contemporary readers need to be aware of these entangled ethical problems within biblical justice, the difficulty is less severe here because the sins of past generations of Canaanite people fuse with those of the present generation.[17] Like the sins of the exiles (see below) that piled up to the sky over many generations, so also did the sins of the Canaanites. The intergenerational aspect of Canaanite sin reaches deep into the biblical story line and is a fascinating one to trace all the way back to Noah's sons (Gen 9:22, 25-27; 10:6, 15-19; 28:1, 6; 36:2; 15:16). The dual focus on sins of both immediate and past generations makes clear the role of Canaanite sin within the driving out/ sacred space theme.

Once again, we come back to the original-audience, broader story-line, justice/ethics question: *Is God just in driving out the Canaanites[E] from the Promised Land in the formation of sacred space?* Though we are eager to answer this question now, if we hold off until the end of the next section on

---

[16]Ancient-world justice often contained within it elements of injustice. These ancient-world (fallen world) pragmatics enter into biblical justice situations at many points.

[17]One could argue that in both/and cases such as this, with *fused* past and present sin, the element of just-justice is even greater.

the exiles, our clarity of thought should be enhanced. At this point, however, one thing should be reasonably certain: the traditional answers—a holy God, the removal of idolatry, and the evil/sin of the Canaanites—fit very well with the generalized story line of Scripture concerning driving out of sacred space. A round peg in a round hole.

THIRD AND FOURTH CANAANITES(L) DRIVEN OUT: NORTHERN KINGDOM AND SOUTHERN KINGDOM ISRAELITES

Within the Hebrew Bible the sacred-space metanarrative finds a new dimension of canonical development in the reflections of those who experienced the exile, whether shortly before, during, or afterward. Exile was by far the most painful experience for the Israelites within the flow of their story. The exile forced them to take a close look in the mirror and think, *We are the Canaanites of our day!* Within the broad story line of Scripture there can be no doubt that Yahweh drove out Israelites from the northern kingdom and the southern kingdom because of their sin; they embraced idolatry and other detestable acts on par with those of the original Canaan land dwellers. The biblical authors repeatedly make the connection between the *original Canaanites(E)* driven out by Joshua and the *literary Canaanites(L)* driven out over the years of exile. Themes of shared idolatry and shared detestable acts (sacrificing children) make it clear that the exiles, like the original Canaanites(E), have polluted the land. It can no longer function as sacred space. Here are a sample of texts that raise this connection to an explicit level (highlighted in italics):

> *Rehoboam* son of Solomon was king in Judah. He was forty-one years old when he became king, and he reigned seventeen years in Jerusalem, the city the Lord had chosen out of all the tribes of Israel in which to put his Name. His mother's name was Naamah; she was an Ammonite.
>
> Judah did evil in the eyes of the Lord. By the sins they committed they stirred up his jealous anger more than those who were before them had done. They also set up for themselves high places, sacred stones and Asherah poles on every high hill and under every spreading tree. There were even male shrine prostitutes in the land; *the people engaged in all the detestable practices of the nations the Lord had driven out before the Israelites.* (1 Kings 14:21-24 [southern kingdom])

There was never anyone like *Ahab*, who sold himself to do evil in the eyes of the LORD, urged on by Jezebel his wife. *He behaved in the vilest manner by going after idols, like the Amorites the LORD drove out before Israel.* (1 Kings 21:25-26 [northern kingdom])

Ahaz was twenty years old when he became king, and he reigned in Jerusalem sixteen years. Unlike David his father, he did not do what was right in the eyes of the LORD his God. He followed the ways of the kings of Israel *and even sacrificed his son in the fire, engaging in the detestable practices of the nations the LORD had driven out before the Israelites.* (2 Kings 16:2-3 [southern kingdom])

Ahaz was twenty years old when he became king, and he reigned in Jerusalem sixteen years. Unlike David his father, he did not do what was right in the eyes of the LORD. He followed the ways of the kings of Israel and also made idols for worshiping the Baals. He burned sacrifices in the Valley of Ben Hinnom and sacrificed his children in the fire, *engaging in the detestable practices of the nations the LORD had driven out before the Israelites.* (2 Chron 28:1-3 [southern kingdom])

The king of Assyria invaded the entire land, marched against Samaria and laid siege to it for three years. In the ninth year of *Hoshea*, the king of Assyria captured Samaria and deported the Israelites to Assyria. He settled them in Halah, in Gozan on the Habor River and in the towns of the Medes.

All this took place because the Israelites had sinned against the LORD their God, who had brought them up out of Egypt from under the power of Pharaoh king of Egypt. *They worshiped other gods and followed the practices of the nations the LORD had driven out before them, as well as the practices that the kings of Israel had introduced. . . .* At every high place they burned incense, *as the nations whom the LORD had driven out before them had done.* They did wicked things that aroused the LORD's anger. (2 Kings 17:5-8, 11 [northern kingdom])

Manasseh was twelve years old when he became king, and he reigned in Jerusalem fifty-five years. His mother's name was Hephzibah. *He did evil in the eyes of the LORD, following the detestable practices of the nations the LORD had driven out before the Israelites.* (2 Kings 21:1-2 [southern kingdom])

Manasseh was twelve years old when he became king, and he reigned in Jerusalem fifty-five years. He did evil in the eyes of the LORD, *following the detestable practices of the nations the LORD had driven out before the Israelites.* He rebuilt the high places his father Hezekiah had demolished; he also erected altars to the Baals and made Asherah poles. He bowed down to all the starry hosts and worshiped them.

He built altars in the temple of the LORD, of which the LORD had said, "My Name will remain in Jerusalem forever." In both courts of the temple of the LORD, he built altars to all the starry hosts. He sacrificed his children in the fire in the Valley of Ben Hinnom, practiced divination and witchcraft, sought omens, and consulted mediums and spiritists. He did much evil in the eyes of the LORD, arousing his anger. (2 Chron 33:1-6 [southern kingdom])

The deep tragedy of exile was that Israel experienced being driven out of the land *twice*—once as the northern kingdom (Israel) and once as the southern kingdom (Judah).[18] Judah—the meager tribe of returning Israelites after exile—would have felt the impact of exile *twice* through family ties to the northern kingdom. Furthermore, two of the ancient world's most powerful war machines—Assyria and Babylon—decimated the people of Israel. The horrific atrocities of war practiced by these two nations make Israel's war methods look comparatively tame and gentle (see chapters five, six, and thirteen). Would exilic readers have been troubled about their wars against the Canaanites—the Israelite version of genocide (chapters eight through twelve, appendixes A through C) or about their version of war rape (chapters five and six)? No. It simply would not have been on their ethical radar.

The exilic question of justice was at the big-picture, story-line level: *Was God just in driving us—the exilic literary Canaanites[(L)]—out of the Promised Land as he did the original Canaanites[(E)] in Joshua's day?* Admittedly, exilic and postexilic authors had difficulty with the evil of the Assyrians and Babylonians (people more evil than the evil Israelites) whom God was using as his holy warriors to do his bidding. Nevertheless, it seems settled in exilic theology that Yahweh was just in driving Israel out of the land. Again, the traditional answers—God is holy, idolatry, evil of the literary Canaanites (past and present), pollution of sacred space—answer this question rather well.

Now back to the question that we postponed: *Is God just in driving out the Canaanites[(E)] from the Promised Land in the formation of sacred space during the time of Joshua to David?* With the exilic horizon and the Edenic horizon in place, we have a helpful orientation with which to view the Joshua-Canaanite scenario. This Joshua-Canaanite question is more difficult to answer than the one concerning the exiles as literary Canaanites[(L)]. No

---

[18]Assyria drove Israel from the land in 721 BC; Babylon drove out Judah in 586 BC.

one seems to have an ethical difficulty with God ousting his own people Israel from the Promised Land when the stench of their sins reaches the heavens. New atheists do not fly into a righteous rage over what Assyria or Babylon did to Israel in the exile. The reason should be obvious. In the one case God seems to function with *direct* causation (Joshua to David), whereas in the latter case he is almost surely using *indirect* causation (Assyria and Babylon).[19] In the latter case God clearly plays in a fallen-world sandbox, bringing about the unfolding plans of salvation history in a mediated sense through the grievous war actions of the Assyrians and Babylonians. No one blames God for *their* horrific war actions.

However, let us challenge one of the assumptions above, namely, that God is functioning with *direct* causation and, by inference, with no accommodation to Israel's war actions in the conquest narratives all the way to the time of David's slaughterhouse establishment of the kingdom. Hold on. Did you catch that expression, "David's slaughterhouse establishment of the kingdom"? Did those words strike you as strange? Here is the problem. Rarely do readers who cheer on the little-David warrior (against the evil giant Goliath) ever speak negatively about David as a warrior. Yet God does (1 Chron 22:7-8; 28:3). That negative perspective was *not* part of our Christian upbringing (we can assure you), but it is clearly part of Yahweh's perspective on *Israel's* war actions. In other words, Yahweh himself declares his accommodating posture in war actions—it is as if he dawns hip waders, venturing reluctantly into the sewer water of *Israel's* war actions, not just for Assyria and Babylon.[20] If we can wrap our minds around this mediated-ethic (or incremental-ethic) concept with holy war and embrace God's own critical assessment of Israel's war narratives, it will go a long way toward resolving ethical problems. (See chapter fourteen on subversive war portraits.) And if we are willing to see Yahweh in hip waders during the Canaanite wars (there is good evidence for doing so), something else happens. In the process of reading about Israel's troubling war actions, we also stumble onto delightful,

---

[19]Israel's covenant and revelatory relationship with Yahweh makes for more direct causation. See appendix G for a discussion of direct versus indirect/truncated causation.

[20]We will argue that the pervasiveness, stench, and depth of the sewer water is greater in one case than the other. Yet readers need to know that God wears his hip waders through sewer water in both cases.

redemptive elements and can appreciate what God is doing. (See especially chapters five, six, and thirteen through sixteen.)

One more stopping place before we move on. Let's go back to the drive-out/sacred-space narrative of Adam and Eve (Gen 3:23-24) and look at the Joshua-Canaanite situation through that related lens. At a conceptual level they share something extremely important, namely, *the broad story-line point that the God of cosmic holiness desires to touch our fallen world with his toes (the footstool) in order to establish sacred space and intimacy with human beings.* As far as we are aware, no one objects to the ethics of Adam and Eve being driven from their Eden-like garden.[21] They broke the rules and were removed from the land/sacred space as a result. End of case. Of course, there is a difference. No troubling issues of military ethics in the concrete-specific dimension about *how* it was done plague contemporary readers. That said, however, kindly go back and read that story-line statement above (the third, italicized sentence in this paragraph), and you should then understand where the traditional answers fit well. Grasping this insight takes us one step further (not done yet—there is more evidence coming) in establishing our square-pegs, round-holes thesis.

FIFTH AND SIXTH CANAANITES(L) DRIVEN OUT: OUTSIDERS TO JESUS' KINGDOM AND CONQUERING SIN

A lot happens with Jesus to transform the story line. The opening chapters of Matthew describe Jesus as God's Son (called out of Egypt) who walks in the pattern of Israel—crossing the Red Sea (baptism), being tempted in the wilderness forty years (forty days/nights), and ascending to Sinai (a mountain) to deliver the law (Jesus' new Torah) for those who would follow him (Mt 2:13–7:29). The pattern is different in at least one striking way—Jesus is the *obedient* son, unlike Israel. Jesus becomes the new temple and dwelling place of God among his followers, and, as their numbers (twelve and seventy) suggest, his followers function in community as the new Israel.[22] No longer is the temple

---

[21]Perhaps one could object to God removing Adam and Eve from their homeland. However, given that the entire earth is God's creation, a relocation of Adam and Eve does not seem problematic.

[22]The seventy-twelve pattern starts deep within the biblical story line. The human race grew from Adam until it reached seventy nations (Gen 10:1-32 [Japheth (14) + Ham (30)

of God a building; it is now a person. Jesus himself embodies sacred space and the meeting place for God and humans (Mt 21:12-13, 42-43; 27:50-54; Mk 14:58; 15:38; Jn 1:14, 51; 2:18-22; 4:7-26; 7:37-39). The Promised Land expands from Canaan to the entire earth, and through repentance of sin (not violence) Jesus' kingdom spreads. (With the coming of the Spirit—the new Jesus in our midst—his community of followers becomes the new temple.[23])

This stage of the drive-out/sacred-space story line incorporates a new kind of literary Canaanites[(L)] in Jesus' day. Those who are removed or cast out of his kingdom are people biblical scholars often call the outsiders. Many studies emphasize Jesus' teachings about kingdom reversal: those who think they are insiders (often *ethnic* Israelites!) become the outsiders.[24] He both taught and lived the insider/outsider reversal. Jesus shares table fellowship (like the shalom meal on the holy mountain) and his most intimate presence with Gentile "dogs," the poor, lepers, tax collectors, criminals, prostitutes, and those of low (women) or no status (children).[25] Jesus heals the daughter of a Canaanite woman who cries out, "Show me mercy!"—probably an intentional play off Old Testament war texts—and commends her great faith.[26] Jesus

---

+ Shem (26)]). The stylized seventy nations represent old humanity under Adam. After the Babel incident God started over with Abraham and a new humanity. By the end of the book of Genesis, the author numbers Jacob's family and this new or second-Adam humanity, which similarly contains seventy in the table-like listing (Gen 45:15-27 [33 + 16 + 14 + 7 = 70]). Of Abraham's offspring who go down to Egypt there are seventy (Ex 1:5; see also Deut 10:22). Israel continues this seventy identity as God's new humanity with its establishment of seventy elders (Ex 24:1, 9; Num 11:16, 24-25; see also Num 33:9). The twelve tribes and seventy elders of Israel make it beyond coincidence that Jesus had twelve close disciples and seventy larger-group disciples among his followers. Jesus himself as well as his community is the new Israel.

[23]We probably should add another seventh or eighth stage to the story line with the advent of the Spirit as the new Jesus. That would be a good idea. However, the objective of the chapter is not to write an exhaustive biblical theology. Rather, it is to show the recurring pattern that connects *sin* with the *driving out* of either Canaanites[(E)] or Canaanites[(L)] as a broad-based, story-line theme.

[24]For a few helpful sources see James D. G. Dunn, *Jesus Remembered*, vol. 1 of *Christianity in the Making* (Grand Rapids: Eerdmans, 2003), 489-541; John O. York, *The Last Shall Be First: The Rhetoric of Reversal in Luke*, JSNTSup 46 (Sheffield: Sheffield Academic Press, 1991); E. P. Sanders, *The Historical Figure of Jesus* (London: Penguin, 1993), 196-204.

[25]Table fellowship in the Gospels anticipates the shalom meal (Passover is a specialized shalom-meal sacrifice celebrating redemption) that will become the meal of Jesus' followers in the church.

[26]For the significance of the conquest language in Mt 15:21-28, see Glenna S. Jackson, *"Have Mercy on Me": The Story of the Canaanite Woman in Matthew 15:21-28*, JSNTSup 228 (New York: Sheffield Academic Press, 2002).

drives out a demon from the daughter of this ethnic Canaanite—no small irony. The physical battle has become a spiritual one, and the physical Canaanites are no longer the enemy. Jesus invites these outsider-type people into his kingdom to share paradise/Eden with him (Lk 23:43); he shuns and casts out (drives out) the religiously smug, the wealthy who need nothing, and hypocritical, self-righteous individuals—idolatry of another form (Lk 13:28-29).[27] Once again, sin plays a major role in sacred space—it drives people out of Jesus' kingdom, whereas faith and repentance allow them to enter.

A theology of the cross plays a key role in moving the drive-out/sacred-space story line forward. Of course, Jesus himself is the *new temple* and also the *sacrifice* for the sins of all humanity. Within the Jesus story the cross sounds the death knell for sin. As the Azazel goat is driven out into the desert, so are even the high-handed, Canaanite-like sins. The exilic "we are the Canaanites" mirror casts a telling reflection on all humans to varying degrees. Unlike the days of Joshua, the cross (not the sword) conquers in this new kingdom. The preaching of the gospel and the forgiveness of sin (not military conquest) extend/expand the kingdom of Jesus to the whole earth (Mt 28:16-20). The new emphasis on individual and spiritual expansion of the kingdom across all ethnic lines breaks down the physical and geographical boundaries over which nations typically fight. No more *physical* wars for sacred space are needed. Jesus' sacrifice on the cross and his resurrection conquer the strongest enemy (death itself) and provide the power for carrying the story line to the final phase of an eschatological Eden. In New Testament theology the Lion of the tribe of Judah conquers/triumphs over his enemies through the *cross* (the Lamb looking as though it has been slain; Rev 5:5-6). The battle has already been won.

SEVENTH CANAANITES[(L)] DRIVEN OUT: ESCHATOLOGICAL CANAANITES AND THE FINAL EDEN

Apocalyptic holy war in the book of Revelation is the final phase in the drive-out/sacred-space story line. Since we cover this topic later (chapter sixteen), our comments here will be short. At the end of the book of Revelation, we

---

[27]People from every ethnicity will be part of the kingdom (north, south, east, and west), but many who think themselves acceptable will be cast out.

encounter the new Jerusalem coming down from heaven (Rev 21:7; see also Rev 3:12) with the dimensions of 12,000 stadia × 12,000 stadia × 12,000 stadia—roughly the distance from Toronto to Cocoa Beach, Florida. The cube shape replicates the upstairs/heavenly temple and holy of holies, with its greatest concentration of God's presence and glory. Once the cosmic cube touches our world, it morphs our fallen planet into a new heavens and a new earth. Sacred space in its most concentrated heavenly sense now covers the entire new/renewed earth.

When the heavenly cubed room touches earth, it ushers in the final chapter of God most holy coming down in order to bring lasting Edenic renewal and intimacy with human beings. As with every other phase in the story line, the removal of sin and idolatry makes possible this kind of Exodus mountain–like, pristine meeting place for God and humans. In this apocalyptic setting the saints are warned not to be seduced by idolatry and false worship of the beast (Rev 13:8, 12, 15; 14:11; 16:2; 19:20; 20:4). Recurring patterns from Old Testament holy war become obvious when the evil players in John's day are being painted with brushstrokes reminiscent of Balaam, Balak, and Jezebel (Rev 2:14; see also Rev 2:20). Those eschatological Canaanites[L] who would rather cling to their idolatry and sin (rather than repent) are banished/driven out from the newly developed sacred space (Rev 21:8, 15). The final Eden cannot sustain the sins of a former world. If we are to embrace God most holy in his most concentrated (heavenly) sense coming to earth, we must leave behind the souvenirs of hell—things such as selfishness, pride, abusive power, and hoarded wealth. Some things simply are not meant to be in this new, Eden-like world because they would ruin the joy of heaven among us.[28]

CONCLUSION

The concept of God most holy and cosmic distance is foundational to understanding holy war and the creation of sacred space. While we summarize here the conclusions of this chapter, to really see it may require working through the successive drive-out/sacred-space stages of the biblical story

---

[28]The last two sentences loosely paraphrase concepts from C. S. Lewis, *The Great Divorce* (New York: HaperCollins, 2001).

line. The exilic material is particularly important for unearthing the concerns of the original audience, which are not the ethical issues readers have today. The optics of exile and the original Eden help shape the broader point at the level of the story line, namely, *that the God of cosmic holy distance desires to touch our fallen world in order to establish sacred space and intimacy with human beings.* This overarching construct ties together all the stages of the drive-out/sacred-space grand story within Scripture. In short, the traditional answers—a holy God, removal of idolatry, the sin of the "Canaanites," anticipation of final judgment, and a new Eden—these all play an indispensable role. At the metanarrative level, the traditional answers fit very well—round pegs in round holes.

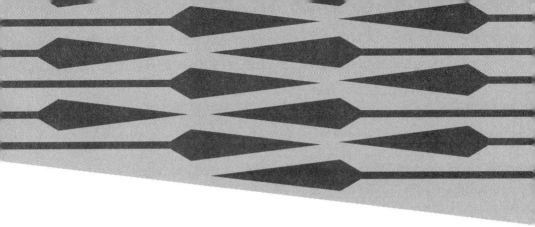

PART 3

BETTER ANSWERS: BETTER FOR QUESTIONS ABOUT GENOCIDE AND WAR RAPE

READING THE BIBLE REDEMPTIVELY

WHILE TRADITIONAL ANSWERS about Israelite warfare provide excellent responses to questions on the minds of the original audience (chapter three), they do not work well in addressing our contemporary ethical questions (chapter two). The better answers to questions about war rape and genocide start here and run through the remainder of the book. They may be loosely grouped as follows:

Methodology: Reading the Bible redemptively (chapter four)

War rape: The ugly and redemptive sides (chapters five and six)

Genocide: Hyperbole thesis (chapters eight through twelve, appendixes A through C)

Better answers to both war rape and genocide: Ancient war atrocities (chapter thirteen), Yahweh as uneasy war God (chapter fourteen), Jesus' cross, resurrection, and ascension (chapter fifteen), Jesus as apocalyptic warrior (chapter sixteen), and reverse holy war (appendix C)

Final answer: The unfinished justice story (conclusion)

Though the genocide issue in Scripture gets more press in contemporary discussions, we have chosen to address war rape before genocide for several reasons. First, the topic of war rape is shorter (two chapters versus five chapters plus three appendixes). Second, the war-rape material with its simple division into two parts (the ugly side and the redemptive side) illustrates well the methodology overviewed in the present chapter on reading the Bible redemptively (chapter four). Third, placing the discussion about war rape first (ahead of genocide) sets up preliminary considerations about the incremental ethic that God uses within Scripture when he gives directives about war. It helps to have this incremental-ethic framework already in mind when approaching genocide and total-kill issues in the biblical text. Finally, the issue of genocide is more complex than war rape. One must first deal with the matter of rhetorical language (hyperbole thesis) to assess exactly what happened. If the hyperbole thesis is correct, that finding itself provides a foundationally better answer concerning the ethics of biblical genocide. However, hyperbole provides only one better answer; it is merely a starting-point better answer to the matter of brutal war killings that we encounter in the Bible. Other better answers carry this starting-point answer further and in ways that are profoundly redemptive.

READING THE BIBLE REDEMPTIVELY:
ENGAGING TWO HORIZONS

One contribution of this book is that it offers a way of reading Scripture redemptively, even its ethically difficult texts. I (Bill) have applied this redemptive-movement or incremental-ethic approach elsewhere to topics such as slavery, women, and corporal punishment.[29] Here we examine the biblical war texts through a similar lens. We also use an eclectic combination of literary, theological, genre, and canonical approaches.[30] Nevertheless, an incremental-ethic or redemptive-movement approach to reading biblical texts across two horizons—ancient and modern—proves useful for seeing and owning real ethical problems within a biblical text while also discovering and celebrating its redemptive side.

Here is what it means to read the Bible redemptively as we talk about it in this book.[31] In figure 4.1 below, notice the different facial expressions of the

---

[29]William J. Webb, *Slaves, Women and Homosexuals: Exploring the Hermeneutics of Cultural Analysis* (Downers Grove, IL: InterVarsity Press, 2001); Webb, *Corporal Punishment in the Bible: A Redemptive-Movement Hermeneutic for Troubling Texts* (Downers Grove, IL: InterVarsity Press, 2011).

[30]Other methods are also helpful, but these are the ones (within our fields of expertise) we have found most fruitful in thinking through ethical issues within the biblical text.

[31]This section has been adapted from *Corporal Punishment in the Bible*, by William J. Webb. Copyright © 2011 by William J. Webb. Used with permission of InterVarsity Press, PO Box 1400, Downers Grove, IL 60515. ivpress.com. All rights reserved.

person reading the Bible. It is the same person but looking at the Bible from two different perspectives or horizons. When people view the Bible from the left side of the diagram, they read Scripture through the lens of its ancient-world context, namely, the ANE for the Old Testament or the Greco-Roman setting and Second Temple Judaism for the New Testament. A person operating from the right side of the diagram reads the Bible through the lens of a contemporary culture. That culture (for purposes of this diagram) in select cases *happens* to have adopted an aspect of biblical truth and applied it in a way that advances in some degree beyond the static form of the biblical text toward something better. Often the right-side reading leaves Christians and non-Christians with a disturbing question mark in their minds about issues of applicability or even relevance of a biblical ethic for our contemporary world. From the right-side vantage point, the Bible looks repressive or regressive.

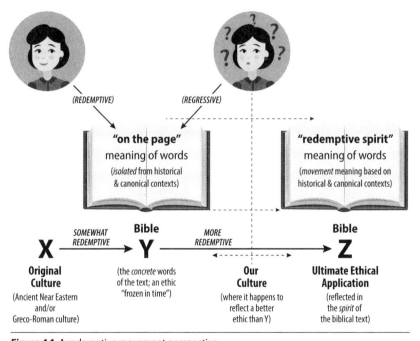

Figure 4.1. A redemptive movement perspective

Let us explore the right-side or the question-mark response through an overview or preamble to the next two chapters, which concern war rape. This brief discussion will serve as a methodological primer. You can understand why the person from the right-side perspective appears perplexed or disturbed. For instance, imagine a contemporary Christian in our Western context reading Deuteronomy 21:10-14. We will cite the passage in full (see also Num 31:25-32):

> When you go to war against your enemies and the LORD your God delivers
> them into your hands and you take captives, if you notice among the captives
> a beautiful woman and are attracted to her, you may take her as your wife.
> Bring her into your home and have her shave her head, trim her nails and put
> aside the clothes she was wearing when captured. After she has lived in your
> house and mourned her father and mother for a full month, then you may go
> to her and be her husband and she shall be your wife. If you are not pleased
> with her, let her go wherever she wishes. You must not sell her or treat her as
> a slave, since you have dishonored her.

One might say that this war text is exposure challenged in Christendom today, that it has in effect been banned from public readings in our contemporary churches. The reason should be obvious. As Christians read this text, it begins to dawn on them that the Bible contains a war ethic that includes "grabbing good-looking women" as wives. This should rightly be a disturbing feature within the text as we read our Bibles today. It is unlikely that Christians will mount a lobby group that attempts to bring this text into legislation through Congress or Parliament as a way in which we ought to treat female prisoners in our modern war context, nor for that matter is it the way we want our enemies to treat their prisoners (us) today.

So what happens as Christians today read a text such as Deuteronomy 21:10-14? Well, most contemporary readers of the biblical war texts (often unknowingly) read these texts through the lens of the Geneva or Hague war conventions. Our everyday, street-level discussions about the treatment of war captives are very much governed by these documents. Whether people are aware of it or not, even media coverage about the ethics of taking pictures of war captives is dominated by these modern treatises on war ethics. However, they reflect developing or emerging treatises on war ethics. First, there has been a long history of development in military ethics, a summary of which is easily accessible on the web.[32] Second, we do not want to give the

---

[32]For the Geneva War Convention and other treaties governing our conduct of war, see "The

impression that even these latest war conventions, as good as they are, have somehow reached an ultimate war or violent-force ethical application that carries forward/further the redemptive spirit within Scripture (position Z in figure 4.1 = ultimate ethical application).

But let us come back to the other, left side of the diagram (position X in figure 4.1). As with the story of James in the introduction to this book, sometimes we talk with Christians (and non-Christians) who are extremely disturbed when they encounter the pretty-women war text of Deuteronomy 21. While not abandoning reflection on the text through the lens of the Geneva and Hague war conventions (i.e., from the right side of the above diagram), we encourage them to begin by reading Scripture from an entirely different vantage point, namely, the ANE contexts within which they originally emerged.[33] That is exactly what we did with James. If we are to understand these biblical texts, we need to be reading ancient war documents from Egypt, Assyria, Babylonia, and so on. Once people do this, they discover that the ancient treatment of women in war was utterly horrendous—it often included bodily mutilation of women (cutting off their breasts and displaying them on poles), torturous deaths, multiple rapes, and a type of concubine enslavement where women would be required to perform perpetual sexual favors and/or produce offspring for their owners (see chapters five, six, and thirteen). In ancient siege warfare, the fate of female captives was considered so dreadful that, if it looked like a city was about to fall, men at times killed their own wives. What an utterly ugly world—the treatment of humanity by humanity is sometimes staggering. In our present-day context, this ancient war portrait shares some commonality with the rape camps of Rwanda.

Placing the biblical text within that sort of war context of the ancient world allows us to see Deuteronomy 21:10-14 in a different light. During the battle conflict and the postbattle context of gathering spoils of war, Israelite

---

Avalon Project at Yale Law School: The Laws of War," http://avalon.law.yale.edu/subject _menus/lawwar.asp (accessed March 7, 2019).

[33]Referring to the ANE context provides a summary way of speaking about the various neighboring countries and the larger ancient-world setting within which Israel was planted and lived out its faith in Yahweh. When Scripture is read in light of the horizon of the ancient world (and not ours), it provides the best vantage point from which to sense its redemptive spirit (with its partial or incremental movement toward something better) because it gives us clues about how God was acting in some sort of redemptive fashion.

warriors were *not* permitted to rape or sexually mutilate women. That restriction alone, when understood against what was normative in ancient warfare (see chapters five and six), provided a major difference and tangible movement in a positive direction. Along with this one large difference, the next two chapters will unfold a dozen or so acts of smaller redemptive movement. By reading the biblical text within its ancient context, one begins to hear its (incremental) redemptive movement. Now Deuteronomy 21:10-14 is a further development or greater fulfillment of this core redemptive trend—*the better treatment of female prisoners in war*—that ought to carry Christians forward in forging new practices and policies that help offset or minimize the atrocities of war. The implications of the initial redemptive movement within the text, which we alternatively call its redemptive spirit, ought to inspire Christians to venture into contemporary war discussions with the intention, wherever possible, of even going beyond the Geneva and Hague conventions. We do not want to stay with an ethic that is static or frozen in time as reflected in the concrete-specific instructions of the Bible; rather, Christians need to embrace the redemptive spirit of the text and journey toward an ultimate ethical application of that spirit.[34]

The essence of a redemptive-movement approach can be captured succinctly in three or four words: *movement is (crucial) meaning.* To be sure, movement is not the only meaning within the text. But redemptive movement, even if incremental (not complete), provides crucial meaning that is often lost by contemporary readers as we wrestle with how to understand ancient biblical texts in today's setting. We might alternatively depict a static type of meaning as one derived by reading the words of a text *only* within its immediate literary context—up and down the page. This literary context for discerning meaning is also important. But it is movement meaning, captured from reading a text in its ancient *historical and social* context and its *canonical* context, that yields a sense of the underlying spirit of the biblical text. It is this redemptive-movement or redemptive-spirit meaning that ought to radically shape the contours of our contemporary ethical portrait.

---

[34]The process of extending Scripture's redemptive spirit or ethical trajectory comes through logical, ethical, and theological reasoning. For an example see Webb, *Corporal Punishment in the Bible*, 119-37.

CONCLUSION

This chapter provides a methodological primer for the next two chapters on how to read the Bible redemptively. We need to think through the meaning of biblical texts from two horizons—the modern and the ancient (see figure 4.1 above). When Christians and non-Christians read the biblical text from a present-day horizon, where contemporary ethics have developed further (ironically, sometimes due in part to Scripture's broader redemptive influence), we often see only one thing—its ethical downside. We become acutely aware of its ethical shortcomings. However, the journey toward *reading the Bible redemptively* means learning to see these ethically troublesome texts also through the lens of the ancient world. Therein lies an opportunity to see and hear a different side to the story—a redemptive side, which often contains partial or incremental movement toward the betterment of human beings. The next two chapters expand on this methodological preview.[35] Appendix E discusses *why* God used an incremental ethic within Scripture.

---

[35]For further methodological discussion beyond the two books cited earlier in this chapter (Webb, *Slaves, Women and Homosexuals*; Webb, *Corporal Punishment in the Bible*) see William J. Webb, "The Limits of a Redemptive-Movement Hermeneutic: A Focused Response to T. R. Schreiner," *EQ* 75 (October 2003): 327-42; Webb, "A Redemptive-Movement Hermeneutic: Encouraging Dialogue Among Four Evangelical Views," *JETS* 48, no. 2 (2005): 331-49; Webb, "A Redemptive-Movement Model," in *Four Views on Moving Beyond the Bible to Theology*, ed. Gary T. Meadors (Grand Rapids: Zondervan, 2009), 215-44; see also 64-74, 133-50, 210-14.

WAR RAPE, PART ONE

The Ugly Side

DEUTERONOMY 21:10-14 IS KNOWN in Judaism as the "pretty woman" text. It describes a situation after a military battle in which an Israelite warrior sees a beautiful captive woman and is strongly attracted to her physical appearance. The text grants the Israelite man permission to take the captive woman as his wife and outlines how it is to be done:

> When you go to war against your enemies and the LORD your God delivers them into your hands and you take captives, if you notice among the captives a beautiful woman and are attracted to her, you may take her as your wife. Bring her into your home and have her shave her head, trim her nails and put aside the clothes she was wearing when captured. After she has lived in your house and mourned her father and mother for a full month, then you may go to her and be her husband and she shall be your wife. If you are not pleased with her, let her go wherever she wishes. You must not sell her or treat her as a slave, since you have dishonored her.

Most contemporary Christians struggle with this Deuteronomy text and its narrative counterpart in Numbers 31. Our ethical thinking about war is framed by the Geneva and Hague conventions and more recent developments in the 1990s that have made war rape a crime. Accordingly, the concept of grabbing "a hot-looking woman" from among prisoners of war as a wife is repulsive and extremely disturbing. When we encounter a biblical text that seemingly treats female war captives like cattle corralled in a stockyard for the picking and with sexual intent, our gag reflex is activated and we may fail to appreciate the text's revelatory and redemptive value.

Yet as we begin to untangle meaning within this disturbing text, we must listen to both sides of the story in order to embrace a full-orbed understanding. On the one hand, there is indeed an ugly, twisted side—replete with ethical problems. But there is also a redemptive side, which causes one to ponder the quiet, subtle, and—in some respects—powerful ways that God is at work. Let's first tackle the more difficult and troubling parts of the situation.

THE TROUBLING SIDE: ETHICAL PROBLEMS

The text of Deuteronomy 21:10-14 contains a series of weighty ethical problems as it permits the taking of beautiful female captives in the context of war.[1]

- ▶ generic issues: patriarchy, war, sexual property, and progeny

- ▶ overvalued external beauty (no focus on a woman's inner beauty)

- ▶ one month to grieve

- ▶ forced or coerced marriage

- ▶ coerced sexuality (all cases)

- ▶ marital rape (some, perhaps many, cases)

- ▶ monthlong delay motivated by concerns for offspring purity (not care for the grieving captive)

- ▶ battlefield rape permitted

- ▶ embedded blinders: arranged marriages, no legal concept of marital rape, and so on

---

[1]Deuteronomy 21:10-14 has garnered much attention over the last twenty-five years beyond the range of standard commentaries: Pearl Elman, "Deuteronomy 21:10-14: The Beautiful Captive Woman," *Women in Judaism* 1 (1997): 1-13; David Stern, "The Captive Woman: Hellenization, Greco-Roman Erotic Narrative, and Rabbinic Literature," *Poetics Today* 19, no. 1 (1998): 91-127; David Resnick, "A Case Study in Jewish Moral Education: (Non-) Rape of the Beautiful Captive," *Journal of Moral Education* 33, no. 3 (2004): 307-19; James A. Diamond, "The Deuteronomic 'Pretty Woman' Law: Prefiguring Feminism and Freud in Nahmanides," *Jewish Social Studies* 14, no. 2 (2008): 61-85; Deborah L. Ellens, *Women in the Sex Texts of Leviticus and Deuteronomy: A Comparative Conceptual Analysis*, LHBOTS 458 (Edinburgh: T&T Clark, 2008), 170-88; Rebekah Josberger, "For Your Good Always: Restraining the Rights of the Victor for the Well-Being of the Vulnerable (Deut 21:10-14)," in *For Our Good Always: Studies on the Message and Influence of the Book of Deuteronomy in Honor of Daniel I. Block*, ed. Jason S. DeRouchie, Jason Gile, and Kenneth J. Turner, CSHB 3 (Winona Lake, IN: Eisenbrauns, 2013), 165-87; Caryn A. Reeder, "Deuteronomy 21.10-14 and/as Wartime Rape," *JSOT* 41, no. 3 (2017): 313-36.

This list is by no means exhaustive.[2] Nonetheless, it illustrates the range of ethical problems and prepares for a focused look at the weightier issues and at several debated ones.

Generic issues: Patriarchy, war violence, sexual property, and the source of progeny. At least four of the ethical problems reflected in Deuteronomy 21:10-14 are seen across a wide spectrum of texts.[3] Here we will simply lament that Deuteronomy 21:10-14 reflects a culture of heavy-handed patriarchy experienced by many within the stories of Scripture. As we are Christians with egalitarian convictions about the equality of men and women in Christ (Gal 3:28), such a passage strikes chords that are not exactly in harmony with that theme. Furthermore, as *almost*-but-not-quite pacifists and supporters of approaches emphasizing the very least violence possible and only if absolutely necessary (preferring nonviolent alternatives, even with greater financial costs) when it comes to war strategies and policing policies, we are troubled to a degree by virtually *all* war texts in the Bible. While we recognize a legitimate role in our present world for highly restricted, strategically decelerating, protective violence by the police force and military, the presence of pervasive war in Scripture is difficult to view as anywhere near the best-possible ethic within a fallen world. War dehumanizes and objectifies the enemy, and such an impact is certainly felt within a text such as this one. War also destroys the participants on all sides with significant psychological costs.[4] Third, the rape laws within the ANE world and within various biblical texts are typically framed as violating sexual property rights; the social honor of the husband and/or father of the woman is what is violated, and the texts do not express a primary concern for violence against women as persons in their own right.[5] The portrait of women

---

[2]One could add the following and more: forced nationality/ethnicity change, the seemingly forced participation in grieving/assimilation rituals, point of view in the text marginalizing women (male author speaks to male warrior), language depicting the sex act objectifies women, and after marriage the captive-turned-wife assumes the gods of her husband (likely implied).

[3]Some of these generic issues are developed in William J. Webb, *Slaves, Women and Homosexuals: Exploring the Hermeneutics of Cultural Analysis* (Downers Grove, IL: InterVarsity Press, 2001).

[4]Dave Grossman, *On Killing: The Psychological Cost of Learning to Kill in War and Society*, rev. ed. (New York: Back Bay Books, 2009).

[5]For a rigorous discussion of women as sexual property in Leviticus and Deuteronomy, see

as sexual property significantly affects our reception of the text before us. Finally, this war-captive text seems to reflect too limited a role for women in the production of offspring. Within an ancient world shaped by agricultural concepts, women were generally seen as providing the "soil" within which a man planted his "seed" for the formation of children. The male contribution to offspring was often viewed as providing the substantive contribution, thus determining purity issues. Such agrarian views of reproduction affected the social status of women throughout the Bible.[6] The text of Deuteronomy 21:10-14 and its narrative counterpart in Numbers 31:17-18, 35 (rounding up of thirty-two thousand virgin women) most likely show a concern for taking virgin wives at least in part because of this underlying ancient-world perspective on progeny.

In sum, these generic issues—patriarchy, war, sexual property, and the source of progeny—converge to make a passage such as Deuteronomy 21:10-14 troubling. We will not examine these underlying generic components here, but we would be remiss not to mention them and identify their *broad-based* contribution. The remainder of the chapter will examine more specific ethical problems within Deuteronomy 21:10-14 and its legislation concerning the treatment of female war captives.

Focus on external beauty. One of the most blatant ethical problems on view in Deuteronomy 21:10-14 is the reduction of women to their physical and sexual attractiveness. The warrior's selection of a wife rests solely on her external beauty—the man "notice[s]" among the captives a "beautiful" woman and he is "attracted" to her (Deut 21:11). When reading Deuteronomy 21:10-11 in a classroom lecture, we purposefully insert a few creative comments that are not in the Deuteronomy text itself to accentuate the problem: "When you go to war . . . suppose you see [and find] among the captives [a young lady who is intelligent—she is your intellectual equal; she delights and challenges your mind with engaging conversation. You connect with her and develop a long

---

Ellens's monograph *Women in the Sex Texts of Leviticus and Deuteronomy*. While any critical exploration into the redemptive side of Deut 21:10-14 is underdeveloped (and we disagree with her assessment of certain problems), her unearthing of the text's ethical downside is excellent.

[6]We became keenly aware of this ancient-world factor when working on a Pauline text that talks about the contributions of women to offspring (compared with that of men). See William J. Webb, "Balancing Paul's Original-Creation and Pro-Creation Arguments: 1 Corinthians 11:11-12 in Light of Modern Embryology," *WTJ* 66 (2004): 275-89.

and lasting friendship. Despite her family background, you discover that she is a deeply devoted follower of Yahweh. The quality of her inner character not only matches but far exceeds whatever might be said about her external beauty] . . ." Obviously, the text does not say that.

Instead of accentuating her internal virtues, Deuteronomy 21 focuses only on the external attractiveness of the female captive to the Israelite male warrior. This unbalanced and reductionist treatment of women should cause contemporary Christians to shake their heads in disgust. There should be a warning here. Some women (and men) who look beautiful on the outside are not that way on the inside.[7] Obviously, this pretty-woman passage in its concrete-specific level of meaning and instruction does not reflect anything close to an ultimate ethic in terms of the way that men should act toward women. While the passage evidences an incremental ethic and a redemptive spirit (as we will see), it nonetheless reflects a deeply scarred and fallen culture. Many other biblical texts point out that true human value is primarily found in a person's character and disposition toward God; external beauty is fleeting and cosmetic, and it can be deceptive (1 Sam 16:7; Prov 11:16, 22; 31:30; Ezek 28:17; 2 Cor 4:16; 1 Pet 3:4-6). On this consideration alone, the passage reveals a real—not simply apparent—ethical problem that Christians ought not to overlook or minimize.

One month to grieve. Another difficulty with the pretty-woman text is the rather short mourning time—only one month—that is given for the captive to grieve the loss of her family before marrying the foreign Israelite warrior. Deuteronomy 21:13 requires that before a marriage can take place, the female captive must remain in the Israelite's house "a full month" and mourn for her father and mother. Most contemporary readers would find this far too short a time for grieving and emotional transition.[8] Harold Washington voices the problem well when he states, "Only in the most masculinist of readings does the month-long waiting period give a satisfactory

---

[7]The text recalls the warning "She ain't pretty, she just looks that way." Used as a street proverb today, this expression originated from the song "She Ain't Pretty," by *The Northern Pikes*, whose video recording of it was posted September 23, 2008, www.youtube.com/watch?v=LUT4sSOlsss.

[8]Imagine giving this Deuteronomy passage to a group of experts in grief counseling and asking them to evaluate what minimal time for grieving would be needed. We suspect they would simply shake their heads or laugh in derision.

veneer of peaceful domesticity," especially in view of having just experienced military defeat and bereavement.[9]

When reading the Deuteronomy text through the lens of contemporary war conventions and egalitarian gender perspectives, the action of grabbing hot-looking women as war captives should be viewed as ethically preposterous and deserving of condemnation. Whatever sort of mourning "fix" one might propose—whether one month, one year, or one decade—it does not solve the ethical dilemmas raised within the passage. Any length of time is categorically inadequate and simply places an ethical Band-Aid on a deep wound because this treatment of captives is inherently problematic from the start. Alongside the inherent wrongness of assuming that captive women will easily become wives, we see from our contemporary horizon that a one-month reprieve is incredibly short. Grief from war trauma involving the deaths of close family members can hardly be resolved in one month.

Forced or coerced marriage. After a month of waiting, the Israelite warrior is permitted to marry the captive woman: "[You may] be her husband, and she shall be your wife" (Deut 21:13). The marriage is essentially forced, and even if the captive woman enters it with a measure of willingness, she surely must be doing so with regret, motivated by the dismal prospects and pragmatics of her newfound life.[10] Entering a marriage covenant without a shared sense of eagerness and commitment from both parties would likely reduce the chance of having a wonderful, joy-filled, trusting marriage. While the husband/wife marital covenant is formally stated in Deuteronomy 21:13, the surrounding circumstances make its functional qualities far less than ideal. It lacks the quality of deep affection grounded in a genuine relationship; instead, desperate pragmatism influences the woman's participation, and physical beauty influences the man's participation.

---

[9]Harold C. Washington, "'Lest He Die in Battle and Another Man Take Her': Violence and the Construction of Gender in the Laws of Deuteronomy 20–22," in *Gender and Law in the Hebrew Bible and the Ancient Near East*, ed. Victor H. Matthews, Bernard M. Levinson, and Tikva Frymer-Kensky, JSOTSup 262 (Sheffield: Sheffield Academic Press, 1998), 205.

[10]Other embedded factors of the ancient world (arranged marriages) might possibly have softened the transition as a result of having lower expectations about controlling one's own destiny. These factors have their own ethical problems. See the discussion of embedded ethical blinders that would have interfered with sensing the gravity of mistreatment in a text such as Deut 21:10-14.

A marriage covenant should be a sacred trust; it requires wholehearted commitment by both parties for the right reasons. Selecting as a wife a pretty woman from among war captives distorts the marital commitment and jeopardizes the proper reasons/basis for entering marriage. The forced or coercive nature of the marriage covenant makes it a weak substitute for what should be happening.

Coerced sexuality. The sexual act is also problematic. Given the spoils-of-war context, the phrase "you may go to her" (Deut 21:13) constitutes coerced sexuality at best. Since the sexual intercourse involved an extremely vulnerable and almost powerless person, one must be mindful of its coercive quality. In our present-day setting the idea of a boss dating and/or having a sexual relationship with a subordinate is viewed as unhealthy and potentially manipulative because of the peril that may befall the subordinate who says no.[11] Sexuality in such relationships, even if ostensibly consensual, can often be coercive and manipulative. If so, how much more likely is the prospect of coercion within the pretty-woman passage? In Deuteronomy 21:10-14 sexual duress is almost certainly the case (even if pragmatic consent is present), since the female war captive (1) has now become one of the spoils of battle; (2) has lost the support of her family, who might protect her honor; (3) lives as a nonnative person within Israel; and (4) faces the unpleasant alternative prospect—should she say no and refuse marriage—of becoming a slave or being abandoned, with even less control over her sexual destiny or livelihood.

Marital rape. A more grievous problem, however, is this: the text overlooks the genuine possibility and horror of marital rape (an anachronistic assessment, to be sure, but a reality nevertheless). In some cases the sex act—"you may go to her" (Deut 21:13)—would have involved something far worse than coercive-but-consensual sex. Should the sexual act have been forced—lacking the woman's consent—then in today's terms the violation would be known as marital rape. Again Washington aptly states, "The fact that the man must wait for a month before penetrating the woman . . . does not make the sexual relationship something other than rape, unless one

---

[11]Also, the person in the position of greater power may be duped into believing that the relationship reflects true love while in fact the subordinate's motives are survival and/or climbing the corporate ladder.

assumes that by the end of the period the woman has consented."[12] We agree with Washington's point here. One should not assume *in every case* that the woman would have consented. But we do not want to assume the converse either, namely, that *in every case* consent of a pragmatic nature was lacking. Some cases were likely consensual (although coercive and pragmatically based); others were not. It is impossible to know how many cases fell on either side of the line.

Coerced sexuality and rape are by far the most disturbing components of Deuteronomy 21:10-14. One shudders to think what the spectrum of real-life scenarios may have looked like. At a concrete-specific level this biblical war instruction does not represent anything near the ideal of how God would want men to treat women.

Clearly, the war ethic of ancient Israel had an ugly and problematic side in how warriors treated female captives. Beyond the generic issues underlying Deuteronomy 21:10-14—heavy-handed patriarchy, war, sexual property, and ancient-world notions about progeny—we need to acknowledge at least five ethical problems as attendant to this text: (1) excessive value is placed on external beauty, (2) one month hardly seems long enough for the grief and adjustment, (3) the marriage is either forced or at least manipulative in view of alternative prospects for the woman, (4) the sexual relationship is coercive due to the extreme vulnerability of war captives, and (5) in any number of cases the level of sexual violation would have been comparable (but not identical) to what we today label as marital rape.[13]

TWO ADDITIONAL ALLEGED ETHICAL PROBLEMS

Two remaining ethical issues associated with the pretty-woman passage require attention: (6) progeny purity is the real/true motive for the waiting period, and (7) battlefield rape is permitted for Israelite warriors. These two problems, however, differ from the former issues. While some scholars see

---

[12]Harold C. Washington, "Violence and the Construction of Gender in the Hebrew Bible: A New Historicist Approach," *Biblical Interpretation* 5, no. 4 (1997): 349.

[13]Concerning the fifth problem: Even in making this comparison between two horizons, the analogy breaks down in some cases. Here is why. All female captives in Deut 21:10-14 suffered a *compounding, two-stage* infraction of (1) a forced and/or coercive marriage covenant and (2) a forced and/or coercive sexual intercourse. In our contemporary context, many cases of marital rape occur with stage (2) but without the compounding infraction of stage (1).

these as ethical problems in Deuteronomy 21:10-14, we will argue that such perspectives need rethinking. Simply put, the evidence does not support those who contend that purity of progeny (*not* compassion) is the *true* reason for the one-month delay. Nor does the evidence support the view that the passage is *only* interested in assimilating female war captives into an Israelite household, and, worse yet, that it allows for and even assumes rape and sexual violence against women on the battlefield. We now turn to these two alleged ethical issues.

Delay for offspring purity. Some argue that the required one-month delay of sexual intercourse was due to concerns about purity of the offspring—wanting to ensure that any children were the legitimate offspring of Israelite men and not those of a foreigner.[14] According to this view, the text's stated concern about a time for grieving (Deut 21:13) is simply a convenient cover for the true motive. Those who make this case appeal to several factors. First, the word "woman" (*'iššâ*) in Deuteronomy 21:11 is a broad term that can be used for either a virgin or a married woman. The use of this broad term for woman (instead of "virgin") may signal an underlying interest in whether the captive woman had been formerly married and so might be carrying a child in the early months. Second, the delay corresponds to the typical length of a woman's ovulation cycle. It is assumed in this argument that one month would reveal whether the female captive had her menstrual period and, if she was found to have it, that would confirm her readiness to have legitimate Israelite offspring—that is, any children would be from the planting of an Israelite (not Canaanite) male seed in the fertile garden. Third, the time of grieving is specified as a "month of days," but this term is not the typical

---

[14]Washington, "Violence and the Construction of Gender in the Hebrew Bible," 349-51. El-lens (*Women in the Sex Texts of Leviticus and Deuteronomy*, 175-79) adopts Washington's view that the controlling purpose of the delay is progeny concerns and not really a concern for the captive woman. With the importance of legitimate progeny in the text we do not disagree. However, a hard-line either-or demarcation unnecessarily discounts multiple concerns. Also, legitimate progeny was in the best interests of the new wife/mother if for pragmatic reasons she wanted the marriage and family to work in this less-than-ideal postwar context. While providing helpful contributions on the side of critical ethics, Wash-ington's and Ellens's development of Deut 21:10-14 is weakest at three points: where they insist that (1) progeny concerns are *only* in the best interests of the male, (2) the stated mourning concerns in the text ought to be dismissed as false concerns, and (3) the three rituals (hair, nails, and clothing) are *only* for assimilation and not for mourning.

expression. Elsewhere in Scripture, the wording is either "seven days" or "thirty days" to describe the grieving period. Perhaps this variance in time designation indicates that something other than grieving is really in view.

Offspring purity ideas and the ancient-world understanding of male contribution to offspring undoubtedly played a role in Israel's war practices. We do not question this and have earlier cited research on the impact of ancient embryology for reading the biblical text.[15] But theorists who argue an *exclusive* progeny motive in Deuteronomy 21:13 need to rethink their position. The text explicitly ties the length of time—"a month of days"—to the duration of grieving. The Hebrew construction literally reads, "she grieves her father and her mother for a month of days." The delayed marriage is unambiguously connected to the woman's grief. One might want to give the benefit of the doubt to the text *at least* in terms of granting two purposes for the month delay: one purpose was for grieving her parents (stated), and one purpose was for assuring offspring purity (unstated). To assert that one purpose is real and the other is not real assumes that the two purposes are mutually exclusive and adopts a naive view of human motives—life often brings together multiple motives for a singular action. If the male Israelite intended to enter a lifelong marriage relationship with this pretty-woman captive (except in the case of divorce), it would have been in his own best interests to treat her kindly. The notion that progeny interests must exist as a singular "real" purpose (while the stated purpose is false) does not provide a persuasive approach.

For that matter, one might suggest numerous levels of purpose for the one-month delay: (1) *a captive-person interest*—allowing the captive woman some time to grieve the loss of her parents and adjust to the new context, (2) *a marriage interest*—the act of kindness and deference toward the captive increases the likelihood of a marriage working, and (3) *a community/nationality interest*—the one-month delay may increase progeny purity. The possibility of progeny interests—should they have been present—does not invalidate other motives. Two more functions may also have been part of the unstated purpose for the one-month delay, namely, (4) *a sexual-deferment interest*—a cooling down period for the Israelite

---

[15]Webb, "Balancing Paul's Original-Creation and Pro-Creation Arguments," 275-89.

warrior, and (5) *a redirection-of-values interest*—a ritualized way to counter the warrior's overt obsession with external beauty. Any assessment should admit the possibility of coexisting motives, rather than succumbing to an approach that suggests a need to uncover the one real and sinister motive. Each motive must be critiqued on its own merits within its textual and ancient-world context.

So let us now evaluate the progeny-purity proposal on its own merit. Was the source of the offspring (progeny purity) a motive in Israelite war practices? In short, a twofold answer seems best. *Yes*—progeny purity does play a role in the background of ANE warfare, and among other reasons, it explains why virgins were viewed as preferable for Israelite men in their selection of war brides.[16] *No*—progeny purity does not seem to be a *primary* underlying or only true motive for the required delay of marriage (Deut 21:13). Several observations are important. First, while the Hebrew word for "woman" by itself could have a broader, nonvirgin meaning, the term has a restricted usage within the immediate context. The woman is said to grieve the loss of "her father and mother" (Deut 21:13)—there is no statement about grief for a husband.[17] This wording seems to imply that the prisoner is a virgin and that a selection from among virgins on the battlefield has already taken place. If so, the text has in view a young virgin girl being taken from the house of her parents (father and mother) to the house of her Israelite warrior (husband). It assumes a typical transfer of authority from the house of the parents to the house/authority of the Israelite husband. Thus the immediate context suggests a restricted understanding of the woman as an unmarried virgin who was living with her parents. This virgin perspective on the text of Deuteronomy 21:10-14 is also supported by the practices of Israelite warriors in Numbers 31:17-18, 35, where they select virgins—that is, women "who had never slept with a man."

---

[16]Aside from progeny purity, other reasons for *virgin* war brides may well have been (1) the greater value placed on the virginity of women entering marriage even among Hebrew women (see Old Testament rape laws) and (2) the overlapping interest in younger women for bearing children and being more adaptable to a postwar marriage within a foreign culture, having fewer ties to the former culture.

[17]One would expect the mention of grieving her husband (along with the parents) since the loss of that *primary* husband-wife relationship would typically be even more grievous than *secondary* losses.

Here is the point. The restrictive expression "her father and mother" in the Deuteronomy text and the existing war customs of the Numbers text imply that a degree of due diligence has *already* happened in this area of selecting virgin captives. As gut-wrenching as it is to imagine, the Israelite soldiers may have rounded up these young virgin girls from their family settings to ensure getting virgins. The mention of "father and mother" most probably alludes to the harsh separation process that would have taken place. The one-month delay for captive females grieving their parents relates very well to an understood virgin context; the grieving motive need not be falsely declared.

Second, a one-month delay of marriage is hardly a reliable method for assuring progeny purity. Rabbinic interpreters with shared virginity and progeny concerns did not find the one-month delay at all reassuring.[18] They were adamant that, if a delay was to be invoked for protecting progeny, then a *three-month or longer delay* would be the actual amount of time required. Only after several months would the pregnancy begin to show. If a foreign woman were clever enough to escape the battlefield assessment for virgins and make it look as though she were in the virgin class of females, then she could easily have continued the deception during the one month before marrying an Israelite. Only a longer delay (at least three months and preferably more) would have fulfilled a progeny-purity purpose. If the one-month delay has the alleged real purpose of protecting Israelite offspring from foreign influence, then the text enshrines an inadequate regulation for achieving those ends.

In sum, it is much more likely that the one-month delay was indeed for the stated purpose of permitting the captive the opportunity to grieve (Deut 21:13) and for the unstated corresponding purpose of an act of kindness (at least in a dehumanized war setting), increasing the chances for a sustained marriage relationship in this dubious war-captive context. While progeny purity clearly ranked as one reason among several likely reasons in the ancient world for choosing virgin war brides, it does not seem to have played a major role in the required one-month delay in the marriage. We should not read a text such as Deuteronomy 21:10-14 in a manner that overlooks its ethical ugliness especially for post–Geneva/Hague readers (see the five points above). Fair enough. But neither should one wrongly strip away the

---

[18]Elman, "Deuteronomy 21:10-14," 8.

redemptive qualities of the biblical text in the name of critical thinking. Critical conjecture based on unreasoned probabilities amounts to *pseudo-critical* thinking.

Battlefield rape permitted. Several scholars also criticize the text of Deuteronomy 21:10-14 by arguing that it permits and even assumes battle-field rape by Israelite warriors.[19] They point out that Deuteronomy 21:10-14 is addressing only an after-the-battle case of assimilating a captive woman into Israelite society as a wife. If an Israelite warrior was attracted to a female captive and wanted to marry her, the text of Deuteronomy 21:10-14 lays out steps for such a marriage and assimilation process. The text does not prohibit battlefield rape. Accordingly, Washington and Carolyn Pressler argue that one should expect that Israelite warriors participated in battlefield rape be-cause they are elsewhere instructed to enjoy the spoils of battle (Deut 20:14) and rape was common in ANE warfare.

One must concede that Deuteronomy 21:10-14 does not explicitly pro-hibit battlefield rape and that the text is indeed addressing the scenario of postbattlefield marriage and assimilation of female war captives into an Is-raelite household. However, those who argue that the rape of foreign women on the battlefield was therefore an acceptable practice for Israelite warriors seem to have missed evidence that suggests otherwise. Also, they have not considered how the postbattlefield actions contained in Deuteronomy 21:10-14 may cast inferential light backward onto the issue of battlefield rape. We will address this issue in the next chapter.

EMBEDDED BLINDERS TO RAPE

Ancients would not have read the pretty-woman text quite like we do today. The ancient-world horizon produced an almost endless number of

---

[19]Washington, "Violence and the Construction of Gender in the Hebrew Bible," 348-49; Washington, "'Lest He Die,'" 203; Carolyn Pressler, *The View of Women Found in the Deu-teronomic Family Laws*, BZAW 216 (New York: de Gruyter, 1993), 11. Following Washing-ton and Pressler, the view that Israelite warriors most likely participated in battlefield rape of women and young girls is widely held as an assumption (no mention of evidence to the contrary). See Richard D. Nelson, *Deuteronomy: A Commentary*, OTL (Louisville, KY: Westminster John Knox, 2002), 258; Sandra Jacobs, "Terms of Endearment? אשת יפת־תאר (The Desirable Female Captive): Her Illicit Acquisition," in *Exodus and Deuteronomy*, ed. Athalya Brenner and Gale A. Yee, Texts @ Contexts Series (Minneapolis: Fortress, 2012), 246; Reeder, "Deuteronomy 21.10-14 and/as Wartime Rape," 318.

embedded blinders that make our assessments both necessary and, admittedly, anachronistic judgments.[20] We will simply mention four blinders directly related to the rape of women: (1) antiquated rape laws in general, with sexual property concepts depreciating women; (2) the dominance of arranged marriages, which still function as a type of rape and/or sexual coercion in many cases; (3) there was no legal concept of rape within a marriage (only in premarital cases); and (4) there was certainly no ancient legal assessment of rape by soldiers as a war crime against humanity. These developments in law—all good ones—have come into being within the last one hundred years.

These factors related to the horizon of the ancient world do not excuse or make acceptable the actions of Israelite soldiers in their Deuteronomy 21:10-14 treatment of female captives. These factors do confirm, however, that making ethical change in a good direction is difficult and complicated by the limits even of our own horizons. One need only read a history of rape-law development in any of these four areas, and it becomes obvious that legal change (especially in hindsight) seems to have come at glacial pace. If anything confirms the idea of an incremental ethic, it is the painstaking steps that have been needed in each of these areas of rape-law development to move ahead even in a conceptual way.

While an ancient horizon and embedded blinders do not excuse or minimize the ethical downside of a text, their existence ought to cause us all to appreciate and even to applaud—in our world as well as in the ancient one—where progress, even if incremental, is made. This positive thought about celebrating incremental change sets the stage for the next chapter.

CONCLUSION

The text of Deuteronomy 21:10-14 (along with Num 31), which governs Israel's treatment of female war captives, contains serious ethical problems. From our post–Geneva/Hague horizon there can be little doubt that these texts enshrine a form or version of war rape (forced marriage of war captives). Such

---

[20]In the next chapter we contest several arguments presented by Ellens (*Women in the Sex Texts of Leviticus and Deuteronomy*). Nevertheless, her work offers one of the clearest and most adept presentations, often tucked in cryptic footnotes, of the two-horizon issues that create ethical blinders.

a conclusion is troubling for modern readers. One must concede that the biblical laws governing the practice of Israel's holy war were far from the best possible ethic. That is one side of the story that must be heard and openly acknowledged.

Nevertheless, there is more to the story, as chapter six will show.

WAR RAPE, PART TWO

The Redemptive Side

THE LAST CHAPTER EXPLORED THE UGLY SIDE of war rape in the Bible, particularly in Deuteronomy 21:4-10 and Numbers 31:17-18, 35. The sexual exploitation of female war captives is a sad and troubling part of the biblical story. Contemporary Christians should be repulsed by what they find in these passages, for they reflect a treatment of women that comes nowhere close to an ultimate or even best-possible ethic. There is, however, a redemptive side to these otherwise ugly war texts. To see this attractive side, we will need to momentarily set aside our contemporary (Geneva) lens of war ethics and instead look at Deuteronomy 21 and Numbers 31 from the vantage point of the world in which they were written. Using this ancient-world lens, we encounter a much-restrained ethic and even some surprisingly positive developments around war rape.

We start by unfolding a picture of war in the ancient world—ancient Mesopotamia, Egypt, Greece, and Rome—where one encounters the common practice of male soldiers raping women.[1]

---

[1]The study of rape in ancient warfare has recently exploded with the contributions of Kathy L. Gaca, which focus on the ancient Greek world: "Ancient Warfare and the Ravaging Martial Rape of Girls and Women: Evidence from Homeric Epic and Greek Drama," in *Sex in Antiquity: Exploring Gender and Sexuality in the Ancient World*, ed. Mark Masterson, Nancy Sorkin Rabinowitz, and James Robson (New York: Routledge, 2015), 278-97; Gaca, "Girls, Women and the Significance of Sexual Violence in Ancient Warfare," in *Sexual Violence in Conflict Zones*, ed. E. D. Heineman (Philadelphia: University of Philadelphia Press, 2011), 73-88; Gaca, "Telling the Girls from the Boys and Children: Interpreting παίδες in the Sexual Violence of Populace-Ravaging Ancient Warfare," *Illinois Classical Studies* 35/36 (2012): 85-109. Unfortunately, the information about war rape in the ANE is far less accessible. Nevertheless, Gaca's work provides a helpful secondary lens through which to reflect on sexual ravaging in ancient war in general.

WAR RAPE IN AN ANCIENT WORLD

Let us warn you that the language of this chapter is graphic and unsettling. Despite this liability, the crude language allows us to contemplate at closer range the horrors of rape in ancient war and the realism of its brutal and violent sex. We must not speak of war rape in dispassionate, clinical, or euphemistic terms. To do so misses the ugliness of the practice and insulates us from a world that, like it or not, we must dare venture into if we are to understand the redemptive side of the Bible. Furthermore, as we will see, the biblical authors themselves talk with offensive, gutter-like vulgarity to visualize and verbalize war-rape sex.

Simply put, within ancient warfare the rape of women and young girls was a common practice. In fact, it was so common that it became part of the honored artwork of the day—artisans chiseled war-rape scenes into stone monuments, engraved them on coins, and painted them on walls. The artistic savoring of this sex-in-war practice provides an important clue, namely, that rape in the ancient world functioned as a way of celebrating the triumph of victory. To talk about war rape as common or pervasive still frames the act too mundanely. It is more accurate to say (looking outside the biblical texts) that the rape of enemy women in ancient warfare was accepted, expected, and celebrated—worn as a badge of honor.[2]

Whether the situation is ancient or contemporary, victory rituals often follow vigorously fought battles. We who are rooted in a contemporary Western society should grasp at least something of the meaning of such rituals. After all, our sports world features victory rituals that have a significant degree of overlap. In the end zone of a football field grown men spike the football (first ritual) and perform a victory dance (second ritual) on the very territory/turf that their opponents failed to protect—flaunting their prowess and driving their message home. So also ancient male warriors

---

[2]The rape of women was so pervasive in ancient warfare that, under threat of war, cities were personified as women and their prospective capture described in the language of rape. See Jer 6:1-8; 13:22; Is 47:1-4; Nah 3:5-6. Rape was the language of dread and horror. See Susan Brooks Thistlethwaite, "'You May Enjoy the Spoils of Your Enemies': Rape as a Biblical Metaphor for War," *Semeia* 61 (1993): 59-75; Alice A. Keefe, "Rapes of Women/Wars of Men," *Semeia* 61 (1993): 79-97; Susanne Scholz, "'Back Then It Was Legal': The Epistemological Imbalance in Readings of Biblical and Ancient Near Eastern Rape Legislation," *Bible and Critical Theory* 1, no. 4 (2005): 36.1–36.22.

celebrated victory with the ultimate "we beat them" ritual that expressed their success in battle and the complete possession and humiliation of their enemies—by phallic penetration, thrusting, and ejaculation within the most protected "territory" of the enemy. Such was the victory dance of warriors in the ancient world. War rape in the ancient world functioned as part of their ritualized triumph. Rape enacted defeat at a far deeper psychological level than mere killing on the battlefield; it took from the opponents the most prized persons and property they had failed to protect. Sexual violation of the enemy's beloved daughters and wives offered a ritualized climax to the killing frenzy on the battlefield. In the case of siege warfare, rape ritually reenacted the invading army's earlier penetration of the city gates. As with our contemporary sports victory rituals—dances, spikes, flipping the bat, punching the air—ancient warriors expressed the finality of their victory with vigor and force, enacting sexual conquest.

It might surprise some readers to find that biblical authors employ equally graphic and disturbing language to describe rape in war. For example, Judges 5:30 talks about the capture and rape of Israelite women by Canaanite warriors as a normal expectation and as part of what it meant to enjoy the spoils of battle, picturing Sisera's mother saying, "Are they [the delayed Canaanite warriors] not finding and dividing the spoils: a woman or two for each man?"[3] The English expression "a woman or two" as a translation removes the unseemly language. The Hebrew text utilizes a graphic body-part expression— "a womb/vagina or two"—which carries sexual and procreative connotations.[4] It could be functionally translated today with disgusting male locker-room talk that uses particular sexual body parts to speak of women.[5]

---

[3]For Deborah's audience the immediate reference would have been to the potential rape of Israelite women. Yet, these words placed within the mouth of Sisera's mother suggest rape as a typical and generalized war practice.

[4]Tammi J. Schneider, *Judges*, BO (Collegeville, MN: Liturgical Press, 2000), 96. Schneider argues that this dialogue both legitimizes her son's actions (hoping he is having a good time raping captive women) and reveals that raping captive females would not have been a unique experience but a standard Canaanite practice. Daniel I. Block similarly comments on the degrading, body-part language in Judg 5: "Preference for this overtly sexual expression ['a womb, a pair of wombs'] reflects the realities of war: to victorious soldiers the women of vanquished foes represent primarily objects for their sexual gratification, another realm to conquer" (*Judges, Ruth*, NAC 6 [Nashville: Broadman & Holman, 1999], 243).

[5]In the ancient world the "womb" was the place where the male planted his semen—a combination of what we now understand as a woman's vagina, fallopian tubes, and uterus. For

While missed by most English readers, these sexualized overtones and the graphic rape language are not lost on Hebrew Bible commentators.[6] In the immediate context, when Jael drives a tent peg with a hammer (repeated and progressive thrusts) pounding ever deeper into the temple of Sisera's head, the irony alludes to sexual penetration in war.[7] The Canaanite armies and their great general intended to penetrate Israelite women—"a vagina or two for each man." But they were defeated (with Sisera representing his army) and ironically were penetrated themselves by a woman.[8] If all of that is offensive for us, how much more so for the original audience? How could the original readers of the Hebrew Bible ever get that picture out of their heads? How can we? We cannot. We are left feeling the horror and violation of war through a graphic image of what it means when warriors ritualize their victory by sexually ravaging women.

The equally disturbing image of "lifting the skirts" of women is used by biblical writers to describe war rape (Is 47:2; Nah 3:5; see also Jer 13:22, 26). This idiom is captured in the movie *Braveheart* in a scene where an English soldier throws the beautiful Scottish bride of William Wallace on a table and lifts her long, flowing skirt—clothing meant for sexual modesty—just before

---

instance, an inscription speaks of the king of Lagash (Eanatum) being birthed by means of his father (a demigod and warrior king) implanting his semen "in the womb" of Eanatum's mother. See William J. Hamblin, *Warfare in the Ancient Near East to 1600 BC: Holy Warriors at the Dawn of History* (New York: Routledge, 2006), 52.

[6] The poem is written by an Israelite author mocking a Canaanite perspective.

[7] The sexually charged language of the tent peg penetrating Sisera reflects double entendre and the symbolism of reversal. Robert B. Chisholm Jr. succinctly captures the point: "Sisera lies raped as it were at the feet of a woman" (Chisholm, *A Commentary on Judges and Ruth* [Grand Rapids: Kregel Academic, 2013], 244). Compare Gale A. Yee: "The author describes the killing scene as the reversal of rape (4:21). The man becomes the woman; the rapist becomes the victim; the penetrator becomes the penetrated. The tent peg in Jael's hands becomes synecdochically the ravaging phallus" (Yee, "By the Hand of a Woman: The Metaphor of the Woman Warrior in Judges 4," *Semeia* [1993]: 116). On sexual overtones in Judg 4–5 see also Susan Niditch, "Eroticism and Death in the Tale of Jael," in *Gender and Difference in Ancient Israel*, ed. Peggy L. Day (Minneapolis: Fortress, 1989), 43-57; Niditch, *Judges*, OTL (Louisville, KY: Westminster John Knox, 2008), 81; Susan Ackerman, *Warrior, Dancer, Seductress, Queen: Women in Judges and Biblical Israel* (New York: Doubleday, 1998), 130-31; Ellen J. van Wolde, "Yael in Judges 4," *ZAW* 107 (1995): 240-46; Ellie Assis, "The Choice to Serve God and Assist His People: Rahab and Yael," *Biblica* 85 (2004): 82-90; Victor H. Matthews, *Judges and Ruth*, NCBC (Cambridge: Cambridge University Press, 2004), 73.

[8] Piercing the temple (a vulnerable spot) may be suggestive of breaking or piercing the hymen of the virgin victims of war rape.

the violent warrior repeatedly thrusts his penis into her. The language of lifting of the skirt is intended to take the reader on a graphic journey right to the edge of the obvious next step—sexual penetration. The biblical authors portray the whole war-rape act by talking about one part of the sequence: grab a woman, throw her down, *lift her skirt*, and penetrate her. A reader shudders when visualizing the image of lifting skirts because of the implied next step. Lifting the skirt is saying far *more*, not less, in its sexual imaging for the reader. These are hard pictures for the brain to erase. Nevertheless, the Bible uses tent-peg images, female body-part language, lifting skirts, and implied next-step pictures to offend a reader's sensibilities. One cannot escape the ugliness and horror of war rape in the ancient world.[9]

In *Ancient Siege Warfare*, Paul Kern describes war rape in the ancient Mesopotamian and Persian world as "undoubtedly the most common atrocity against noncombatants" and as an act that expressed complete victory:

> Rape was the ultimate violation of women, marking the complete possession of them by the soldiers who had taken possession of their city. From the phallic shape of the battering ram trying to penetrate the walls of the city to priapic soldiers pillaging and raping in a violated city was a logical progression. All warfare has a strong sexual undercurrent, but siege warfare was an explicit battle for sexual rights. The defending soldiers were attempting to protect their sexual rights to their wives as well as protect the sexual integrity of their tribe or ethnic group. The raping that frequently followed the fall of a city starkly symbolized total victory in a total war.[10]

---

[9]The biblical authors understood rape as an inevitable and terrifying part of war: Is 13:16; Zech 14:2; Lam 5:11.

[10]Paul Bentley Kern, *Ancient Siege Warfare* (Indianapolis: Indiana University Press, 1999), 81, 83. For allusions to war rape in ANE curse formulae and biblical texts see Paul A. Kruger, "Women and War Brutalities in the Minor Prophets: The Case of Rape," *OTE* 27, no. 1 (2014): 157-70. The biblical language of penetrating the city (by the battering ram or any means) often included double entendre in the domain of rape-penetration imagery since the city itself/herself was frequently cast in feminine terms and personified as a woman; the attacking armies were bent on raping the woman/city—penetrating both the city and her women inside. In addition to Kruger, see J. Cheryl Exum, *Plotted, Shot, and Painted: Cultural Representations of Biblical Women*, JSOTSup 215 (Sheffield: Sheffield Academic Press, 1996), 101-28; Pamela Gordon and Harold C. Washington, "Rape as Military Metaphor in the Hebrew Bible," in *A Feminist Companion to the Bible: The Latter Prophets*, ed. Athalya Brenner (Sheffield: Sheffield Academic Press, 1995), 308-52; Susanne Scholz, *Sacred Witness: Rape in the Hebrew Bible* (Minneapolis: Fortress, 2010), 179-208.

Frankly, we cannot envision the graphic biblical images or read about rape in ancient warfare books without feeling numbness and nausea. Part of us wishes to skip over this opening section. But it is the utterly grotesque reality of ancient warfare that sets the stage for understanding the redemptive actions within Scripture, even if they are limited or incremental. For the rest of this chapter we will explore ways in which the biblical text is far different from the sexual conquest that was so flagrant in ancient war practices. Herein lies the encouraging side of the war-rape texts in Scripture.

NO BATTLEFIELD RAPE

In an ancient world where the battlefield rape of women was common practice, we encounter one of the most dramatic differences within the biblical story. For Hebrew warriors, no rape (no sex of any kind) was allowed on the battlefield or on the journey from the battle site back to Jerusalem. This military difference is huge. No sexual ravaging of women typical of ancient warfare. None. At the very time when the frenzy of bloody fighting was at its height or just completed, Hebrew warriors were *not* permitted to carry their violence further into the domain of sexual conquest. After a successful battle, when celebration in some fashion would be expected, Israelite warriors were *not* allowed to ritualize their victory through the sexual ravaging of women.

Not all scholars see it this way. Contrary to the view that we will develop, that battlefield rape did not occur, several scholars argue the opposite, namely, that Israelite soldiers did rape women on the battlefield. They make their case from several pieces of evidence. First, they rightly point out that the text of Deuteronomy 21:10-14 does not close the door to battlefield rape.[11] Deuteronomy 21:10-14 addresses only an after-the-battle situation of assimilating a captive woman into Israelite society as a wife. If an Israelite warrior is attracted to a female captive, the text of Deuteronomy 21:10-14 lays out the steps for the marriage and assimilation process. That text does *not* prohibit battlefield rape. Furthermore, based on ANE war practices, Washington and Pressler both argue that one should assume that Israelite

---

[11]Carolyn Pressler, *The View of Women Found in the Deuteronomic Family Laws*, BZAW 216 (New York: de Gruyter, 1993), 11; Harold C. Washington, "Violence and the Construction of Gender in the Hebrew Bible: A New Historicist Approach," *Biblical Interpretation* 5, no. 4 (1997): 348.

warriors participated in battlefield rape. Also, certain biblical texts (Deut 20:14; Num 31:25-54) instruct Israelite warriors to enjoy the spoils of battle: women, children, animals, and all the goods of the city. One might assume, given no explicit prohibition of battlefield rape in Israel's war instructions, that sexual ravaging of women was simply an understood part of the process.

Nevertheless, the case for Israelite warriors engaging in battlefield rape is problematic. True, Deuteronomy 21:10-14 does not explicitly prohibit battlefield rape, and the text is instead addressing postbattlefield marriage back in the homeland and the assimilation of female war captives into Israelite households. However, those who argue that the rape of foreign women on the battlefield was an acceptable practice for Israelite warriors use an argument from silence and, even more damaging, omit significant evidence that suggests otherwise (see below). Also, they have not considered how certain redemptive elements in the postbattlefield actions contained in Deuteronomy 21:10-14 may cast inferential light backwards onto the issue of battlefield rape.[12] Finally, the passages concerning the spoils of war (Deut 20:14; Num 31:25-54) are at best general descriptions of the goods taken and do not give us any specific statement about what Israelite soldiers did with these women either before or after their capture. Given the normal patterns of ancient warfare, rape on the battlefield is a reasonable conjecture. But here is the crucial question: *Did Israel's sexual practices in war fit the normal patterns of the ancient world?* The question is a fascinating one and permits an unusual glimpse into a strange but redemptive side of the biblical text.

---

[12]While it is true that Deut 21:10-14 does not prohibit battlefield rape, that does not mean it provides no logical inferences about the issue. Many actions within Deut 21:10-14 as read within an ANE world push for greater dignity in the treatment of female war captives. Within that ancient world the monthlong waiting period before sexual intercourse/marriage, the prohibition against later selling the woman as a slave, and the verbal denouncement of "violating" her in the case of divorce were virtually unheard-of actions. These highly redemptive elements are developed later in this chapter. At this point, however, they are at least suggestive: the *postbattlefield* treatment of women says something about the *battlefield* treatment of women. If Israelite men were free to rape and ravage women during battle, why place any restrictions at all on warriors in the postbattlefield treatment of captives? Why care one whit about postponement of the marriage/sexual intercourse, about a time for grieving (see chapter five's discussion), about violating the woman, or about selling her as a slave? These compassionate markings within the biblical text make little sense if a warrior had unrestricted sexual access to raping foreign women during the time of battle before the captives were formally gathered and Deut 21:10-14 came into play.

A comparatively stronger case can be made that Israelite warriors were prohibited from engaging in battlefield rape. Several pieces of evidence support no battlefield rape as the more likely conclusion. First, consider that the patterns of sexuality in ancient Israel in certain ways were dramatically different from surrounding ANE countries. For instance, Israelites were not permitted *any* sexual acts within the temple setting as part of the worship of Yahweh (Lev 21:7, 9; Num 15:39; 25:1-4; Deut 23:17-18; 1 Kings 14:24; 15:12; 22:46; Hos 4:4; 2 Maccabees 6:4; see also Rev 2:14, 20). Unlike practices in ancient pagan cults/temples, where sexuality seems to have played a role in the worship setting (see discussion below), in Israel the presence of male and female temple prostitutes and ritual sex in worship were completely banned.[13]

When approaching Yahweh at Mount Sinai—the paradigm of worship—the people are instructed to wash their clothes and abstain from all sexual intercourse (Ex 19:14-15).[14] Instructions later in Exodus about making the priests' garments and the building of altars are explicit about avoiding nakedness (Ex 28:42; 20:26). Cultic purity laws in Leviticus create yet another layer of temporal and spatial distance from sexual intercourse—even distance from an everyday married sex life (let alone sexual activity in temple worship; Lev 15:16-18).

These restrictive sexual mores in the temple context and the worship of Yahweh seem to have flowed into Israel's military practices. Here is why. God's presence in battle is symbolically conveyed through the ark of the covenant. In preparation for battle, the ark is taken from the most holy place in the temple and carried by the priests to accompany the army to the battlefield (Num 10:35-36; Josh 6:7-13; 1 Sam 4:3-11; 11:11): *Yahweh's temple-like presence moves with the army.* With Yahweh's ark (his footstool) in the army's midst, participation in war is viewed as a holy or sacred act and thus requires a raised state of devotion of the warriors and of the battle activity—both are consecrated to the Lord (Is 13:3; Jer 6:4; 22:7; 51:27-28; Joel 3:9; Mic 3:5).[15] This raised sacral state means that the Israelite warriors can eat the consecrated

---

[13]When temple prostitution does occur within Israel (2 Kings 23:7), it is viewed by biblical authors as a heinous violation of God's law and one of the reasons (along with idolatry) for Israel's removal from the land.

[14]Recall chapter three and its discussion of God most holy in Exodus.

[15]See chapter three concerning the footstool.

bread normally reserved for priests but, as with worship at Sinai, they cannot participate in any sex. As the biblical text puts it, male warriors are obligated to keep themselves from women. Abstinence from sexual intercourse during war seems to have been a standard part of Israel's military practices, as is noted by David in a conversation with Ahimelek:[16]

> David said to Ahimelek the priest, ". . . Now then, what have you at hand? Give me five loaves of bread, or whatever you can find."
>
> But the priest answered David, "I don't have any ordinary bread at hand; however, there is some consecrated bread here—provided the men have kept themselves from women."
>
> David replied, "Indeed *women have been kept from us, as usual whenever I set out.* The men's bodies are holy even on missions that are not holy. How much more so today!" (1 Sam 21:2-5)

This Israelite practice of abstaining from sexual intercourse during war—Israel's military men keeping themselves from women—makes David's sexual immorality with Bathsheba even more hideous because it happens "at the time when kings go off to war" (2 Sam 11:1). This subtle comment about what kings generally do in war is the narrator's way of raising the question of why King David is at home (having sex!) and not out on the battlefield with his men. When David invites Bathsheba's husband, Uriah, back home from the battle, he hopes that Uriah will sleep with his wife and thus cover up the pregnancy. Instead, Uriah's behavior serves as a contrastive foil to David's wrongful indulgence. Uriah sleeps on the palace floor with the servants; he does not go home and sleep with his wife.[17] In his explanation to David, Uriah points to the presence of the ark on the battlefield and suggests that he could not have done otherwise considering the conditions of his fellow warriors. Thus, Uriah responds to David with an adamant refusal: "The ark [Yahweh's footstool] and Israel and Judah are staying in tents [near the battlefield], and my commander Joab and my lord's men are camped in the open

---

[16]Even for a nocturnal emission a soldier had to leave the camp, wash in the evening, and return to the camp only after sunset (Deut 23:9-14). On the other hand, newly married men were to stay home with their wives and not go to war (Deut 24:5)—an instruction due *in part* to the comparatively restricted sexual activities permitted to Israelite warriors.

[17]Uriah's abstinence is especially notable because none of his army mates on the battlefield would have known (or would need to have known) about his sexual intercourse while back home. This furthers the contrast to David, who tries to hide his actions.

country. How could I go to my house to eat and to drink and make love to my wife? As surely as you live, I will not do such a thing" (2 Sam 11:11). Within this sex-and-war discussion the ark depicts the *temple-like presence of Yahweh* (like the Exodus mountain), the raised consecration levels, and the (resultant) restriction on Israelite warriors from participation in sexual acts. The text's implied question is obvious: How could Uriah possibly engage in such sexual enjoyment when his fellow warriors could not?

Given the complete prohibition of sexual intercourse in Israel's worship and in war contexts (overlapping domains of sacred space in relation to the ark), it makes little sense to suggest that Israelite soldiers were free to rape foreign women as part of daily military life while they were at war. Uriah's reflections about his fellow men on the field would be rather hollow if they were engaging in sexual intercourse with foreign women on the battlefield as part of capturing and enjoying the spoils of battle. In the same way, David's earlier comments to Ahimelech regarding no sex during war (1 Sam 21:2-5) can hardly be split into a bipolar answer—a negative answer for sexual intercourse with Israelite women and an affirmative response to sexual intercourse with foreign women. Sacral defilement would have been even greater in the second case. Abstinence from sexuality in both areas—worship and war—is intended by Yahweh to be total/absolute for the Israelites; it does not depend on the nationality of the women.

Some might still argue that there was yet a brief window of opportunity for raping women when the battle was finished and Israel's army was gathering up the spoils and returning to Jerusalem. With the victory of battle already sealed and the threat of danger considerably lessened, this time of gathering of spoils would have provided an opportune moment for raping women. A couple of considerations suggest that rape even in the lingering, postbattle aftermath was not permitted. First, the continued presence of the golden ark all the way back to Jerusalem made the postbattle collection of goods and travel back to Jerusalem a sacred space.[18] Yet again, we encounter the *temple-like* presence of Yahweh, which requires no sexual activity regardless of the stage of battle. Even during the liminal period following a battle, the Israelites are still under the ban of sexual intercourse. Only when

---

[18]The ark symbolizes sacred space even while en route outside the temple (2 Sam 5:1–6:23).

the ark is returned to the temple in Jerusalem is the sacred "war space" reconfigured. Second, certain battles stretched over several months. Acquiring captives—both men and women—often happened throughout the time of a prolonged battle because of unsuccessful attempts to flee an advancing army or the siege of a city and the multiple stages of capturing parts of a city or territory. It would make little sense to prohibit sexual intercourse with captive women during the various stages of a *prolonged* war but make it acceptable for a *brief* period once the battle was over.

Yahweh's prohibition of sexual activity in the temple and on the battlefield—acts of worship and acts of war—involves two domains where women were most vulnerable to rape and coerced sexuality within the ancient world. Is this a coincidence? Perhaps. But maybe these sexuality laws at least in part had something to do with changing the way human beings related to each other in these highly vulnerable contexts, where sexuality was widely open to abuse. One might also reflect on the prophets who rail against men (presumably husbands) who violate—a strong term, close to what we would consider rape in our culture—women during their menstrual periods (Ezek 22:10-11). From a Western perspective the laws of Leviticus about cultic purity, menstruation, and sexual prohibitions seem dauntingly fastidious and often baseless. However, the biblical taboos against *sex during menstruation, war, and worship* seem to connect with a related theme, namely, a concern to curb unchecked male power and opportunities for forced or coercive sexual intercourse with women in vulnerable settings.

NO GLORIFICATION OF WAR RAPE IN ISRAEL'S ART OR ANNALS

Over the last fourteen years while writing this book, we have gathered more than thirty electronic portraits and numerous published pictures of war art from the ancient world—each of which portrays male soldiers raping enemy women.[19] After a battle in the ancient Mesopotamian, Greek, and Roman worlds, the sponsoring government would often hire its best artisans to place portraits of (implied) war rape—the sexual ravaging of

---

[19]The earliest item of this sort that we have found is a stone relief that depicts two Assyrian soldiers raping a woman; it dates to the time of Ashurbanipal. For a photograph of it, see Simo Parpola and Kazuko Watanabe, *Neo-Assyrian Treaties and Loyalty Oaths*, SAA 2 (Helsinki: Helsinki University Press, 1988), 47 [BM 124927].

women and girls—on city walls, coins, statues, columns, and paintings. In these ancient war-rape scenes artists typically displayed soldiers grabbing women by their clothes or hair, overpowering a resisting female, carrying girls off with their sideways bodies flailing, and often with partial nakedness such as a bare breast. The disheveled clothing, pulled hair, and partial nakedness are telltale signs of groping hands in the struggle and symbolic of more sexual unveiling (rape) to follow.

Imagine living in a nation that proudly hired its artists to enshrine "glorious" rape scenes in their war memorials. This *artistic* war-rape practice is utterly baffling. If we struggle to fathom such a practice, perhaps it is because the difference between our horizons creates a canyon-sized gap of inconceivable horror. The chasm is too large to cross. Of course, we have examples of war rape in our world—conservative estimates in the Congo war have risen to over eleven hundred women raped each day.[20] But acts of rape tend to be hidden. In our contemporary context, worldwide abhorrence and censure of rape in war (now a war crime) are so pronounced that sexual conquest of women in war becomes a matter of military shame, not pride, as soon as it is known and for future generations.[21]

No evidence exists from ancient artwork that Israel glorified its battle memories by portraying its soldiers raping foreign women. Granted, little ancient Israelite war art has been found.[22] Even an exhaustive search would reveal only whatever items had managed to survive. Without survival and access to all ancient Israelite state-sponsored artwork, it is impossible to say that glorified rape art never existed in Israel.

---

[20] See chapter one, footnote 3.

[21] Only two decades ago the International Criminal Tribunals of Yugoslavia and Rwanda (1990s) and the Roman Statute (1998) officially made rape in a war context a crime against humanity, a form of genocide, and a war crime. For a fascinating story of the development of this legislation see Tuba Inal, *Looting and Rape in Wartime: Law and Change in International Relations* (Philadelphia: University of Pennsylvania Press, 2013).

What United Nations country today would dare hire artists to capture its male warriors sexually ravaging enemy females? Perhaps a country full of Isis-like warriors would do such a thing. Even so, most of our world would be repulsed by that art and would want it kept (like lamps made of human skin from Nazi concentration camps) only in war museums as evidence of sick and twisted human minds.

[22] Unlike the prolific war art from other ANE countries, Israel seems to have produced little or no war art (at least none that survived). An informal survey of several leading biblical scholars on Israelite and ANE warfare yielded no undisputed examples.

Nevertheless, the difference involving Israel's so-far-nonexistent war art is confirmed on a corresponding literary level. The tale of rape visualized by foreign artists has parallels in their literary world. For example, an Assyrian war scene of two soldiers raping a woman finds its counterpart in written documents (1) with explicit threats of rape and sexual ravaging of enemy women in curse formulas, (2) with the inclusion of rape in the victory records of war annals, and (3) with the seeming allusion to war rape in an annual celebration festival.[23] A ritual commentary on the Enuma Elish festival recounts a battle in which the male god Marduk is said to have "defeated [the female goddess] Tiamat with his penis."[24] The narrative timing

---

[23]Cynthia M. Chapman points out that treaty curses typically focused on "the vassal king's failure to protect his family by threatening his wife and children with both physical and sexual harm" (*The Gendered Language of Warfare in the Israelite-Assyrian Encounter* [Winona Lake, IN: Eisenbrauns, 2004], 41-43). Chapman cites several examples. In one Aramaic treaty the wives of Mati-'ilu, king of Arpad, are threatened with being stripped naked like a prostitute: "[And just as a pros]ti[tute is stripped naked] so may the wives of Mati'el be stripped naked, and the wives of his offspring and the wives of [his] no[bles]." Along similar lines, Esarhaddon's *Succession Treaty* threatens the wives of the assembled vassals with sexual conquest: "May Venus, the brightest of stars, before your eyes make your wives lie in the lap of your enemy." Any vassals who broke the treaty would see their women being sexually ravaged. See Parpola and Watanabe, *Neo-Assyrian Treaties*, 46 [#6, line 428]; see also 49 [#6, lines 481-84]. In another curse formula with magical overtones Bel-etir, the ruler of Bit-Iba, is warned to be loyal if he does not want to be treated like "a raped [female] captive . . . slave girl, woman . . . 'beard' of raped girls!" The curse seems to be talking about the military rape of a male vassal ruler as would typically happen with female war captives. See Alasdair Livingstone, *Court Poetry and Literary Miscellanea*, SAA 3 (Helsinki: Helsinki University Press, 1989), 30 [#30; lines 1-4]. See also the threat announcement by King Ben-Hadad of Syria when laying siege against Israel/Samaria: "Your silver and gold are mine, and the best [most beautiful] of your wives and children are mine" (1 Kings 20:3).

On inclusion of rape in victory records of war annals, see Elisabeth Meier Tetlow, *Women, Crime, and Punishment in Ancient Law and Society*, vol. 1, *The Ancient Near East* (New York: Continuum, 2004), 168-71. Shalmanesser III records that "for *nine days* he pillaged his [Erartu's] place" (italics added), and afterwards he drove the women of the land in front of his troops. The nine days of place pillaging may have included war rape similar to Absalom's sexual conquest of David's concubines on the palace rooftop (2 Sam 16:22). See Livingstone, *Court Poetry and Literary Miscellanea*, 46 [#17; line r. 18]; see also 120 [#50, line 21]. For implied sexual ravaging of women (seized and placed in the holds of ships) and the ruling vassal's wives (carried off before his eyes) in Egyptian conquest accounts, see K. Lawson Younger Jr., *Ancient Conquest Accounts: A Study in Ancient Near Eastern and Biblical History Writing*, JSOTSup 98 (Sheffield: JSOT Press, 1990), 80-81.

[24]Alasdair Livingstone, "A Cultic Commentary [on Enuma Elish]," in *Court Poetry and Literary Miscellanea*, no. 37:18 (pp. 92-95). The penis in this late Assyrian ritual commentary should be identified as Marduk's bow. See also Jerrold S. Cooper, "Female Trouble and Troubled Males: Roiled Seas, Decadent Royals, and Mesopotamian Masculinities in Myth and Practice," in *Being a Man: Negotiating Ancient Constructs of Masculinity*, ed. Ilona Zsolnay (New York: Routledge, 2017), 115-16.

of unsheathing the male penis weapon (*after* the enemy armies are slaughtered and *before* victory celebrations) is highly suggestive of sexual conquest, since such would have occurred in the human war realm at that very point.[25] By way of contrast, however, biblical accounts do not glorify war rape in their annals or threaten their enemies with the sexual conquest of their women. While God threatens Israel herself with *being* raped by foreign armies, the action is obviously different. This latter case involves truncated or short-form causation where the simplified rhetoric represents a far more complex causation process and reality; a sovereign God can use sinful/evil human agency (the moral choices of human beings) to accomplish his will.[26]

We might ponder the connection between there being no glorified rape scenes (with a positive connotation) in Israel's war art and annals and the earlier point about no battlefield rape. A logical correlation exists between the absence of war-rape art in Israel and our last point about no sex on the battlefield or during postbattlefield journeys. Here is the link. In almost all non-Israelite artistic samples of ancient war-rape scenes, the artists chose the pictured setting for sexual ravaging as the battlefield/plundering context. So our first two redemptive points are closely connected. If Israelite warriors were *not* permitted sexual contact before battle, on the battlefield, or on their way back to Jerusalem (first point), it would follow that artistic representations that glorified rape in its war art (this second point) would not be likely among Israelite artifacts. The one anticipates the other.

NO RAPE OF TEMPLE SLAVES

War captives in Israel would not have been vulnerable to sexual exploitation in the temple (perpetual rape of female slaves) to the same extent that they would have been in other ANE countries. At least to the degree that Israel followed Yahweh's instructions about no temple prostitutes, there would

---

[25]At the very least this cultic commentary on the New Year's festival—"Marduk . . . [defeat]ed Tiamat with his penis"—confirms the openly sexualized nature of ancient war. However, its placement in the unfolding battle scene suggests an intentional comparison with war rape on the human level.

[26]See appendix G. The few exceptions (Judg 21; 2 Sam 16:22) are viewed by the biblical narrator as abominable war actions. The horror of wartime rape was a national shame for Israel, *not* a mark of pride and glory.

have been no opportunity to use slaves in this context.[27] This third re-demptive feature in the biblical material on war rape returns to the temple theme. We have already argued that Israel's theology that sex was not to be part of temple worship had a profound impact on changing ancient expectations and practices related to battlefield rape. The presence of the ark on the battlefield made a dramatic difference in the sexual practices of Israelite warriors. Now we will examine how war rape in other ANE cultures often carried over into *perpetual rape* in the pagan temple setting or at least in a connected relationship to ancient foreign temples.

In ancient war a victorious army would forcibly march captives back to the army's homeland and use many of the captives in temple estates as forced labor. War was a standard means by which kings could readily fill the labor pools for the temple precincts and lands owned by the temple. Records exist of temple donations of war slaves by various Egyptian pharaohs, Hittite kings, and Babylonian rulers—all giving captive war slaves to their temples, often as an act of thanking their gods for victory.[28] In fact, the slave pool in foreign temples was so plentiful that it was one of the rare contexts where the king or temple supervisor could exercise extreme collective-punishment measures against not only slaves who committed a crime but also against their

---

[27]Yahweh's prohibition of temple prostitution is very clear (Deut 23:17-18; see also Lev 21:7, 9; Num 15:39; 25:1-4); exceptions/violations are strongly censured (1 Kings 14:24; 15:12; 22:46; 2 Kings 23:7).

[28]Egyptian pharaohs: Mark D. Janzen, "The Iconography of Humiliation: The Depiction and Treatment of Bound Foreigners in New Kingdom Egypt" (PhD diss., University of Memphis, 2013), 237-40. Thutmose III, Seti I, Ramses II, and Ramses III each make similar statements about giving many war captives (sometimes the vast majority) to fill Amon's temple with male and female slaves. See also Jeffrey J. Niehaus, *Ancient Near Eastern Themes in Biblical Theology* (Grand Rapids: Kregel, 2008), 66. Sennacherib gave forty-one men, women, and children to a temple as slaves (Tetlow, *Women, Crime, and Punishment*, 292n124).

Hittite kings: In one Hittite cult/temple drama the players representing Hittite warriors and enemy troops fight a mock battle. Naturally, the Hittites win. Then the Hittite soldiers take the captives and present them to their deity, which probably reflects the real-life practice of donating some prisoners of war to the temple estates of Hittite deities—a practice confirmed by Hattusili I's annals. See Harry A. Hoffner Jr., "The Treatment and Long-Term Use of Persons Captured in Battle According to the Masat Texts," in *Recent Developments in Hittite Archaeology and History*, ed. K. Aslihan Yener and Harry A. Hoffner Jr. (Winona Lake, IN: Eisenbrauns, 2002), 63.

Babylonian rulers: The Babylonian king at times personally presented slaves to various gods and temples. See Andrea Seri, *The House of Prisoners: Slavery and State in Uruk During the Revolt Against Samsu-Iluna*, SANER 2 (Boston: de Gruyter, 2013), 131-32.

entire family or group by means of collective executions (see appendix D).[29] Such was the vulnerable status of slaves in ancient temples and the extent of control by temple administrators.

Now *if* sex was a part of the ancient worship setting, then war-captured slaves donated to the temple would become a natural resource for performing ritualized temple sex and/or sacred prostitution. We intentionally began the last sentence with an italicized "if" because this is a hotly debated subject. For years biblical scholars have held the view that sexual intercourse in religious rituals and/or prostitution was a dominant part of ancient foreign temple practices. Statements within the Bible and in other external or non-Mesopotamian sources seem to support this conclusion.[30] But many recent scholars have challenged these *external* (non-Mesopotamian) sources as having propagandistic agendas and have concluded from the scant internal evidence that no such practices occurred in Mesopotamian temples. This view of ancient Mesopotamian temples is currently held by many ANE scholars and by a large group within the biblical-studies guild.[31]

However, the pendulum is starting to swing back. A significant number of scholars have pieced together a more rigorously developed case supporting the fact that sex occurred in ancient Mesopotamian temples using a variety of internal/Mesopotamian sources.[32] If we were to engage this

---

[29]As Tetlow points out, "The temple probably could sustain such a loss [from collective/group executions] because it regularly received fresh supplies of war captives to be temples slaves." See *Women, Crime, and Punishment in Ancient Law and Society*, 306n83.

[30]Within the Bible see Lev 19:29; Deut 23:17-18 (MT 23:18-19); 1 Kings 14:24; 15:12; 22:46 (MT 22:47); 2 Kings 23:7; Is 57:7-8; Jer 2:20; 3:2; 5:7-8; Ezek 16:16, 24-25, 31; Hos 4:14; Mic 1:7. Scholars are split over whether citations from Herodotus (*History*, 1.199), Lucian, and Strabo (*Geography*, 16.1.20) carry any weight. For whether these three ancient sources, external to Mesopotamia, should be dismissed or should not, see the sources cited in the next two notes.

[31]For example, Julia Assante, "The Kar.kid/harimtu, Prostitute or Single Woman: A Reconsideration of the Evidence," *UF* 30 (1993): 5-96; Assante, "From Whores to Hierodules: The Historiographic Invention of Mesopotamian Female Sex Professionals," in *Ancient Art and Its Historiography*, ed. A. A. Donohue and Mark D. Fullerton (Cambridge: Cambridge University Press, 2003), 13-47; Martha T. Roth, "Marriage, Divorce and the Prostitute in Ancient Mesopotamia," in *Prostitutes and Courtesans in the Ancient World*, ed. C. A. Faraone and L. K. McClure (Madison: University of Wisconsin Press, 2006), 21-39; Stephanie Lynn Budin, *The Myth of Sacred Prostitution in Antiquity* (New York: Cambridge University Press, 2008).

[32]Edward Lipiński, "Cult Prostitution and Passage Rites in the Biblical World," *Biblical Annals* 3 (2013): 9-27; Lipiński, "Cult Prostitution in Ancient Israel?," *BARev* 40, no. 1 (2014): 48-56, 70; Richard M. Davidson, *Flame of Yahweh: Sexuality in the Old Testament*

debate, it would take the next twenty pages just to survey the evidence. Our summary comment here is that the pendulum will likely continue to swing back with a better contextualized understanding of prostitution (not exactly like in our world) and a more balanced and rigorously established position using internal evidence. A collection of evidence within a wide range of Mesopotamian sources creates a case for seeing sexual activities as a likely part of temple worship (ritual sex) and/or temple economic practices (sacred prostitution-*like* sex).

Therefore, *if* sexual intercourse played a role in worship rituals to connect with the deity, and possibly in sacred prostitution to fund the temple (and we would argue there is evidence of both), we have bumped into yet another redemptive aspect of Israel's war practices in relation to the rape of women and girls within the ANE. As mentioned above, in ancient Mesopotamia and Egypt the taking of war captives was a primary means for stocking temples and temple-owned lands with slaves. These war slaves (as well as domestic debt slaves) were extremely vulnerable to the whims of temple managers, as evidenced by collective punishments. This much is certain. Now *if* ancient temples included sexual intercourse as either part of their ritual practices or sponsored sacred prostitution-*like* enterprises (reasonable evidence here), then female war captives would have been particularly vulnerable to rape in this setting.

Before leaving this point about temple/sacred sex, let us highlight a few Mesopotamian sources to make a connection between slavery and the role of women as temple prostitutes for the goddess Ishtar. An Akkadian composition called "Ishtar Will Not Tire" presents the sex goddess Ishtar as a having unlimited sexual stamina for satisfying men with her erotic pleasures:

(Peabody, MA: Hendrickson, 2007), 85-113; Morris Silver, "Temple/Sacred Prostitution in Ancient Mesopotamia Revisited: Religion in the Economy," *UF* 38 (2008): 631-36; James E. Miller, "A Critical Response to Karin Adam's Reinterpretation of Hosea 4:13-14," *JBL* 128, no. 3 (2009): 503-6; John Day, "Does the Old Testament Refer to Sacred Prostitution and Did It Actually Exist in Ancient Israel?," in *Biblical and Near Eastern Essays: Studies in Honour of Kevin J. Cathcart*, ed. John F. Healey, Carmel McCarthy, and Kevin J. Cathcart (New York: T&T Clark, 2004), 2-21; Jerrold S. Cooper, "Prostitution," in *Reallexikon der Assyriologie* (Berlin: de Gruyter, 2006), 11:12-22. See also Gernot Wilhelm, "Marginalien zu Herodot Klio 199," in *Lingering over Words: Studies in Ancient Near Eastern Literature in Honor of William L. Moran*, ed. Tzvi Abush, John Huehnergard, and Piotr Steinkeller, HSS 37 (Atlanta: Scholars Press, 1990), 503-24; Tetlow, *Women, Crime, and Punishment*, 162, 249n85.

Since I'm ready to give you all you want,

Get all the young men of your city together,

Let's go to the shade of a wall!

Seven for her midriff, seven for her loins,

Sixty then sixty satisfy themselves in turn upon her nakedness.

Young men have tired [sexually], Ishtar will not tire.[33]

Given Ishtar's role as a sex goddess (and, interestingly, as the goddess of war), it is not surprising that girls and women were pledged to work for her in the temple or sacred service to perform sexual acts with patrons. An early Nuzi source describes a father who dedicated his daughter to Ishtar as a prostitute. The daughter seems to have worked in sex services for the goddess as a debt-slave prostitute under the name *kar.kid/ḫarīmtu*, translated "prostitute," to repay money owed to the temple.[34] Two other Mesopotamian documents include curses where the breaking of a contract will result in the offender's seven daughters being "led forth as prostitutes to Ishtar." These sources bring together the concept of sexual prostitution and debt slavery in ancient temples. If female debt slaves (temporary and domestic) could be dedicated to the temple gods as prostitutes or sexual servants of the gods, it is highly probable that (permanent and foreign) war captives/slaves were placed in temples to serve as sex slaves for various gods.[35]

Ancient Egyptian sources provide a somewhat similar window into the sexual function of female war captives and, once again, with obvious temple connections. The Egyptians were known for recurring wars aimed at capturing slaves who would work in various parts of their economy. A considerable number of the captive women and girls were segregated into all-women settlements or "houses of women" with the dedicated purpose of producing children for the Egyptian slave industry. This systematic, forced production of slave children by female war captives presents a disturbing picture:

---

[33]Benjamin R. Foster, *Before the Muses: An Anthology of Akkadian Literature*, 3rd ed. (Bethesda, MD: CDL Press, 2005), 678.

[34]The terms *kar.kid/ḫarīmtu* are explained at times by the juxtaposed expression "one who knows the penis."

[35]The significant role of slaves in domestic prostitution (see next point) suggests at least that slaves in other settings where they were prominent (temple estates) may have been used for similar sexual purposes without transgressing cultural norms.

Clearly the Egyptian implementation of slavery varies in profound ways from Colonial American conceptions, though some aspects are understandably disconcerting to modern minds. Such is doubtless the case with the "houses of female slaves" which were, as Loprieno puts it, "devoted to the 'industrial production' of children." Papyrus Harris I (47.8-9) refers to an "all-women settlement," whose purpose seems to have been production of *slave labor for the temple of Ptah.*[36]

These all-female slave settlements raise many questions. Why were these enslaved females kept separate? Did certain males benefit from the sexual services of these captive women? Someone had to be impregnating these women. Was it Egyptian males, foreigners, or both? What was the connection to the temple? The evidence argues at least in a broad sense that the sexual services of female war captives were exploited on an ongoing basis for the benefit of Egyptian temples. The remaining question is whether that benefit derived from purely procreative outcomes or from providing sensual pleasure as well. In other words, would the temple benefit economically from the sexual services of the women or only from their production of more slave offspring? It is hard to imagine the exploitation of sexual service for procreation of future slaves without some benefit for the temples coming from sexual intercourse itself—pleasure for adult male participants. The abuse of female sex slaves seems highly probable given this benefit.

In sum, female captives of war *likely* functioned in positions vulnerable to perpetual rape (nonconsensual, forced sex) as slaves owned by and serving ancient Egyptian and Mesopotamian temples. It seems reasonable to conclude that at least some of the attractive females (as well as males) among the captives were given to these ancient temples for their sexual services as a part of that religious setting.[37] The good news with Israel's war-rape story is temple

---

[36]Janzen, "Iconography of Humiliation," 261 (italics added). See also Antonio Loprieno, "Slaves," in *The Egyptians*, ed. Sergio Donadoni (Chicago: University of Chicago Press, 1997), 208.

[37]Since captive women would have been dedicated to the temple goddess, the local Mesopotamian population would have seen sex with them as part of religious devotion. Some scholars are willing to concede the possibility of sacred/religious sexual rituals as part of Mesopotamian temples but with women as devotees to the god/goddess and not with a prostitution element as we understand it. See Johanna H. Stuckey, "Sacred Prostitutes," *MatriFocus* 5, no. 1 (2005): 1-7, www.matrifocus.com/SAM05/spotlight.htm.

sex with war captives (or anyone else in the temple) was not permitted.[38] Israel's sexual boundary lines in the religious domain were clear and absolute. Since no temple prostitution or sacred-ritual sex of any kind was permitted in the worship of Yahweh, Israel's war practices did not result in women being repeatedly raped as sex slaves for religious purposes.

REDUCED RAPE OF DOMESTIC SLAVE PROSTITUTES

Ancient war practices made women vulnerable to yet another form of rape, namely, as slave prostitutes among the general population. Many women who survived a war were taken captive and sold into slavery (war slaves). That alone would have been a horrid experience. However, some women had the further ill-fated prospect of belonging to a soldier or slave purchaser who would then rent them out for sexual use. After a war victory the military commander would distribute the spoils of battle among his valiant soldiers, and the king of the land would similarly reward loyal subjects by giving them war slaves.[39] Slaves obtained as war captives were a major source for domestically based prostitution. The slave owner kept the female slave within his household and had the right to hire her out for sexual purposes. While one might not think of general prostitution as war rape, clearly it functioned as such in the ANE. As a result of war some slaves would experience perpetual rape through forced prostitution, with their owner reaping monetary benefits.

What is the redemptive upside within Israel's war-rape story? We cannot say that war-slave prostitution never happened in Israel. After all, there are no explicit biblical commands against using war slaves for prostitution, and certainly no guarantees of unwavering obedience, even if there were. However, several factors suggest that Israelite males were socially restricted

---

[38]In 1 Sam 2:22-25 Yahweh punishes Eli's sons (with death) for sleeping with the women who served at the entrance of the tabernacle/temple. Seemingly the heightened censure (and temple location of the sacrificial violations) indicates that the sexual intercourse occurred within the temple precinct itself. This violation of the rule against temple sex, although not with war-captive women, clearly confirms that no women (slaves or free) were permitted to engage sexually with men in the temple.

[39]Based on Babylonian sources, Tetlow (*Women, Crime, and Punishment*, 108-9) states: "Soldiers were often paid with war booty and thereby came to own slave women. Some they used or sold, and others they rented out as prostitutes. . . . Slave women who were young and beautiful had a higher value than those who were old and ugly. Some slave owners hired their slave women out as prostitutes, both in brothels and to individuals."

in their use of prostitutes and that the dominant perspective that sex was acceptable only in the context of marriage in Israel had at least some redemptive impact on the issue at hand. Unlike other ANE countries, where prostitution was legal and a moderately accepted practice, Israel's view of both cultic and common prostitution was highly negative and monolithically so.[40] Also, tighter limits on approved avenues of sexual intercourse within Israel would have significantly restricted any practice of war-slave prostitution in Israel.[41] The influx of prostitutes during the first century of our era was primarily due to Roman presence, as seen in Jewish response to tax gatherers and prostitutes, which confirms the generalized Hebrew restriction on frequenting prostitutes.[42]

Furthermore, the pretty-woman text of Deuteronomy 21:4-10 establishes the normative route for achieving a sexual relationship with an attractive captive woman. Since Deuteronomy 21:4-10 makes the Israelite male jump a series of hurdles to have sex with a war captive, certain logical implications follow for prostitution of war slaves. We do not have an either-or scenario offered to Israelite males: if you are sexually attracted to a war captive woman, *either* (1) go the Deuteronomy 21:4-10 route *or* (2) enjoy her sexually by hiring her services as a prostitute from another Israelite owner. The latter option would amount to repeated war-captive rape, have the social stigma of frequenting a prostitute, and wrongly circumvent the protective benefits of Deuteronomy 21:4-10. Within Israel the only acceptable course of action was to marry the war captive. While Deuteronomy 21:4-10 does not address battlefield

---

[40]When discussing women who served as domestic slaves and were rented out by their owners as sex slaves, Tetlow (*Women, Crime, and Punishment*, 109) comments: "Since prostitution [in Babylonia] was legal, it was not a crime. But insofar as prostitution forced women into unwanted sex, it victimized women."

[41]While Hebrew law does not directly ban male promiscuity, neither does it leave men with any legitimate sexual partners outside marriage. See Davidson on the restrictive measures in Israel that limited available sex partners for males (*Flame of Yahweh*, 363). Recall also the prohibition of adultery in the Ten Commandments and warnings in Proverbs.

[42]The increased prostitution in first-century Palestine was most likely due to the presence of the Roman army and the more normative role that prostitutes played in the sexual service of that foreign army. The connection in the Gospels between tax gatherers and prostitutes is not accidental—*both* groups were very much related to the presence of the hated Romans. Tax gatherers were known for throwing parties for the elite Roman rulers and likely maximized these occasions with prostitutes for their guests (foreign/Roman military and government elites).

rape, it does carry strong implications for postwar slave prostitution that typically happened in ancient households through hiring out slaves.

REDEMPTIVE ELEMENTS IN DEUTERONOMY 21:4-10

For our final task we return to the text of Deuteronomy 21:4-10. Reading this disturbing text against its ancient social context allows contemporary readers to see the ways—some minor, others major—in which it moved a violent, rape-saturated war world in incremental steps toward something better. We will highlight five redemptive elements:

1. a monthlong waiting period

2. mourning/assimilation rituals: hair, nails and clothing

3. marriage covenant before sex

4. prohibition against selling the woman as a slave

5. concern voiced for the woman's honor

A monthlong waiting period. An Israelite warrior has to wait one month before marrying a female war captive. The biblical text explicitly ties the waiting time to the right of the captive to mourn. The marriage is to take place after the captive woman has "mourned her father and mother for a full month" (Deut 21:13). As pointed out earlier, some scholars take great pains to argue only self-serving purposes for the one-month delay (progeny purity) in an attempt to discredit the motive stated in the text (grieving father and mother). To the contrary, we have argued that the mourning motive in the text is genuine and in fact the primary motivation for the one-month delay (see chapter five). If our reasoning and evidence are correct, then one important redemptive element emerges in the Deuteronomy 21 text—the granting of a time for mourning, and a relatively long one at that. Even Washington recognizes the month of mourning as a "relatively *long* period of time" within ancient-world grieving patterns.[43] Where one week was the cultural norm for grieving family loss, the biblical legislation required four times that standard length of time.[44]

---

[43]Washington, "Violence and the Construction of Gender," 350 (italics added).

[44]When Bathsheba mourns Uriah's death before joining David as his wife, commentators suggest a one-week grieving period (see 1 Sam 31:13). See Philip F. Esler, *Sex, Wives, and Warriors: Reading Biblical Narrative with Its Ancient Audience* (Eugene, OR: Cascade,

This comparison is helpful but not quite accurate. We must understand the redemptive element in the text in much larger proportions—the ratio is four to zero, not four to one. After all, the comparison of four weeks with one week involves compassion extended to one's family and fellow citizens, *not* to one's defeated enemy. Ancient war captives were typically granted no mourning rights (zero). This biblical requirement of a mourning time for enemy captives stands alone as a monument—an unrivaled statement of compassion—within ancient warfare. Yet its contextualized redemptive qualities of greater compassion do not stand alone within Israel's war practices. For a broader understanding of Israel's kinder and gentler treatment of war captives, see chapter thirteen.

We might add one speculative note here. Other *unstated* motives—such a cooling-down time for the warrior (if intentional but not voiced)—may have provided further positive, redemptive value to the month delay.

Mourning/assimilation rituals: Hair, nails, and clothing. In addition to the warrior having to wait a month before marrying the woman, Deuteronomy 21 requires that the captive woman shave her head (removing her hair), trim her nails, and change her clothes. These three rituals fit within widely practiced mourning customs of the day and are most likely connected to the month of grieving and waiting period. In addition, these actions offer a ritualized way of assimilating the foreign woman into the new household. The two functions—assimilation and grieving—need not be mutually exclusive.[45]

So what is redemptive here? Several elements. First, if the thirty days of waiting highlights the *length* of grieving (much longer than normal), then the three rituals—hair, nails, clothing—accentuate the *intensity* of grief permitted. In an ancient world intense verbal wailing in grief was often accompanied by dramatic acts—cutting off or tearing out the hair on one's head, cutting off anything else that might grow back (beard, nails, etc.) and tearing

---

2011), 316. On the typical one-week length of mourning in the ANE and biblical traditions, see Xuan Huong Thi Pham, *Mourning in the Ancient Near East and the Hebrew Bible*, JSOTSup 302 (Sheffield: Sheffield Academic Press, 1999), 16-27.

[45]Contra Washington ("Violence and the Construction of Gender," 349-51) and Ellens (*Women in the Sex Texts of Leviticus and Deuteronomy*, 175-79), who see progeny purity as the real reason for the one-month delay. See a critique of their position in chapter five.

one's clothing (also replaceable).[46] All three rituals relate to the concept of destroying in grief what was a standard or symbol of joy in one's former world. The text is redemptive in giving room for this intensity of grief and its dramatic enactments. It permits the captive through three removal/destruction rituals to voice the pain of war: "My world has been torn apart, cut off, irrevocably changed. Joy and beauty are removed from me."

Here is the flip-side implication. The biblical text implicitly forbids the warrior's joy in victory to muzzle or squelch the captive woman's pain in grief. Her grief is not to be silenced or suppressed. The three rituals suggest intense grief and grant permission for these rituals to puncture the joy bubble of the victorious warrior. For one month war grief as a right for the captive ritually trumps the victorious joy of the captor. While far from perfect, the Deuteronomy 21 text requires that the woman's grief be given a ritualized voice.[47] It sounds contrived and mechanical; it probably was to some extent. But look at the alternative offered to female captives in ancient war: no period of grieving at all, no rituals of grieving or transition, and the male warrior could simply have forced sex with his captive female whenever and wherever he pleased.

The redemptive function of the hair, nails, and replaced clothes may go a step further. The three grief-related rituals may have been intentionally selected by the biblical author to highlight the folly of pursuing external beauty alone. A woman's hair within the ancient world and the Bible clearly functions as a sexually attractive feature for males.[48] Head coverings often hid

---

[46]Saul M. Olyan, "The Biblical Prohibition of the Mourning Rites of Shaving and Laceration: Several Proposals," in "A Wise and Discerning Mind": Essays in Honor of Burke O. Lang, ed. Saul M. Olyan and Robert C. Culley, BJS 325 (Providence, RI: Brown Judaic Studies, 2000), 181-89; G. A. Anderson, A Time to Mourn, a Time to Dance: The Expressions of Grief and Joy in Israelite Religion (University Park: Pennsylvania State University Press, 1991); Saul M. Olyan, Biblical Mourning: Ritual and Social Dimensions (New York: Oxford University Press, 2004), 28-61, 111-23. See also Pham, Mourning in the Ancient Near East, 16-27.

[47]The particular selection of grieving rituals (hair, nails, and clothing) permitted intense grieving while curbing the extreme of self-mutilation prevalent in the ancient world.

[48]A woman's hair was one of her primary attractive features for men in the ancient world. See Preston T. Massey, "The Veil and the Voice: A Study of Female Beauty and Male Attraction in Ancient Greece" (PhD diss., University of Indiana, 2006), 19-49. In Mesopotamian culture both hair and clothing played a dominant role in female sexual attractiveness. See Aubrey Baadsgaard, "Trends, Traditions, and Transformations: Fashion in Dress in Early Dynastic Mesopotamia" (PhD diss., University of Pennsylvania, 2008), 32-41, 42-45, 221-57; Amy Rebecca Gansell, "Women of Ivory as Embodiments of Ideal Feminine Beauty

this feature of female beauty, making it even more alluring. While we know less about nails, ancient women frequently painted them and wore them longer as a sign of wealth and beauty.[49] The style of a foreign woman's clothing—its color, texture, visual look, and shaping—may also have played a role in attracting the male warrior.[50] Perhaps modesty issues in the cut of a foreign woman's dress were a factor. Or if mourning rituals had begun among the captive women (and tearing their clothing), there may have been a need to regain modesty and offset unseemly exposure. In sum, giving the captive woman Israelite clothing would also have removed any unusual beauty features and possibly replaced her torn garments. While a generalization, a woman's hair, nails, and clothing are visual features (see how in the text the warrior "notice[s]" her) that have attracted men for millennia in almost every culture. Contemplate the opposite: a bald woman with short-cut nails and plain, modest clothes. The three cutting rituals (hair, nails, and [possibly] clothes) and their likely symbolic connection to grief may also offer a subtle rebuke to the disproportionate emphasis that the male warrior has placed on outward beauty.[51]

Marriage covenant (before sex). Deuteronomy 21:10-14 is not an anti–battlefield rape passage in the direct expression of its words as read in an isolated fashion (all on their own). It is an assimilation text—navigating foreign female captives into legitimate family roles in Israel. However, if Israelite warriors were not permitted battlefield rape of foreign women on other grounds/texts (as we have argued), then the Deuteronomy 21:10-14

---

in the Ancient Near East During the First Millennium BCE" (PhD diss., Harvard University, 2008), 51-56, 180-81, 258-59.

[49]Ancient Egyptian women painted their nails with henna; longer nails were associated with a life of leisure and wealth. See Richard Corson, *Fashions in Makeup: From Ancient to Modern Times* (London: Peter Owen, 1972), 9. With a few comments on ancient nail painting and cosmetics, see Baadsgaard, "Fashion in Dress in Early Dynastic Mesopotamia," 97-97, 102, 277-82.

[50]Clothing styles for women were clearly one aspect of their beauty in an ancient world. See for example Janet M. Johnstone, "Wrapping and Tying Ancient Egyptian New Kingdom Dresses," in *Wrapping and Unwrapping Material Culture: Archaeological and Anthropological Perspectives*, ed. Susanna Harris and Laurence Douny (Walnut Creek, CA: Left Coast Press, 2014), 59-82. The clothing style, hair, and jewelry of war captives in Egyptian reliefs was often so detailed that it reflects the different ethnic origins of the captives. See Janzen, "Iconography of Humiliation," 56, 102-3.

[51]The change of clothing in the context of the other two rituals (that clearly involve cutting and most likely grief) may assume the grief-torn garments of captivity being replaced.

text by inference offers the only legitimate avenue for male warriors to have sex with an attractive female captive. He must wait a month and then marry her. A formal marriage covenant is expressed in the wording "you may go to her and be her husband and she shall be your wife," increasing the woman's protection and benefits (Ex 21:10-11). For Israelite warriors living in an ancient world where the sexual ravaging of girls and women upon military victory was the pervasive reality, Deuteronomy 21:10-14 becomes the alternative by default. When Deuteronomy 21:10-14 is read alongside the prohibitions against battlefield sex, then the collective message to soldiers sexually attracted to a pretty captive woman becomes the following: "You must wait a month and marry her before sex." While this collective message has the ethical downside outlined in the last chapter, it nonetheless communicates incremental redemptive movement within the horizon of an ancient world.

Prohibition against selling the woman as a slave. If things do not work out and the man divorces the woman, he is prohibited from selling her as a slave (Deut 21:14). Given the wider context in which men could do virtually whatever they wanted with their female war slaves, this restriction is profoundly meaningful. In that ancient setting, it spoke loudly.[52] The prohibition brought full status as a free woman after a divorce. That much is obvious. But it also meant reduced male power over the woman even within the marriage itself because it denied the husband any monetary gain from a potential divorce. It confirmed that in the act of marriage she in some respects already had the status of nonslave or free woman—no strings attached; if divorced, she could go wherever she pleased. The ancient-world prospects for a divorced foreign woman would not have been great. But her life as a free woman would likely have been better than being sold as a permanent chattel slave.[53]

Concern voiced for the woman's honor. The closing statement "you have dishonored her" (Deut 21:14) adds a further positive element in that it raises concern for the honor of the woman and quietly denounces the man's actions in the event of divorce. We agree with Rebekah Josberger's analysis that the

---

[52]Recall the ANE practice of using female slaves captured in war as domestic prostitutes.

[53]If biblical total-war language is hyperbolic (as we will argue in later chapters and appendixes A through C), the former captive woman would even have been free to return to her people/ethnic group.

lowered status and humiliation of the woman is inherent in the act of divorce itself.[54] However, the dishonoring language may include, even if secondary, more than the husband's actions in merely the divorce. Josberger dismisses the role of sex as part of the dishonoring: "The only reference to sexual conduct occurs within the context of a marriage situation and is *a facet, not a focus*, of the text."[55]

However, such a limiting perspective overlooks (1) the label on female war captives elsewhere in Scripture as "virgins"—a highly sexual term anticipating their sexual function for men within Israel; (2) that the opening verse of Deuteronomy 21:10 describes the warrior seeing a beautiful captive and wanting to marry her—a major focus on sexual attraction and anticipated sex; (3) that the lack of pleasure/delight ("pleased") in Deuteronomy 21:14 as the husband's divorce motive surely includes sex as one domain, even if not exclusively so, particularly with the opening emphasis being that of sexual attraction in Deuteronomy 21:10; (4) that the lowering of the captive's status includes both "divorced" and "nonvirgin" status issues, with the latter carrying an obvious sexual-liability component; and (5) that the larger ANE social context of sexual conquest in war provides an obvious sexual framework, even if this particular text does not directly speak to the battlefield setting. Therefore, it seems better to view both divorce and sex as factors in the dishonor language, but in a primary and secondary manner. If this dual focus is correct, then the biblical author may include both the divorce *and* some tacit aspect of the failed sexual relationship as connected to how the man has humiliated the captive woman. The consequent restriction on the male (not selling her) and the framing of the language (you humiliated her) are redemptive, for they together place blame on the one with power.[56] That the biblical authors would care at all about the honor of a divorced female war captive is nothing short of amazing, given their ancient horizon.

---

[54]See Rebekah Josberger, "For Your Good Always: Restraining the Rights of the Victor for the Well-Being of the Vulnerable (Deut 21:10-14)," in *For Our Good Always: Studies on the Message and Influence of Deuteronomy in Honor of Daniel I. Block*, ed. Jason S. DeRouchie, Jason Gile, and Kenneth J. Turner, CSHB 3 (Winona Lake, IN: Eisenbrauns, 2013), 180-85.

[55]Josberger, "For Your Good Always," 182 (italics added).

[56]Given the specific emphasis on grieving (one month for mourning and three related rituals), the text at least tacitly suggests that the new husband should help the captive woman with *any* hurdles that might jeopardize marriage.

CONCLUSION

The ethical problems with the treatment of female captives in Israel's war texts make it almost impossible for modern readers to appreciate anything redemptive within them. Nevertheless, if readers intentionally journey back into the horizon of the ancient world (markedly different from ours), they have an opportunity to see the redemptive side of the biblical text. That journey takes us to a gruesome and violent war context, where warriors sexually ravaged women as part of their victory rituals, spoke about female captives in terms of their sexual body parts, and proudly displayed rape scenes in their nationally sponsored war art—corresponding to literary bravado about war rape. This backdrop of pervasive sexual violence in war is needed to appreciate the biblical perspective. Israel's war story pushes the margins of a rape-crazed war world in some dramatic ways:

- ▶ no battlefield rape
- ▶ no artwork or literary counterpart that glorifies war rape
- ▶ no rape of temple-slave prostitutes (war captives as a source)
- ▶ reduced rape of domestically owned slave prostitutes (war captives as a source)
- ▶ restrictive measures placed on Israelite warriors attracted to a beautiful captive woman
  - ▶ a one-month delay for mourning
  - ▶ mourning/transition rituals that permit intense grieving
  - ▶ marriage covenant before sex
  - ▶ in the event of divorce, no selling the woman as a slave (she is a free woman)
  - ▶ concern voiced for her honor (placing blame for the divorce on the male)

When sex and violence in war collide within Scripture, we nonetheless discover something that is worth embracing: the real and sometimes even bold actions of an incremental ethic that embodies an underlying redemptive spirit. When read within the horizon of an ancient world, the heavy darkness of war-rape texts such as Deuteronomy 21 and Numbers 31 are pierced by numerous shafts of bright, redemptive light—meaning easily missed from our present-day horizon. Such light and beauty amid the darkness is consistent with, and even quietly inviting toward, a journey of faith.

7

WAR RAPE MEETS GENOCIDE

THE TRADITIONAL VIEW KEEPS the war-rape texts of Deuteronomy 21 and Numbers 31 ethically separate from genocide texts—texts that command killing the entire enemy population. Proponents of the traditional position, should they discuss the war-rape passages in the context of biblical holy war, typically treat them differently from the total-kill texts. They consider that the war-rape instructions in the Bible exemplify God's *accommodated* ethic (affected by a fallen world, involving real ethical problems) whereas the total-kill instructions exemplify his *unaccommodated* ethic (pure and pristine, involving only perceived ethical problems).[1] In other words, ancient-world war practices and fallen-world ethics affected the war-rape texts but not the total-kill texts. Real ethical problems exist in the former but not in the latter.

The purpose of this transitional chapter is to create a conversation between war rape (the past two chapters) and genocide, the next topic (five chapters and three appendixes that lie ahead). We intentionally want to bring these two ethical issues—war rape and genocide—closer together, not further apart. Our realigned-traditional position will argue that *the war-rape and total-kill texts, while obviously describing different human acts, both reflect God's accommodated ethic as he communicates within a fallen world.*

---

[1]We have confirmed this accommodated view of the war-rape texts through personal conversation with published and unpublished proponents of the traditional view. While unwilling to acknowledge accommodation in the total-kill commands, there was generally a willingness to do so in the war-rape passages. The reason was based on the difference of command versus permission.

KEEPING THEM ETHICALLY SEPARATE

Why might one be inclined to place war-rape and total-kill instructions in separate ethical categories? The reason is simple: God *permits* the one, but he *commands* the other. If you look closely at the Deuteronomy 21 passage, God does not command Israelite men to take good-looking women as their wives. Rather, the biblical text simply permits the action: "When you go to war against your enemies and the LORD your God delivers them into your hands and you take captives, *if* you notice among the captives a beautiful woman and are attracted to her, *you may take her* as your wife" (Deut 21:10-11).

The conditional "if" clause does not demand that all male warriors notice a beautiful woman. Nor does it demand that they all be attracted to a female captive. Even if an Israelite warrior did notice a captive and found her attractive, no imperatival obligation requires him to take the next step. Instead, the instruction requires the warrior's choice to participate: "you may take her as your wife." Deuteronomy 21 communicates permission, not command.

On the other hand, total-kill instructions such as those in Deuteronomy 20 include the command to kill all breathing Canaanites within the land. The complete destruction of Israel's enemy within the Promised Land is clearly a command: "However, in the cities of the nations the LORD your God is giving you as an inheritance, do not leave alive anything that breathes. Completely destroy them—the Hittites, Amorites, Canaanites, Perizzites, Hivites and Jebusites—as the LORD your God has commanded you" (Deut 20:16-17).

The command language makes this total-kill military action a required obligation. It is not optional, like the taking of a bride from among virgin war captives. Even if these total-kill passages reflect hyperbole (as we will argue in the chapters ahead), there is still a command to take possession of the land with some (reduced, not total) killing involved.

We agree with the traditional position that there is a very clear difference in language (permission versus command) when the war-rape text of Deuteronomy 21 is compared with the total-kill passages. However, we disagree with the inference drawn that the presence of command language places the total-kill instructions into a different ethical category, namely, one that is pristine and good in all respects (no fallen-world ethical components). We will make a case for the converse: *total-kill instructions are just as much part of our fallen-world, enculturated ethic as are the war-rape instructions.* Both require us to acknowledge real ethical liabilities. Both need to be read redemptively within an understanding of an incremental ethic. Readers should bring the two sets of war instructions—war rape and war killings—together and not separate them ethically.

KEEPING THEM ETHICALLY TOGETHER

That something in Scripture is communicated in command language does *not* mean that it has escaped the impact of fallen-world ethics and divine accommodation. As we will see below, in the final analysis it is an *ethical assessment* and not the presence or lack of command language in the biblical text that helps us appreciate God's accommodation. In what follows we will argue that the war-rape texts and total-kill texts should be brought under the same accommodated-ethic umbrella.

God-sanctioned war instructions. If we assume for a moment that war-rape texts are accommodated but total-kill texts are unaccommodated, a measure of ethical trouble remains for the traditional view. First, proponents of the traditional position must acknowledge holding a mixed ethical bag that includes *both* war rape and total-kill warfare. That would be more realistic than the "all is good" image of the war texts that the traditional view tends to project. Second, the argument that "God sanctioned it" for arriving at a pristine-ethic view in the total-kill passages seems weak in light of the war-rape passages. For a moment, let us come back to Merrill's statement: "The issue then cannot be whether or not genocide is intrinsically good or evil—its *sanction* by a holy God settles that question."[2] Substitute "war rape" for "genocide" and it reads, "The issue then cannot be whether or not war rape is intrinsically good or evil—its *sanction* by a holy God settles that question."[3] The standard understanding of the word *sanction* means "to grant official permission or approval for an action."[4] So clearly God *does*

---

[2]Eugene H. Merrill, "The Case for Moderate Discontinuity," in C. S. Cowles, Eugene H. Merrill, Daniel L. Gard, and Tremper Longman III, *Show Them No Mercy: Four Views on God and Canaanite Genocide,* ed. Stanley N. Gundry (Grand Rapids: Zondervan, 2003), 93 (italics added).

[3]Our modified citation with the substitution of "war rape" instead of "genocide."

[4]"Sanction," The Oxford Dictionary online, https://en.oxforddictionaries.com/definition/sanction (accessed March 20, 2017).

sanction war rape (at least of a certain type) in Deuteronomy 21, and a command is not required to do so. Therefore, just because something is *sanctioned* in the biblical (war) texts does not mean it is "intrinsically good" (contra Merrill).

Some readers may suggest that Merrill's argument that God sanctioned it can be fixed by adding a qualifying component, "God sanctioned it through *a divine command*." All right, we now have two categories: (1) war rape *sanctioned by divine permission* and (2) genocide *sanctioned by divine command*. Fair enough. Let us reflect on that option. The added qualification of command language still makes for a mixed ethical bag within Israel's warfare—both (1) and (2) are part of holy war—and perhaps we, on the basis of war-rape texts, ought to ponder whether we got the genocide equation right. In what follows, a permission-versus-command distinction, much as we might like it to, does *not* help us determine whether something in the biblical text functions at an accommodated or unaccommodated level. The traditional position's distinction is an (incorrect) artificial construct.

Command language is part of war rape. Proponents of the traditional view may think that commands separate biblical war-rape texts from total-kill texts. But this distinction is faulty. We agree that there are no imperatives in *Deuteronomy 21* and that text leaves it open for some warriors to participate in the (coercive/forced) marrying of good-looking captives and others to not do so. However, such is not the case in the war-rape text of Numbers 31. In Numbers 31:18 an imperative verb is used for *all* the warriors to participate in sparing and collecting female, virgin captives: "Now *kill* [imperative] all the boys. And *kill* [imperative] every woman who has slept with a man, but *save for yourselves* [imperative] every girl who has never slept with a man" (Num 31:17-18).

There seems to be no choice here.[5] As part of God/Moses' sanctioned war directives, the entire Israelite army (not just some) is commanded to participate in gathering thirty-two thousand female virgins. True, the marrying of

---

[5]Perhaps there is an unstated condition such as, "Those of you who want female captives . . ." While possible, this option is unlikely, since (1) all three commands in Hebrew are plural, inferring the entire army, and (2) the action of killing (boys and nonvirgins) juxtaposed with sparing (virgins) seems to place the decision to kill or spare on the shoulders of the entire army.

these captive women is not required for every single soldier. Yet, in Numbers 31 the entire army of male warriors is required to gather up these young virgins for the express purpose of saving them "for yourselves" (in other words, an implied offer of a female captive is extended to all warriors). Furthermore, all Israelite warriors play a commanded part in the chain of events that enables war rape even if not all of them participate in a coercive/forced marriage to a captive. If command language is part of the war-rape texts themselves (and it is in Num 31), then the traditional view's appeal to command language to verify pristine, unaccommodated ethics starts to crumble. Or, better put, command language is not a reliable indicator of pristine biblical war ethics.

Divine commands often reflect an accommodated and incremental ethic. We come back to the corporal punishment/mutilation text of Deuteronomy 25:11-12 for insight on whether the distinction between command and permission works as a reliable factor in determining whether a biblical text reflects an unaccommodated ethic.[6] The passage reads, "If two men are fighting and the wife of one of them comes to rescue her husband from his assailant, and she reaches out and seizes him by his private parts, *you shall cut off* [imperative] her hand. *Show her* [imperative] no pity" (Deut 25:11-12).

This passage contains two imperatives. Both are commands from Moses and God, and the punishment instruction here is expressed with command language (an imperative). As in the war texts, the initial command is backed by an ominously familiar additional imperative, "Show her no pity [no mercy]." Most importantly, this mutilation-punishment text (cutting off a wife's hand) reflects God's accommodated and incremental ethic within the horizon of punishments in the ancient world.[7] The presence of command language does not provide a reliable indicator that something is unaccommodated.

The mutilation text of Deuteronomy 25 offers an important window of understanding into biblical war texts because, as will be developed later, ANE warfare functioned as a way of punishing crimes and thus mirrored domestic punishment texts (see chapter thirteen). Aside from cutting off a

---

[6]We raised this text in chapter two.

[7]For an ethical assessment of Deut 25:11-12 see William J. Webb, *Corporal Punishment in the Bible: A Redemptive-Movement Hermeneutic for Troubling Texts* (Downers Grove, IL: InterVarsity Press, 2011), 97-118.

wife's hand, numerous other punishment texts within the Bible are stated with command language and yet do not reflect an ultimate ethic in terms of justice and the treatment of human beings—they express God's accommodated ethic, which functions in relation to the wider context of punishments in the ancient world. As a sample of crime and punishment, we might begin with capital punishment cases. Most include instructions communicated with divine command language: "You shall put him/her to death."[8] Yet these texts are heavily affected by the ethics of the ancient world around the Israelites; few Christians today would want to argue for no ethical modifications in the capital punishment texts in view of their severity and finality, their lack of restorative justice, the range of offenses covered, and the methods (burning, stoning) that are part of these commands. Even if modern-day Christians advocate for capital punishment, it is (unlike Scripture) usually limited to cases of premeditated murder. Accommodated ethics affect many punishment texts. Should we flog adults today in public at the gates of the city?[9] Or should we still require a rapist to marry his victim?[10] Most crime and punishment texts, whether adultery, rape, or property infractions, have the punishment factor stated in the imperative. Yet many of these passages reflect an enculturated ethic with redemptive elements, but hardly an ultimate or best-possible ethical development.[11]

---

[8]Ex 21:12, 15-17; 22:19-20; 31:13; 35:2; Lev 20:1-5, 9-17, 27; 21:9; 24:14-17, 23; Num 15:32-36; 35:16-21; Deut 13:1-19; 17:2-7; 18:20; 19:16, 19; 22:20-21, 22-25; 24:7.

[9]On the ethics of *adult* corporal-punishment texts, see Webb, *Corporal Punishment in the Bible*, 97-118.

[10]On the ethics of biblical laws regulating rape, virginity, and adultery in the biblical text and the ANE, see as a small sampling: Deborah L. Ellens, *Women in the Sex Texts of Leviticus and Deuteronomy: A Comparative Conceptual Analysis*, LHBOTS 458 (New York: T&T Clark, 2008); Susanne Scholz, *Sacred Witness: Rape in the Hebrew Bible* (Minneapolis: Fortress, 2010); Sandie Gravett, "Reading 'Rape' in the Hebrew Bible: A Consideration of Language," *JSOT* 28, no. 3 (2004): 279-99; Caryn A. Reeder, "Wives and Daughters: Women, Sex, and Violence in Biblical Tradition," *Ex Auditu* 28 (2013): 122-41; Cynthia Edenburg, "Ideology and Social Context of the Deuteronomic Women's Sex Laws (Deuteronomy 22:13-29)," *JBL* 128, no. 1 (2009): 43-60; Tikva Frymer-Kensky, "Virginity in the Bible," in *Gender and Law in the Hebrew Bible and the Ancient Near East*, ed. Victor H. Matthews, Bernard M. Levinson, and Tikva Frymer-Kensky, JSOTSup 262 (Sheffield: Sheffield Academic Press, 1998), 79-96.

[11]Rigorous ethical reflection and reasoning (e.g., contemporary developments in war ethics like Hague/Geneva [and beyond—the relatively recent inclusion of rape as a war crime], the abolition of slavery, etc.) along with the biblical and theological trajectory of ethics make it possible to posit better ethical positions in many human domains.

The plentiful use of commands within these biblical punishment texts should dispel the notion that the language of command rather than permission indicates an unaccommodated text. In fact, the reverse is true here. If command language in the domestic realm of biblical punishment is so heavily affected by the broader cultural norms (many not exhibiting an ultimate or best-possible ethic in the just treatment of human beings), it should create a reasonable expectation for such an accommodated ethic in the war realm as well. Why is that? We will discover that the realm of *domestic* (court) punishments and *foreign* (war) punishments within the ancient world were closely connected, and the one was viewed as an extension of the other. Again, see chapter thirteen. If so, the divine accommodation that is so evident in domestic/court punishment texts makes it likely that divine accommodation is at work in punishment aspects (total kill) of the biblical war texts as well. The types, weighting, and harshness of biblical punishments are best understood as God's accommodation to the punishments of an ancient world.

More evidence of accommodation in the chapters ahead. In the chapters that lie ahead we will develop three *more* reasons (beyond this transitional chapter) for viewing *both* war-rape and total-kill texts as an accommodated (incremental) ethic. First, chapters eight through twelve and appendixes A through C show that biblical authors used clear rhetorical markings in the total-kill language that describes their war practices. The biblical war texts are so highly enculturated they share the *same* hyperbolic language as the rest of the ANE world. This shared language is a good clue that the biblical war ethic in some way correlates with the broader ethics of warfare in the ancient world.

Second, like in the chapters on war rape—its ugly side (chapter five) and its redemptive side (chapter six)—a two-sided picture will become evident in analyzing the killing practices of the Israelite army. Biblical warriors were not inclined toward inflicting lingering pain and torture as a means of expressing their battle victory and bringing about the agonizing deaths of their enemies (chapter thirteen). The victory rituals of the ancient world that were equivalent to spiking a football in the end zone made their way into *both* war rape *and* killing methods; these areas—raping and killing—share more in common than one might think.[12] It makes little sense to separate their ethics. As with war rape, Israel's total-kill texts offer numerous examples where we can celebrate the redemptive betterment of Israel's killing practices relative to the horrors of the context of the ancient world. Yet if thinking carefully about war ethics helps us discover what is redemptive about the biblical scene, it also makes us painfully aware of how much further the ethic needs to go. It is the redemptive spirit of both the war-rape and war-kill texts that carries us to (and surges far beyond) Hague and Geneva.

Finally, the subversive war texts of chapter fourteen present Yahweh as an unhappy, reluctant war God—a portrait with which most Christians are unfamiliar. This chapter provides evidence that at least a significant portion of Israel's war killing should be understood as divine accommodation. While Yahweh nudged Israel's war ethic along in incrementally redemptive ways (chapter thirteen), the situation was hardly what he wanted for his people (chapter fourteen).

CONCLUSION

This chapter has argued for handling biblical war rape and genocide with the same incremental-ethic approach and not as two separate entities. The traditional position appeals to the divine commands (imperatival sanctions) within the total-kill texts as indicating God's unaccommodated ethic. To the contrary, we have suggested that such reasoning creates an artificial construct within the biblical evidence. Both the war-rape and genocide texts in Scripture reveal an accommodated, incremental ethic.

---

[12]On modern sports celebrations, see discussion of rape as a victory ritual in chapter six. The anal penetration of male war captives with a pole (impalement) had clear sexual overtones and mimicked ANE courtroom punishments for adulterous wives. See chapter thirteen.

8

TOTAL-KILL HYPERBOLE, PART ONE

Ancient Near Eastern Warfare

WARFARE WAS, UNFORTUNATELY, such a commonplace experience in ancient Israel and the ANE that certain times of the year became synonymous with expectations of military conflict (2 Sam 11:1). Ancient Israel shared not only the experience of combat with its neighbors but also the use of similar weapons, strategies, tactics, and even beliefs about the right conduct of war.[1] Recent scholarly work comparing war in the Bible and elsewhere in the ANE shows a significant degree of overlap between the ways that ancient peoples *talked* about battles. As a result, our exploration of better answers to the ethics of genocide in the Bible will look at ways in which ancient Israel's neighbors and battle opponents thought and talked about their battles. This will allow us to place our discussions within the larger context of how ancient wars were fought and how scribes described those wars in the ANE. This background exploration will allow us to recognize various forms of hyperbole evident in texts that describe Israel's battles with the Canaanites (see chapter nine).

ANE battles were fought at the command of the gods, and victories were attributed to divine assistance. Thus, the victory of the king was also the victory of the king's patron deity (or deities). Defeat, on the other hand, indicated divine displeasure and pointed to some deficiency either in the king

---

[1]For a helpful survey of the technology, tactics, and strategies of ancient armies contemporaneous with ancient Israel, see Boyd Severs, *Warfare in the Old Testament: The Organization, Weapons, and Tactics of Ancient Near Eastern Armies* (Grand Rapids: Kregel, 2013).

or among his people.[2] Repeated military defeats in the realm of the king's foreign affairs brought growing internal dissatisfaction and could spark a coup d'état fueled by talk of regaining divine approval and support. Accordingly, ANE kings were motivated to publicly present their battles in the best possible light.

One of the ways in which kings showcased their military prowess and successes was to inscribe their accomplishments for public display in temples, on palace walls, or on erected stones called steles. These inscriptions enshrined the military conquests and exploits of ancient kings. Accounts of military achievements served a variety of purposes: to foster the worship of a king's patron deity, to memorialize a king's accomplishments for future generations, to instill fear and obedience among conquered populations, and to legitimate the king's power, position, and territorial ambition.[3] ANE battle reports were commissioned by kings or possibly other leaders and were initially written to persuade elite leaders (or *literati*) of the crucial role of the king in establishing and/or maintaining the order that legitimized their position.[4] This was because coups most often began *within* the palace rather than among the general populace. However, we cannot restrict the intended audience of these battle reports to the social elites, for the king's great deeds in battle were also written for the consumption of the general

---

[2]See for example the Mesha Stele, where the Moabite king Mesha indicates that his god Kemosh allowed the Israelite king Omri to oppress his land for a time because he was angry with his people (*COS* 2:23, 137). A similar perspective is evident in the book of Judges, where Israel's sin prompts Yahweh to give Israel into the hands of foreign oppressors for a time, before raising up judges who deliver Israel from these foreign oppressors via military success (e.g., Judg 2:11-18). For a general discussion of the intersection of military activity and national identity/ideology, and particularly for defeat as divine displeasure and in its extreme form as divine abandonment, see Daniel I. Block, *The Gods of the Nations: Studies in Ancient Near Eastern National Theology*, 2nd ed., ETS Studies 2 (Grand Rapids: Baker, 2000), 113-47.

[3]Concerning memorialization, compare the function of the stones erected by Joshua to memorialize Yahweh's work in bringing Israel across the Jordan (Josh 4:6-7).

Legitimacy is not a static quality but a dynamically changing status that can be diminished or supplemented depending on the words and actions of a power holder. Power holders must retain and build legitimacy to keep their power—they must persuade others of the continuing legitimacy of their power. See the discussion in Dennis H. Wrong, *Power: Its Forms, Bases and Uses* (New York: Harper & Row, 1979).

[4]Concerning who commissioned battle reports, 2 Kings 25:19; Jer 52:25, for example, mention the scribe of the commander of the army, suggesting military elites in Israel also had access to writing.

populace.[5] They paid heavy taxes and so needed to understand the benefits brought by the king. Consequently, it was in the king's interest to present his accomplishments in the best possible light for all to see. To accomplish this goal when describing a battle or campaign, scribes at times omitted negative details such as setbacks or the loss of troops or key resources.

One well-known example of this type of battle reportage is seen in the Assyrian king Sennacherib's account of his campaign against Judah in 701 BC.[6] Sennacherib portrays his campaign as a complete victory, laying siege to, conquering, and then plundering forty-six cities of Judah and deporting 200,150 people. As for the Judahite king Hezekiah, Sennacherib says, "Himself I made a prisoner in Jerusalem, his royal residence, like a bird in a cage. I surrounded him with earthwork in order to molest those who were leaving his city's gate." When he finally retreated, Sennacherib suggests that "Hezekiah himself, whom the terror-inspiring splendor of my lordship had overwhelmed and whose irregular and elite troops which he had brought into Jerusalem, his royal residence, in order to strengthen (it), had deserted him, did send me, later, to Nineveh, my lordly city," bringing with them all manner of tribute in acknowledgement of his greatness.[7] The biblical account mentions Sennacherib's invasion and the dire circumstances faced by Hezekiah and Jerusalem (2 Kings 18:13–19:37; Is 36–37; 2 Chron 32:1-22), but it points out that Hezekiah was ultimately able to hold out because of his trust in Yahweh. Sennacherib's troops left the city unconquered, pushed away by the sudden death of 185,000 Assyrian soldiers (Is 37:30-37). Sennacherib correctly describes a successful campaign in Judah but fails to include information indicating that he was not completely successful, such as why he left the rebellious Hezekiah alive and Jerusalem unconquered.[8] This

---

[5]W. Hallo writes, "Monumental inscriptions are not addressed to a literate readership but rather to a largely illiterate *audience*, who would be read to by the minority of trained scribes and other literate alumni of the scribal schools" (*COS* 2:xxv).

[6]See Antti Laato, "Assyrian Propaganda and the Falsification of History in the Royal Inscriptions," *VT* 45 (1995): 198-226; Bustenay Oded, "History Vis-à-vis Propaganda in the Assyrian Royal Inscriptions," *VT* 48 (1998): 423-25.

[7]*ANET*, 288.

[8]For a helpful discussion of the interplay between the Assyrian description of the events and the biblical text, see Paul S. Evans, *The Invasion of Sennacherib in the Book of Kings: A Source-Critical and Rhetorical Study of 2 Kings 18–19*, VTSup 125 (Leiden: Brill, 2009), 139-85.

should alert us to the fact that ANE battle accounts could at times overstate the severity of a defeat or gloss over an unsuccessful battle to paint the best possible portrait of the king.

It is in this process that figurative language or hyperbole could help a king put the best face on his military accomplishments without falsifying the essential gist of the events. Hyperbole is a common literary and rhetorical device that uses emotionally charged overstatement to persuade an audience of a particular point. As the following brief survey will show, ANE kings and scribes made use of several different forms of overstatement (or understatement in the case of a defeat or setback) to offer the brightest picture of their accomplishments.

NUMERICAL HYPERBOLE

The number of troops that faced off in battle or were killed is seldom related with specificity in ANE battle accounts. Quantification of booty or prisoners, however, frequently includes the use of rounded numbers, particularly for numbers over one hundred.[9] On occasion, numerical hyperbole was employed to emphasize the bravery of the king or his army in the face of seemingly overwhelming numbers. Egyptian king Seti I boasts that his power in battle is such that "he cares nothing for even hundreds of thousands gathered," though this is surely bluster.[10] Hundreds of thousands of troops arrayed against any king would be a concern for even the most confident military leader.

Assyrian king Shalmaneser III seems to have recycled tallies of past victories to highlight his military accomplishments. In a reconstructed inscription from the Calaḫ Bulls, Shalmaneser says that in his tenth regnal year he captured, razed, destroyed, and burned the city of Arnê and one hundred surrounding cities in the land of Arame. In his eleventh year, he returned to Arame and again captured, razed, destroyed, and burned one hundred cities.

---

[9]Marco De Odorico notes that statements such as "he killed 1,000 men" are unlikely to be exact, for it would be unusual to kill exactly one thousand men in a battle. Even some numbers such as 14,400, which seem exact, may actually be a combination of several round numbers (e.g., $4 \times 3,600 = 14,400$) and could also be represented as 15,000 (*The Use of Numbers and Quantifications in the Assyrian Royal Inscriptions*, SAAS 3 [Helsinki: Neo-Assyrian Text Corpus Project, 1995], 5).

[10]*COS* 2:4E, 29.

While it is possible that Shalmaneser razed and destroyed one hundred cities in Arame in two successive years, it is unlikely that he would find exactly one hundred cities of significance left to destroy the very next year.[11]

Shalmaneser III's scribes have a rather flexible approach to the tally of opponents that he and his army killed in battle. On the Kurkh Monolith, Shalmaneser boasts that he struck down 14,000 enemy troops at the battle of Qarqar.[12] However, on the Aššur clay tablets, the Calaḫ Bulls, and a marble slab inscription from Aššur, which also describe the results of the battle of Qarqar, the number increases to 25,000.[13] On the other hand, when he reports the number of troops felled in the same battle on the Black Obelisk, it drops to 20,500 troops, while on the Aššur basalt statue, the number of troops defeated increases to 29,000.[14] This variation in the numbers reported by Shalmaneser suggests flexibility in the way that the number of enemy troops killed in a battle might be reported.

The Gebel Barkal Stele of Egyptian king Thutmose III proclaims, "I repeat further to you—hear, O people! He entrusted to me the foreign countries of Retenu on the first campaign, when they had come to engage with my majesty, *being millions and hundred-thousands of men*, the individuals of every foreign country, waiting in their chariots—330 princes, every one of them having his (own) army."[15] The extent of Thutmose III's opposition here seems significantly inflated for this era. The tally for the army fielded by Egypt at the battle of Qadesh in 1275 BC is twenty thousand soldiers, while Egyptian sources suggest that the Hittites also fielded an army of approximately twenty thousand troops.[16] The available evidence from Egypt's glory days in the New Kingdom period suggests that the Egyptian army numbered

---

[11]The likelihood that Shalmaneser only destroyed one hundred cities of Arame once is heightened when we observe his repeated "decisive defeats" of Hadad-ezer the Damascene, Irḫulēni the Hamathite, and a coalition of twelve kings in consecutive years of his reign (see below for further discussion).

[12]*COS* 2:113A, 264.

[13]*COS* 2:113B, 265; 2:113C, 266; 2:113D, 267.

[14]*COS* 2:113F, 269; 2:113G, 270. The date of the defeat of Hadad-ezer's troops is not clearly relayed.

[15]*ANET*, 238 (italics added).

[16]Severs, *Warfare in the Old Testament*, 110-11. Later in the thirteenth century BC, Egyptian kings Merneptah and Ramses III faced Libyan armies in various battles totaling 9,300, 13,500, and 4,200 troops.

somewhere in the low ten thousands, so it is unlikely that even a coalition of kingdoms could have fielded an army larger by a factor of ten or more than Egypt's army. In this light, Thutmose III's claim to have faced hundreds of thousands of opponents is clearly hyperbolic.[17]

SPEED HYPERBOLE

A second aspect of ancient battle accounts that could include an element of hyperbole is the length of time required for either a battle to be engaged or for a defeat to be secured. Egyptian king Thutmose III boasts of his hunting prowess, saying,

> I speak to the water of what he did, without lying and without equivocation therein, in the face of his entire army, without a phrase of boasting therein. If he spent a moment of recreation by hunting in any foreign country, the number of that which he carried off is greater than the bag of the entire army. *He killed seven lions by shooting in the completion of a moment.* He *carried off a herd of twelve wild cattle within an hour,* when breakfast time had taken place, the tails thereof for his back.[18]

While not directly describing a battle, this anecdote is part of a larger display inscription that switches between descriptions of the king's military victories and his hunting skill. Thutmose claims to have carried out these incredible feats in front of his whole army, with the implication that the king's hunting skills were another demonstration of his military prowess. In a similar vein, the annals of Tiglath-pileser I claim that he marched from the edge of Suhu to Carchemish in a single day, a distance more than 250 miles![19] Egyptian King Seti I, after a campaign in Palestine, says of his enemies, "His majesty kills them *all at one time,* and leaves no heirs among them. He who is spared by his hand is a living prisoner, carried off to Egypt."[20] Seti's claim to have

---

[17]Gary Rendsburg notes a similar use of hyperbole when he points to the Ugaritic Kirta Epic, where King Kirta claims he could marshal a force of three million troops ("An Additional Note to Two Recent Articles on the Number of People in the Exodus from Egypt and the Large Numbers in Numbers I and XXVI," *VT* 51, no. 3 [2001]: 393).

[18]*ANET*, 243-44 (italics added).

[19]K. Lawson Younger Jr., *Ancient Conquest Accounts: A Study in Ancient Near Eastern and Biblical History Writing,* JSOTSup 98 (Sheffield: JSOT Press, 1990), 215-17. Younger lists a number of other examples of conquest in a single day.

[20]*ANET*, 254 (italics added). In a Neo-Sumerian text, Ibbi-Sin claims to have subdued Susa, Adamshah, and the land of Awan in a single day (*COS* 2:141B, 391); Lugalbanda is said to

killed *all* of his foes at one time, leaving no survivors, is immediately followed with a line that indicates that those he spared were carried off to Egypt. So his claim to have *completely* killed his enemies *all at once* is best understood as hyperbole. These examples show that one of the ways in which ancient kings and warriors spoke about their battles was to use hyperbole to express the swiftness with which they engaged and conquered their enemies, thereby highlighting the king's military expertise and status as a powerful warrior, and hence his position at the head of his armies.

SEVERITY HYPERBOLE

Severity hyperbole occurs when a battle report heightens the extent of the defeat inflicted on an enemy. An extreme form of this is evident in the Egyptian account of the Battle of Qadesh, an epic battle between the two superpowers of the time, the Egyptians and the Hittites. Ramses II's account of the battle highlights his bravery and suggests an overwhelming Egyptian victory:

> I found the mass [literally "the 2,500 chariots"] of chariots in whose midst
>   I was
> Scattering before my horses;
> Not one of them found his hand to fight,
> Their hearts failed in their bodies through fear of me.
> Their arms all slackened, they could not shoot,
> They had no heart to grasp their spears;
> I made them plunge into the water as crocodiles plunge,
> They fell on their faces one on the other.
> I slaughtered among them at my will,
> Not one looked behind him,
> Not one turned around,
> Whoever fell down did not rise.[21]

Upon reading Ramses II's account of the battle, it would seem that Egypt scored a decisive victory. Yes, the Hittites suffered heavy losses, but most scholars acknowledge that the battle likely resulted in a draw. Ramses was

---

have traversed the land between Aratta and Unug (Uruk) in a single day (H. L. J. Vanstiphout, trans., *Epic of the Sumerian Kings: The Matter of Aratta*, ed. Jerrold S. Cooper, SBLWAW 20 [Atlanta: Society of Biblical Literature, 2003], 5).

[21]*AEL* 2:66.

unable to capture Qadesh, which remained under Hittite control, and his Hittite opponent, Muwatalli, harried the Egyptians as they fled south after the battle, even taking control of the Egyptian-controlled city of Upi (Damascus) for a year's time. Additionally, Amurru, an Egyptian ally up to that point, came under Hittite control after the battle.[22] These are not the actions of a decisively defeated army. Thus, while not totally falsifying his accomplishments, Ramses II's portrait of the battle of Qadesh paints an excessively rosy picture of what transpired.

ANE battle accounts frequently used hyperbole to overstate the severity of a defeat laid on enemy forces. One of the clearest examples of overstated defeat is Pharaoh Mernepthah's account of his battles in the Levant:

> The princes are prostrate saying: "Shalom!"
> Not one of the Nine Bows lifts his head:
> Tjehenu is vanquished, Khatti at peace,
> Canaan is captive with all woe.
> Ashkelon is conquered, Gezer seized,
> Yanoam made nonexistent;
> *Israel is wasted, bare of seed,*
> Khor is become a widow for Egypt.
> All who roamed have been subdued
> By the King of Upper and Lower Egypt, *Banere-meramun,*
> Son of Re, *Merneptah, Content with Maat,*
> Given life like Re every day.[23]

The idiom "bare of seed" conveys the idea that no offspring remain—that no survivors are left to carry on the name of Israel.[24] While likely describing an actual battle not recorded in the Bible between the forces of Mernepthah and the people of Israel, the idea that no Israelite survivor was left by Mernepthah is clearly an exaggerated claim.

With similar hyperbole, Egyptian king Seti I says upon his triumphant return to Egypt after his northern wars:

---

[22]See Billie Jean Collins, *The Hittites and Their World*, SBLABS 7 (Atlanta: Society of Biblical Literature, 2007), 53-55; *CANE*, 549.

[23]*AEL* 2:77, italics for "Israel is wasted . . ." added.

[24]See Gen 12:7, where God promises Abram that his seed (*zera^c*) will inherit the land and the repeated references to Abram's "seed" or offspring as the recipients of God's covenant with Abram (Gen 15:3, 5, 13, 18; 17:7-10, 12, 19).

Lo, as for the Good God, he rejoices to begin battle, he is delighted to enter into it, his heart is satisfied at seeing blood, he cuts off the heads of the rebellious-hearted, he loves an hour of battle more than a day of rejoicing. His majesty slays them at one time. *He leaves not a limb [i.e., heir] among them, and he that escapes his hand as a living captive, is carried off to Egypt.*[25]

In this case, Seti claims to have left no heirs among his enemies in one sentence, while in the next sentence, he allows that some who escaped death were brought as prisoners back to Egypt. A similar overstatement of the extent of the Egyptian king's victory is found in Ramses II's account of his battle at Qadesh (discussed above). In the context of this battle Ramses describes his role as follows:

His majesty charged into the force of the Foe from Khatti and the many countries with him. His majesty was like Seth, great-of-strength, like Sakhmet in the moment of her rage. *His majesty slew the entire force of the Foe from Khatti,* together with his great chiefs and *all* his brothers, as well as *all* the chiefs of all the countries that had come with him, their infantry and their chariotry falling on their faces one upon the other. His majesty slaughtered them in their places; they sprawled before his horses; and *his majesty was alone, none other with him.* My majesty caused the forces of the foes from Khatti to fall on their faces, one upon the other, as crocodiles fall, into the water of the Orontes.[26]

As we saw above, the Battle of Qadesh likely ended in a draw. Thus, while Ramses and his forces left a tremendous amount of carnage in the wake of the battle, his claim that he slew *all* the hostile forces of the king of Hatti is hyperbolic, along with his claim that he accomplished this singlehandedly.

Assyrian leaders were also wont to overemphasize their battlefield successes. Assyrian governor Ninurta-kudurrī-uṣur relates his victory over the Arameans by saying his triumph was so complete that he was able to capture even those who escaped:

I decisively defeated them. I annihilated them. I scattered their substantial auxiliary troops; and I broke up their troop contingents. *I captured those who attempted to escape.* I caused their blood to flow like waters of a river. The road with their corpses was visible to the eagles and vultures. I filled the

---

[25]*ARE* 3:52 (italics added).
[26]*AEL* 2:52 (italics added).

mountains and wadis with their skulls like mountain stones. Birds made nests in their skulls.[27]

However, just a few lines later, he admits that while he killed 1,846 of the enemy's troops, 254 soldiers escaped. Thus, while he may have decisively defeated the enemy, his claim of having captured those who attempted to escape is hyperbolic—he captured *some* but also allowed others to escape.

Assyrian king Shalmaneser III inscribed the Kurkh Monolith with his battle exploits, including a description of his encounters with Aḫuni of Bīt-Adini.[28] After attacking the city of Tīl-Barsip, Aḫuni's city, Shalmaneser says he decisively defeated him and confined Aḫuni to his city before going on to capture Burmarʾina, another city of Aḫuni. He then decisively defeated Aḫuni's lands across the Euphrates, laying waste his cities, filling the plain with his warriors, and capturing the city of Paqaruḫbuni. However, despite apparently being confined to his city and having been soundly defeated *twice* already, Aḫuni gathers a coalition that is again *decisively defeated* by Shalmaneser as he dyes the mountains with his opponents' blood and razes, destroys, and burns their cities. Yet despite being *decisively defeated*, the forces of Aḫuni and his coalition then find refuge in the city of Alişir (or Alimuš) with Sapalulme, the Patinaean. Again Shalmaneser captures the city and plunders it. Presumably the next year (though the date is not given), Shalmaneser again captures the city of Tīl-Barsip, Aḫuni's city, though Aḫuni yet again escapes the clutches of the king. In this case, Shalmaneser can claim decisive defeat over Aḫuni three times and attack his city twice within a short time span, while Aḫuni, despite being decisively defeated and confined to his city, is able to lead a coalition of kings against Shalmaneser, escaping his clutches numerous times. One wonders how decisive Shalmaneser's victories were if Aḫuni remained an ongoing problem for several years.[29]

---

[27]*COS* 2:115B, 280 (italics added).

[28]*COS* 2:113A, 261-63.

[29]There are many further examples of severity hyperbole. Moabite king Mesha claims that Israel "has gone to ruin forever" (*COS* 2:23, 137). Assyrian king Shalmaneser claims to have "decisively defeated" a coalition of twelve kings at Qarqar, though he fought against the same coalition four times in a span of eight years (*COS* 2:113B, 264 and n35). Assyrian king Sennacherib claims to have destroyed Babylon so completely that "the site of that city, its temples and its gods would not be identifiable" (*COS* 2:119E, 305), but his son Esarhaddon could identify it well enough to rebuild the city (*COS* 2:120, 306). In 605 BC, Nebuchadnezzar

EXTENT HYPERBOLE

Closely related to severity hyperbole is the use of hyperbole to emphasize the geographical extent of a military victory or the reach of a king's dominion.[30] Claims about the extent of an army's victories usually included the immediate theater of combat and lands associated with any opposing forces in the battle. A victorious king might claim dominion over lands controlled by the defeated nation (whether they actually submitted to their new overlord or not). For example, after the defeat of an unnamed enemy, Thutmose III claims, "Everyone on whom the sun shines is bound under my sandals."[31] He surely cannot have conquered the entire world! In the "Bulletin" Text of the Battle of Qadesh, Ramses II lists fifteen forces allied with Muwatalli of Hatti, and he describes his victory by noting he slew all the forces of Hatti, and then he extends the reach of his victory even beyond Hatti and its allies to include all hostile forces everywhere: "I was after them like a griffin, *I defeated all the*

---

king of Babylon claims to have annihilated the army of Egypt so thoroughly that no member of its army returned home (Jean-Jacques Glassner, *Mesopotamian Chronicles*, ed. Benjamin R. Foster, SBLWAW 19 [Atlanta: Society of Biblical Literature, 2004], 227-29), yet four years later, he met such a determined resistance that he was forced to turn away (James M. Lindenberger, *Ancient Aramaic and Hebrew Letters*, 2nd ed., SBLWAW 14 [Atlanta: Society of Biblical Literature, 2003], 114). Seti I of Egypt claims to kill all his enemies at one time and leave no heirs among them, but in the next line says he spares some to take them captive (*ANET*, 254). Thutmose III claims that he "annihilated completely like those who had not existed" the army of Mitanni and did so "by himself, alone" (*COS* 2:2B, 14-15). Tiglath-pileser boasts of having defeated the Ahlamu Arameans twenty-eight times—twice in one year (*ANET*, 275), yet the extent of the defeat is called into question by its frequency. See also the discussions in the following secondary literature: James K. Hoffmeier, *Israel in Egypt: The Evidence for the Authenticity of the Exodus Tradition* (New York: Oxford University Press, 1997), 38-43; Baruch Halpern, *David's Secret Demons: Messiah, Murderer, Traitor, King* (Grand Rapids: Eerdmans, 2001), 124-32; Paul Copan, *Is God a Moral Monster?: Making Sense of the Old Testament God* (Grand Rapids: Baker, 2011), 170-74.

[30]There are more examples of extent hyperbole. Hittite king Muršili II claims to have conquered "all the land of Arzawa . . . Arawanna . . . Tipiya," but this should better be understood as *control* of these lands (Younger, *Ancient Conquest Accounts*, 244-45). Egyptian queen Hatshepsut claims that the god Amon "set all lands beneath her sandals" before setting off for a more limited expedition to Punt (*ARE* 2:116). Ramses II of Egypt says his might and victory "are in all lands and all countries," yet he could only fight the Hittites to a draw at Qadesh (*ARE* 3:201). Ramses III boasts that he slayed "all lands" and that no one could stand up against him (*ARE* 4:47). Thutmose III of Egypt had inscribed on the Gebel Barkal Stele "My majesty subdued all lands," but then he specifies that this means Retenu and Nubia in the next line (*COS* 2:2B, 16). For further secondary literature see James K. Hoffmeier, "Understanding Hebrew and Egyptian Military Texts: A Contextual Approach," *COS* 2:xxv-xxvi; Younger, *Ancient Conquest Accounts*, 241-47.

[31]*COS* 2:2B, 17.

foreign lands, being alone, my troops and chariotry abandoned me, none of them stood looking back."[32] In the context of a battle with sixteen enemies, the claim to have defeated *all* foreign lands is an overstatement meant to imply the wide geographical scope of the king's victory, but it clearly did not mean the defeat of every possible enemy. The poetic account of the Battle of Qadesh even goes so far as to recount the Egyptian gods' greeting to Ramses II upon his return, saying, "'Welcome, our beloved son, King *Usermare-sotpenre*, the Son of Re, *Ramesse, Beloved of Amun*, given life!' They granted him millions of jubilees forever on the throne of Re, *all lowlands and all highlands* lying prostrate under his feet for ever and all time."[33] Even though the Battle of Qadesh was a draw and its aftermath included the temporary loss of control of Damascus, Ramses is still greeted with a salutation claiming eternal victory over all other lowlands and highlands. While a claim to limited victory might be understandable, a claim to have *eternally* defeated *all foreign lands* is hyperbolic.

Examining the reporting practices in Tiglath-pileser I's battle accounts, Baruch Halpern notes differences between the descriptions of military activities in the king's annals and those in public display inscriptions. Halpern observes that Tiglath-pileser's annals distinguish between various kinds of battle victories:

- ▶ places the king loots and burns
- ▶ places that must pay tribute *after* the looting and burning of their towns
- ▶ places that must pay tribute *without* their towns having been looted and burned (voluntary submission)
- ▶ places that are *annexed*
- ▶ places that he cannot *fully* defeat

Yet in the king's display inscriptions, each of these battle outcomes is described as a resounding victory. Thus, Halpern notes, "In Assyrian royal inscriptions, then, the torching of a grain field is the conquest of a whole

---

[32]*COS* 2:5B, 40 (italics added). See the discussion of the Battle of Qadesh above.
[33]*AEL* 2:71 (emphasis added).

territory beyond it. A looting raid becomes a claim of perpetual sovereignty. But this does not mean that campaigns can be confected. The technique is that of putting extreme spin on real events."[34] In essence, Assyrian royal display inscriptions present the most generous interpretation of the extent of territories conquered or controlled, and this was common practice throughout the ANE.[35]

ATTRIBUTION HYPERBOLE

One additional type of hyperbole commonly found in the ANE is what we might call attribution hyperbole. ANE descriptions of war commonly attributed victories to the king, even though the entire army fought the king's battles. These victories were credited to the king not only because he organized and led his army into battle but because he *embodied* his people.[36] At the same time, to manage the king's continuing need to legitimize his leadership in the eyes of his people, kings were often described in glorified terms, particularly when it came to their military expertise and persona as ultimate warrior.

One form of this type of claim is found in battle descriptions using the first-person singular pronoun. For example, Assyrian king Tiglath-pileser III says, "I laid siege to and conquered the town Hadara," and Sargon II says, "I besieged and conquered Samaria."[37] In both cases, the king did not personally lay siege to a city all on his own; he did so as the leader and head of his army, even though they are not mentioned. Likewise, the Hittite king Muršili's actions in the Ten Year Annals of Muršili are recounted in the first person. In these cases, rather than hyperbole, we should understand the claims as using synecdoche, where the king stands for his entire army. However, several ANE examples extend beyond the use of synecdoche to attribution hyperbole, ascribing victory to the exploits solely of the king.

---

[34]Halpern, *David's Secret Demons*, 125-26.

[35]Steven W. Holloway ("Use of Assyriology in Chronological Apologetics in *David's Secret Demons*," *SJOT* 17 [2003]: 245-67) disputes Halpern's use of Tiglath-pileser's descriptions of his accomplishments as a valid parallel for an early dating of the Solomon narrative, but he affirms the practice of hyperbole in Assyrian royal display inscriptions: "If Tiglath-Pileser I exaggerated the comprehensive nature of his political mastery over areas briefly overrun by his troops, his torture of reality was neither innovative nor extreme in comparison with his successors" (259).

[36]For further development of this topic see appendix A.

[37]*ANET*, 284, 285.

Egyptian battle accounts from the New Kingdom period, for example, can take the representative function of the battle leader to the extreme, suggesting that the king, and the king alone, was responsible for victory. King Amenhotep II recounts one conflict in Syria by saying, "There was *no one with his majesty except himself* with his valiant, powerful arm. His majesty slew them with arrows."[38]

Amenhotep's father, Thutmose III, goes even further on the Gebel Barkal Stele, claiming that he himself overthrew the armies of Mitanni by himself:

> *He is a king who fights alone,* without a multitude to back him up. He is more effective than a myriad of numerous armies. An equal to him has not been, (he is) a warrior who extends his arm on the battlefield, no one can touch him. . . . Numerous armies of Mitanni were over-thrown in the space of an hour, annihilated completely like those who had not existed, in the manner of those who are burned, because of that which the arms of the good god performed, great of might in the mêlée, *who slaughters everyone, by himself alone,* the king of Upper and Lower Egypt, Menkheperre, may he live forever.[39]

Ramses II's account of the battle of Qadesh essentially throws his entire army under the bus as he berates them for failing to stand and fight with him, claiming at one point to have fought against twenty-five hundred enemy chariots on his own as his army raced off in fear. He goes on to emphasize how he, and he alone, was responsible for the victorious battle:

> Have I not done good to any of you,
> That you should leave me alone in the midst of battle?
> You are lucky to be alive at all,
> You who took the air while I was alone!
> Did you not know it in your hearts:
> I am your rampart of iron!
> What will men say when they hear of it,
> That you left me alone without a comrade,
> That no chief, charioteer, or soldier came,
> To lend me a hand while I was fighting?
> I crushed a million countries by myself
> On Victory-in-Thebes, Mut-is-content, my great horses;

---

[38]*COS* 2:3, 19 (italics added).
[39]*COS* 2:2, 14-15 (italics added).

It was they whom I found supporting me,
When I alone fought many lands.[40]

CONCLUSION

Hyperbole played an integral part of the genre of ANE war rhetoric. The ancient world thought about and talked about warfare with an array of language that went well beyond what actually happened in order to communicate not only the military action itself but also the emotive perspective on what took place. As we have seen, ANE scribes could accentuate the speed at which victory took place (speed hyperbole) or the number of troops involved in a battle (numerical hyperbole) to emphasize a king's military prowess. They could relate the complete annihilation of the enemy while later history shows that this was not the case or while even the same battle account acknowledges the presence of survivors (severity hyperbole). ANE battle reportage at times claimed the conquest or control of entire regions or people groups when other data (either within the battle report itself or other historical information) indicates that the victory was not as complete as described (extent hyperbole). Sometimes such war victories are ascribed solely to the king when he was clearly accompanied and aided by his army (attribution hyperbole).

War-genre hyperbole complicates the reading of ancient battle reports for modern readers attempting to understand ancient accounts, but awareness of these techniques becomes a hermeneutical key for correctly reading descriptions of warfare in the Old Testament. Along these lines, hyperbole in ANE war rhetoric provides an essential backdrop for the next chapter.

---

[40]*AEL* 2:69-70.

9

TOTAL-KILL HYPERBOLE,
PART TWO

Joshua and Judges

WHEN WRESTLING WITH THE ETHICS of warfare in the Bible, it makes a difference whether the language of Scripture of total kill or leaving no survivors is understood in a hyperbolic (not literal) sense. If this hyperbole option is correct, the implications for understanding the ethics of biblical warfare are substantial. No longer is the object of Israel's warfare against the Canaanites to kill (literally) every man, woman, and child, combatant and noncombatant alike, as many readers have thought. Rather, the conquest of Canaan meant defeating the Canaanite armies in battle and driving out of the land at least a significant portion of the Canaanite population. Did the biblical authors in fact think and talk about warfare in hyperbolic terms similar to what we saw in the last chapter on ANE war language? To answer that question, Joshua and Judges will have our main attention, along with some discussion of total-kill language in Deuteronomy and the Prophets.

THE PROBLEM OF JOSHUA AND JUDGES

The books of Joshua and Judges include some of the best-loved stories in the Old Testament. Yet they also contain descriptions of brutal warfare. Israel's battle conduct in these books takes its cues from Yahweh's directives set out in Deuteronomy:[1]

---

[1]Gordon J. Wenham, "The Deuteronomic Theology of the Book of Joshua," *JBL* 90 (1971): 140-48. Scholars have long recognized the close links between Deuteronomy and Joshua, though it was Martin Noth's hypothesis that placed Deuteronomy at the head of the collection of Deuteronomy, Joshua, Judges, 1 and 2 Samuel, and 1 and 2 Kings, which he called

> When the LORD your God brings you into the land you are entering to possess and drives out before you many nations—the Hittites, Girgashites, Amorites, Canaanites, Perizzites, Hivites and Jebusites, seven nations larger and stronger than you—and when the LORD your God has delivered them over to you and you have defeated them, then *you must destroy them totally*. Make no treaty with them, and *show them no mercy*. (Deut 7:1-2; see also Deut 7:16, 23-24; 20:16-18)

The book of Joshua describes Israel's faithful obedience to Yahweh's instructions, recounting the annihilation of entire villages and cities, including women and children: "Everyone in [Hazor] they put to the sword. They *totally destroyed them, not sparing anyone that breathed*" (Josh 11:11); "The city [Libnah] and everyone in it Joshua put to the sword. *He left no survivors there*" (Josh 10:30). These samples represent numerous others (Josh 8:26; 10:1, 28, 35, 37, 39, 40; 11:11, 12, 20-21). Their descriptions of wholesale annihilation—killing even the elderly, women, and children—are very disturbing. How should we understand these descriptions of brutal violence?

In the previous chapter, we saw that ANE kings and scribes commonly used various forms of hyperbole to describe the results of battles. In this chapter we turn directly to the accounts of Israel's battles in the book of Joshua. At a rhetorical level they indicate that Israel killed everyone, left no survivors, and conquered all the land of Canaan. However, when we look at the book of Judges, we see evidence that *the entire land was not conquered and that Canaanites were left alive*—some in cities that Joshua "totally destroyed" and where he left "no survivors." We can then turn back to the book of Joshua itself to highlight often overlooked evidence that Israel did not conquer the entire land and did not kill every living being. With ANE war genre as a backdrop, this biblical evidence makes a strong case for hyperbole.

TOTAL-LAND AND TOTAL-KILL ASSERTIONS IN JOSHUA

Well-known accounts in Joshua 6–12 describe Joshua's first battles at Jericho (Josh 6) and Ai (Josh 7–8), as Israel established a central bridgehead in the Promised Land. The battle descriptions in Joshua 10–11 are much briefer and

---

the Deuteronomistic History (*The Deuteronomistic History*, trans. Jane Doull, rev. trans. John Barton, JSOTSup 15 [Sheffield: JSOT Press, 1981]).

summarize Israel's battles to the south and north respectively. The accounts emphasize that these battles were fought (except for the first battle of Ai) in compliance with the directives of Yahweh and in accord with the instructions of Moses as seen in Deuteronomy, including the application of total-kill warfare protocols specifying the complete annihilation of the Canaanites. Thus, after the capture of Jericho, Israel "devoted the city to the LORD and *destroyed with the sword every living thing in it*—men and women, young and old, cattle, sheep and donkeys" (Josh 6:21). Similarly, in the second battle of Ai, "Joshua did not draw back the hand that held out his javelin until he had *destroyed all who lived in Ai*" (Josh 8:26). (Aside: Throughout this book we have chosen to focus on a wide range of *total-kill* language [e.g., "kill all," "leave no survivors," "put all to the sword," "destroy all," etc.]. Since the meaning of *ḥērem* is currently debated within scholarly circles, we have chosen not to make our argumentation dependent on that term.[2])

The descriptions of Israel's southern campaign relay similar results, such as when Israel attacked the city of Hebron: "They took the city and put it to the sword, together with its king, its villages and everyone in it. They *left no survivors*. Just as at Eglon, they *totally destroyed it* and everyone in it" (Josh 10:37; see also Josh 10:28, 35, 39). The description of Israel's campaign in the north also includes the complete annihilation of the Canaanites: "Everyone in [Hazor] they put to the sword. They *totally destroyed them, not sparing anyone that breathed*, and [Joshua] burned Hazor itself" (Josh 11:11).

---

[2]C. Brekelmans notes that there are two primary contexts for the word *ḥērem*, one cultic and one martial, and sees these two as interrelated (*THAT* 1:637-38), while Jason R. Tatlock emphasizes the sacrificial component of the word ("How in Ancient Times They Sacrificed People: Human Immolation in the Western Mediterranean Basin with Special Emphasis upon Ancient Israel and the Near East" [PhD diss., University of Michigan, 2006], 167-74). Jannica A. De Prenter, on the other hand, holds that the word denotes a polysemous taboo (something either consecrated or desecrated), signifying overlapping meanings of "separation" and "irredeemability" ("The Contrastive Polysemous Meaning of חרם in the Book of Joshua: A Cognitive Linguistic Approach," in *The Book of Joshua*, ed. Ed Noort, BETL 250 [Leuven: Peeters, 2012], 473-88). Philip D. Stern views *ḥērem* as ad hoc and largely figurative (*The Biblical Ḥerem: A Window in Israel's Religious Experience*, BJS 211 [Atlanta: Scholars Press, 1991] 217-26), similar to Douglas S. Earl's position that *ḥērem* is symbolic, emphasizing radical separation ("Holy War and חרם: A Biblical Theology of חרם," in *Holy War in the Bible: Christian Morality and an Old Testament Problem*, ed. Heath A. Thomas, Jeremy Evans, and Paul Copan [Downers Grove, IL: InterVarsity Press, 2013], 152-75), while John H. Walton and J. Harvey Walton advance the position that *ḥērem* means to remove from human use and has to do primarily with the removal of identity (*The Lost World of the Israelite Conquest* [Downers Grove, IL: InterVarsity Press, 2017], 169-77).

Similarly, Joshua 11:14 says, "All the people they put to the sword until they *completely destroyed them, not sparing anyone that breathed.*" The narrator summarizes the northern campaign, emphasizing yet again that all of these things took place at Yahweh's instigation and in full compliance with his instructions and the directives to Moses: "For it was the LORD himself who hardened their hearts to wage war against Israel, so that he might *destroy them totally, exterminating them without mercy, as the LORD had commanded Moses*" (Josh 11:20), and, "As the LORD commanded his servant Moses, so Moses commanded Joshua, and Joshua did it; he *left nothing undone of all that the LORD commanded Moses*" (Josh 11:15).

Not only do battle accounts in the book of Joshua describe the total annihilation of the Canaanites, but the book also emphasizes the complete conquest of the lands formerly held by the Canaanites. Joshua 10:40-42 summarizes the results of the southern campaign, reporting the conquest of the entire region:

> Joshua subdued the whole region, including the hill country, the Negev, the western foothills and the mountain slopes, together with all their kings. He left no survivors. He totally destroyed all who breathed, just as the LORD, the God of Israel, had commanded. Joshua subdued them from Kadesh Barnea to Gaza and from the whole region of Goshen to Gibeon. *All these kings and their lands Joshua conquered in one campaign*, because the LORD, the God of Israel, fought for Israel. (Josh 10:40-42)

Similarly, Joshua 11:16-17 summarizes the results of both the northern and southern campaigns, indicating that Israel under Joshua's command "took this entire land." Joshua 11:23 concludes Israel's military campaigns, saying, "So Joshua took the entire land, just as the LORD had directed Moses, and he gave it as an inheritance to Israel according to their tribal divisions." Joshua 21:43-45 serves as a concluding summary of all of Israel's activities in Joshua's day, including both the conquering and the apportioning of the land to the tribes of Israel:

> So the LORD gave Israel *all the land* he had sworn to give their ancestors, and they took possession of it and settled there. The LORD gave them rest on every side, just as he had sworn to their ancestors. *Not one of their enemies withstood them*; the LORD gave all their enemies into their hands. Not one of all the LORD's good promises to Israel failed; every one was fulfilled.

Consequently, when reading these passages in the book of Joshua, we might conclude that the Israelites obtained complete control of Canaan in a blitzkrieg-like charge by putting to death not only the kings of the cities Israel conquered but their entire populations as well, leaving alive no survivors or anything that breathes. Moreover, all of this happened with Yahweh's full blessing, at his command, and even with his participation (see Josh 10:11; 11:20). This literal or face-value approach to the total-kill language is how many people have read the descriptions of battle in the book of Joshua. But we need to look at further evidence to know how to read these passages.

EVIDENCE FOR HYPERBOLE IN JOSHUA AND JUDGES

When we look at the accounts of Joshua and Judges more closely, we see that, despite what is affirmed in the texts at a rhetorical level, not *all* the Canaanites were killed and not *all* their lands were conquered. Several biblical passages paint quite a different picture of how the people of Israel came into possession of the Promised Land. We will start with Judges and then turn again to Joshua.

Judges: Conquest of the entire land? The book of Joshua ends with Joshua's death, which is also the point at which the book of Judges picks up the story: "After the death of Joshua, the Israelites asked the LORD, 'Who of us is to go up first to fight against the Canaanites?'" (Judg 1:1). If we read Joshua along the lines of what we saw above, the thoughtful reader should ask, "What Canaanites?" and, "Where did they come from?" It stretches credulity to believe that the control of the entire land described in Joshua 10:42; 11:23 was lost immediately after the death of Joshua. Based on the narratives of Joshua 6–12, it seems that the entire land was conquered; none of their enemies stood up against them (Judg 1:34; Josh 21:44). Yet, Judges 1 goes on to describe battles not of the unified tribes of Israel, but of individual tribes in the mode every tribe for itself as they struggled to take possession of their allotted territory, beginning with Judah and ending with Dan. When each tribe battled on its own, they met with varying degrees of success. Judah (when paired with Simeon) had significant success, while Dan failed completely in possessing the land within its tribal allotment (Josh 19:47). Yet even Judah, the most successful tribe, failed to take all the cities within its allotted territory. Judges 1:19 points out: "The LORD was with the men of Judah. They took possession of the hill country, but they were *unable to drive the people from the plains*, because they had chariots fitted with iron." The region taken by Judah and Simeon falls within the area Joshua 10:40-42 describes as completely conquered. Based on Judges 1, it appears that Israel had not literally conquered *all* the land.

Judges: Annihilation of entire city populations? Not only does Judges 1 suggest that Israel was unable to conquer all the lands allotted to the various tribes, but it also indicates that quite a few Canaanites survived the total-kill warfare described in Joshua. Judges 1 reports that Judah conquered the cities of Hebron (Judg 1:10; see Josh 10:36-37), Debir (Judg 1:11-13; see Josh 10:38-39), Jerusalem (Judg 1:8; see Josh 10:5, 23-26; 12:10) and Zephath, also called Hormah (Judg 1:17; see Josh 12:14).[3] Yet these are all cities and/or their kings that Joshua has *already* defeated within total-kill regions.[4] Similarly, Manasseh was not able to drive out the people of Taanach, Dor, or Megiddo (Judg 1:27), and Ephraim was unable to overcome Gezer (Judg 1:29). Yet the rulers of these cities are among the list of thirty-one kings conquered in Joshua's campaigns (Josh 12:21, 23).[5] Other evidence indicates that several of these Canaanite enclaves remained unconquered and relatively unassimilated into Israelite culture until the time of Solomon, when he conscripted the remaining Canaanite peoples for his work projects (1 Kings 9:20). In short, the cities "totally destroyed" by Israel in the book of Joshua needed to be reconquered almost immediately after the death of Joshua in Judges.[6]

---

[3]Deborah and Barak battle Jabin king of Hazor (Judg 4:2, 23-24), a city and king whom Joshua had already decisively defeated (Josh 11:1, 11-13; 12:19). For a helpful discussion of Jabin king of Hazor, see Daniel I. Block, *Judges, Ruth*, NAC 6 (Nashville: Broadman & Holman, 1999), 188-90. Kenneth Kitchen suggests that Jabin is a dynastic name and distinguishes between Jabin I of Joshua's day and Jabin II of Deborah and Barak's day (*On the Reliability of the Old Testament* [Grand Rapids: Eerdmans, 2003], 213).

[4]See the discussion in chapter ten: "Four Conquest-Summary Statements."

[5]While one might consider defeat of a king (and his army) at first glance as not including the conquest of his city, the defeat of a king often entailed the submission of his city to the conqueror (for the city was left defenseless after the defeat of the king and army). Joshua's defeat of the kings of Taanach, Dor, Megiddo, and Gezer implies control if not conquest of these cities. Nevertheless, it would seem that Manasseh and Ephraim did not exert enough control to compel forced labor from these cities until much later (Judg 1:28).

[6]A rather strange but corroborating example of extent hyperbole with respect to city annihilation appears at the end of the book of Judges. When the city of Jabesh Gilead failed to send warriors to aid Israel in its battle against the tribe of Benjamin, Israel sent a force of

Joshua: Conquest of the entire land? Lest we think that only the book of Judges raises questions about the complete conquest of Canaan and the total annihilation of the Canaanites, we need look no further than the book of Joshua itself to see that it also indicates that Israel did not conquer the entire land of Canaan. Joshua 13:1-2 says: "When Joshua had grown old, the LORD said to him, 'You are now very old, and there are still very large areas of land to be taken over. This is the land that remains.'"[7] Joshua 13:2-5 lists territory yet to be conquered. Moreover, while Joshua 12:8, 10 indicates that the Israelites conquered the land of the Jebusites and its king, just three chapters later Joshua 15:63 says, "Judah could not dislodge the Jebusites, who were living in Jerusalem; to this day the Jebusites live there with the people of Judah." The Jebusites were not fully dislodged until the time of the monarchy, when David's army finally conquered the city of Jerusalem (2 Sam 5:6-8). Joshua 12:21-23 indicates that Joshua defeated the kings of Dor, Taanach, and Megiddo; yet later Joshua 17:12 indicates that "the Manassites were not able to occupy these towns [including Dor, Taanach, and Megiddo], for the Canaanites were determined to live in that region," and only when Israel grows stronger do they put the people to forced labor. These examples show that while Joshua 1–12 indicates that the Israelites controlled the "entire land," other passages in the book of Joshua itself show that the land was not fully conquered.[8]

---

twelve thousand warriors with total-kill instructions (*ḥāram*—Hiphil) for every male and every female who slept with a man (Judg 21:10-11). The total-destruction language used here suggests that the entire city was wiped out except for four hundred virgins, who were given as brides to the men of Benjamin (Judg 21:12-13). However, not too much later, in 1 Sam 11:1-11 Saul must rescue the city of Jabesh Gilead from the Ammonites. It is possible that the city was reestablished sometime after the Judg 21 fiasco (see the excursus on city re-settlement below), but given the already acknowledged selective nature of the action and the hyperbolic language of total kill (see below), it is more likely that the narrators have used hyperbole to paint the chaos at the end of the book of Judges in the worst possible light.

[7]Joshua 13:1 immediately follows the summary statements in Josh 11 about the central/south/ north conquest of all the land (Josh 11:16-17, 23) and the lengthy list in Josh 12 of conquests of kings and cities. It would have been obvious to the original audience that hyperbolic "all the land" conquest statements coexisted with the reality of "still very large areas to be taken" conquest statements.

[8]The book of Joshua in its canonical form is generally attributed to the Deuteronomists, who combined earlier sources with their own editorial bridges and additions (see, e.g., R. Nelson, *Joshua*, OTL [Philadelphia: Westminster John Knox, 1997], 5-9; Robert L. Hubbard, *Joshua*, NIVAC [Grand Rapids: Zondervan, 2009], 30-33). The tensions noted here are not washed away by simply appealing to the use of different sources in the composition of Joshua. The

Joshua: Annihilation of entire city populations? Several indicators within the book of Joshua itself also show that the Israelites did not completely destroy all the Canaanite cities and the people living in those cities. Rahab and her family are, of course, famously permitted to live among the Israelites "to this day" (Josh 6:25) because of Rahab's acknowledgement of Yahweh and her pact with the spies. The Gibeonites serve as woodcutters and water carriers for the altar of Yahweh "to this day" (Josh 9:27) because of the covenant they finagled with Joshua.

More significantly, other people groups are described as having "no survivors" and being "completely destroyed" by Israel's war initiative, and yet survivors existed—people who clearly were alive and not completely destroyed, that is, put to death. In Israel's southern campaign, Joshua 10:33 indicates that "Horam king of Gezer had come up to help Lachish, but Joshua defeated him and his army—*until no survivors were left,*" which complies with the summary in Joshua 10:40 indicating that in Joshua's southern campaign, he not only subdued the whole region but *"left no survivors. He totally destroyed* [ḥāram—Hiphil] *all who breathed,* just as the LORD, the God of Israel, had commanded" (Josh 10:40). Yet a few chapters later we learn that the Ephraimites "did not dislodge the Canaanites living in Gezer; to this day the Canaanites live among the people of Ephraim but are required to do forced labor" (Josh 16:10).[9] Now, it is possible that Joshua 10:33 indicates the annihilation of only the king of Gezer and his army, but Joshua 10:40 indicates that Joshua captured *all* the lands of the Canaanites and left *no* survivors among the populace of the cities he conquered.

Other peoples seem also to have survived the total kill of ḥērem warfare. Joshua 10:41 includes Gaza in the region that Joshua controls and in which he applies the ḥērem (see Josh 10:40). However, Joshua 11:22 indicates that the Anakites of Gaza, Gath, and Ashdod survived. Thus, not *all* the inhabitants of Gaza were destroyed. Joshua 10:38-39 says that Joshua put all the

---

editors would still have been left with the tensions brought by combining different sources that could presumably have been harmonized but were allowed to stand.

[9]The people of Gezer continued to live among the Israelites until the time of Solomon, when the king of Egypt finally wiped the city out and then gave it as a wedding gift to Solomon (1 Kings 9:16).

city of Debir to the sword and totally destroyed (*ḥāram*—Hiphil) the town, leaving no survivors; yet Caleb must fight against Debir a few chapters later (Josh 15:15-16). How could Caleb conquer an entire city full of people that had already been completely annihilated just a short while beforehand?

Similarly, Hoham king of Hebron fights in a coalition of kings against Joshua at Gibeon and is killed along with his army (Josh 10:3, 23-26). Joshua's army subsequently attacks Hebron, "took the city and *put it to the sword*, together with its king, its villages and *everyone in it. They left no survivors. Just as at Eglon, they totally destroyed it and everyone in it*" (Josh 10:37). Hebron is part of Caleb's reward for his faith in Yahweh's promise to give the Israelites the land when the ten other spies caused Israel to fearfully abandon entry into Canaan (see Num 13:30; 14:24; Deut 1:36). Yet before Caleb can go up and take possession of his inheritance, he must drive certain Anakites out from Hebron (Josh 15:13-14), even though Joshua employed total kill at Hebron and its surrounding villages, leaving no survivors and, more specifically, eliminating all the Anakites within Israelite territory (Josh 11:21). Upon receiving their tribal allotment, the house of Joseph (the tribes of Manasseh and Ephraim) complains that its allotment in the hill country of Ephraim is not big enough because it has such large tribal groups; yet even they cannot overcome the remaining Canaanites: "The hill country is not enough for us, *and all the Canaanites who live in the plain* have chariots fitted with iron, both those in Beth Shan and its settlements and those in the Valley of Jezreel" (Josh 17:16). Thus, Joshua counsels them to use their size and power to patiently drive the remaining Canaanites out of their allotted inheritance (Josh 17:18), even though we read that Joshua had already taken the entire land (Josh 11:16, 23).

The end of the book of Joshua also indicates that many Canaanites survived total-kill warfare. Joshua's first farewell speech warns about the dangers of fraternizing with the Canaanites remaining in the land (Josh 23:7). Joshua emphasizes that the reason the Israelites were able to gain any measure of success in taking possession of the land was their complete obedience to Yahweh, their divine warrior, who fought on their behalf. But "if you turn away and ally yourselves with the *survivors of these nations that remain among you* and if you intermarry with them and associate with them, then you may be sure that the LORD your God will no longer drive out these nations before you" (Josh 23:12-13). Thus, plentiful evidence within the book of Joshua itself shows that at the end of Joshua's life significant numbers of Canaanites still lived within the land, some in the very places where Joshua is said to have left no one alive.

EXCURSUS: RUN, RETURN, REPOPULATE

Some early readers of this material have asked us about the possibility of Canaanites *fleeing and returning* to their cities. Such a scenario might lead one to understand the total-kill language literally as describing the death of all those who remained in the cities. Perhaps then cities that needed to be reconquered (such as Hebron) were rebuilt or repopulated by Canaanites who evaded Joshua's forces by fleeing ahead of time. One might speculate that they hid out in the country and later returned to their city. If this were the case, some might say that hyperbole was not being used in the total-kill language; Israel literally killed everyone—men, women, and children—who were *in those cities* at the time of the battle but not those who fled and hid out only to later return and reoccupy conquered cities. Thus, the total-kill language would be *limited* in its referential meaning to *only* those who remained in the cities.

While some Canaanites may have fled and later returned (we have no problem affirming this may have happened to some extent and in certain cases), the limited-referent argument does not work as a response to the hyperbole thesis. First, speculation about fleeing ahead of a battle appears to go directly against the biblical descriptions of how the Canaanites responded to the threat of the approaching Israelite army. Any fear of the coming Israelites did not lead to fleeing before battle but instead motivated the Canaanites to build coalition armies (Josh 10:1-5; 11:1-5; see chapter ten on hear-fear-flee sequences). Also, the return of any who had fled is purely speculative. While it may have happened, it is not spoken of even once in Scripture. Second, many of the battles that were said to wipe out (hyperbolically) entire city populations and destroy total people groups were not physically located at the city. Rather, the armies from a number of cities gathered as coalition forces to fight the Israelites on open ground away from their cities. The destruction of a city's king and its armed forces meant that the biblical authors could speak of the total-kill (representative, i.e., part for the whole) destruction of *all* the people, even those in the cities, in a hyperbolic sense.

Third, in the regional summary of the southern campaign in Joshua 10:40, not only does Israel subdue cities, but also Joshua subdues the *whole* region and "left no survivors. He totally destroyed all who breathed." This passage claims the total destruction not just of individual cities but the entire region. The totality of the conquest of the entire southern region is framed by the double emphasis on leaving no survivors and totally destroying all who breathed. Thus, one cannot argue against hyperbole by simply positing a speedy return of survivors to cities (i.e., a flee-then-return scenario). Fourth, such a limited literal reference to killing all nonfleeing city dwellers does not square with the ANE phenomenon of hyperbolic severity and extent language in the broader context of ancient warfare (see chapter eight). Fifth, the accumulating weight of evidence for hyperbole that we have yet to present in this and following chapters would need to be discounted. In sum, a flee-then-return scenario does not sufficiently handle the multilayered evidence for hyperbole.

A more likely explanation, one that embraces hyperbole, is that taking a city was described using total-kill (hyperbolic) language, but only the key leaders of that city (the king and a sufficient number of the fighting force to remove the military threat) were defeated and killed by the Israelites in battle. A fivefold scenario accounts better for the evidence: (1) Perhaps a small percentage of Canaanites fled before battle to live in different regions or outside the land, since this counters the biblical text in its descriptions of prebattle fear, as noted above. (2) Others may have fled over time, when it became clear the Israelites controlled the land. Yet (3) other city populations seem to have been assimilated into Israel without battle (e.g., Shechem, Josh 8:30-35; 21:21; 24:1, 25; Judg 8:31; 9:1). Another type of situation includes (4) a description of the total kill of a Canaanite city (using hyperbole) but whose population was not eradicated and continued to hold on. Cities such as these were weakened seemingly to the point of not being a military threat, but the population remained until they were later driven out (e.g., Hebron, Josh

10:36-37; see Josh 15:13-14). Finally, (5) there is evidence that some kings and their armies (with no mention of total kill of the city) were initially defeated (Josh 10:23-26; 12:10) but not fully conquered (that is, not quelling any lingering military threat) until much later, at which point they were assimilated into Israel, as was the case with the Jebusites and other groups put to forced labor (e.g., 2 Sam 5:6-8; Josh 16:10; 17:13; see Josh 24:16-25; Zech 9:7). The hyperbole thesis best accounts for these diverse scenarios.

To summarize our findings up to this point: Joshua 1–12 suggests that the Israelites conquered and controlled all the land of Canaan through a series of relatively quick (though note Josh 11:19) battles. Some battles (Jericho, the second battle of Ai) were fought at Yahweh's instigation, while others were fought in reaction to the attacks of Canaanite kings (Josh 10–11). During these battles, the Israelites used total-kill warfare against the kings they conquered and their cities' inhabitants so that there were "no survivors," and the "whole region" was conquered (Josh 10:40-42; 11:14, 23). All of this occurred because Yahweh fought for Israel (Josh 10:14, 42) and Israel was completely obedient to Yahweh: "As the LORD commanded his servant Moses, so Moses commanded Joshua, and Joshua did it; he left nothing undone of all that the LORD commanded Moses" (Josh 11:15).

However, other passages in Joshua and Judges 1 reveal that several Canaanite enclaves, though described in Joshua 10–12 as completely conquered and annihilated, continued to exist and in fact were strong enough to resist Israelite advances (contra Josh 21:43-44). Thus, the book of Joshua itself acknowledges that Canaanite districts continued to exist.

This raises a difficult question: How can Joshua claim to have completely conquered the land of Canaan, fought total-kill battles, and left no survivors —seemingly perpetrating a program of genocidal extermination—yet also acknowledge that Canaanite enclaves remained, some in places where Israel is said to have left no survivors? We contend that the hyperbole answer offers an important piece of the puzzle as we struggle to come to terms with the ethical implications of Israel's battles within the land of Canaan.

The next section develops further the evidence for hyperbole in the biblical war texts and how to understand their various types of expression.

WHY HYPERBOLE MAKES SENSE

Our positive case for hyperbole in the biblical war texts began with insights into how people in the ANE described their victories in battle. Recent comparisons of biblical conquest stories and ANE conquest accounts (see chapter eight) have noted significant overlap in these descriptions; a common feature is the use of figurative or hyperbolic language.[10] Obviously, we believe that this hyperbolic way of thinking about and describing ANE battles was also a part of how Israel described its own battles. But let us press the comparison at even a closer, more intricate level by examining certain types of hyperbole.

In the previous chapter we noted several types of hyperbole that ANE scribes used in their descriptions of battles. The battle accounts recorded in Joshua 6–11 also use elements of hyperbole to describe Israel's wars in Canaan. Let's review the evidence:

▶ Joshua 6; 8; 10:42 give the impression of a *speedy* conquest, while passages such as Joshua 11:18; 16:10; 17:13; Judges 1 suggest a more protracted process of taking possession of Canaan.

▶ Joshua 21:44 says that *none* of Israel's enemies withstood them, and passages such as Joshua 10:33, 37, 38-39, 41 suggest that Israel destroyed entire cities *without leaving any survivors.* However, passages such as Joshua 13:13; 16:10; 17:13 indicate that some of the original inhabitants of Canaan did resist, and passages such as Joshua 15:13-14, 15-16, 63; 17:16; 23:7, 12-13 indicate that Israel did leave survivors in cities elsewhere described as completely annihilated with no remaining survivors.

▶ Passages such as Joshua 11:16-17, 23; 21:43 suggest Israel *conquered the entire land of Canaan,* but others, such as Joshua 13:1-5; 15:13-14, 63; 16:10; 17:12-13, indicate that Israel did not completely conquer the entire land of Canaan.[11]

---

[10]On the overlap between biblical and ANE conquest accounts, see K. Lawson Younger Jr., *Ancient Conquest Accounts: A Study in Ancient Near Eastern and Biblical History Writing,* JSOTSup 98 (Sheffield: Sheffield Academic Press, 1990); David Howard, *Joshua,* NAC (Nashville: Broadman and Holman, 1998), 259-60; Kitchen, *On the Reliability of the Old Testament,* 173-74; Hubbard, *Joshua,* 301n79. For general examples of hyperbole in the Bible see E. W. Bullinger, *Figures of Speech Used in the Bible: Explained and Illustrated* (London: Eyre and Spottiswoode, 1898; repr., Grand Rapids: Baker, 1968, 423-28).

[11]The "all the land" summary statement in Josh 10:40-42 is likely a summary of the central

Some of these tensions (and others referred to earlier) can best be explained through the biblical writers' use of hyperbole. The impression of a speedy conquest of the land of Canaan by Joshua and Israel in some passages, though other sources indicate an extended process of settling in the land, may best be viewed as an example of speed hyperbole. The existence of survivors in areas for which there are claims of complete annihilation (often using total-kill warfare) offers a good example of severity hyperbole, and claims of complete control of regions when other passages indicate that supremacy had not yet been fully secured serve well as examples of extent hyperbole.[12] K. Lawson Younger draws this important conclusion at the end of his seminal study comparing ANE conquest accounts with the battle reportage of Joshua 9–12:

> This study has shown that one encounters very similar things in both ancient Near Eastern and biblical history writing. While there are differences . . . the Hebrew conquest account of Canaan in Joshua 9–12 is, by and large, typical of any ancient Near Eastern account. In other words, there is a common denominator, a certain commonality between them, so that it is possible for us to speak, for purposes of generalization, of a common transmission code that is an intermingling of the texts' figurative and ideological aspects.[13]

This form of reportage sounds strange to most modern readers, for it seems to describe events in ways that are contradictory, possibly even to the point where we might question their reliability. To be sure, an awareness of the use of hyperbole in ancient battle reports, and particularly when it is found in the biblical text, does make the process of understanding what was described in the book of Joshua more complex. However, several factors may help us consider the implications of this style of hyperbolic writing in the Bible.

---

and southern campaigns described to that point in the book of Joshua. Yet, even if limited to the central and southern campaigns, it should still be understood as extent hyperbole. On the other hand, the "all the land" statements in Josh 11:16-17, 23; 21:43 are *comprehensive* conquest statements that include all of Joshua's central, southern, and northern campaigns. A correct understanding of these summary statements makes a solid case for hyperbole (see chapter ten for further discussion on arguments against hyperbole).

[12]War hyperbole affects the Joshua text at many levels: the northern coalition of armies is "as numerous as the sand on the seashore" (Josh 11:4; *numbers* hyperbole); Caleb at eighty-five years old is "still as strong as the day Moses sent me out [forty-five years ago]" (Josh 14:11; see Josh 14:7); and the capability of Israel's warriors, of which the text says, "One of you routs a thousand" (Josh 23:10).

[13]Younger, *Ancient Conquest Accounts*, 265.

First, biblical statements that line up claims that are in tension with each other, sometimes even side by side, would seem to falsify these claims for modern readers. However, this is a modern assumption that was not shared by ancient writers. We need to read the biblical text from the perspective of and using the literary methods of its ancient writers and ancient audiences. We obviously do not have ANE individuals to ask for opinions about the use of hyperbole in battle reportage, but the phenomenon can be found throughout the second and first millennia BC and across ANE cultures. It was simply an accepted part of battle reports.[14] For example, James Hoffmeier points out how the Tomb Biography of Ahmose of Nekheb describes Nubian tribesmen "carried off in neck constraints, without losing one of them," but then the next sentence says, "The one [i.e., every person] who fled was laid low like those who did not exist."[15] Hoffmeier further remarks, "While to a western audience, such statements appear to be contradictory, clearly it was not to the Egyptians," and he points to a similar phenomenon in Joshua 10:20, where readers are told that Israel completely destroyed their enemies, but then the next line tells of how some survivors escaped.[16]

Second, the presence of hyperbole need not invalidate a text for use in historical studies. For example, while the Moabite king Mesha obviously overstates his claim that "Israel has perished forever," his declaration in the same inscription that he took Nebo (an Israelite city) finds support in the Old Testament (2 Kings 3:4-5; see also Is 15:2; Jer 48:1-2).[17] The use of hyperbole does not negate a toned-down reality version of what was described in the text: that a battle took place, that one side was defeated by another,

---

[14]Manfred Weippert, "'Heiliger Krieg' in Israel und Assyrien: Kritische Anmerkungen zu Gerhard von Rads Konzept des 'Heiligen Krieges im alten Israel,'" *ZAW* 84 (1972): 460-93; Moshe Weinfeld, "Divine Intervention in War in Ancient Israel and the Ancient Near East," in *History, Historiography and Interpretation: Studies in Biblical and Cuneiform Literatures*, ed. Hayim Tadmor and Moshe Weinfeld (Jerusalem: Magnes, 1984), 121-47; Jeffrey J. Niehaus, "Joshua and Ancient Near Eastern Warfare," *JETS* 31 (1988): 37-50; James K. Hoffmeier, "The Structure of Joshua 1–11 and the Annals of Thutmose III," in *Faith, Tradition, and History: Old Testament Historiography in Its Near Eastern Context*, ed. A. R. Millard, James K. Hoffmeier, and David W. Baker (Winona Lake, IN: Eisenbrauns, 1994), 165-79; Kitchen, *On the Reliability of the Old Testament*, 173-74; Hubbard, *Joshua*, 301n79.

[15]*COS* 2:1, 6.

[16]*COS* 2:1, 6n30.

[17]*ANET*, 320.

and that lives were lost as the battle was fought. It simply makes us work a little harder to interpret these accounts.[18]

Third, modern readers may throw up their hands in frustration, saying, "Well then, how can we know what to take literally and what is hyperbolic?" That is a fair question. In short, it requires getting used to the idea and looking for clues in the text (much like we have already done) that suggest a literal understanding is simply implausible. While modern readers of the Bible may struggle to read ancient battle accounts and to distinguish the literal from the figurative, an awareness of a war-language genre in the biblical text and its conventions is an essential starting place. The original ancient audience would have picked up on the subtleties of battle accounts (knowing also their genre expectations) and would have readily distinguished the literal from the figurative.

Modern people actually do this as well. Imagine for a moment switching places and letting a person from the ANE hear a commentator read a National Hockey League report that says, "The Boston Bruins totally slaughtered the Toronto Maple Leafs; they wiped them off the map!"[19] Later in the broadcast one learns that the score was seven to three. We hear this statement and are immediately attuned to its hyperbolic elements. No one complains about wrongful reporting, because we all understand that sportscasters use colorful, figurative language to describe a sound victory and the emotive excitement about the win (or the pain of a loss). Hockey fans know that the reporter's language is *not* to be taken

---

[18]Younger (*Ancient Conquest Accounts*, 266) concludes his book with this statement: "We do not wish to give the reader the impression that we believe that none of the data in the ancient texts is trustworthy or that all is rhetoric and stereotyped vocabulary. It is simply that the use of a common transmission code underlying the ancient texts must be taken into account; the commonality of such set language does not negate the fact that a war took place, that someone won or that the army performed certain specific actions. The use in the biblical narrative of such stereotyped syntagms as 'YHWH gave the city into Israel's hand,' 'Joshua put the city and everyone in it to the sword,' 'he left no survivors,' or 'he conquered all the land' does not invalidate them any more than the use of such syntagms as 'a great slaughter was made' or 'his majesty dispatched' invalidates the Egyptian accounts. The fact that there are figurative and ideological underpins to the accounts should not make us call them into question *per se*—it should only force us to be cautious!"

[19]This is obviously a fallacious news report. Everyone knows that the Leafs always slaughter the Bruins (not the reverse) and within a matter of few minutes on the ice! (Forgive our extent, speed, and severity hyperbole. Canadian fans are very passionate about their hockey.)

literally. Similarly, sportscasters might say that a baseball team annihilated an opposing pitcher or that a defensive back obliterated a receiver in football, and no one will balk. Because of familiarity, we know how to interpret those statements accurately; they indicate a lopsided defeat or a ferocious tackle. Familiarity with the conventions of genre (whatever genre it is) aids in proper interpretation.[20] ANE scribes and their audiences were familiar with the genre of battle reportage and understood its conventions. Our understanding of what Joshua and Judges intended to communicate is greatly enhanced by picking up on the presence of hyperbole in the ancient war texts.

Fourth, it helps to note that the hyperbole found in the battle language of Joshua and Judges is not unique to those books; it appears throughout the Old Testament. The prophets frequently speak of the demise of certain peoples or nations with rhetorically inflated language that was never intended to be understood literally. Numerous examples demonstrate the ease with which the prophets engage in total-kill language to depict in hyperbolic form a significant (but *not* complete) destruction of various nations or people groups:

▶ Israelites: "Not one will get away [from death by the sword], none will escape" (Amos 9:1); an attack against the city of Jerusalem will completely wipe out all its inhabitants; even the survivors of the siege will meet with death: "I will put the survivors to the sword before their enemies" (Jer 15:9).

▶ Assyrians: "Whoever is captured will be thrust through; all who are caught will fall by the sword" (Is 13:15); the nation will be "overthrown

---

[20]Hyperbole especially accentuates the *emotive* element of meaning. Beyond the realm of sports, here is an example from the everyday marital setting. Recently my wife, Marilyn, said, "Bill, this war book has taken you [and Gord] *forever* to write. [As I recall, the context was comparing the war book to other things I had written.] I responded to Marilyn with a smile (and a twinkle in my eye) by saying, "No, love. That is not true. It only took me 14 years and, in fact, only 7 years after Gord joined me. What do you mean then by saying it took me/us 'forever'?" Without a moment's pause, I quickly followed up with the crucial question, "Instead of using the word 'forever' literally, perhaps you were using it hyperbolically and wanted to convey some *emotive* meaning through the word?" We both chuckled because Marilyn has caught the gist of this war book at many spots. She responded, "I mean it *feels* like forever!" After that, we had a long conversation unpacking the emotive component of what exactly "forever" felt like for each of us.

. . . like Sodom and Gomorrah" (Is 13:19); "I will wipe out Babylon's [= Assyria] name and survivors, her offspring and descendants" (Is 14:22).[21]

▶ Babylonians: "Attack the land of Merathaim and those who live in Pekod. Pursue, kill and completely destroy them" (Jer 50:21); "Pile her up like heaps of grain. Completely destroy her and leave her no remnant" (Jer 50:26); "Encamp all around her; let no one escape" (Jer 50:29); "Do not spare her young men; completely destroy her army" (Jer 51:3).

▶ Philistines: "Your root I will destroy by famine; it [the famine] will slay your survivors" (Is 14:30); "The day has come to destroy all the Philistines and to remove all survivors" (Jer 47:4); "I will turn my hand against Ekron, till the last of the Philistines are dead" (Amos 1:8); "I will destroy you, and none will be left" (Zeph 2:5).

▶ Arameans: "They flee far away, driven before the wind like chaff on the hills, like tumbleweed before a gale. In the evening, sudden terror! Before the morning, they are gone!" (Is 17:13-14).

▶ Cushites: "They will *all* be left to the mountain birds of prey and to the wild animals" (Is 18:6).

▶ Moabites and Ammonites: "Moab shall become like Sodom, the Ammonites like Gomorrah [an idiom for total destruction with no survivors; see Is 1:9]" (Zeph 2:9); "I will wipe you [Ammon] out from among the nations and exterminate you from the countries. I will destroy you" (Ezek 25:7); Ammon will "not be remembered among the nations" (Ezek 25:10).

▶ Edomites: "'As Sodom and Gomorrah were overthrown, along with their neighboring towns,' says the LORD, 'so no one will live there; no people will dwell in it'" (Jer 49:18); "there will be no survivors from Esau" (Obad 18).

▶ Phoenicia/Tyre: "When I make you a desolate city, like the cities no longer inhabited . . . I will bring you to a horrible end and you will be no more. You will be sought, but you will never again be found" (Ezek 26:19, 21);

---

[21]Both the Assyrian and Babylonian empires are referred to in different texts under the same city name of "Babylon."

"All your soldiers, and everyone else on board will sink into the heart of the sea on the day of your shipwreck" (Ezek 27:27); "All the nations who knew you are appalled at you; you have come to a horrible end and will be no more" (Ezek 28:19).

▶ Elamites: "All of them are slain, fallen by the sword" (Ezek 32:24).

▶ Meshech/Tubalites: "All of them are uncircumcised, killed by the sword" (Ezek 32:26).

▶ Egypt: "I will drench the land with your flowing blood all the way to the mountains" (Ezek 32:6); "When I snuff you out, I will cover the heavens" (Ezek 32:7); "I will cause your hordes to fall by the swords of mighty men . . . and all her [Egypt's] hordes will be overthrown" (Ezek 32:12); "I will destroy all her [Egypt's] cattle" (Ezek 32:13); "When I strike down all who live there" (Ezek 32:15).[22]

We know that this total-destruction language is hyperbolic and not literal because at certain points the prophets themselves speak of continuing remnants of people *after* total-kill battles (e.g., Is 1:8-9; Ezek 29:13-16; Amos 9:12). Also, as far as we know, no total-kill destructions ever took place against any of these nations. Not one was (literally) wiped out without any survivors.[23] Yes, these nations encountered major battles and shifts in power, and they generally fell from prominent positions. But total-kill destruction was simply not accomplished in a literal sense.

The hyperbolic total-kill language was intended to communicate on an emotive level just how displeased Yahweh was with a nation's behavior. While the total-war rhetoric spoke of the complete destruction of every living human being, the reality of these prophetic statements was much more a matter of losing some (occasionally many) people in war but, even more importantly, losing their former power, dominance, and prestige within the ancient world and with that the prestige of their gods. Clearly the language is that of emotive hyperbole, not intended to be taken in a strictly literal sense.

---

[22]In context, the meaning of "strike down" the living is probably the idea of death by the sword (see Ezek 32:6, 12).

[23]While *some* of these groups eventually faded from history (years later), that appears to strain the notion of prophetic fulfillment. The biblical rhetoric does not indicate a gradual dissipation but immediate military conquest and total-kill destruction.

EXCURSUS: EVEN GOD'S COMMANDS?

Some readers have posed this question: Should even *God's commands* to kill *all* the Canaanites be understood as hyperbole? Answer: "Yes, they should." Here is evidence that supports this conclusion:

▶ The battle summary reports within Joshua discussed in this chapter are best understood in hyperbolic terms. The biblical authors view these reports as confirmation of fulfilling God's commands (Josh 10:40-42; 11:11-12, 15-18, 21-23; 21:43-45); they do not see any dissonance between their reports and God's commands. In fact, the summary reports are repeatedly and directly tied to God's commands.

▶ Some scholars understand God's commands as misconstrued communication or human misrepresentation (Moses', Joshua's, etc., incorrect understanding) of what God said.[24] We do not take this misrepresentation or miscommunication view. While we affirm an accommodated ethic within God's communication (including commands), we see God speaking to Moses and others using war language and total-kill rhetoric in the same hyperbolic manner as the biblical authors themselves.[25]

▶ In issuing total-kill commands God is fully aware of and intentionally using the broader war-genre context of an ANE setting.[26] God speaks in ancient-world semantic domains that people in that culture typically used to talk about war.

---

[24]Gregory A. Boyd, *Cross Vision: How the Crucifixion of Jesus Makes Sense of Old Testament Violence* (Minneapolis: Fortress, 2017), 9-10, 117-19; Boyd, *The Crucifixion of the Warrior God* (Minneapolis: Fortress, 2017), 2:924-27, 963. Boyd uses expressions such as "Yahweh is depicted as telling Moses," "Scripture reports that Yahweh told Moses," and "Moses believed Yahweh has told him" to leave room for Moses misunderstanding (and in turn misrepresenting) what God was communicating even if it was not intentional on his part. Boyd ultimately views the total-kill commands as words from Moses, not from Yahweh. Other scholars widen the gap further and argue that the conquest commands and the conquest events themselves are merely literary creations with no historical basis within the time frame that the text purports. The conquest itself (let alone any total-kill commands attributed either to Moses or God) did not actually happen. See Eric A. Seibert, *Disturbing Divine Behavior: Troubling Old Testament Images of God* (Minneapolis: Fortress, 2009); Seibert, *The Violence of Scripture: Overcoming the Old Testament's Troubling Legacy* (Minneapolis: Fortress, 2012). For sake of space (reasonable book length) and quality (not our expertise) we have curtailed any attempts to make an archaeological-historical case here.

[25]For a discussion of God's commands and fallen-world ethics see chapters two and seven.

[26]See chapter eight.

▶ Further evidence is found in war texts where God *himself* is speaking and conveying total-kill ideas but most probably in hyperbolic terms: (1) the woe oracles against the nations, (2) the double-merism language of killing men and women, young and old in reverse holy war against Israel and at times against the nations, and (3) the side-by-side placement of *drive-out* commands that by inference affirm hyperbole in the *total-kill* commands.[27] While the grammatical form varies between these examples, the divine source (God himself speaks), the substance of his total-kill rhetoric, and its intended hyperbolic meaning remain the same.

HYPERBOLE AND THE ETHICS OF ISRAEL'S CONQUEST

A hyperbolic understanding of the total-kill and total-land language of biblical warfare (like that of ANE warfare) texts helps in significant ways to alleviate *some* of the ethical difficulty that contemporary readers sense in these war texts. Hyperbole speaks to the ethics of Israel's war passages based on the evidence presented thus far in at least these ways: (1) reduced severity, (2) no genocide, and (3) an ethical baseline for viewing redemptive elements.

Reduced severity. Not everyone was killed in Israel's battles against the Canaanites, contrary to the war rhetoric of some texts. The ancient audience understood this reality, despite the inflated rhetoric. Saying that biblical accounts contain war hyperbole does not mean that lives were not lost, nor does it mean that noncombatants were never killed. However, it does suggest that Israel's battles were not quite as bloody and brutal as they might at first seem to contemporary readers who understand those words in a literal fashion. To the degree that hyperbolic language translated into Israel *not* killing everyone (and that was acceptable), the ethical tension is reduced.[28]

---

[27]On the woe oracles, see the list above in this chapter. On double-merism language, see chapter ten and appendix C. On the side-by-side placement of *drive-out* commands that by inference affirm hyperbole in the *total-kill* commands, see chapter twelve.

[28]Later chapters will provide evidence for what the gap between rhetoric and reality probably looked like. Most likely to be killed were the enemy king, royal family (to some extent), ruling leaders, and resisting armies (those who continued to fight rather than flee).

No genocide. Israel's warfare should not be considered genocide *in the sense of military action taken to (literally) eliminate an entire ethnic people/ group.*[29] Yes, the rhetoric of Israel's battle language sounds genocidal to us. And it *would* be genocidal if taken literally. But since the inflated war language simply meant a sound defeat of the enemy (as in other ANE war texts), it is inaccurate to label the biblical accounts as genocide. If one insists on labeling Israel's battles as genocide, then we must logically attach the *same* label to all warfare throughout the entire ancient world (chapter eight). Labeling all warfare in the ancient world as genocidal misunderstands the ancient war genre and blunders into a single-horizon and anachronistic ethical assessment.[30]

Ethical baseline within an ANE world. Establishing hyperbole within the biblical text (this chapter) and the ANE world (chapter eight) provides something of an ethical baseline for more detailed comparative work. It provides an ethical starting point for understanding normative war expectations. What it says is that Israel's total-kill and total-land (hyperbole) warfare was much like that of the rest of the ancient world.[31] The use of battle hyperbole and other literary devices in Israel's battle reportage suggests that Israel fought its battles in roughly the same way that other ANE peoples did.[32] The importance of this ethical baseline is that we can now examine, based on what we know of standard war practice, where there is deviation. In short, an ethical baseline allows us to better look at what might be redemptive in Israel's war practices. The more detailed examinations found in chapters five and six (war rape), chapter thirteen (other ancient war atrocities), and chapters fourteen through sixteen (war portraits of Yahweh/Jesus differ from those of ANE war gods) highlight what is ethically redemptive in the biblical war material.

---

[29]Some definitions add (1) "in whole or in part" and (2) "land displacement," etc. These more encompassing definitions of genocide by some moderns would then include much or perhaps all ancient warfare.

[30]See Markus Zehnder, "The Annihilation of the Canaanites: Reassessing the Brutality of the Biblical Witness," in *Encountering Violence in the Bible*, ed. Markus Zehnder and Hallvard Hagelia, The Bible in the Modern World 55 (Sheffield: Sheffield Phoenix Press, 2013), 263-90.

[31]See Walton and Walton, *Lost World of the Israelite Conquest*, 195-211 (proposition 17).

[32]Our argument is focused on the language found in Deuteronomy, Joshua, and Judges here.

CONCLUSION

Recognizing the use of hyperbole and heightened rhetoric in ANE and biblical battle reportage does not completely solve the ethical dilemmas raised by the battles described in the book of Joshua for modern readers of the Bible. It is one of several better answers to ethical problems within the biblical war texts; each answer provides a piece to the ethical puzzle. However, compared to traditional answers that do not work (chapter two) and need to be realigned with the justice questions of the original audience (chapter three), hyperbole is indeed a much better answer. Furthermore, the previous chapter and this one, which set Israel's hyperbolic war rhetoric within its ancient world, tell us that Israel would not likely have had a problem with using common, well-understood inflated language. The issue of using genocide-like language (rhetoric) to indicate a decisive win (reality) would not likely have been on their ethical radar.

If the hyperbole thesis proves true, it holds important implications for questions about the ethics of the conquest accounts in Joshua and Judges. The use of hyperbole in describing Israel's battles against the Canaanites reduces the severity of Israel's actions so that, while lives were undoubtedly lost, not everyone was killed and *genocide did not take place*. Genocide did not take place in the biblical accounts any more than it did in the rest of ANE warfare. Israel fought its wars in much the same way as did other ancient armies. Making a solid case for total-kill language as hyperbole provides an *ethical baseline* within the ancient war horizon from which we can view— within the ancient horizon—where the biblical war actions are markedly different and—thank God (!)—reflect either minor or major (incremental) redemptive movement. These redemptive differences within an ancient world have been explored in chapters four through six with respect to war rape. More redemptive movement will be explored in chapter thirteen on war atrocities and chapters fourteen through sixteen on theological portraits.

10

ARGUMENTS AGAINST HYPERBOLE

DESPITE THE STRENGTH OF THE HYPERBOLE EVIDENCE, some scholars have been unconvinced and have raised arguments in support of a literal (rather than hyperbolic) understanding of the total-kill and total-land conquest language. This chapter aims to answer those arguments. Working on it, much to our surprise, led to strengthening the hyperbole thesis with new evidence that we might otherwise have overlooked. So, while the chapter on the one hand answers objections, on the other hand it also adds evidence for the hyperbole thesis.

ISRAEL WAS DISOBEDIENT IN NOT KILLING (LITERALLY) ALL THE CANAANITES

One argument against hyperbole is the disobedience argument: the continuing presence of Canaanites in already-conquered areas is due to Israel's disobedience to Yahweh's command to annihilate (literally) *all* the Canaanites. Beale contends that failure to annihilate *all* Canaanites equals disobedience when he writes, "This appeal to highly exaggerated claims of defeat [hyperbole] fails to take into consideration that the ongoing presence of the Canaanites in the land was due to Israel's *unfaithfulness* in carrying out God's command to *exterminate them all*. This is apparent from the narrative flow in Joshua and Judges, and is made explicit in Judges."[1] The

---

[1] G. K. Beale, *The Morality of God in the Old Testament*, Christian Answers to Hard Questions (Phillipsburg, NJ: P&R, 2013), 40-41 (italics added). For a similar disobedience/failure argument, see Wes Morriston, "Did God Command Genocide? A Challenge to the Biblical Inerrantist," *Philosophia Christi* 11, no. 1 (2009): 12.

disobedience argument appeals primarily to Judges 2:2-3 (as it relates to the portrayal of Israel's repeated failure to drive out the Canaanites in Judg 1:21-36) and secondarily to Judges 2:10-13, 20-23; Joshua 18:3; 23:12-13.

While the argument that disobedience equals the failure to annihilate (literally) *all* Canaanites sounds plausible, it fails on two grounds. It involves *oversimplification* of Israel's disobedience and, more importantly, *incorrect representation* of what the text states. Let's start with the oversimplification problem.

Oversimplifying levels/types of disobedience. Beale's analysis oversimplifies the issue of disobedience in the biblical text. We agree that the making of covenants with the Canaanites is cast in a negative (disobedience) light in the Judges text:

> The angel of the LORD went up from Gilgal to Bokim and said, "I brought you up out of Egypt and led you into the land I swore to give to your ancestors. I said, 'I will never break my covenant with you, and *you shall not make a covenant with the people of this land, but you shall break down their altars.'* Yet you have disobeyed me. Why have you done this? And I have also said, 'I will not drive them out before you; they will become traps for you, and their gods will become snares to you.'" (Judg 2:1-3)

The command to "not make a covenant" likely refers to making peace treaties with Canaanites residing in the land.[2] Thus the subsequent "you have disobeyed me" statement casts a negative light on Israel's permitting various Canaanite groups to stay as forced labor within the land (Judg 1:28, 30, 33, 35). Up to this point we agree with Beale.

However, the prohibition against covenant making in Judges 2:1-3 is immediately connected to the far more severe problem of Israel not breaking down Canaanite altars. The close connection between "you shall not do this . . . but do this" implies that when Israel made these covenants

---

[2]Judges 2:2-3 should be read in conjunction with Josh 23:11-16, where the issue of marrying Canaanites is explicitly connected with the "covenant" (Josh 23:16) of exclusive worship of Yahweh and not turning to worship other gods. Both in turn relate back to Ex 23:20-33 (compare Ex 34:11-15) but do *not* pick up the explicit extermination language of Deut 7:1-5 (compare Deut 20:16-18) and make disobedience fundamentally about idolatry. See also the emphasis on a covenant of exclusive Yahweh worship in Josh 24:14-27 (especially Josh 24:23-25). On the relationship of Judg 2:2-3 to Ex 23 (and Ex 34) see Daniel I. Block, *Judges, Ruth*, NAC 6 (Nashville: Broadman & Holman, 1999), 115-16.

with Canaanites staying in the land, they wrongly permitted them to continue with their public and communal places of worship to their gods. Therein lies the *deeper* disobedience rub. Had the Israelites destroyed the altars of subservient Canaanite peoples remaining in the land and made the disallowance of Canaanite altars part of their agreement, the issue would not have been the same.

That the biblical authors had a nuanced understanding of different types or levels of disobedience is displayed in at least four ways. First, idolatry is the definition of the *deepest* disobedience in the books of Joshua and Judges. If we trace the theme of disobedience—not listening, doing evil in the eyes of the Lord, sinning, rebelling, provoking Yahweh's anger—throughout Joshua and Judges, we discover that it is almost always related to idolatry.[3] The issue of Canaanites remaining in the land is problematic, but on a much lesser and different level. *Deeper* disobedience is leaving Canaanite idols undestroyed; *deepest* disobedience is worshiping Canaanite gods.[4] This becomes clear in the downward spiral of disobedience in Judges, where it is the repeated worship of Canaanite gods that begins a new cycle of oppression, not the failure to drive out the remaining Canaanites (Judg 2:11-13, 19; 3:5-7; 6:10; 8:33-34; 10:6-7, 10-16; 17:1-6; 18:14-25, 30-31).

---

[3]For a sampling of texts concerning disobedience within Judges, see Judg 2:2-3, 11-13, 17, 19-20; 3:7-8; 6:9-10; 8:27; 10:6-16; see also Judg 17:3-6; 18:14-17, 30-31. For Joshua see Josh 22:16-18; 23:7, 16; 24:14-15. Israel's sin/disobedience in (1) their struggle to drive out (or kill) every single Canaanite was on a completely different level from (2) not tearing down their altars and (3) succumbing to the temptation to worship their gods and the gods of the other nations around them. As a consequence of Israel's idolatry, Yahweh resolved to no longer drive out the peoples left by Joshua (Judg 2:19-23). In fact, "the LORD had *allowed* [*nûaḥ*—Hiphil] those nations to remain; he did not drive them out at once by giving them into the hands of Joshua" (Judg 2:23). They were left to test Israel's obedience to Yahweh's commands and to teach them warfare (Judg 3:1, 4).

[4]Different levels of disobedience can be seen in the evaluation of Israel's kings. Josiah, who does the most to eradicate Canaanite-style worship, is the only king who receives unqualified praise in the book of Kings. Hezekiah receives similar praise for eliminating Canaanite forms of worship (2 Kings 18:1-7, but see also 2 Kings 20:14-19). However, a king could be viewed as *mostly good* (that is, like David) except for leaving Canaanite-style altars and high places (Asa: 1 Kings 15:11-15; Jehoshaphat: 1 Kings 22:43; Joash: 2 Kings 12:2-3; Amaziah: 2 Kings 14:3-4; Azariah = Uzziah: 2 Kings 15:3-4; Jotham: 2 Kings 15:34-35). The kings of Israel perpetuate Jeroboam's sin of worshiping at the altars of Dan and Bethel and at the high places, and they are consistently evaluated negatively in Kings. Judahite kings who furthered Canaanite-style worship such as idolatry and worship at high places are said to do evil in the eyes of Yahweh and are also viewed negatively (2 Kings 16:3; 21:2-8; see also 1 Kings 11:4-10; 14:21-24; 2 Kings 8:18, 26-27; 21:19-22; 23:31-32, 36-37; 24:8-9, 18-19).

Second, remaining Canaanites in the land cannot be viewed on the level of the deeper or deepest disobedience because even within Judges 1 there is variance in this portrait of disobedience. God is said to be "with them"— Judah and Joseph (= Manasseh and Ephraim)—in their battles with the Canaanites, and their thwarted efforts to drive out Canaanites are not viewed as their fault or as overt disobedience.[5]

Third, Canaanite groups are present in the land during the reigns of David and Solomon. Neither David nor Solomon receives even a slap on the wrist for permitting Canaanites to remain in the land.[6] Rather, their utilization of subjugated Canaanites for building the temple as well as for supplying its wood-and-water needs is viewed positively as part of the grandeur of Solomon's kingdom.[7]

Fourth, the greatest litmus test on the question of Canaanites still living in the land is whether God's glory will fill the temple built by Solomon (1 Kings 8:11; 2 Chron 5:14; 7:1-2), *while Canaanites still live in the land* (and before we are told of Solomon putting them to forced labor). There is no rush or pressure to rid the land of all breathing Canaanites before Yahweh can live there. The point is that God chooses to live in the land with Canaanites present: his temple glory sets the bar (not our all-or-nothing, perfectionistic readings of the biblical text) for what it means to create sacred space, or *terra sancta*, within a fallen world (see chapter twelve). All subsequent Davidic

---

[5]While one can make a case for a *lesser level* of drive-out disobedience in the case of the cited forced-labor scenarios in part of Judg 1 (Judg 1:28-36), Judg 1 gives a mixed assessment of the house of Joseph—they fail in some areas (Judg 1:26, 27, 29) but succeed in others (Judg 1:22-25). Judah is largely successful in its efforts. The inability to drive out the Canaanites due to a lack of strength is significantly tempered in both cases by the positive statement that Yahweh is with them (Judg 1:19, 22).

[6]The lack of disapproval by biblical narrators correlates well with the real issue being idolatry and not the ethnicity of any remaining Canaanites.

[7]First Kings 9:20-22 views Solomon's conscription of Canaanite descendants in a positive light and mentions even the Jebusites, whom David did not totally exterminate (in any literal sense) in taking Jerusalem: "There were still people left from the Amorites, Hittites, Perizzites, Hivites and Jebusites (these peoples were not Israelites). Solomon conscripted the descendants of all these peoples remaining in the land—whom the Israelites could not exterminate—to serve as slave labor, as it is to this day. But Solomon did not make slaves of any of the Israelites; they were his fighting men, his government officials, his officers, his captains, and the commanders of his chariots and charioteers." This passage and other statements about forced labor during the days of David and Solomon (2 Sam 20:24; 1 Kings 4:6; 5:14; 9:15) correlate well with the "to this day" statements in Joshua and Judges that specify the ongoing presence of the Canaanites (Josh 9:27; 13:3; 15:63; 16:10), often in a forced-labor role.

kings were measured by whether they followed Yahweh exclusively and wholeheartedly *like David*; this "like David" bar of obedience is never set in terms of the number of Canaanites remaining in the land. Thus the canonical story line develops a clear distinction between (1) the presence of Canaanites and (2) the worship of idols or the need to destroy idols.[8] There is a growing canonical recognition by biblical writers that, while the presence of subjugated Canaanites in the land is/was problematic (a potentially negative influence), it is not a controlling factor in the assessment of David or Solomon's obedience, nor does it make the land impure to the extent that Yahweh's glory cannot reside there.[9] In sum, the notion that Israel was disobedient because they did not (literally) kill *all* the Canaanites disregards the far more nuanced and complex development by the biblical authors.

Misrepresentation of what the biblical text states. Even more problematic in Gregory Beale's handling of the Judges material is his allegation that Israel's disobedience is based on their unwillingness to kill or "exterminate" (Beale's language) every breathing Canaanite in the land. Beale's view simply misrepresents the biblical text. In every text that Beale cites (Judg 2:2-3, 10-13, 20-23; Josh 18:3; 23:12-13) the explicit emphasis is on the need to *drive out* (not kill all) the Canaanites. If the Canaanites wanted to practice their idol worship of Baal, Ashtoreth, and Molek *outside* the land (like all the other nations), they could do so. In other words, Israel was just as obedient to Yahweh by pushing the Canaanites outside the sacred space that he wanted to create. (See chapter twelve on drive-out equivalency.)

To make his disobedience argument work, Beale must find passages in Joshua and Judges where a lack of (literal) *total extermination* equals

---

[8]For example, it appears that although David takes the city of Jerusalem (1 Chron 11:4, 6), he does not totally drive out or kill (literally) all the Jebusites in Jerusalem (1 Kings 9:20; 1 Chron 21:15, 18, 28; 2 Chron 8:7; Ezra 9:1; Zech 9:7; see Josh 15:63; Judg 1:21). Ultimately the Jebusites are absorbed into Israel.

[9]This later canonical clarity begins to emerge in the Joshua texts themselves. Even at that early stage in biblical war texts the original audience would have realized that there was not a *necessary* connection between Israel's obedience and/or disobedience and the number of still-breathing Canaanites in the land. After the complete central, south, and north conquest, the generation that enters with Joshua and Caleb lives obediently for many years with the presence of numerous Canaanites. Thus, obedience does not mean killing every Canaanite. However, the next generation lives disobediently with the presence of Canaanites because they adopt idolatrous worship practices and break their covenant of exclusive worship with Yahweh. For the contrast in obedience between the two generations, see Judg 2:7-13.

disobedience. A case could be made for *drive-out* disobedience (although levels of disobedience and canonical development make it a faulty argument against hyperbole). Nevertheless, such a case cannot be made for *total kill.* Judges *never* condemns Joshua for failing to fully eliminate or completely exterminate the Canaanites.[10] Instead, we are told—in contrast to Israel's behavior under the judges—"The people served the LORD throughout the lifetime of Joshua and of the elders who outlived him" (Judg 2:7; see also Josh 24:31).[11] Similarly, Israel's failure to kill all the Canaanites is *never* condemned in the book of Joshua.[12] To the contrary, the book of Joshua goes out of its way to highlight Joshua's *complete obedience* to the words of Yahweh and to the instructions of Moses (Josh 8:30-31; 11:15), even bestowing on Joshua the honorific title "servant of Yahweh" after his death, a title reserved elsewhere in the Old Testament only for the likes of Moses (e.g., Deut 34:5) and David (e.g., Ps 18:1).[13] In short, the books of Joshua and Judges level no charge of disobedience for failing to eliminate all the Canaanites.[14]

---

[10]This silence about disobedience corresponds to where the narrator clearly speaks of obedience (Judg 2:6-10; Josh 4:10, 14; 8:35; 11:12, 15, 23). One might expect silence on this matter because the explicit badge of obedience is that they have accomplished what they understood as the purpose of the total-kill language. On the contrast between Joshua's leadership and the succeeding generations in Judges 2, see Dennis T. Olson, "The Book of Judges," in *The New Interpreter's Bible*, vol 2 (Nashville: Abingdon, 1998), 752-53.

[11]Yahweh intentionally does not give the Canaanites into Joshua's hands (Judg 2:23); they are left to teach the Israelites warfare after Joshua (Judg 3:1-2) and to test their obedience, especially with respect to intermarriage and idolatry (Judg 2:19-23; 3:4-5). This gradual conquest of the land is anticipated in Ex 23:30; Deut 7:22, but more reasons are added as the story line progresses.

[12]One might wonder whether the narrator's silence is implied and not explicitly stated. However, the silence on disobedience correlates with the narrator's positive evaluations of Joshua throughout the books of Joshua and Judges. Even Joshua's covenant with the Gibeonites (Josh 9) is not expressly condemned, despite the warning in Deut 7:2.

[13]Israel's obedience is emphasized even more by the account of Achan's disobedience (Josh 7), for that event highlights the consequences of disobedience to Yahweh's *herem*-warfare protocols.

[14]Beyond the two main issues we have already discussed, arguing that all Canaanites had to be killed in order for Israel to be obedient has other difficulties. First, it tends wrongly to collapse the ideas of temptation and sin. Of course, it would have been safer to a degree to eliminate the temptation. Temptation and sin are related, but they are separated by human choice. Israel chooses to succumb to the allure of Canaanite worship during the tenure of many of the judges and kings; Israel also chooses not to succumb during the days of Joshua and Caleb and the days of a few judges and kings. Second, the biblical authors identify other temptations and sins as part of living in the desert (for example, grumbling because of lack of food or water) and in the Promised Land (for example, much food and wealth turning people away from God). Warnings related to these temptations should not be equated with

THE FOUR CONQUEST-SUMMARY STATEMENTS
ARE LITERAL (NOT HYPERBOLE)

In the previous chapter we argued for recognition of extent hyperbole and severity hyperbole. Joshua's statements about conquering *all* the land and killing *all* the people in the land should be understood in a hyperbolic (not literal) manner. Alternatively, Beale understands the four major "all the land" conquest statements in the book of Joshua—Joshua 10:40-43; 11:16-18, 23; 21:43-45—in a literal (not hyperbolic) manner. While the evidence for extent and severity hyperbole is much broader than these four summary statements, this is a good place to test Beale's literal total-land conquest view. The four conquest-summary statements in Joshua are as follows (with certain "all" and "none" language highlighted):

Summary statement one: Central + southern campaigns

1. Joshua 10:40-43: So Joshua subdued *the whole region* [*kol hāʾāreṣ*], including the hill country, the Negev, the western foothills and the mountain slopes, together with *all their kings* [*kol malkêhem*]. He left *no survivors* [*lōʾ hišʾîr śārîd*]. He totally destroyed *all who breathed* [*kol hannəšāmâ*], just as the LORD, the God of Israel, had commanded. Joshua subdued them from Kadesh Barnea to Gaza and from the whole region of Goshen to Gibeon. *All these kings and their lands* [*kol hamməlākîm hāʾēlleh wəʾet-ʾarṣām*] Joshua conquered in one campaign, because the LORD, the God of Israel, fought for Israel. Then Joshua returned with all Israel to the camp at Gilgal.

---

disobedience. Total elimination of the Canaanites would not have guaranteed Israelite faithfulness. Third, Israel is also influenced toward idolatry (and other temptations—wanting a king, etc.) by nations *outside* the land. Killing or driving out every Canaanite from *within* the land would not have been a magical fix for the problem of idolatry. Conquering and taking enough of the land, cities, and ruling elite meant that Israel would have sufficient strength to destroy Canaanite idols and at least resist intermarriage. But it was not automatic. The Israelites are obviously influenced toward both idolatry and intermarriage by the nations around them just as much as (if not more than) by the Canaanites who remain in the land (note the wives chosen by Solomon). Fourth, taking the land is also viewed positively as a *gift and inheritance* for Israel. Having less of the gift (land possession) than Israel would have liked makes it odd to view failing to drive out as categorical disobedience. Accordingly, surviving Canaanites in the land are often viewed by the biblical authors as a *struggle* (not disobedience on the level of idolatry) for Israel's hope to achieve their much-longed-for inheritance, whether during the days of Joshua and Caleb, the judges, the kings, or the postexilic community.

Summary statements two, three, and four: Central + southern + northern campaigns

2. Joshua 11:16-18: So Joshua took *this entire land* [*kol hā'āreṣ hazzō't*]: the hill country, all the Negev, the whole region of Goshen, the western foothills, the Arabah and the mountains of Israel with their foothills, from Mount Halak, which rises toward Seir, to Baal Gad in the Valley of Lebanon below Mount Hermon. He captured *all their kings* [*kol malkêhem*] and put them to death. Joshua waged war against *all these kings* [*kol hamməlākîm hā'ēlleh*] for a long time.

3. Joshua 11:23: So Joshua took *the entire land* [*kol hā'āreṣ*], just as the LORD had directed Moses, and he gave it as an inheritance to Israel according to their tribal divisions. Then the land had rest from war.

4. Joshua 21:43-45: So the LORD gave Israel *all the land* [*kol hā'āreṣ*] he had sworn to give their ancestors, and they took possession of it and settled there. The LORD gave them rest on every side, just as he had sworn to their ancestors. *Not one of their enemies* [*wəlō' 'āmad 'îš bipnêhem mikkol-'ōyəbêhem*] withstood them; the LORD gave *all their enemies* [*kol 'ōyəbêhem*] into their hands. Not one of all the LORD's good promises to Israel failed; every one was fulfilled.

As we discuss the total-land conquest language, it will be helpful to flip back to these four summary texts.

Beale uses two strategies to argue for a literal understanding of the total-land conquest language in these four summary statements. His two strategies are (1) *limited geography* and (2) an *already-and-not-yet* perspective. The first strategy he applies to the first summary statement, the second strategy to the latter three summary statements.

Limited geography (summary statement one): "To that point" summary. In arguing for a literal understanding of the total-land conquest language Beale, in the case of the first summary statement, limits the geographical referent. He views this statement as an "up to that point" summary in the conquest narrative. In other words, Joshua 10:40-43 functions as a summary of the central and southern campaigns but not the northern campaign. Beale argues that "the whole region" in Joshua 10:40 refers to only the central and southern campaigns covered earlier in the book, since this first summary (1) comes immediately after the listing of southern cities and kings conquered in Joshua 10:29-39 and (2) comes just before the northern campaign begins to take shape in Joshua 11:1-5. Furthermore, (3) the place names mentioned in summary statement one focus predominantly on central and southern regions and not northern regions.[15] So the geography in the first summary statement must be understood in a limited sense because other unconquered regions are mentioned immediately after that: "Joshua 11:1-5 reveals other areas not mentioned in 10:40-42 [summary statement one] that Joshua had not yet engaged in battle. Since 11:1-5 follows right on the heels of 10:40-42, it is likely that the language of the latter is to be understood in a more limited manner than referring to every single part of the Promised Land."[16]

We agree that it makes good sense to understand "all the land" in this summary statement within the flow of the narrative and as expressing complete or total-land conquest to that point in the story line. Along these same lines (contra Beale), the other three summary statements *also* need to be understood as "to that point" summaries within the narrative flow. More about that in a moment.

The recognition, with which we agree, that the first summary statement is talking about a limited area of land, however, does nothing to support taking the total-land conquest language literally. Even with the perspective that summary statement one is speaking in terms of limited geography or up to that point, the author of Joshua *still* intends his "all the land" language (Josh 10:40) in a hyperbolic manner. We know this because some cities included in the central and southern total-land-conquest campaigns need to be reconquered later.[17] To say "Not one city or area cited as defeated in Joshua 10–11 is mentioned in these following chapters" is simply incorrect.[18] The *total*-land and *total*-kill language in Joshua 10:40 with its fourfold punch ("the whole region" and "all their kings [/cities]"; "no survivors" and "all who breathed"), even with the reduced-geography perspective in summary statement one, should be

---

[15]Beale, *Morality of God*, 34-35.

[16]Beale, *Morality of God*, 34-35.

[17]Gaza (Josh 10:41; see Josh 11:21-22), Debir (Josh 10:38-39; see Josh 15:15-16), Hebron (Josh 10:37; see Josh 15:13-14); see summary-statement recap below.

[18]Beale, *Morality of God*, 35.

understood as hyperbolic descriptions of conquest within the region covering the central and southern regions (but not northern).[19]

Already-not-yet summaries (summary statements two, three, and four): Let's include future conquests. Since the next three summary statements involve all of Israel's campaigns within the land (central, southern, and northern) during Joshua's lifetime, Beale argues that "all the land" conquered in the other three summary statements should be taken in a literal sense. He appeals to the biblical phenomenon of already-and-not-yet fulfillments. In other words, these conquest statements include as their referential meaning not only the conquest under Joshua but also all future Israelite battles against the Canaanites—for example, the conquest battles fought by King David. If the summary statements in Joshua 11:16-17 (statement two), Joshua 11:23 (statement three), and Joshua 21:43-45 (statement four) were in fact meant to include all future battles to the point of David and Solomon, then Beale would come closer to his literal (not hyperbolic) understanding, though not completely there.[20]

However, an already-and-not-yet perspective on certain of Joshua's summary statements (statements two through four) suffers serious problems. First, even if already-and-not-yet thinking could explain how to understand these summaries, it would not support seeing complete extermination (or even driving out) of the Canaanites in the conquered regions. First Kings 9:20-22 states that neither David nor Solomon (literally) exterminates or drives out all the Canaanite groups in the Promised Land. Instead, Solomon conscripts the remaining Amorites, Hittites, Perizzites, Hivites, and Jebusites for slave labor. So a literal fulfillment (total kill of *all* Canaanites) *never* happened, even in David and Solomon's day. While a pattern-type fulfillment does happen in the eschaton (the ultimate new Eden), in that final day the land parameters have shifted to the whole earth, and the Canaanites are no

---

[19]Consider the conclusion of K. Lawson Younger Jr. about Josh 10:40-42: "The phrase 'all the land' must be understood as hyperbole. The claims to conquest have been overstated. This is a very similar situation in the vast majority of ancient Near Eastern conquest accounts" (*Ancient Conquest Accounts: A Study in Ancient Near Eastern and Biblical History Writing,* JSOTSup 98 [Sheffield: Sheffield Academic Press, 1990], 244; see also 241-47).

[20]The last mention of ethnic Canaanites in the land is during the reign of Solomon (1 Kings 11:20-21; 2 Chron 8:7). Other later biblical references to the Canaanites are either figurative (e.g., Zech 14:21) or references to the historical past (e.g., Neh 9:8).

longer defined ethnically. They are literary Canaanites (see chapter three). This sort of pattern fulfillment is hardly literal (something needed for literal reading of the Joshua summaries), and its meaning has moved far from what the author of Joshua envisions with these summary statements.

Second, the best way to understand the latter three summary statements is within the literary flow of the Joshua narrative. In short, they each look backward as summary statements about Joshua's land conquest (not forward to David's conquests). They recap what has already happened up until that point in the narrative flow. Note the overlapping king and geographical links between summary statements one and two:

> So Joshua subdued the whole region, including the hill country, the Negev, the western foothills and the mountain slopes, together with *all their kings*. He left no survivors. He totally destroyed all who breathed, just as the LORD, the God of Israel, had commanded. Joshua subdued them from Kadesh Barnea to Gaza and from the whole region of Goshen to Gibeon. *All these kings and their lands* Joshua conquered in one campaign, because the LORD, the God of Israel, fought for Israel. Then Joshua returned with all Israel to the camp at Gilgal. (Josh 10:40-43)

> So Joshua took this entire land: the hill country, all the Negev, the whole region of Goshen, the western foothills, the Arabah and the mountains of Israel with their foothills, from Mount Halak, which rises toward Seir, to Baal Gad in the Valley of Lebanon below Mount Hermon. He captured *all their kings* and put them to death. Joshua waged war against *all these kings* for a long time. (Josh 11:16-18)

The place names and slain kings mentioned in the second statement provide an overlapping historical link with the first statement (concerning the central and southern regions) and extend the conquest to include the northern region. In turn, these two summary statements anticipate the similar list of slain kings and captured cities in Joshua 12—from the king of Jericho (the first) to the king of Tirzah (the last). Joshua's total-land and total-people conquest covered the regions belonging to thirty-one kings. The referential meaning of the four summary statements is rooted in the king-city-land list of Joshua 12, which picks up on earlier material (especially Josh 10:28-39) and summarizes conquest actions mentioned earlier in the book. All four

summary statements about conquering the Promised Land rehearse conquest activities under Joshua (not under David or Solomon).

Joshua's summary statements cover both the extent and the severity of
Israel's actions. Joshua 10:40 says that Israel "left no survivors," destroyed "all
who breathed," and "subdued the whole region." Beale interprets this as Israel
killing "the majority" of living beings in all the parts of Canaan that Joshua
attacked.[21] But leaving "no survivors," as the biblical text says, if taken literally, is very different from killing the majority of living beings.[22] These
adjustments to the Joshua text within Beale's view signal the failure of his
quest for literal renderings.

Moreover, even within the areas mentioned in the summary statements,
survivors and cities need to be reconquered or remain unconquered. In
maintaining that the summary statements of Joshua do not contain any hyperbole but refer to complete conquest only of cities in the area specifically
mentioned, Beale writes, "Significantly, not one city or area cited as defeated
in Joshua 10–11 is mentioned in the following chapters. . . . The language is
describing complete and decisive defeats in the particular areas cited but
that such defeats did not include other areas and cities cited later in Joshua
and Judges."[23] However, as we have already seen, the evidence does not bear
out Beale's claims.

Recapping the summary-statement evidence. In short, evidence for
understanding all four summary statements in a hyperbolic manner includes
the following. Joshua 10:40-42 summarizes Israel's conquest primarily in the
southern parts of Canaan, saying that Israel conquered the entire region and
left no survivors. Specific instances in Joshua 10 seem to bear this out at first.
Joshua 10:36-37 says that Israel captured the city of Hebron, totally destroying
it and leaving "no survivors," while Joshua 10:38-39 says they did the same to
Debir. Moreover, Joshua 10:33 indicates that Israel completely defeated
Horam king of Gezer so that "no survivors were left" of his army. However,
just five chapters later, Joshua 15:13-14 says that Caleb must drive the Anakites

---

[21]Beale, *Morality of God*, 34.
[22]One wonders whether the majority language on Beale's part was simply an oversight. After
all, *majority* can mean anything over 50 percent. Beale provides no explanation for using
the term *majority*.
[23]Beale, *Morality of God*, 35.

out of Hebron (despite the claims in Josh 11:21-22 stating that Joshua destroyed the Anakites in Hebron and Debir). Similarly, Joshua 15:15-17 indicates that Othniel, Caleb's relative, must reconquer Debir to win the hand of Caleb's daughter Achsah. Clearly there were more than a few stray survivors in these cities, despite statements indicating Israel had left no survivors.

Moreover, Joshua 16:10 says that the Ephraimites were unable to dislodge the Canaanites living in Gezer, even though Joshua 10:33 says that Israel had completely destroyed its king and his army. It is unlikely that a new king could rebuild the army of the city of Gezer quickly enough to hold out "to this day" of the later author (Josh 16:10) against the powerful tribe of Ephraim just a short while after being completely wiped out. In this light, even within just the southern reaches of the land of Canaan (i.e., the area to which the summary statement in Josh 10:40-42 refers) there are cities with enough survivors that they must be reconquered just a little later in the book of Joshua. A literal reading of Joshua 10:40-42 claiming total-land conquest and no survivors does not mesh with this evidence. A reading that factors in extent and severity hyperbole upholds the truth of the claims of Joshua 10:40-42 while also allowing for survivors later in the book.

A similar argument can be made for the summary statement in Joshua 11:16-18 (statement two), which summarizes Israel's conquest of the combined northern and southern reaches of the land, saying, "Joshua took the entire land." Joshua 11:11, 13 says that in Joshua's northern campaign, Israel exercised total-kill warfare against Hazor, killing every living thing in the city and burning it to the ground. Yet Jabin, the king of Canaan who reigned in Hazor, was strong enough to marshal a force of nine hundred chariots to fight Israel in the days of the judges Deborah and Barak (Judg 4:2-3). The continued existence of Canaanites in these cities that were completely destroyed counters Beale's claims and shows that cities and areas conquered by Joshua needed to be reconquered not long after Israel is said to have completely destroyed them. The continued existence of Canaanites in cities belonging to the areas referenced in the summary statements of Joshua 10:40-42; 11:16-18 is thus best explained by extent and severity hyperbole.

The summary statement in Joshua 11:23 (statement three) is closely linked to the previous summary in Joshua 11:16-18, for both follow the central, southern, and northern campaigns, and the phrase "Joshua took [this] entire land" forms an inclusio, or envelope, around these two passages, linking the two summaries. Joshua 11:21-22 relates additional information about Israel's conquest and the Anakites, which took place "at that time," that is, at the same time as the events described earlier.[24] The book of Joshua again emphasizes their complete destruction and their total elimination from within Israel (except from Gaza, Gath, and Ashdod):[25]

> At that time Joshua went and *destroyed the Anakites* from the hill country: from Hebron, Debir and Anab [notice Hebron in this "all the hill country" list], from *all the hill country* of Judah, and from *all the hill country* of Israel. Joshua *totally destroyed them and their towns. No Anakites were left in Israelite territory*; only in Gaza, Gath and Ashdod did any survive. (Josh 11:21-22)

The summary that follows in Joshua 11:23 again relates the entire conquest of the land (now, in case there was any question, including the dreaded Anakites). But this summary too includes hyperbole, for when the land is apportioned later in the book, Caleb must still drive Anakites out of Hebron, even though Joshua 10:36-37 says that the city was completely destroyed, and even though the summary in Joshua 11:23 says that Israel took the entire land, and even though Joshua 11:21-22 says that *no Anakites* were left in Israelite territory and specifies that none were left in Hebron. Thus, the summary statement in Joshua 11:23 also contains extent and severity hyperbole.

The final summary statement, in Joshua 21:43-45, says not only that Yahweh gave the Israelites all the Promised Land but that Israel had taken possession of it and that none of their enemies stood up against them. This

---

[24]See R. Hubbard, *Joshua*, NIVAC (Grand Rapids: Zondervan, 2009), 332-33. The Anakites are regarded as particularly fearsome, in part because of their extraordinary height (see Num 13:22-33; Deut 2:21; 9:2); they were descended from the Nephilim (Num 13:33).

[25]Even the highlighted/explicit exceptions (Gaza, Gath, and Ashdod) provide unambiguous evidence from the biblical author that the "totally destroyed" and "no survivors" war language within these verses is hyperbolic and should not be taken literally. The exceptions right after total-destruction language (Josh 11:21-22), and the fact that the author immediately returns to more total-destruction language, which enfolds those exceptions (Josh 11:23)—without a whit of pause—show that the language should not be taken literally. Had the biblical author wanted to write this war account in a literal fashion, it would have required removing the emotive element of hyperbole and changing significant parts of the wording to a far less emotive wording than what we encounter: "*all* the hill country" (Josh 11:21; 2×), "*totally* destroyed" (Josh 11:21), "*no* Anakites" (Josh 11:22), "the *entire* [*all* the] land" (Josh 11:23). But that is not how impassioned biblical authors wrote battle narratives.

statement is appropriate, for it summarizes both the conquest portion of the book (Josh 1–12) and the portion relating the distribution and possession of the land (Josh 13–21). But this summary also contains hyperbole, for even in the land-distribution phase of the conquest, the book of Joshua mentions enemies whom Israel was unable to conquer (even though Josh 21:44 says that none of their enemies stood up against them). Unconquered resistance against Israel is clear. Canaanites of Geshur and Maakah, Jerusalem, Gezer, Beth Shan, Ibleam, Dor, Endor, Taanach, and Megiddo (Josh 13:13; 15:63; 16:10; 17:13, 18) all resisted attempts to possess their towns and remained as holdouts in the land. Again, arguments for a literal (no hyperbole) reading of the summary statements cannot hold. The evidence simply does not support a literal reading of any of the summary statements.

YOUNG/OLD, MAN/WOMAN PAIRING LANGUAGE IS LITERAL (NOT HYPERBOLE)

Biblical authors at times use double-paired terms—old/young and men/women—either in killing instructions or in descriptions of the results of Israel's warfare. Similar triads—men, women, and children—at times describe their total-kill war destruction. Double-pairing (and triad) language is part of the way biblical texts portray Joshua's conquest battles and later battles under Saul and David—the classic case is 1 Samuel 15:3.

Beale contends that the language about killing "young and old" and "man and woman" in the war texts should be understood literally and not as hyperbolic descriptions of a decisive battle.[26] He appeals to Deuteronomy 20:10-18, which allows Israel to spare noncombatant women and children *outside* the borders of the Promised Land but not *inside* its borders. Also, for Beale, Deuteronomy 2:34; 3:3-7, which describe the destruction of women and children earlier in Deuteronomy's battle accounts, support this literal perspective.[27] Our response to his literal understanding of the old/young,

---

[26]We agree with Beale in part. These are figures of speech (merisms), and their usage in themselves does not automatically imply hyperbole. Other contextual evidence must be used to affirm hyperbole.

[27]Beale argues here against Paul Copan, *Is God a Moral Monster?: Making Sense of the Old Testament God* (Grand Rapids: Baker, 2011), 175-77. Beale, *Morality of God*, 38, also points to support from Josh 7:24; 1 Sam 22:19, and probably also Josh 6:21; 1 Sam 15:3.

man/woman pairings will examine the nature of these pairings in Deuteronomy 20:10-18; 2:34; 3:3-7, and four other passages.

Figures of speech: old/young, men/women pairings as merisms.
Merisms are figures of speech where two polar terms stand in place of the whole. The paired expression "old and young" means old, young, and everything in between—all ages. "Men and women" means all/both genders. A combination of these two merisms thus means *every living human being* within the writer's focus.[28] We might have guessed this expansive or totality definition, since the other total-kill language that we have looked at is equally encompassing: *all* that breathes, *no* survivors, *all/every* Canaanite, *all* the land. The merisms old/young and men/woman are simply alternative expressions for "every breathing person"—part of the hyperbolic war vocabulary we have already considered. Given the extensive evidence already presented in favor of taking these other totalistic war statements as hyperbolic, perhaps we should (contra Beale) at least be open, if not predisposed, toward taking them also as hyperbole. Nevertheless, let us unpack the evidence further.

Seven passages employing merisms. After citing the entire text of Deuteronomy 20:10-18 as the prime example of merism/triad language (men, women, and children) that should be taken literally, Beale claims that Deuteronomy 2:34; 3:3-7, and four other passages—a total of seven biblical texts—should in like manner either "clearly" or "probably" be understood as calling for or describing the literal killing of *all* men, women, and children. He writes as follows:

> [After citing the full text of *Deut 20:10-18* . . .] It is clear that in cities farther
> out from the Palestinian area, the latter to be given as an inheritance to Israel,
> "the women and the children and the animals and all that is in the city" could
> be spared and taken as spoils by Israel. But in the nearby land of the Canaanites,
> Israel was "not [to] leave alive anything that breathes." Therefore, when *Deuteronomy 2:34* and *3:6* say that not only the "men" but also the "women and
> children" in every city, who were "breathing" beings, were to be "utterly destroyed," the reference to the women and children should be taken literally, not
> figuratively [hyperbole] (as is clearly the case also in *Joshua 7:24* and *1 Samuel*

---

[28]The triadic expression "man, woman, and child" means roughly the same thing (every living human being) because it covers both age and gender variations across the three terms.

22:19, and probably also in *Joshua 6:21* and *1 Samuel 15:3*, where a literal interpretation is best). This indicates that both literal men, elderly people, women, children, and animals were to be destroyed in these close-lying cities. Thus, "women and children" is not figurative [hyperbole] in these expressions for extermination but is literally meant.[29]

We will explore these seven texts by moving from where we agree with Beale's literal assessment (two texts) to where we disagree (five texts).

Joshua 7:24: Yes, literal, but. We agree that stoning and then burning Achan, his "sons and daughters," and "all that he had [belonging to him]" (Josh 7:24) should be understood literally. The pairing of "sons and daughters" in that context likely stands for his whole family. This one case does not, however, prove literalism in every usage of paired merisms (or triads) within the biblical war texts, especially since the Achan case has features that undermine holy war literalism. First, Yahweh's announcement of what happened in Israel's loss of the first battle against Ai displays the same *ḥērem* label of "complete destruction" that is used against the Canaanites: "That is why the Israelites cannot stand against their enemies; they turn their backs and run because they have been made *liable to destruction [laḥērem]*" (Josh 7:12). Yet the whole of Israel was not destroyed. Not even the whole army was wiped out. Rather, Israel suffered a relatively minor military loss (only thirty-six out of three thousand men died).

Second, when the real culprit(s)—the person(s) most responsible for the wrongful/rebellious actions—are caught and punished (death for the instigator[s] and often his/their immediate families), there is a sense that sufficient punishment for the crime has been completed. The part (Achan's punishment and Israel's minor war losses) stands as sufficient for the whole (all Israel punished). We will discover in appendixes A and D that this kind of collectivism helps bridge the tension between (1) total-kill *rhetoric* that references all the people/population and (2) the corresponding *reality* of destruction aimed at the persons most responsible and their immediate

---

[29]Beale, *Morality of God*, 38 (italics added). For sake of clarity we have inserted in the word *hyperbole* in square brackets where Beale uses the wording "figuratively" and "figurative." We are reasonably certain that Beale would agree that "old/young" and "man/woman" are figures of speech called merisms. In this quote he is using the term *figurative[ly]* to mean "hyperbole."

families. The literal phenomenon of killing Achan's immediate family along with the actual perpetrator of the crime (Achan) is a typical ANE way of making a pronounced and severe judgment statement (see appendix D). It also exhibits a type of collective thinking that, while foreign to moderns, is essential to understanding biblical war texts, where the killing of some could be thought of as destroying an entire nation.

First Samuel 22:19: Yes, literal, but. Driven by almost insane hatred for David and the priests who help him, Saul entrusts a foreigner—Doeg the Edomite (no Israelite would attack the priests)—with performing the heinous act of killing eighty-five priests and later their families: "men and women, its children and infants." After Doeg slaughters the priests who committed the "crime" of helping David, he travels from Gibeah to Nob and kills their families. Here the double merism is likely literal. At least one person, Abiathar, escapes and joins David (1 Sam 22:20), and it is possible that more family members escape.[30] But the narrator mentions only Abiathar. Even if others escaped, it was Saul's intention to literally kill all eighty-five priests and all their families living in Nob. Treason in the ANE world was frequently punished in this manner—killing the persons and their families.

Nevertheless, even though the double merisms are correctly understood literally in 1 Samuel 22:19, this does not substantially support asserting that such double-merism language is literal within the holy war texts. Several considerations are important. First, the context is a king's judgment against local/Israelite "criminals" for alleged treason, not holy war against a foreign nation.[31] Saul's judgment is limited to eighty-five priests plus their families (the focus of the text); it is a pronounced-severity, collective-punishment scenario that was well known in the ANE world, particularly for the crime of treason.[32] Appendix D provides numerous examples where the punishment of key leaders is extended to their

---

[30]The text does not say that only Abiathar escapes. His escape could be representative of others. Given that none of Saul's (Israelite) officials are willing to kill the assembled priests (Saul's own officials and guards are insubordinate to his enraged commands!), it is possible that word of the killings in Gibeah reaches the town of Nob (well before the Edomite Doeg did) and that others escape as well.

[31]The biblical narrator obviously does not believe this is a case of treason.

[32]First Samuel 22 seems to focus primarily on killing the *families* of the priests who came at Saul's request: "You will surely die, Ahimelek, you and your whole family" (1 Sam 22:16); "Nob, the town of the [eighty-five] priests" (1 Sam 22:18-19); "Saul had killed the priests of the Lord" (1 Sam 22:21); "the death of your [Abiathar's] whole family" (1 Sam 22:22).

immediate families but not to entire populations. It makes a statement of control to the larger population but does not include them. These severe punishments of perpetrator(s) and their family(ies) were typically enacted against a limited number of leaders or prime instigators and not literally against the entire population base. With the leaders and their families put to death, such killings often enabled broader social control but did not necessitate wiping out whole nations composed of many cities.

Second, the cause is Saul's personal vendetta and, from the biblical narrator's point of view, a pseudo-judgment that is wholly illegitimate. Saul's evil killing rampage against the priests who helped David is not biblical holy war. Saul continues to spiral morally downward here into even deeper darkness than the actions that led to his rejection by Samuel and Yahweh (1 Sam 15); the narrator views Saul's killings in an entirely negative, shameful, and immoral light. So we need to be careful about bringing this story about a crazed king's evil killing with its double merisms into an equation with Israel's holy war actions that are directed by Yahweh.

Third, unlike the Saul case, within Yahweh's war initiatives (viewed *positively* by the biblical authors) the double-merism descriptions—old/young, men/women—are intended in a hyperbolic (not literal) fashion. Saul's actions are not a part of Yahweh-sanctioned holy war. Unlike Saul, Yahweh war never intends for Israel to carry out (literally) total-kill destruction; the totalistic language conveys significant defeat and an important emotive component.

We now turn to five Yahweh war texts where the evidence favors understanding the language of double merisms (or triads) as hyperbole.

Deuteronomy 20:13, 15 within Deuteronomy 20:10-18: Hyperbole. In Deuteronomy 20:10-18 two important "all" statements require attention in the process of understanding the use of double merisms in this section. When cities outside the land refuse to submit to forced labor for Israel and reject Israel's peace (at a price) agreement, Israelite warriors are instructed to "put to the sword *all* [*kol*] the men in it" (Deut 20:13) and to do so in such cases with "*all* [*kol*] the cities" outside the Promised Land. Are Israelite warriors under a moral obligation to kill (literally) *every* adult male in (literally) *every* resistant city outside the land of Israel? Our answer: no. There is good reason for taking this war instruction about killing *all* men in *all* such non-Canaanite cities

(Deut 20:13, 15) as hyperbole. First, one must ask whether this ever happened in any of Israel's battles with non-Canaanite cities or nations beyond the boundaries of the Promised Land. Again, the answer is no, we have no indicators that this ever happened in Israelite military encounters with those outside the land of Israel who would not accept paying tribute (agreements to peace at a price).[33] When Yahweh war is extended to foreign nations beyond Israel the double-merism language is used but clearly with a hyperbolic sense.

Second, the instruction to kill (literally) *all* adult males when Israel fights against cities outside the land is best understood as hyperbole for killing any male who fights in the battle (the armies) along with the key decision makers (the king and supporting leaders). It makes little sense to understand Israelite warriors as required to kill anyone other than those who would threaten an agreement to forced labor or tribute payment. After all, forced labor was the explicitly stated objective of these subjugation battles (Deut 20:11), and that language strongly shapes the meaning of all other particulars. Not every shepherd, gardener, scribe, lame person, or aged male threatened the functional objective of this war battle; to kill all adult males would have been profoundly counterproductive. We need to place the *reality-based goals or objectives* (a good tape measure for discerning literal intent) up against the *heightened rhetoric* of how to accomplish those goals.[34]

---

[33]For Israel's battles against foreign nations *outside* the land see Judg 3:7-11; 2 Sam 8:2, 11-14; 10:1-14 // 1 Chron 19:1-15; 2 Sam 10:15-19 // 1 Chron 19:16-19; 2 Sam 12:29-30 // 1 Chron 20:1-3; 1 Kings 11:15-17; 22:29-40; 2 Kings 3:1-27; 8:20-22 // 2 Chron 21:8-10; 2 Kings 8:28 // 2 Chron 22:5-6; 1 Chron 5:10, 19-22; 18:1-2, 3-9, 12-13; 2 Chron 20:7; 25:11-12, 14-15; 27:5 // 2 Kings 14:7; Is 11:14. In most of these examples the larger male population is left alive and subjected to sending tribute to Israel and/or forced labor. On one occasion a significant number of males are killed, but not the entire population of adult males. In the killing of Moabite men (2 Sam 8:2), David lets every third one live, and this figure should likely be further limited beyond the stated two-to-three kill ratio to either the captured army or men of fighting age. David's garrisons in Edom and the Aramean kingdom of Damascus further indicate that there was no (literal) total slaughter of the male adult population. Only one case—Joab killing "all the men in Edom" (1 Kings 11:15)—comes even close in its language to Deut 20:10-15. However, this single example that is close to Deuteronomy ought to be understood as hyperbole because, only a short time later, Hadad the Edomite is able to gather enough Edomite military men to serve as a thorn in Solomon's side (1 Kings 11:17-22). In sum, the wars of Israel outside the land support taking the two "all" statements in Deut 20:13, 15 as hyperbole and functionally related to subduing nations so that they send tribute and/or provide forced labor. Killing all the adult males was never intended in a literal sense.

[34]Beyond explicit statements about subjugating by forced labor in the biblical text, this post-battle reality fits well within the norms of the ANE world. See the discussion on enslaved captives in references in chapters six and thirteen.

Third, the evidence we have amassed for total-kill and total-land hyperbole in Joshua's battles inside the land helps our understanding of similar instructions outside the land (Deut 20:13, 15). If biblical authors understood total-kill and total-land war language *inside* the land as hyperbolic, that sheds light on instructions for killing all adult males in warfare *outside* the land.[35] Here is why. For warfare inside the land, Israel's war objectives include the establishment of *terra sancta*, or sacred space (see chapter twelve). If Israel understood its total-kill language inside the land in a hyperbolic and functional sense where *terra sancta* was at stake, how much more does such hyperbolic and functional meaning (related to lesser goals) play a role in the directives for war outside the land? Finally, to recognize the killing component of Deuteronomy 20:13, 15 for outside the land in a functional (i.e., goal related) and hyperbolic sense undermines the argument contrasting inside against outside the land for taking the killing of (literally) all "men, women, and children [implied triad]" as required within the land. If the killing component on one side of the border is understood in a nonliteral sense, that tilts the likelihood of the meaning on the other side of the border in a similar nonliteral direction.

Deuteronomy 2:34; 3:6; 20:10-18: Hyperbole. Three Deuteronomy texts either explicitly (Deut 2:34; 3:6) or implicitly (Deut 20:10-18) use triad language to describe Israel's killing of "men, women, and children" in totalistic terms. These triads are simply another way of expressing the point of the double merisms: old and young, men and women. Both the triads and double merisms describe killing that encompasses both genders and all ages. On first glance these three Deuteronomy triad texts appear to be literal. The language itself is strong, concrete, and vivid. However, for several reasons we should not understand the triads of men, women, and children or the double merisms in Yahweh war as inciting or describing literal total kill.

We should note that Deuteronomy 20:16-17 does not specifically call for the destruction of women and children. Its command for the destruction of cities inside the land is broader and more general: "Do not leave alive anything that

---

[35]The "if" clause of this sentence guards against any charges of circular reasoning in this third argument. The argument works to the degree that readers have found the evidence and argumentation persuasive.

breathes. Completely destroy them" (Deut 20:16-17). It clearly involves an *implied* triad of men, women, and children within the statement about killing "anything that breathes." We do not fault Beale for raising this implied language while comparing commands for cities inside and outside the land. Rather, the problem with Beale's analysis is that the evidence that supports hyperbole for war *outside* the land (the "all" men in Deut 20:13) makes it likely that hyperbole is understood in the "anything that breathes [implied: men, women, and children]" for total-kill wars *inside* the land. So the evidence in the last section feeds into our discussion here. Let's preview the arguments for hyperbole in steps:

1. The hyperbole of "all" men and "every" city in Deuteronomy 20:13, 15 argues via the inside/outside contrast for hyperbole in the implied killing of men, women, and children in Deuteronomy 20:10-18.

2. The weight of hyperbole evidence for the triad language of Deuteronomy 20:10-18 (step one) ought to affect our understanding of the triads in Deuteronomy 2:34; 3:6.

3. We need to read Deuteronomy 2:34; 3:6 within the genre of battle reports and thus in the same manner as the battle reports of Joshua.

4. The synoptic account of Numbers 21 (covering the same Sihon and Og battles as Deuteronomy 2:34; 3:6) provides two clues that the killing was primarily focused on the king, his sons, and his army.

5. We should compare the double-merism language of Deuteronomy 32:25 (as it was written by the same author), which describes Yahweh war against Israel, who will be treated just like the Canaanites if they worship idols. The use of double-merism war language in Deuteronomy 32:25 is clearly hyperbole.

6. We should not limit ourselves to Beale's seven cases but look at many other totalistic merisms and triads in Yahweh war advanced against either Israel or against the nations. These clearly support hyperbole.

7. Now we can investigate the double merisms in Joshua 6:21 and 2 Samuel 15:3.

The first two steps we can handle quickly. Step one points out that we have already argued the case for hyperbole with the implied triad—men, women, and children—in Deuteronomy 20:10-18. Step two suggests that hyperbole in the triad in Deuteronomy 20:10-18 ought to inform our thinking about Deuteronomy 2:34; 3:6. While not clinching the case, perhaps it should set a positive disposition toward finding hyperbole in Deuteronomy 2:34; 3:6.

The third step looks at the war account genre shared by Deuteronomy 2:34; 3:6 and Joshua. Both Deuteronomy 2:34 and Deuteronomy 3:6 fall into the genre of battle report and are followed by an account of Moses' distribution of the land of Sihon and Og to a portion of the Israelites (Deut 3:12-20).[36] This is the same sequence of genres found in the book of Joshua. Joshua 10–12 contain battle reports from Israel's southern and northern campaigns, which are followed by Joshua's division of the land (Josh 13–19). As we have seen from both ANE battle reports and the book of Joshua, conquest accounts often use hyperbole to emphasize the extent of the victory. Given the use of similar genres, it is certainly possible, even likely, that Moses' account of the severity of Israel's battles with the Amorites contains heightened language about the extent of the defeat.

The fourth step looks for any evidence within Numbers 21:21-35, which recounts the same Israelite battles against Sihon and Og as Deuteronomy 2–3. A couple of clues suggest that Numbers 21 presents a closer-to-reality version of these two battles, while Deuteronomy describes the same battles with more emotive hyperbole. The first clue is that Numbers 21 limits the killing to that of the king, his sons, and the entire king's army (not the entire population).[37] While one could take both accounts literally, with

---

[36]On the genre of battle report, see Daniel I. Block, *Deuteronomy*, NIVAC (Grand Rapids: Zondervan, 2012), 89.

[37]While Deut 2:34; 3:6 indicate the annihilation of everyone, including women and children (leaving no survivors), the parallel passages in Num 21:24-25, 31 *only* indicate that Israel put Sihon to the sword, took possession (*yārāš*) of his land, captured (*lāqaḥ*) his cities, and occupied (*yāšab*) his lands, while Num 21:35 says Israel struck down (*nākāh*) and left no survivors among Og, his sons, and his army. The most significant difference is between no survivors among the army (Numbers) and no survivors among the people (Deuteronomy). Furthermore, Numbers says nothing about the annihilation of women and children (either implicitly or explicitly) in its parallel account of these same battles.

In Num 21:23-24, 33-35 we should note the distance traveled by the kings and their armies (not their entire populations) to reach their battle sites: "But *Sihon* [the king] would not let Israel pass through his territory. He mustered *his entire army* [kol 'ammô] and marched out into the wilderness against Israel. When *he* reached Jahaz [a twenty-mile march from Heshbon], *he* fought with Israel. Israel, however, put *him* [King Sihon and (implied) his entire army] to the sword and took over *his* land from the Arnon to the Jabbok,

Numbers choosing not to mention killing the entire population (which is possible), it is more likely within the broader evidence of this chapter that Numbers presents a version that is *closer to being literal* and Deuteronomy a *hyperbolic* version.[38]

A second clue comes from the poem in Numbers 21:27-30, which ultimately describes Israel's experience of conquering Sihon.[39] The poem highlights that what Sihon/the Amorites did to Moab, Israel did to Sihon. The delightful irony of the poem is that it was taken from the lips of Amorites and thus analogically celebrates Israel's own war experience.[40] Sihon's taking of *Moabite* sons and daughters as "fugitives" and "captives" (Num 21:29) would then parallel in Israel's experience the taking of *Amorite* sons and daughters as captives (i.e., not total kill).[41] This typical warfare practice of

---

but only as far as the Ammonites, because their border was fortified" (Num 21:23-24). "Then they [Israel] turned and went up along the road toward Bashan, and *Og king of Bashan* and *his whole army* [*kol 'ammô*] marched out to meet them in battle at Edrei [a twelve-mile march from Ashtaroth]. The LORD said to Moses, 'Do not be afraid of *him*, for I have delivered *him* into your hands, along with *his whole army* [*kol 'ammô*] and *his* land. Do to *him* what you did to Sihon king of the Amorites, who reigned in Heshbon.' So they struck *him* [King Og] down, together with *his sons* and *his whole army* [*kol 'ammô*], leaving them *no survivors* [i.e., no army survivors]. And they took possession of *his* land" (Num 21:33-35).

Imagine if you had to march with King Sihon a full *twenty miles* while carrying heavy military equipment. Most of us would be exhausted. Now, imagine adding women, children, babies, the elderly, the sick, and the lame. One of the purposes of that march would have been to meet the enemy away from Sihon's home city. Our point is this: the NIV translation is *correct* in its interpretive decision to recognize the referential meaning of *kol 'ammô* in Num 21 as "his army" (nothing about killing the entire population). The ESV translation replaces the NIV's "entire *army*" with "entire *people.*" While the ESV preserves the broad sense of the Hebrew term for "people" (that is its strength), it does so at the cost of skewing for English readers what was actually happening in the Numbers account and what would have been obvious to the original audience, who would have been familiar with the terms, army mustering practices, and geography. This Num 21 text should help us see why war hyperbole (about killing the entire population) worked so well in the ancient world. From their perspective, the *literal* killing of the king, his sons, and the king's army was equivalent to *figuratively* (thus hyperbole language) killing the entire nation.

[38] Even the "*no* survivors [in the army]" and "*all* the army [dies]" language in Numbers is likely hyperbolic. So, technically, it would be better to say that Numbers has a less hyperbolic (entire army) description, whereas Deuteronomy has a more hyperbolic (entire population) one.

[39] Each of the three poems in Num 31:14-15, 17-18, 27-30 describes some aspect of Israel's experience in the journey.

[40] As with Israel, Sihon "destroyed" (*ʾābad*) their enemy. Yet this does not mean (literal) total kill.

[41] Of course, analogies do not always match in every detail. Perhaps the taking of captives (instead of killing everyone) is part of the analogy that should have been cut in a more precise analogical rendering. This clue provides some weighting but is not conclusive.

taking captives after defeating the king and his army fits nicely with Israel's treatment of its enemies in Numbers 21.

The fifth step in the argument for hyperbole in Deuteronomy 2:34; 3:6 appeals to Deuteronomy 32:25, which is a Yahweh war text by the same author that includes a double merism to describe war destruction against Israel: "In the street the sword will make them childless; in their homes terror will reign. The *young men* and *young women* will perish, the *infants* and *those with gray hair* [the old]" (Deut 32:25).[42] The double merism in this verse shows that the author was familiar with using such merisms and in a context of Yahweh war that intended to communicate a hyperbolic (not literal) total-kill sense. Both the historical evidence and literary evidence from reverse holy war (see appendix C) make it clear that a literal approach to these double merisms fails; not all the people of Israel perished, nor did the nation or people group perish. The inflated language of hyperbole captures the urgency and emotive dimension of Yahweh's parental/spousal heart.[43]

The sixth step in our investigation of Deuteronomy 2:34; 3:6 looks at a broader biblical collection of merisms and triads in Yahweh war. This broader selection of young/old, man/woman texts (beyond Beale's seven samples) further confirms our hyperbole findings because, despite their totalistic wording, they contextually do not describe events where (literally) everyone dies. In each case these all-inclusive double merisms or triads are intended to say something important on the emotive level (the point of hyperbole) but not affirm literal total-population kill.[44] Placed in italics are the merisms or triads themselves and other related totalistic words or expressions. The first group of Yahweh-war texts comes from reverse holy war passages, instances

---

[42]The sword making them (Israelites) "childless" does not mean that everyone of parental age lives. The double merism covers both genders and all ages—infants, [young], aged. The further parallelism of erasing their people's name from human memory (mentioned in the next verse, Deut 32:26) is itself hyperbolic of the extent and severity.

[43]See chapter fourteen.

[44]While this collection of merisms and triads does not come from Israel's wars against the Canaanites, they are examples from Yahweh war either against Israel or against the nations. One of Beale's seven examples (1 Sam 22:19) is not even from a Yahweh war passage; it is just Saul on a self-interested killing rampage. So some latitude ought be permitted. More importantly, in the case of the reverse holy war texts, this type of Yahweh war involves explicit statements about the *same thing* happening to Israel as Yahweh had done to the Canaanites if Israel was unfaithful. See chapter three.

where Yahweh fights against Israel in order to drive the Israelites out of the Promised Land as he had done with the Canaanites:[45]

> In the street the sword will make them childless;
>> in their homes terror will reign.
> The *young men* and *young women* will perish,
>> *the infants* and *those with gray hair*. (Deut 32:25)

> He brought up against them the king of the Babylonians, who killed their young men with the sword in the sanctuary, and did not spare *young men* or *young women, the elderly* or *the infirm*. God gave them *all* [*hakkōl*] into the hands of Nebuchadnezzar. (2 Chron 36:17)

> But I am full of the wrath of the LORD,
>> and I cannot hold it in.
> Pour it out on the *children* in the street
>> and on the *young men* gathered together;
> both *husband* and *wife* will be caught in it,
>> and the *old*, those weighed down with years. (Jer 6:11)

> Why bring such great disaster on yourselves by cutting off from Judah the *men* and *women*, the *children* and *infants*, and so leave *yourselves without a remnant* [*ləbiltî hôtîr lākem šəʾērît*]? (Jer 44:7)

> The LORD is righteous,
>> yet I rebelled against his command.
> Listen, all you peoples;
>> look on my suffering.
> My *young men* and *young women*
>> have gone into exile [merism for exile, not death]. (Lam 1:18)[46]

> *Young* and *old* lie together
>> in the dust of the streets;
> my *young men* and *young women*
>> have fallen by the sword.

---

[45]For further double merisms or triads in reverse holy war see Jer 16:3. For single reverse holy war merisms see Deut 28:5; Amos 8:13. Also see the reversal of war where triads (Jer 31:13) are used to celebrate recovery.

[46]The single merism young men/young women for the living exiles (not killed) in reverse holy war emphasizes the youth of both genders, perhaps because the youth would have been the choice captives taken back to Babylon. The elderly and infirm Israelites would have been left in the land, since they could not make the journey and the youth were more valuable as captives.

You have slain them in the day of your anger;

you have slaughtered them without pity. (Lam 2:21)

Slaughter the *old men*, the *young men* and *women*, *the mothers* and *children*, but do not touch anyone who has the mark. Begin at my sanctuary. (Ezek 9:6)

A second group of totalistic merisms comes from total-kill war passages where Yahweh fights against the nations. The important connection with Deuteronomy 2:34; 3:6 is that these cases reflect Yahweh war, employ similar everything-included merisms, and never happened literally. One example from Jeremiah should suffice, since it offers a record-breaking eightfold merism and connects contextually with plenty of other total-destruction language:

"You [Persians] are my war club,

my weapon for battle—

with you I shatter nations,

with you I destroy kingdoms,

with you I shatter [1] *horse* and *rider*,

with you I shatter [2] *chariot* and *driver*,

with you I shatter [3] *man* and *woman*,

with you I shatter [4] *old man* and *youth*,

with you I shatter [5] *young man* and *young woman*,

with you I shatter [6] *shepherd* and *flock*,

with you I shatter [7] *farmer* and *oxen*,

with you I shatter [8] *governors* and *officials*.

"Before your eyes I will repay Babylon [Babylonians[47]] and *all who live in Babylonia* [*ûləkōl yôšəbê kaśdîm*][48] for all the wrong they have done in Zion," declares the LORD.

"I am against you, you destroying mountain,

you who destroy the whole earth,"

declares the LORD.

"I will stretch out my hand against you,

roll you off the cliffs,

and make you a burned-out mountain.

---

[47]Babylonians (not Assyrians) are the referent here.

[48]This "all" refers to every person in the entire Babylonian kingdom/nation!

No rock will be taken from you for a cornerstone,
    nor any stone for a foundation,
    for you will be desolate forever,"
    declares the LORD. (Jer 51:20-26)

The war oracle against Babylon from which these lines come covers a lengthy section of 110 verses in Jeremiah (Jer 50:1–51:64). It includes the eightfold merism (Jer 51:20-26) and abounds with hyperbolic total-kill language: "Attack the land . . . and *completely destroy them*" (Jer 50:21); "Pile her up like heaps of grain. *Completely destroy her; and leave her no remnant*" (Jer 50:26); "Encamp all around her; *let no one escape*" (Jer 50:29); "Spare not her young men; *completely destroy her army*" (Jer 51:3).

Here is the point of step six in our argumentation from the merisms and triads in the Yahweh wars against the Israelites and the foreign nations: *it would be absurd to take these Yahweh war merisms and triads in even a remotely literal sense.* Yes, the horrors of ancient war affected everyone. No person was left untouched. The pain and suffering was immense. But that hardly meant absolutely everyone was killed. Such total-kill extermination of *entire* nations across their *entire* land never happened in any of these examples. The historical realities that this war language describes are decisive battles that led to a new configuration of power, dominance, and control. Furthermore, in the vast majority of cases these merisms and triads, as a *literary phenomenon,* were not intended by the biblical authors (see the list in chapter nine) or by other ANE authors (chapter eight) to be understood in a literal sense.

Joshua 6:21; 1 Samuel 15:3: Hyperbole. We come now to two double-merism texts that Beale views as probable cases calling for the extermination of literally all women and children. The language of total-kill merisms and other totalistic expressions are evident in both biblical texts:

They devoted the city [Jericho] to the LORD and destroyed with the sword *every living thing* [kol ʾăšer bāʿîr] in it—*men* and *women, young* and *old*, cattle, sheep and donkeys. (Josh 6:21)

Now go, attack the Amalekites and *totally destroy all* [wǝhaḥăramtem ʾet kol] that belongs to them. Do not spare them [wǝlōʾ taḥmōl]; put to death *men* and *women, children* and *infants*, cattle and sheep, camels and donkeys. (1 Sam 15:3)

In the case of double-merism language in Joshua 6:21 we have nothing more to say. We have already developed in this chapter three lines of evidence that argue for a hyperbolic understanding of the merisms there, namely, the total-kill language elsewhere in the book of Joshua; the total-kill merisms in Yahweh war against the Canaanites in Deuteronomy 2:34; 3:6; 20:10-18; and the total-kill merisms in Yahweh war against Israel and foreign nations. These three lines of evidence make a good case for hyperbole in Joshua 6.[49] Enough said. On the other hand, 1 Samuel 15 with its double merism and other total-kill language deserves further consideration. We will devote an entire chapter—chapter eleven—to understanding the totalistic language in the text of 1 Samuel 15.

DRIVE THEM OUT BY ANNIHILATING THEM

Finally, any case for *literal* total kill must do something with the drive-out language. After all, driving out the Canaanites seems to leave them alive after they have been forcefully relocated outside the land. With the same drive-out language the Egyptians push the Israelites out of Egypt (Ex 6:1; 11:1). Killing was not required for residents to be driven out of a land.

Gregory Beale responds to the challenge of drive-out language by giving priority to the (literal) total-kill commands over the drive-out commands. He contends that the drive-out language could "just as easily and more probably" imply that "the way Israel was to 'drive out' and 'dispossess' the Canaanites was *by* annihilating them."[50] He places drive-out and total-kill into a temporal sequence, prioritizes one over the other, and insists on a physical requirement for the one (killing), while the other happens as a result of the first and typically without any physical action on the part of the Israelites (driving out):

▶ *required action for Israelite warriors:* physically kill (literally) all Canaanites as they encountered them

---

[49]It is unlikely that the rules of engagement at Jericho differed greatly from those in the rest of Josh 7–12. The Battle of Jericho was paradigmatic for the other conquest narratives in Joshua, as noted by Richard D. Nelson, *Joshua*, OTL (Louisville, KY: Westminster John Knox, 1997), 91; Sarah Lebhar Hall, *Conquering Character: The Characterization of Joshua in Joshua 1–11*, LHBOTS 512 (New York: T&T Clark, 2010), 91.

[50]Beale, *Morality of God*, 41 (italics added).

▶ *resultant outcome but not a physical action by Israelite warriors:* God will use the dread/fear of Israelite warriors' physical action—killing (literally) all Canaanites they meet—to drive out the Canaanites from the land

In other words, when news got out about Israel's policy of literal and complete annihilation, the Canaanites would flee for their lives. Some may have fled before or during Israelite attacks and some may have made peace with Israel (though this was not the norm). Any Canaanites who escaped went into exile in lands outside Canaan, or if they remained, "It was because of Israel's disobedience in not destroying them when they were found."[51]

The question of how to interpret drive-out language is too important to skip over lightly. We will devote chapter twelve to examining the relationship between annihilation language and drive-out/dispossess language. Can Beale's literal approach and his understanding that driving out should be by (literal) total killing be sustained in terms of this relationship? In short, we will show that the drive-out passages support the hyperbole thesis. The driving out of the Canaanites and the military defeat of the Canaanites are two different means of accomplishing the same goal, which is preparation of the land to become Yahweh's sacred space. But first let's look at 1 Samuel 15.

CONCLUSION

This chapter examined objections to hyperbole in the language of Yahweh war, primarily in Deuteronomy, Joshua, and Judges. We countered these objections by showing that the weight of evidence still supports the hyperbole thesis. Addressing these objections uncovered even *more* evidence in favor of taking the total-land conquest and total-kill language as *extent* hyperbole and *severity* hyperbole. We have postponed two other objections for upcoming chapters about the total-annihilation language in 1 Samuel 15 (chapter eleven) and the relationship between drive-out and wipe-out language (chapter twelve). Three more appendixes (A through C) will provide further evidence for the hyperbole thesis, but they also stand on their own (beyond the hyperbole discussion) as better answers to the ethics of holy war.

---

[51]Beale, *Morality of God*, 41.

FIRST SAMUEL 15

Hyperbole Thesis Undone?

RECENT CHAPTERS HAVE ARGUED that the total-kill or genocide language in the Bible needs to be understood in a hyperbolic (not literal) manner. The weight of evidence in Joshua, Judges, the prophetic books, and the broader ANE world make the hyperbole view much more probable than a literal understanding. More evidence for the hyperbole thesis comes in chapter twelve and appendixes A, B, and C. But first, some features in 1 Samuel 15 may seem to support a literal total-kill view; further attention, however, finds support for the hyperbole thesis.[1]

This chapter builds on three readings:

1. *A first-glance reading.* At first glance, a face-value reading of 1 Samuel 15 seems to overturn the hyperbole thesis. Saul is told to completely destroy the Amalekites. When Saul leaves one survivor, Samuel severely reprimands Saul for his disobedience (1 Sam 15:19, 26). On the surface, it seems that Samuel's intense displeasure relates to Saul's not killing every single breathing Amalekite, since he has kept one remaining survivor (the king) alive. Along this line of reasoning, one thinks: if only Saul had killed just one more person—every Amalekite would have been wiped out! If King Agag is understood as the last of all Amalekites, then indeed the hyperbole thesis has a problem. First Samuel 15 might be its undoing.

---

[1]We thank Bill Henderson, a student in the Untangling Hermeneutics, Ethics, and Story line of Holy War class at Tyndale Seminary (summer 2012) for his very stimulating paper, which prompted aspects of this investigation.

2. *A second-look reading.* If we take a second look, however, and more closely understand what Saul was attempting to do, we see that 1 Samuel 15 does not overturn the hyperbole thesis. In fact, good arguments have already been made (by others) for recognizing hyperbole in 1 Samuel 15. We will critique those arguments and, if need be, strengthen them.

3. *A third, sustained-look reading.* A third, more protracted examination of the passage will develop further evidence for the hyperbole thesis especially along the lines of legitimation. The issue is not so much that Saul let one stray peasant live (and otherwise everything would have been fine). Rather, it is *whom* he let live (the king!) and *why* (his motives).

A FIRST GLANCE: SEEMING TO OVERTURN HYPERBOLE

At the outset of the 1 Samuel 15 story, Yahweh instructs Saul through the prophet Samuel to completely destroy the Amalekites. Total-kill language extends to the Amalekite people and their animals:

> This is what the LORD Almighty says: "I will punish the Amalekites for what they did to Israel when they waylaid them as they came up from Egypt. Now go, *attack* [or strike down] the Amalekites and *totally destroy* all that belongs to them. *Do not spare them; put to death men and women, children and infants, cattle and sheep, camels and donkeys."* (1 Sam 15:2-3)

> Samuel said, "Although you were once small in your own eyes, did you not become the head of the tribes of Israel? The LORD anointed you king over Israel. And he sent you on a mission, saying, 'Go and *completely destroy* those wicked people, the Amalekites; wage war against them *until you have wiped them out.'"* (1 Sam 15:17-18)

Furthermore, in the description of actual battle events the narrator of 1 Samuel affirms that in fact all Amalekites *were* destroyed (except one). The always-reliable narrator communicates total kill of the Amalekite people through three elements: (1) the wide-ranging geography, (2) the explicit "all" language, and (3) the contrast with the one survivor: "Then Saul attacked the Amalekites [1] *all the way from Havilah to Shur, near the eastern border of Egypt.* He took Agag king of the Amalekites alive, and [2] *all* [*kol*] his people *he totally destroyed with the sword.* [3] *But*

Saul and the army spared Agag and the best of the sheep and cattle, the fat calves and lambs" (1 Sam 15:7-9). It is important to note that this is the *narrator's* version of what happened (not Saul's) and that the narrator has *both* Saul and the army at fault for sparing Agag and the animals (contra Saul's later version). Concerning the total kill of the Amalekite people (animals aside), the narrator affirms Saul's complete obedience except for one living person.

Finally, the story closes with Samuel slaying the one person Saul had allowed to live—Agag, king of the Amalekites. This final dramatic act of the sword makes the point that Samuel, by finishing Saul's job, embodies the obedience that Saul lacked.[2] Emphasis on the sword as the instrument of battle casts a shadow back on what Saul should have done with his sword on the battlefield: "Then Samuel said, 'Bring me Agag king of the Amalekites.' Agag came to him in chains. And he thought, 'Surely the bitterness of death is past.' But Samuel said, 'As your *sword* has made women childless, so will your mother be childless among women.' And Samuel put Agag to death before the LORD at Gilgal" (1 Sam 15:32-33). From Yahweh's original instructions (1 Sam 15:2-3 [see 1 Sam 15:17-18]), to the narrator's review of what happened in the battle (1 Sam 15:7-9), to Samuel's killing the Amalekite king (1 Sam 15:32-33), all readers should agree: *the total-kill commands directed toward the Amalekite people (animals aside) would have been fulfilled had Saul (like Samuel) killed the king.* In fact, based on the well-established pattern of Joshua's obedience, Saul should have *killed Agag on the battlefield, hung his dead body outside his defeated city for one day (until sunset), and then buried him there* (Josh 8:2; 10:1, 26, 28, 30, 37; 11:10).[3] Saul should never have brought Agag (dead or alive) back to Bethel.[4]

---

[2]First Samuel 15:33 implies that Samuel kills Agag with a sword. That Samuel is finishing Saul's job may be further confirmed if he used Saul's own sword to kill Agag—a distinct possibility (see 1 Sam 13:19-22).

[3]See chapter thirteen and the discussion of impaling.

[4]Bringing home the *live* enemy king in chains (NIV; other versions translate the word for "in chains" differently) was an action by Saul to legitimize his kingship. It gave him the ability to project the image of a successful war king versus the defeated Amalekite king. Yet, even if Saul had dragged home Agag's dead body and fulfilled the killing instructions, it would have still broken with Joshua's pattern and functioned as a prideful act of legitimation.

In view of the obedience in 1 Samuel 15 coming with the sword action of Samuel, one may have the impression that the chapter's total-kill language must be taken literally. It seems as if the text does not allow for even one (literal) Amalekite person to remain alive. Such a conclusion obviously is a literal (not hyperbolic) understanding of the total-kill language in 1 Samuel 15.

A SECOND LOOK: SOME ARGUMENTS FOR HYPERBOLE

Apologists Paul Copan and Matthew Flannagan have argued that the description of Saul's slaughter of the Amalekites "appears highly hyperbolic and contains obvious rhetorical exaggeration" based primarily on three factors: (1) that 210,000 men as the number of Saul's army seems inordinately large (1 Sam 15:4), (2) that the geographical scope of the battle seems impossibly large, and (3) that a massive contradiction would result from a literal reading of 1 Samuel 15 in light of the continued survival of the Amalekites witnessed later in the Bible (1 Sam 27:8; 30:1, 18; 2 Sam 1:1; 8:11-12; 1 Chron 4:43; see also Esther 3:1; 9:24).[5] However, we need to examine Copan and Flannagan's arguments and the biblical text more closely. Not all their supporting evidence carries equal weight or is equally persuasive, and so the question merits reexamination.

Saul's muster of 210,000 men. Copan and Flannagan point out that the 210,000 men mustered by Saul to fight against the Amalekites in 1 Samuel 15:4 is "larger than any army known at this time in antiquity" and so is likely hypberbolic.[6] The figure, however, does not differ much from other large numbers in the premonarchic era and the era of the united monarchy:

▶ Saul musters 300,000 men from Israel and 30,000 from Judah (1 Sam 11:8).

▶ Israel musters 400,000 men (Judg 20:2, 17).

▶ David musters twelve divisions of 24,000, totaling 288,000 men (1 Chron 27:1-15).

---

[5] Paul Copan and Matthew Flannagan, "The Ethics of 'Holy War' for Christian Morality and Theology," in *Holy War in the Bible: Christian Morality and an Old Testament Problem*, ed. Heath A. Thomas, Jeremy Evans, and Paul Copan (Downers Grove, IL: InterVarsity Press, 2013), 223; see also Copan and Flannagan, *Did God Really Command Genocide? Coming to Terms with the Justice of God* (Grand Rapids: Baker, 2014), 109-17. This second work provides similar (though more developed) arguments for hyperbole in 1 Sam 15.

[6] Copan and Flannagan, "Ethics of 'Holy War' for Christian Morality and Theology," 223.

The large number of men mustered by Saul to fight against the Amalekites is not, in and of itself, out of line with what we find elsewhere in the Bible. The question, however, is how to best understand these large numbers.[7]

Copan and Flannagan, following David Fouts, hold that the number mustered by Saul is best understood as hyperbolic.[8] This may be the case, since the hyperbolic use of numbers in ANE warfare contexts is pervasive. For example, in the Ugaritic Keret epic, King Keret marshals 3,000,000 soldiers to his side.[9] Similarly, Assyrian king Shalmaneser III boasts of defeating an alliance of 14,000 troops at the battle of Qarqar, but that number grows to 20,500 and 25,000 in subsequent accounts of the battle.[10] Presumably, then, the 210,000 soldiers marshaled for Saul's attack on the Amalekites reflects a similar approach on the part of the biblical writer, attributing to Saul an army so vast in size that he would be left completely without excuse for his failure to fully obey Yahweh. A hyperbolic approach may also be supported by the Septuagint, which further expands the size of Saul's army, doubling the soldiers marshaled from Israel (400,000) and tripling the men mustered from Judah (30,000).

However, large numbers in the Hebrew Scriptures are notoriously difficult.[11] The Hebrew root translated "thousand" ('elep) can refer to either a precise or a round number, and it can also describe a variety of levels of social connectedness or kinship in Israel. The root can serve as an equivalent

---

[7]For a survey of options related to the large numbers in the book of Numbers, which often form the basis of discussion of other large numbers in the Old Testament, see Aaron Goldstein, "Large Census Numbers in Numbers: An Evaluation of Current Proposals," *Presbyterion* 38, no. 2 (2012): 88-108.

[8]Copan and Flannagan, *Did God Really Command Genocide?*, 115; compare David M. Fouts, "A Defense of the Hyperbolic Interpretation of Large Numbers in the Old Testament," *JETS* 40, no. 3 (1997): 377-87; Eryl W. Davies, "A Mathematical Conundrum: The Problem of the Large Numbers in Numbers I and XXVI," *VT* 45, no. 4 (1995): 467.

[9]Gary Rendsburg, "An Additional Note to Two Recent Articles on the Number of People in the Exodus from Egypt and the Large Numbers in Numbers I and XXVI," *VT* 51, no. 3 (2001): 393; noted also in Fouts, "Defense of the Hyperbolic Interpretation of Large Numbers," 386. For further examples see Fouts, "Defense of the Hyperbolic Interpretation of Large Numbers," 383-86; Davies, "Mathematical Conundrum," 467.

[10]Shalmaneser boasts of defeating 14,000 troops in the battle of Qarqar (*COS* 2:113B, 264), but on the first bull of Caleh the number increases to 25,000 (*COS* 2:113C, 266) and then appears as 20,500 on the Black Obelisk of Shalmaneser (*COS* 2:113F, 269).

[11]John Wenham notes, "There is evidence that the Old Testament text is on the whole marvelously well preserved. There is also evidence from the parallel passages in Samuel, Kings and Chronicles and (especially) in Ezra 2 and Nehemiah 7 that numbers were peculiarly difficult to transmit accurately." Wenham, "The Large Numbers in the Bible," *JBQ* 21, no. 2 (1993): 116.

term to a clan (e.g., 1 Sam 10:19-21; Mic 5:1), region (1 Sam 23:23), and even tribe (e.g., Num 10:4, 36).[12] Based in part on the polyvalence of the term *'elep*, and in part following George Mendenhall, Colin Humphreys has made a persuasive argument that the root *'elep* need not be understood exclusively as a numeral but can also refer to a fighting unit or a troop/squad in certain contexts. This seems to be supported by Numbers 31:5, where each tribe supplies an *'elep* for the army of Israel, and by 1 Samuel 10:19-21, where the terms *'elep* and *mišpāḥâ* ("clan") seem to refer to similar levels of social organization. Thus, 1 Samuel 15:4 could indicate that (1) Saul mustered 200,000 soldiers from Israel and 10,000 soldiers from Judah *or* (2) Saul mustered 200 fighting units from Israel and 10 fighting units from Judah.[13] Humphreys's analysis of Numbers 1 and Numbers 26 found that the average *'elep* or squad consisted of approximately nine to ten men.[14] Saul then would have mustered 200 squads/fighting units (2,000 warriors) from Israel and 10 squads/ fighting units (100 warriors) from Judah. If this were the case, then the number of troops mustered by Saul would still represent a formidable fighting force, but it would not exhibit the presence of hyperbole.

In short, the numbers used in 1 Samuel 15 *may* support the hyperbole thesis but should at best be viewed as tentative evidence.

---

[12]On clan references, see Francis I. Anderson, "Israelite Kinship Terminology and Social Structure," *BT* 20 (1969): 36. On tribe references, see *HALOT*, "אֶלֶף," III, I.59-60.

[13]Colin J. Humphreys, "The Number of People in the Exodus from Egypt: Decoding Mathematically the Very Large Numbers in Numbers I and XXVI," *VT* 48 (1998): 196-213; Humphreys, "The Numbers in the Exodus from Egypt: A Further Appraisal," *VT* 50 (2000): 323-28. Note the ensuing discussion in Jacob Milgrom, "On Decoding Very Large Numbers," *VT* 49 (1999): 131-32; M. McEntire, "A Response to Colin J. Humphreys's 'The Number of People in the Exodus from Egypt: Decoding Mathematically the Very Large Numbers in Numbers I and XXVI," *VT* 49 (1999): 262-64; Rendsburg, "Additional Note," 392-96; Rüdiger Heinzerling, "On the Interpretation of the Census Lists by C. J. Humphreys and G. E. Mendenhall," *VT* 50 (2000): 250-52. Humphreys also notes that his hypothesis for large numbers should be applied on a case-by-case basis rather than across the board. From a different standpoint but generally arriving at a similar conclusion see N. Gottwald, *The Tribes of Yahweh: A Sociology of the Religion of Liberated Israel, 1250–1050 BCE* (Sheffield: Sheffield Academic Press, 1999), 270-76. David Firth points to the possibility that the word *'elep* in 1 Sam 15:4 could refer to a military unit or clan instead of "thousand" (*1 & 2 Samuel*, AOTC [Downers Grove, IL: InterVarsity Press, 2009], 173).

[14]Humphreys figures the size of each fighting unit or troop to be about nine to ten men, which is consistent with roughly contemporary numbers described in the Amarna Letters ("Number of People," 203-4). These numbers fall broadly in line with the archaeological findings of J. D. Schloen, *The House of the Father as Fact and Symbol: Patrimonialism in Ugarit and the Ancient Near East*, SAHL 2 (Winona Lake, IN: Eisenbrauns, 2001), 153-55.

Geographical scope of the battle. Copan and Flannagan also identify the impossibly large size of the battlefield as another marker of hyperbole in 1 Samuel 15. They point to 1 Samuel 15:7, which indicates that Saul strikes down the Amalekites from Havilah to Shur, pointing out that "Shur is on the edge of Egypt, and Havila is in Saudi Arabia. This is an absurdly large battle field!"[15] This would indeed be a massive field of battle, particularly for the defeat of a relatively small opposing force such as Amalek. However, the Amalekites were a nomadic people group who are connected elsewhere in Scripture with places as distant as Edom (Gen 36:16) in the east, the Negev in the south (Num 13:29), Philistine Ziklag in the west (1 Sam 30:1-2), and the Ephraimite hill country in the north (Judg 12:15). Moreover, while scholars are generally agreed that Shur lies along the northwest border of Egypt along the Sinai Peninsula, the precise location of the land of Havilah is uncertain.[16]

In addition, Genesis 25:18 notes that the territory in which the nomadic Ishmaelites settled (*šākan*) also stretched "from Havilah to Shur."[17] Judges 8:24 identifies the Midianite kings Zeba and Zalmunah as Ishmaelites, while Judges 6:3 links the Midianites with the Amalekites, who together raided Israelite territory in the days of the judges. Thus the nomadic Amalekites may be associated with a large amount of territory—territory similar in scope to that covered by the Ishmaelites. Furthermore, 1 Samuel 15:7 states that Saul strikes them from Havilah to Shur, not Shur to Havilah.

---

[15]Matthew Flannagan and Paul Copan, "Does the Bible Condone Genocide?," in *In Defense of the Bible: A Comprehensive Apologetic for the Authority of Scripture*, ed. Steven B. Cowan and Terry L. Wilder (Nashville: B&H Academic, 2013), 316; Copan and Flannagan, "Ethics of Holy War," 223-24.

[16]On Shur, see Yohanan Aharoni, *The Land of the Bible: A Historical Geography*, rev. ed., trans. A. Rainey (Philadelphia: Westminster, 1979), 10, 142, 197, 287; Alice Mandell, "Shur, Wilderness of," *NIDB* 5:246. On Havilah, see C. Mark McCormick, "Havilah," *NIBD* 2:751. McCormick comments that in the end, "The location of the land of Havilah is unknown." Havilah seems to be a diminutive of *ḥwl*, Hebrew for "sand" or "stretch of sand" (*HALOT*, I.297). Consequently, Havilah is generally associated with the Arabian Peninsula, though other possibilities exist, and it has been variously located in northwest Arabia, southern Arabia, and even on the northwest African coast (see Gen 10:7). See Claus Westermann, *Genesis 1–11: A Commentary*, trans. J. J. Scullion (Minneapolis: Augsburg, 1984), 217-18; W. W. Müller, "Havilah," *ABD* 3:82.

[17]The Hebrew verb *šākan* can describe permanently dwelling within a defined space, or it can refer to temporary settlement: "The accent of *škn* is on the aspect of settling without any enduring ties, i.e. without legal possession of property. The key feature here is an open orientation to an as yet undefined living space" (Manfred Görg, "שָׁכַן *šakan*," *TDOT* 14:696; see also A. R. Hulst, "שָׁכַן *škn*," *THAT* 2:906; *HALOT*, 1497).

When biblical narratives describe the geographical scope of a battle scene, they typically begin by naming the region *closest* to the initial field of battle before describing its widest geographical extent.[18] In this light, it is extremely unlikely that Havilah served as the initial point of conflict, particularly if Havilah was located in northern Arabia (or even less likely if it was in southern Arabia), because of its remoteness from Israelite territorial concerns and interests. The next time 1 Samuel mentions the Amalekites, it connects them with ancestral regions on the way toward Shur—in the direction of Egypt (1 Sam 27:8).

Consequently, the mention in 1 Samuel 15:7 of the field of battle stretching from Havilah to Shur is best understood as a general reference to the region in which the nomadic Amalekites were *known to roam* rather than a *specific indication of the theater of battle*. As a result, hyperbole on the part of the narrator need not be implied based on what seems at first to be an extremely large field of battle.[19] However, that does not mean the geography fails to help the hyperbole case in 1 Samuel 15. Geography does favor hyperbole, but through a slightly different line of argument that places a highly *localized* battle against the backdrop of an extremely large region. We will examine this different geographical argument in the third-reading section (below).

Total kill affirmed by the narrator in 1 Samuel 15 versus later living Amalekites (affirmed by the same narrator). The final and most persuasive argument that Copan and Flannagan offer for hyperbole is the continuing existence of the Amalekites *after* their defeat by Saul and Samuel. In 1 Samuel 15 the *narrator himself* (not just Saul's words) affirms that indeed *all* Amalekites *were* destroyed (except one). The biblical narrator confirms the total-kill language through his description of the battle events: "He [Saul] took Agag king of the Amalekites alive, and *all* [*kol*] his people *he totally destroyed with the sword. But Saul and the army spared Agag*" (1 Sam 15:8-9). Agag's death by the hand of Samuel also confirms the narrator's point of view, namely, that *all* Amalekites *were* destroyed (and at that point without the exception of one).

---

[18]E.g., Gen 14:11, 15; 31:11; Ex 14:5-9; Josh 2:7; 10:10; 24:6; Judg 4:14-16; 7:21-23; 11:33; 20:43; 1 Sam 7:11; 17:51-53; 2 Sam 2:24; 1 Kings 20:29; 2 Kings 9:27; 25:5; 2 Chron 14:10-13; Jer 39:4-5; 52:7-8.

[19]See Gerald Mattingly, "Amalek," *ABD* 1:170.

Nevertheless, this cannot mean that Saul killed every last Amalekite person (other than Agag) because the Amalekites reappear in statements made by the *same* narrator (1 Sam 27:8; 30:1-2, 18; 2 Sam 1:1) and elsewhere (1 Chron 4:41-43; see also Haman the Agagite in Esther 3:1; 8:3; 9:24). In fact, the Amalekites still have a sufficient population to later sustain raids against Israel. One might also ponder this discrepancy through the lens of later canonical editing of the Hebrew Bible. As Copan and Flannagan argue, "It becomes untenable to think that those who edited these works into the final sequence were affirming that God literally commanded Saul to destroy the Amalekites."[20] The continued existence of the Amalekites strongly indicates that 1 Samuel 15 uses hyperbole in its characterization of God's command and the reports by the narrator of Saul's thoroughness—Saul could not possibly have killed *all* the Amalekites except one.

To this evidence for hyperbole, we should probably add the existence of later-living Amalekite animals. The use of hyperbole in 1 Samuel 15 in the slaughter of *all* Amalekite people seems to be replicated in the total-kill slaughter of *all* Amalekite animals (other than those brought back by Saul). First, it seems unlikely that Saul and the Israelites slaughtered every last Amalekite animal in the vast region between Havilah and Shur except for a few of the best calves and lambs (1 Sam 15:7, 9). But, there is also the matter of those later 1 Samuel references to Amalekite animals. Not more than 10-12 years later[21] David twice attacks the Amalekites and on *both* occasions takes spoils of battle including an array of animals—"sheep and cattle, donkeys and camels"—and what appears to have been a mammoth supply of Amalekite animals (1 Sam 27:8-12 [esp. v. 9]; 1 Sam 30:1-31 [esp. vv. 17-20]).[22] Consequently, the supposed total-kill or

---

[20] Flannagan and Copan, "Does the Bible Condone Genocide?," 315. Considering the correspondence between divine command (1 Sam 15:3) and execution (1 Sam 15:8, 33), Copan and Flannagan point out, "It seems implausible to suggest that we ought to interpret the command in verse 3 as literal but the fulfillment just four verses later, as hyperbolic; the text requires that the command and fulfillment be read in the same sense."

[21] Leslie McFall, "The Chronology of Saul and David," *JETS* 53 (2010): 475-533 [esp. 502].

[22] In the first attack David *explicitly* brings back Amalekite animals (1 Sam 29:9). In the second attack David brings back his own re-captured animals but most likely (*strongly inferred*) also Amalekite animals. After all, the later distribution of goods was so plentiful that he gave spoils to both groups of his men—the 400 fighting soldiers and the 200 soldiers who remained with the supplies (1 Sam 30:9, 21). Also, David further extends the spoil distribution to a long list of thirteen Israelite and non-Israelite benefactors (1 Sam 30:26-31) and to an additional group of "those in all the other places where he [David] and his men

slaughter of *all* Amalekite animals (like that of killing *all* the Amalekite people) "except those brought back" in 1 Samuel 15 further supports, at least in a secondary manner,[23] the hyperbole thesis.

In short, the references to Amalekite people (and animals) later in 1–2 Samuel by the *same* narrator and in other, later canonical books can best be explained through the common biblical and ANE practice of using hyperbole to describe the execution and outcome of battles.

A THIRD, SUSTAINED LOOK: MORE HYPERBOLE EVIDENCE

With the evidence already in hand, we could happily end this chapter now and feel secure in its conclusions. When 1 Samuel 15 is read within its literary context of 1–2 Samuel, it affirms (not overturns) the hyperbole thesis. However, some readers may want further confirmation. If so, the rest of this chapter—an even deeper, third read—is for you. In the remaining section, we develop the hyperbole understanding of 1 Samuel 15 through three more lines of evidence: (1) hints of a localized battle with hyperbolized outcomes, (2) reading 1 Samuel 15 through the lens of comparable Deuteronomy/Joshua total-kill language, and (3) God's disapproval of Saul's self-serving motives. This look at evidence about the *why* (motives) and the *who* (the Amalekite king, not a peasant) allows us to think more deeply about what exactly was so upsetting to God, Samuel, and the biblical narrator.

Geography again: Localized battle; hyperbolized outcomes. Several hints of a localized battle in 1 Samuel 15 suggest that Saul did not actually attack or kill all the Amalekites, even if the (hyperbolic) language sounds like

---

roamed" (1 Sam 30:31). The narrator seems to be saying that David got back from the Amalekites exponentially more spoils than the Amalekites originally took from him. The likelihood that this far-greater spoils taking (well beyond what he distributes to his 600 men) would have included *Amalekite animals* is very high. Here are several reasons: nomadic wealth was typically measured in terms of portable goods such as animals, the recaptured originally-Israelite animals probably went back to David's men, and the overwhelming extent of broader postbattle distribution of spoils suggests that Amalekite animals played a role here (not only recaptured Israelite animals).

[23] We do not wish to overstate the evidence for hyperbole in the total-kill of the Amalekite animals because the transference of animals between raiding nomads would have been more fluid than Amalekite people (it is easier to change the ownership-identity of animals than the transference of ethnically identified human beings). Nevertheless, it remains an important secondary consideration based upon the weight of probabilities.

it.[24] First, 1 Samuel 15:5 indicates that Saul came to the city of Amalek and laid an ambush in a nearby ravine. The location of the "city of Amalek" is unknown, and its association with the nomadic Amalekites is surprising, though it may have referred to an unwalled encampment frequented by the Amalekites.[25] However, the reference to an ambush at a single location suggests this was a localized action against a smaller group of Amalekites rather than a sustained effort to annihilate the entire Amalekite people group. Second, Saul's warning (1 Sam 15:6) urging the Kenites to depart from the midst of the Amalekites assumes relatively close proximity between the Kenites (or at least some Kenites) and where Saul was attacking the Amalekites. This also presumes a localized battle. Third, while Amalek is generally connected with the desert regions in the southern portions of Judah (Gen 14:7; Ex 17:8-16; Num 13:29; 1 Sam 30:1, 13-14; 1 Chron 4:40-43; but see Num 14:25, 45), it was also connected with areas such as Edom in the east (Gen 36:16) and Israel's north, near Ephraim.[26] This may simply point to the nomadic nature of the Amalekites, but it may also indicate the existence of multiple Amalekite tribes.

Therefore, considering the continued presence of the Amalekites in the region going down to Shur during the time of David (1 Sam 27:8; see 1 Sam 15:7), Saul's attack was likely against one Amalekite group encamped in the southern regions of Judahite territory, rather than the entire ethnic group or nation.[27] Broad total-kill instructions and total-kill reporting of events that sound like they wiped out the entire Amalekite people are fulfilled through a far more narrow, localized event. One reason such military hyperbole worked well in the ancient world is that Saul chose to go after an Amalekite

---

[24]Copan and Flannagan also argue for a localized battle on similar though not identical grounds (*Did God Really Command Genocide?*, 116-17).

[25]David T. Tsumura, *The First Book of Samuel*, NICOT (Grand Rapids: Eerdmans, 2007), 393-94. Anson Rainey notes that the city of Amalek has sometimes been identified with Tel Masos, but Masos is more likely Baalath-beer (*The Sacred Bridge* [Jerusalem: Carta, 2006], 246-47).

[26]Judges 6:33 indicates that Amalek raided in the Valley of Jezreel, and the Amalekite claiming to have killed King Saul says he came from the battle site at Mount Gilboa (2 Sam 1:6). Judges 5:14 parallels Amalek with Ephraim, and Judg 12:15 also places the Amalekites in the western Samarian hills, though this reading is controverted. See Diana V. Edelman, "Saul's Battle Against Amaleq (1 Sam. 15)," *JSOT* 35 (1986): 71-84.

[27]Firth comes to a similar conclusion (*1 & 2 Samuel*, 173).

city and, even more importantly, the place where the Amalekite king resided. To the ancient mindset, focused on collective identity, the king represented larger groups of people—his army and/or his nation (see appendix A).

Localized total kill of the Amalekites. Some may point out that postulating a localized action against the Amalekites makes a literal reading of 1 Samuel 15 more likely. Perhaps Saul may not have wiped out every last Amalekite everywhere, but a small-scale, confined confrontation makes it more probable that he totally destroyed all the Amalekites living in the "city of Amalek"—with the exception of Agag—as Yahweh seems to demand (1 Sam 15:3), as the narrator implies (1 Sam 15:8), and as Saul claims (1 Sam 15:13, 20). This interpretation is possible, but several factors make this reading unlikely.

At a rhetorical level, the language of 1 Samuel 15 is comprehensive in its scope, focusing on the Amalekites (all Amalekites, not just some) as a people group. (1) In 1 Samuel 15:2, the Amalekite people are juxtaposed against the entire people of Israel. (2) In 1 Samuel 15:3, the instructions to attack and kill the Amalekites similarly focus on the destruction of the entire people group (not just a part). (3) Once again, in 1 Samuel 15:6, the rhetoric is inclusive of *all* the Israelite people in relationship to *all* of the Kenites (despite the reality being localized).[28] (4) In 1 Samuel 15:7-8, the reference to destroying all (*kol*) the Amalekite people with the sword is paired with equally comprehensive rhetoric about all the places where Amalek was known to roam. At a rhetorical level, this infers that all the Amalekite people in all the places where they lived were killed, not just some. If we may draw an analogy, this would be like finding Egyptian records indicating Egypt killed all of David's people (the entire Israelite nation) from Beersheba (south) to Dan (north), and the Great Sea (west) to the Jordan (east), when in reality they only conquered Jerusalem and captured David.

So how do we respond to the idea that total-kill language is literally fulfilled in the narrow (one city) scene but not the broader (entire people group) scene? First, we must confess that we cannot know with certainty what actually happened. All we can do is work with reasoned probabilities. Within that probability framework, we can determine some things. Here is what

---

[28]Even though, in reality, only one subgroup of Kenites moves away from one subgroup of Amalekites.

seems clear to us: the biblical rhetoric about punishment, kindness, and killing is at a comprehensive level concerning total people groups. So, if the narrator is comfortable with creating a gigantic chasm between rhetoric (kill everyone) and reality (not everyone killed) at the national level, how much more so at the local level? Second, appendix A on royal-family equivalency will show how the city as well as the larger people group is represented by the king (and sometimes his armies). This evidence shows that the dislocation at a national level also happened at a local, city level. We could go on, but this must suffice for here, because the focus on the biblical rhetoric in this passage is at the national level.[29]

Reading 1 Samuel 15 through the lens of Deuteronomy/Joshua total-kill language. With yet another piece of evidence, the hyperbole conclusion becomes more likely when we compare the language used in 1 Samuel 15 with the language used in Deuteronomy and Joshua to describe total-kill warfare, as in table 11.1.

Table 11.1

1 Samuel 15	Deuteronomy/Joshua
Command to strike down (*nākâ*) the enemy: 1 Sam 15:3, 7	Strike (*nākâ*) the enemy: Num 21:35; Deut 1:4; 2:33; 3:3; 7:2; 20:13; Josh 10:10, 20, 26, 28, 30, 32-33, 35, 37, 39-41; 11:8, 10-12, 14, 17; 12:1, 6-7
Devote to destruction (*ḥāram*) everything: 1 Sam 15:3, 8, 15, 18, 20	Devote to destruction (*ḥāram*): Deut 2:34; 3:6; 7:2; 13:16; 20:17; Josh 2:10; 6:18, 21; 8:26; 10:1, 28, 35, 37, 39-40; 11:11-12, 20, 21
Do not have mercy (*ḥāmal*) on them: 1 Sam 15:3; see also 1 Sam 15:15	Do not show mercy (*ḥāmal*) to them: Deut 7:2
Put to death (*mût*—Hiphil) men and women, child and baby, cattle and sheep, camel and donkey: 1 Sam 15:3	Put them to death (*mût*—Hiphil): Josh 10:26; 11:17
Put them to the sword (*ləpî-ḥāreb*): 1 Sam 15:8	Put to the sword (*ləpî-ḥāreb*): Deut 13:16; 20:13; Josh 6:21; 8:24; 10:28, 30, 32, 35, 37, 39, 11:11-12, 14; see also Judg 1:8; 18:27; 20:37

---

[29]For example, Samuel's pronouncement of judgment on Agag, "As your sword has made women childless, so will your mother be childless among women" (1 Sam 15:33), is problematic for a literal, total-kill reading. If this statement is read literally, then at the very least, Agag's mother would have been left alive to experience the pain of Agag's death. However, Samuel's statement reflects a talionic sense of justice and is likely figurative (i.e., not literal), much like the hyperbolic language of conquest in the passage.

As we saw in chapter nine, the book of Joshua uses hyperbole in its descriptions of Israel's total-kill warfare against the Canaanites. The common terminology and similar contexts (battle against Canaanite foes) that we see in table 11.1 build the expectation that if the language of Deuteronomy and Joshua is hyperbolic, then the language of 1 Samuel 15 likely also indicates the presence of hyperbole.

Although 1 Samuel 15 and Deuteronomy/Joshua share common total-kill terminology, Yahweh's explicit condemnation of Saul for his failure to kill King Agag is a striking difference. This difference fits well with a hyperbole thesis. Saul is vilified not because he left one last Amalekite alive (and so did not follow Yahweh's command in a literal sense down to the last letter), but because of *whom* he left alive—the king, the living embodiment of the Amalekite threat.[30] Joshua, on the other hand, is not condemned even though Canaanites are left alive, because in each case he kills the king and thereby neutralizes the threat posed by that city (Josh 8:1-2, 29; 9:10; 10:26, 28, 30, 33, 37, 39, 40, 42; 11:10, 12, 17-18; 12:1-24). Both 1 Samuel 15 and Deuteronomy/Joshua use total-kill hyperbole to describe the extent and scope of battle. Saul's failure is rooted in leaving the king alive (contra the Joshua pattern) and, as we will see, his motives for doing so.

Saul's self-serving motives. First Samuel 15 does not provide any explicit rationale or motives for Saul's actions, but clues in the text allow us to reconstruct his probable motives.[31] Once we see the larger picture of what Yahweh and Samuel are truly upset about (not the need to kill every Amalekite peasant), we recognize that Saul's failure to kill the Amalekite *king* is symptomatic of the larger problem lying at the root of his actions—his pride and self-glorification.[32] Several pieces of evidence in 1 Samuel 15 lead to the

---

[30]The king by himself would not be much of a threat if everyone else in his kingdom had been killed (total-kill literalism). However, the king would have been a threat to the degree that he was still a viable leader and could rally any people who were left alive. See discussion above about Amalekite survivors.

[31]Robert Alter notes, "The masters of ancient Hebrew narrative were clearly writers who delighted in an art of indirection, in the possibilities of intimating depths through the mere hint of a surface feature, or through a few words of dialogue fraught with implication" (*The World of Biblical Literature* [New York: Basic Books, 1992], 65-66).

[32]Even if Saul's army pressured him for plunder or to enjoy the spoils of war, his decision to give in to them was likely motivated by a desire to look good in their eyes, similar to his desire to look good in the eyes of the leaders and people (1 Sam 15:30).

conclusion that Saul's self-serving desire to legitimize his role as king rather than trust Yahweh to establish his kingship lies behind his actions and Yahweh's condemnation.

Literary context: Saul as Israel's failed war leader. Within its literary context 1 Samuel 15 culminates in the description of Yahweh's rejection of Saul as king (1 Sam 13–15). It is no accident that each episode in 1 Samuel 13–15 depicts Saul's failure as the war leader of Israel. The original request for a king had as its goal that Israel would "be like all the other nations, *with a king to lead us and to go out before us and fight our battles*" (1 Sam 8:20). Israel wanted a warrior king to lead them in battle. But Saul repeatedly shows himself to be ineffective as a war leader because he is not fully obedient to Yahweh.

Early on, Saul seizes Yahweh's prerogative to initiate battle by offering prebattle sacrifices before the arrival of Samuel, Yahweh's appointed spokesman. Because of his disobedience, Saul loses Yahweh's endorsement of his dynasty (1 Sam 13:13). When Saul's son Jonathan uses his bravery and courage to secure Israel's routing of the Philistines (1 Sam 14:45), Saul's inept leadership costs Israel a decisive victory. In his zeal to pursue the fleeing Philistines, Saul forbids his soldiers to slow down to grab some food and threatens the death penalty for anyone who does so. Jonathan, not knowing of Saul's order, quickly takes a bit of honey before resuming his pursuit. Because Saul failed to recognize his soldiers' need, their energy levels fall and they miss an opportunity to decisively defeat the Philistines. Saul's endeavor to enforce his vow further undercuts his credibility and compels the army to rescue Jonathan—the actual hero of the battle—from Saul's belated attempt to make good on his death threat. These portrayals of Saul's bungling battle leadership climax in 1 Samuel 15 with Saul's failure to fully obey Yahweh and Yahweh's subsequent rejection of Saul as king (1 Sam 15:23).[33]

First Samuel 16 introduces the promised "one better than [Saul]" (1 Sam 15:28) by narrating how Samuel anoints David as the next king of Israel.

---

[33]First Samuel depicts Saul's military leadership as a mixture of some successes (1 Sam 11:1-11; 14:47-48; 18:7-8) and some key failures (1 Sam 13:13-14; 15:23). Saul's failures ultimately lead to his rejection as king.

The anointing of David inaugurates what some have called the History of David's Rise (1 Sam 16 through 2 Sam 5).[34] This block of narrative contrasts Saul's doomed attempts to hang onto his kingship with David's refusal to prematurely grasp the kingly position for which he was designated (1 Sam 16:13; see also 1 Sam 24:6, 10; 26:9, 16, 23; 2 Sam 1:14-16). Thus, 1 Samuel 15 culminates the portrayal of Saul's failed leadership in war and in obedience to Yahweh, thereby paving the way for the introduction of Saul's successor, David.

King Saul and the desire for legitimacy. Considering this portrayal of Saul's failure to live up to expectations, 1 Samuel 15 displays Saul's last-ditch attempts to reestablish his flagging status in the *eyes of his people* by trying to do what other ANE warrior kings did: legitimate his role as a warrior king. Such acts, however, reveal Saul's pride in his own accomplishments and lead him away from full obedience to Yahweh, the true source of his legitimacy in the eyes of the biblical narrator.

Though the concept of kingship was not novel to the ancient Israelites (see Deut 17:14-20; Judg 8:22-23; 9:1-6; 17:6; 18:1; 19:1; 21:25), the installation of an Israelite king inaugurated a dramatic change in the exercise of authority in ancient Israel. Samuel enumerates several examples of the new powers that kingship implies:

- ▶ the ability to conscript Israel's young men for the king's army (1 Sam 8:11)
- ▶ the ability to command work for the king's agricultural benefit (1 Sam 8:12)
- ▶ the need to make the king's instruments of war (1 Sam 8:12)
- ▶ the ability to conscript Israel's young women to serve the king's domestic needs (1 Sam 8:13)
- ▶ the ability to appropriate the best arable land (1 Sam 8:14)
- ▶ the ability to command a 10 percent tithe (1 Sam 8:15)
- ▶ the ability to redistribute wealth as he sees fit (1 Sam 8:16-17)
- ▶ the ability to enslave his people (1 Sam 8:17)

---

[34]Firth, *1 & 2 Samuel*, 27-28; see also Kyle P. McCarter, "The Apology of David," *JBL* 99 (1980): 489-504.

These negative aspects of kingship represent a monumental change in Israel's power and authority structures, a shift that could not be instituted or maintained without establishing the legitimacy of these structures.[35]

Legitimation has multiple dimensions, but divine sanction was crucial for the ongoing legitimation of leaders in ancient Israel and throughout the ANE. The initial legitimation of Saul's kingship, for example, is conveyed through both Samuel's anointing and his words: "Has not [Yahweh] anointed you as ruler over his inheritance?" (1 Sam 10:1). However, legitimacy dissipates unless a king works to sustain and develop it. The loss of Yahweh's full sanction (1 Sam 13:13-14) and Saul's inconsistent war leadership in 1 Samuel 13–14 set the stage for his attempts to regain and rebuild his legitimacy in the eyes of his people in 1 Samuel 15 by attempting to do the kinds of things that ANE kings did to build themselves up in the eyes of their people.

While 1 Samuel 15 does not explicitly mention the concept of legitimation, that is exactly what is happening. The text provides us with some dramatic clues. Saul's perceived need to bolster his legitimacy in the eyes of his people is evident when he explains why he violated Yahweh's commands. He says, "*I was afraid of the men* and so I gave in to them" (1 Sam 15:24). Saul desperately seeks approval, and so rather than risk his people's disapproval, he gives in to them. Similarly, even after Samuel has informed Saul that Yahweh has given his kingdom to someone else, Saul is still concerned about elevating his status in the people's eyes and says to Samuel: "I have sinned. But please *honor me before the elders of my people and before Israel*" (1 Sam 15:30).

---

[35]Anthropologists, along with political and social scientists, have recognized that such changes in power bring inequities, particularly as societies transition from prestate to state forms, requiring significant and ongoing legitimation. See Donald V. Kurtz, "The Legitimation of the Aztec State," in *The Early State*, ed. Henri J. M. Claessen and Peter Skalník, Studies in the Social Sciences 32 (New York: Mouton, 1978), 186. See also Donald V. Kurtz with Margaret Showman, "The Legitimation of Early Inchoate States," in *The Study of the State*, ed. Henri J. M. Claessen and Peter Skalník, Studies in the Social Sciences 35 (New York: Mouton, 1981), 181-82. Ronald Cohen observes, "The realities of power and inequity once set into place through competition and conflict are a culture-creating force that interacts with human consciousness, especially its cause-effect rationality, to produce an explanation for both the acceptance of the inequity—legitimacy—and its rejection or resistance—illegitimacy." But legitimacy is a fluid state that ebbs and flows in response to power holders' words and actions—they must also continue to act in ways that retain and build on their legitimacy, or risk losing it. See Cohen, "Legitimacy, Illegitimacy, and State Formation," in *State Formation and Political Legitimacy*, ed. Ronald Cohen and Judith D. Toland, Political Anthropology 6 (New Brunswick, NJ: Transaction Books, 1988), 82.

In short, Saul's actions throughout 1 Samuel 15 should be understood in view of his concern to legitimate his position. In trying to legitimate his rule as other ANE kings did, Saul loses the one indicator of his legitimacy that truly matters—Yahweh's endorsement. The issue in 1 Samuel 15 is not violation of a literal total-kill command but rather (1) violation of hyperbolic total kill that resides in the king as representative of the nation (collective identity) and (2) Saul's self-serving attempt to use the enemy king and the best animals to honor himself. Saul's desire to honor himself (not Yahweh) and make himself look good in the victory over Amalek can be seen in three self-serving acts of legitimation.

Legitimation act one: King Saul and the monument. The narrator relays the seemingly random bit of information that the morning after his battle with the Amalekites, Saul goes to Carmel to set up a monument (*yād*) in his own honor (1 Sam 15:12). Saul, and possibly David, are the only two recorded Israelite kings to set up a postbattle monument.[36] Moreover, Saul sets up the monument *for himself* rather than to honor Yahweh's role in the victory (see 1 Sam 15:2). In the ANE, kings set up monuments as shameless self-promoting propaganda recounting their accomplishments, thereby reminding their enemies of the futility of resistance and rebellion, and by implication reminding their supporters of the values of supporting the king. William Hallo remarks, "Near Eastern kings celebrated their achievements and the 'sacraments' of their own lifetimes not only in monumental inscriptions but also in royal hymns, date formulas, and statuary. The bombastic tones in which they glorified their roles is unmistakable even when they assigned due credit to their deities."[37] Monuments thereby acted as projections of a king's power. For example, the Kurkh Monolith regales readers with the victories of Shalmaneser III, noting,

---

[36]It is unclear whether the description of David's *yād* in 2 Sam 8:3 // 1 Chron 18:3 denotes the restoration of his "monument" (NIV, NRSV) or his "power/rule/control" (ESV, KJV, NASB, NLT) over Zobah. Furthermore, it is grammatically ambiguous whether it is David or Hadadezer who sets out to restore his monument/power in these verses. Thus, it is possible that David set up a monument for himself, but we cannot definitively say this is the case. Second Samuel 18:18 indicates that Absalom erected a monument for himself to perpetuate his name because he had no children, but this was not a postbattle display inscription. Isaiah 56:5 describes Yahweh's promise to set up a monument to remember the eunuchs, but this is not a postbattle monument and is clearly metaphorical, set up by Yahweh himself.

[37]*COS* 2:xxvi.

At that time, I paid homage to the greatness of (all) the great gods (and) extolled for posterity the heroic achievements of Ashur and Shamash by fashioning a (sculptured) stela with myself as king (depicted on it). I wrote thereupon my heroic behavior, my deeds in combat and erected it beside the source of the Saluara river which is at the foot of the mountains of the Amanus.[38]

Similarly, an inscribed stela of Tiglath-pileser III says, "I caused a stela to be made in the vicinity of the mountain, (and) I depicted on it (the symbols of) the great gods, my lords, (and) I engraved upon it my own royal image; and the mighty deeds of Aššur, my lord, and achievements of [my] hands, which were done throughout all the lands, I wr[ote] on it."[39]

As noted above, Saul is the first and only unambiguous example of an Israelite king to erect such a monument. Unlike other ANE kings who also honored their patron deities, Saul apparently sets up his monument to honor only himself. Thus, Saul, like other ANE kings, seems to be attempting to engage in a self-serving projection of kingly power.

This self-serving element seems even more likely because Saul erects his monument at Carmel (1 Sam 15:12). The Carmel of 1 Samuel 15:12 is not Mount Carmel, which lies far to the north on the Mediterranean coast. Rather, this Carmel was a small Judahite town at the edge of the Negev (1 Sam 25:2) in the general area where the battle with the Amalekites took place. Carmel was also squarely in Judahite territory (see Josh 15:55). First Samuel 15:4 already hints at a division between Judah and other Israelites by distinguishing the Judahite soldiers mustered by Saul from those he mustered from the other Israelite tribes. Judah was also David's tribe, the first to support David (2 Sam 2:4) and to abandon Saul and his descendants. Considering the previous chapters, which highlight his waning legitimacy as a warrior, mention of Saul's monument for himself (and significantly not for Yahweh) in Judahite territory is likely the narrator's way of drawing attention to Saul's attempts to project kingly power in the heart of opposition territory.

Through this self-promotion, Saul has left behind the humble posture that accompanied his appointment as king, and more importantly the acknowledgment that his legitimacy stems from Yahweh. Samuel reminds Saul

---

[38]*ANET*, 277.
[39]*COS* 2:117B, 287.

accordingly, "Although you were once small in your own eyes, did you not become the head of the tribes of Israel? The LORD anointed you king over Israel" (1 Sam 15:17).

Legitimation act two: Sparing the spoils of war. Saul's rationale for sparing the best of the Amalekite livestock can also be understood as a twisted attempt to hold on to kingly power. ANE protocol saw the plunder of war as the king's rightful due, the spoils of victory, given to him to disperse after he presented the gods with their share.[40] Kings would disperse plunder among battle participants, in part to resupply their army and in part as a reward for support or participation in a successful campaign.[41] Large disbursements of plunder kept warriors happy and fostered increased loyalty to the king. Most of all, the distribution of plunder was a kingly show of strength. For example, the account of Ashurnasirpal II's campaign into Lebanon includes a description of how he conquered the king of the city of Carchemesh, saying, "In order to (show the) strength of my rule, the possessions of his palace I plundered. A valuable image of my likeness for his temples I glorified."[42] In an inscription Egyptian pharaoh Sethos I boasts of his exploits in a campaign against the Lybians that included the taking of plunder to highlight his military prowess:

> His Majesty has returned from the foreign lands, his at[tack] having succeeded. He has plundered Retenu (Syria), he has slain their chiefs. He has caused the Asiatics to say: "Who is this? He is like a flame in its shooting forth, unchecked by water!" He causes all rebels to desist from all boasting with their mouths— he has taken away the (very) breath of their nostrils.[43]

A four-line inscription from Sennacherib's palace describes the king's public display of spoils taken from the Judahite city of Lachish in order to showcase his military might:

---

[40]For Egypt see *COS* 2:4A, 24-25; Boyd Severs, *Warfare in the Old Testament* (Grand Rapids: Kregel, 2013), 112; see also Num 31:29-30.

[41]Pharaoh Mernepthah says that after he thoroughly defeated the prince of Rebu, "all his goods were food for the troops" (*ANET*, 377). Similarly, Sennacherib boasts in his first campaign against Merodach-Baladan that he provisioned his troops with barley from enemy fields and dates from their groves (*COS* 2:119A, 302). Sennacherib recounts how he plundered Hezekiah's towns and gave them to Mitini king of Ashdod, Padi king of Ekron, and Sillibel king of Gaza (*ANET*, 288).

[42]*COS* 2:139, 471.

[43]*COS* 2:4F, 31.

> Sennacherib, king of the universe, king of Assyria,
> Seated upon a sedan chair,
> The spoils of Lachish
> Passed before him.[44]

In these examples, the display and dispersal of plunder exemplify the king's military might and bountiful largesse to solidify the support of elite leaders and common soldiers.

The leaders of ancient Israel seem to have had a similar view of plunder. Typical postbattle protocol viewed the plunder as Yahweh's possession, since he won the victory.[45] The best of the spoils of battle belonged to Yahweh (Num 31:28-31, 41, 47; Deut 13:16; Josh 6:24; 1 Chron 26:27), though Yahweh could choose to divide the plunder among the warriors (Num 31:12; Josh 8:2, 27; Jer 17:3; Ezek 7:21). Human war leaders had a similar responsibility (Num 31:27; Josh 22:8; 1 Sam 30:26; Ezek 29:19; Dan 11:24). The division of plunder by Israel's war leaders was meant to secure the loyalty of those who fought in or supported their campaigns, as when David divided the plunder equally among all his troops and also sent a portion to the elders of Judah and all those who backed him (1 Sam 30:26-31). These are the same people who later anointed David as their king after Saul's death (2 Sam 2:4). Consequently, in both the ANE generally and in ancient Israel, the distribution of plunder, whether for Yahweh's use or for the people's, acted as a projection of power and authority.

These perspectives are embedded in 1 Samuel 15. Yahweh's instructions were to destroy everyone and everything (1 Sam 15:3). Saul, however, spared the best sheep and cattle, destroying only the least desirable animals (1 Sam 15:9). When questioned (1 Sam 15:15, 21), Saul indicated that the people spared the best animals to sacrifice (*zābaḥ*) them to Yahweh while the rest were destroyed (*ḥāram*—Hiphil). To Saul's (incorrect) way of thinking, sacrificing the animals to Yahweh was equivalent to destroying them, for both actions—sacrificing and destroying—involved the death of the animal in an act of worship to Yahweh. But the difference between these two actions is significant.

---

[44]*COS* 2:119C, 304.
[45]Tremper Longman III and Daniel G. Reid, *God Is a Warrior*, SOTBT (Grand Rapids: Zondervan, 1995), 45-47.

When an animal was offered by destruction (*ḥāram*), the whole animal was given to Yahweh with no part available for human consumption. On the other hand, some sacrifices allowed for humans to eat parts of the animal (Ex 34:15; Lev 7:15-21; Deut 12:5-7, 21; 1 Sam 2:13; 28:24-25; 1 Kings 19:21).[46] For example, the fellowship offering (*šelem*) included large portions that were eaten as part of a sacrificial meal (Lev 7:15-18; 19:5-7; see also 1 Sam 10:8), which was sometimes enjoyed after victory in battle (1 Sam 11:15). A great victory was often followed by sacrifices of thanksgiving (1 Sam 11:15; see also Lev 7:12-15; 22:29-30; Judg 16:23; Ps 50:14-15; Jon 1:16) and festal sacrifices that included major portions consumed by the worshiper, much like the one in which Saul participates when he first meets Samuel (1 Sam 9:12, 24-25; see also 1 Kings 8:62-66).

Saul wants to have his cake and eat it too. By saving the best animals for sacrifice and bringing them home, Saul could give the impression of obeying God by killing the animals while also serving a feast for the warriors and people that would bring *himself* honor. Here is the rub. He clearly violates *ḥērem* by using the animals for his own purposes even if the temple/worship context makes it *look like* everything is given over to Yahweh. Perhaps Saul could have petitioned Yahweh before the battle for this modified-*ḥērem* approach and use of the animals in this dual function, but he did not.[47] In fact, his actions against the "don't bring back any loot" instructions proclaim his arrogance and desire to inflate himself before the

---

[46]The verb *zābaḥ* can refer both to the general act of slaughtering an animal and to the act of slaughtering an animal as part of a religious ritual in which the participant sometimes consumes part of the sacrifice (*TDOT* 4:11, 25-27).

[47]Saul's claim to have followed Yahweh's instructions (1 Sam 15:13, 20) despite not fully destroying all the animals has some precedent. Deuteronomy 20:16-17 commands Israel to leave nothing alive that breathes (presumably including animals) when fighting the Canaanites. However, Israel under Joshua is sometimes allowed to take livestock as plunder without recrimination (Josh 11:14; see also Josh 8:2, 27). Thus, Saul can claim to have carried out Yahweh's instructions, especially because all the animals would eventually be killed, while at the same time using them to throw a huge party in Yahweh's name, which also just happens to raise his status in the eyes of his people. This line of reasoning is supported by 1 Sam 15:19, where Samuel says that Saul "pounce[d] on the plunder" (*wattaʿaṭ ʾel-haššālāl*). This expression is used elsewhere only in 1 Sam 14:32, where it describes the excessive haste of Saul's army in slaughtering and consuming the sheep, cattle, and calves taken as spoil from the Philistines before their blood had been fully drained (see Lev 19:26). Saul's haste to take up the spoils of war in 1 Sam 15:19 hints at his desperation to use the plunder to further his own agenda instead of Yahweh's agenda, and it suggests that he had already made plans to divide the booty in ways that would build his stature in the people's eyes.

people, as when he usurped Samuel's priestly role by rushing to perform prebattle sacrifices by himself (1 Sam 13:9-14).

Legitimation act three: Sparing the king. Saul's sparing of King Agag may also be understood as an attempted projection of kingly power.[48] ANE kings might spare the kings or leaders of other nations for a variety of reasons: to appoint a person indebted to the conquering king as leader over a rebellious area and so ensure his continuing loyalty, to serve as hostages, to impose tribute on them, or to later mock a leader, thereby displaying the victor's might and military prowess.[49] Similar perspectives are reflected in the Bible, where David repeatedly spares Saul's life (1 Sam 24:10; 26:10-11), refusing to seize kingship for himself and also building his reputation as a good and merciful leader.[50] The king's ability to take or spare a life is reflected in passages such as 1 Kings 20:31, when Ben-Hadad's officials suggest that he surrender to the king of Israel because, they say, "We have heard that the kings of the Israelites are merciful kings." In a much later text, Daniel 5:19 describes Nebuchadnezzar's absolute power: "All the nations and peoples of every language dreaded and feared him. Those the king wanted to put to death, he put to death; those he wanted to spare, he spared; those he wanted to promote, he promoted; and those he wanted to humble, he humbled." Thus, in both ANE and biblical texts, sparing the life of another king was a projection of power, designed to instill fear, reverence, and loyalty in his subjects and enemies.

We cannot know with certainty Saul's exact motives in sparing Agag. However, given the portrayal of Saul's other attempts to act like the kings of the nations in 1 Samuel 15, it is not unreasonable to suppose that Saul's decision to

---

[48]Commentators speculate as to why Saul spared Agag. Keith Bodner suggests Agag was Saul's war trophy (*1 Samuel: A Narrative Commentary* [Sheffield: Sheffield Phoenix Press, 2009], 152-53). Bill T. Arnold holds that Saul wanted to display Agag as a royal slave (*1 & 2 Samuel*, NIVAC [Grand Rapids: Zondervan, 2003], 219-20). Louis H. Feldman notes that Pseudo-Philo speculated that Saul thought Agag would show him hidden treasures, while in Josephus Saul saw the beauty of Agag and so spared him ("Josephus's View of the Amalekites," *BBR* 12, no. 2 [2002]: 175, 179).

[49]Ashurbanipal spared Necho and appointed him as king in Egypt after his first campaign (*ANET*, 295). Ashurnasirpal II's expedition to Carchemish and Lebanon included kings taken as hostage in his vanguard (*ANET*, 275). Egyptian king Piye spared King Namart and gladly received his tribute (*COS* 2:7). Sargon of Agade brought Lugalzagesi king of Uruk to the gate of Enlil wearing a dog collar (*ANET*, 267).

[50]Compare the sparing of Mephibosheth, Jonathan's son and Saul's heir, in 2 Sam 21:7.

spare Agag was an attempted projection of power. This interpretation is also supported by the words of Saul and the actions of Samuel. Even if we do not know the precise motive, the presence of Agag as a defeated and captured king clearly casts the spotlight on Saul as the victorious king. As with the monument built to honor Saul and the cattle/sheep being used to honor Saul in the public worship gathering, it is most likely that Agag (even if understood as a broad contrastive foil) played a role in bringing greater honor to Saul than if he had followed Joshua's example by killing the king with the sword, hanging the dead body outside the king's city until sunset, and burying him there.

Even after being told that Yahweh has rejected Saul as king over Israel and has given his kingdom to one better than Saul (1 Sam 15:28), Saul is still concerned about his status before the elders, for he briefly admits, "I have sinned," but then with shocking juxtaposition says to Samuel, "*Honor me before the elders of my people and before Israel*; come back with me, so that I may worship the LORD your God" (1 Sam 15:30). Moreover, the task of dispatching an enemy king was usually the responsibility of the war leader or king, for it was a humiliation to be slain by a warrior of lesser status.[51] This explains Agag's relief when he realizes that it is Samuel the prophet who has sent for him and not King Saul, for he reasons, "Surely the bitterness of death is past" (1 Sam 15:32). Samuel's slaying of Agag not only deprives Saul of the boost to his status that would have come by dispatching King Agag, but it also illustrates the demotion of Saul from kingly status.

In this way, 1 Samuel 15 insinuates that Saul's motives are self-serving and prideful in (1) building a monument to honor himself, (2) sparing Agag and keeping him presumably as a bound capture (highlighting Saul as a successful king), and (3) likely hoping to use the sheep (a small portion of each animal) as sacrifice for Yahweh but (a larger portion) also as meat for a victory banquet to reward his army and bring himself even greater honor. Each of these actions is driven by Saul's desire to make himself look good as

---

[51]Gideon instructs his son Jether to kill the Midianite kings Zebah and Zalmunnah, but he refuses, and the Midianite kings say to Gideon, "Come, do it yourself. 'As is the man, so is his strength'" (Judg 8:21). Deborah warns Barak that his failure to willingly go into battle against Hazor will result in the glory for battle passing to a woman (Judg 4:9), and Abimelech's wound at the hands of a woman is so horrifying to him that he asks his armor bearer to dispatch him so that he will not go down in infamy as killed by a woman (Judg 9:52-54).

king—doing the kinds of things that the kings of the nations are known to do. But Saul's attempts to elevate himself in the eyes of his people come at the expense of full obedience to Yahweh, whose approval is far more important than that of the people. Because of his attempts to project kingly power, Saul's own power and status are taken away from him.

The biblical narrator in 1 Samuel 15 clearly accepts that total kill has happened with the (glaring) exception of the enemy king. However, the same narrator fully understands this total-kill language to mean that not every common Amalekite was literally killed—as seen by the later Amalekites, localized battle, Joshua's use of similar hyperbole language—and that hyperbolic language simply means a decisive battle win.

To kill the king is to destroy the people/nation. By keeping the Amalekite king alive Saul has broken the clear obedience patterns of Joshua and done so to boost his own honor (not Yahweh's honor). But another factor in play with hyperbole is the overlapping identity of the king and his people/nation (also the king and his army). In the Old Testament and in the ANE generally, the king served not only as the commander in chief of the army but also conceptually as the embodiment of the army and the nation. As a result, the actions of the entire army were attributed to the king. For example, 2 Samuel 5:6-7 attributes the conquest of Jerusalem to David, though we are specifically told that David and his men march up to capture the city, and 1 Chronicles 11:6 suggests that Joab strikes the decisive blow. Similarly, 2 Samuel 5:17-25 indicates that David defeated the Philistines at Baal Perazim, though his entire army fought there. More importantly for our purposes, to kill the king was to defeat his entire army and the nation. In many instances a nation or people group are finally defeated only when the king has been defeated and killed. This thinking manifests itself in a variety of ways. Deuteronomy 1:4 describes the defeat of King Sihon and King Og without reference to their armies. Joshua 10 describes Joshua's defeat of a coalition of five cities, along with a prolonged chase from Gibeon all the way to Azekah and Makkedah (Josh 10:10). But the defeat is not consummated until the death of the five kings at the head of the coalition is narrated as the final battle act (Josh 10:26; see also Judg 8:27). The death of the king terminates the battle and neutralizes the threat posed by that group.

If we view Yahweh's condemnation of Saul in this light, the implications of Saul's failure to kill King Agag become clearer. Saul might be thinking he is in compliance with Yahweh's commands because he has defeated the Amalekite army and captured its king. But his motives are self-serving, and his actions fall short. Samuel can rightly chastise Saul. He was disobedient, not because he failed to kill every last Amalekite peasant but because (1) he failed to kill the Amalekite king, the embodiment of the Amalekite army/nation and the threat they represented, and because (2) Saul's prideful motives kept him from doing so. Only when Samuel kills Agag are Yahweh's instructions to destroy the Amalekites completed.

CONCLUSION

The evidence favors understanding the total-kill language of 1 Samuel 15 in a hyperbolic (not literal) sense. A literal rendering is possible only if we understand Yahweh's (also Samuel's and the biblical narrator's) intense displeasure with Saul's act of sparing Agag as due to not killing every surviving Amalekite. Along these lines we must then understand the narrator himself as saying that except for one person, Saul obeyed God and literally killed all breathing Amalekites. If only Saul had gone one further! Yet this is not what provokes Yahweh's displeasure. Several lines of evidence support understanding the total-kill language in 1 Samuel 15 in hyperbolic terms:

▶ The same biblical narrator speaks of other living Amalekites later in 1–2 Samuel.

▶ Other later biblical texts confirm living Amalekites.

▶ The evidence for a localized battle in 1 Samuel 15 against the backdrop of an expansive Amalekite territory suggests that the narrator and original audience would have known full well that total kill was not literally intended.

▶ Finding the same total-kill language in 1 Samuel 15 and Deuteronomy/Joshua (see table 11.1) strengthens the case for hyperbole in 1 Samuel 15.

▶ Saul's motives are self-serving and prideful in his attempts at legitimation with actions that honor himself (but not Yahweh): erecting the monument, sparing animals, and keeping King Agag alive for subjugated display are each designed to honor Saul.

God's displeasure at Saul's failure to kill Agag is not because Saul has failed to kill every breathing Amalekite—merchant, shepherd, farmer, and so on. The status and role of King Agag means that he is not an average Amalekite. Only by killing the embodiment of the Amalekites—the Amalekite king—in battle could Saul have claimed obedience to Yahweh. At root, the issue is with Saul's pride, his self-aggrandizing acts honoring his own military prowess and not Yahweh for victory in battle, and his failure to trust in Yahweh to establish his kingship.

12

DRIVE OUT

An Equivalent Alternative

A PROBLEM FACING ANY READER of the Bible is that the total-kill instructions seem to contradict the drive-out instructions if both are taken literally. If the Israelites are instructed to kill (literally) *all* Canaanites, why are they also commanded to drive them out of the land? This chapter examines three proposals for relating total-kill and drive-out commands and reports within the biblical war texts. The three options can be configured along these lines:

▶ *Contradictory sources:* total kill (one source) and drive out (another source)

▶ *Literal means:* drive out by means of (literal) total kill

▶ *Shared-goal equivalency:* total kill (hyperbole) and/or drive out

Along with critiquing the competing options, we argue that total kill and drive out are equally acceptable ways of achieving the same goal.

In ancient Israel's understanding, the land was sacred space—Yahweh's temple land, *terra sancta*—and the goal of Israel's battles with the Canaanites was to create conditions for the exclusive worship of Yahweh in the land. This made the land as new Eden and sacred space (chapter three) the foundational issue and not necessarily killing every breathing Canaanite. If total-kill and drive-out instructions were both acceptable options for achieving the primary goal of restoring *terra sancta*, then this chapter provides yet another good piece of evidence for understanding total-kill language in a hyperbolic (not literal) sense.

CONTRADICTORY SOURCES: TOTAL KILL (ONE SOURCE)
AND DRIVE OUT (ANOTHER SOURCE)

Baruch Schwartz reconciles the seemingly contradictory total-kill and drive-out instructions by appealing to two different sources. He argues that different Pentateuchal compositions lie behind these varying descriptions of how Israel was to possess the land of Canaan.[1] Schwartz says that the pre-Deuteronomic (J and E) sources held that Yahweh would cause the Canaanites to flee the land (no total kill), while the Deuteronomic tradition held that if the Israelites waged a war of annihilation (total kill) against the Canaanites, then Yahweh would terrify them with his hornet (Deut 7:20), drawing any remaining Canaanites out of hiding so that Israel could completely eradicate them.[2] A problem with Schwartz's proposal is that many of the Old Testament texts using eradication language for Israel's battles with the Canaanites also describe their expulsion from the land:

> My angel will go ahead of you and bring you into the land of the Amorites, Hittites, Perizzites, Canaanites, Hivites and Jebusites, and *I will wipe them out* [*kāḥad*; **total kill**] . . . I will send my terror ahead of you and will throw into confusion every nation you encounter. I will make all your enemies turn their backs and run. I will send the hornet ahead of you to *drive* [*gāraš*—Piel; **drive out**] the Hivites, Canaanites and Hittites from out of your way. (Ex 23:23, 27-28)

> When the LORD your God brings you into the land you are entering to possess and *drives out* [*nāšal*; **drive out**] before you many nations—the Hittites, Girgashites, Amorites, Canaanites, Perizzites, Hivites and Jebusites, seven nations larger and stronger than you—and when the LORD your God has delivered them over to you and *you have defeated them* [*nākâ*—Hiphil], *then you must destroy them totally* [*ḥāram*—Hiphil; **total kill**]. (Deut 7:1-2)

> You must *destroy* [*ʾākal*; **total kill**] all the peoples the LORD your God gives over to you. Do not *look on them with pity* [*lōʾ hûs*; **total kill**] and do not serve

---

[1]Baruch J. Schwartz, "Reexamining the Fate of the 'Canaanites' in the Torah Traditions," in *Sefer Moshe: The Moshe Weinfeld Jubilee Volume*, ed. Chaim Cohen, Avi Hurvitz, and Shalom M. Paul (Winona Lake, IN: Eisenbrauns, 2004), 153-59. Compare Moshe Weinfeld, who proposes a three-stage development within the Pentateuchal sources (*The Promise of Land: The Inheritance of the Land of Canaan by the Israelites* [Berkeley: University of California Press, 1993], 76-98).

[2]Schwartz, "Reexamining the Fate of the 'Canaanites' in the Torah Traditions," 153-59.

their gods, for that will be a snare to you. You may say to yourselves, "These nations are stronger than we are. How can we *drive them out* [*yāraš*—Hiphil; **drive out**]?" (Deut 7:16-17)

The LORD your God will drive out [*nāšal*; **drive out**] those nations before you, little by little. You will not be allowed to eliminate them [*kālâ*—Piel; **total kill**] all at once, or the wild animals will multiply around you. But the LORD your God will deliver them over to you, throwing them into great confusion *until they are destroyed* [*šāmad*—Niphal; **total kill**]. He will give their kings into your hand, and you will *wipe out their names* [*ʾābad*—Hiphil; **total kill**] from under heaven. No one will be able to stand up against you; you will destroy them [*šāmad*—Hiphil; **total kill**]. (Deut 7:22-24)

But be assured today that the LORD your God is the one who goes across ahead of you like a devouring fire. He will *destroy them* [*šāmad*—Hiphil; **total kill**]; he will *subdue* [*kānaʿ*—Hiphil; **total kill**] them before you. And you will *drive them out* [*yāraš*—Hiphil; **drive out**] and *annihilate* [*ʾābad*—Hiphil] *them quickly* [**total kill**], as the LORD has promised you. After the LORD your God has *driven them out* [*hādap*; **drive out**] before you, do not say to yourself, "The LORD has brought me here *to take possession* [*yāraš*; **drive out**] of this land because of my righteousness." No, it is on account of the wickedness of these nations that the LORD is going to drive them out before you. (Deut 9:3-4)

The LORD your God will *cut off* [*kārat*—Hiphil; **total kill**] before you the nations you are about to *invade and dispossess* [*yāraš*; **drive out**]. But when you have *driven them out* [*yāraš*; **drive out**] and settled in their land and after they *have been destroyed* [*šāmad*—Niphal; **total kill**] before you, be careful not to be ensnared by inquiring about their gods, saying, "How do these nations serve their gods? We will do the same." (Deut 12:29-30)

When the LORD your God has *destroyed* [*kārat*—Hiphil; **total kill**] the nations whose land he is giving you, and when you have *driven them out* [*yāraš*; **drive out**] and settled in their towns and houses, then set aside for yourselves three cities in the land the LORD your God is giving you to possess. (Deut 19:1-2)

The LORD your God himself will cross over ahead of you. He will *destroy* [*šāmad*—Hiphil; **total kill**] these nations before you, and *you will take possession* [*yāraš*; **drive out**] of their land. Joshua also will cross over ahead of you, as the LORD said. And the LORD will do to them what he did to Sihon and Og, the kings of the Amorites, *whom he destroyed* [*šāmad*—Hiphil; **total kill**] along with their land. The LORD will deliver them to you, and you must do to them all that I have commanded you. (Deut 31:3-5)

The eternal God is your refuge,
   and underneath are the everlasting arms.
He will drive out [*gāraš*—Piel; **drive out**] your enemies before you,
   saying, *"Destroy them!"* [*šāmad*—Hiphil; **total kill**]. (Deut 33:27)

Remember how I have allotted as an inheritance for your tribes all the land of the nations that remain—the nations *I conquered* [*kārat*—Hiphil; **total kill**]— between the Jordan and the Mediterranean Sea in the west. The LORD your God himself will *push them out* [*hādap*; **drive out**] for your sake. He will *drive them out* [*yāraš*—Hiphil; **drive out**] before you, and you will take possession of their land, as the LORD your God promised you. (Josh 23:4-5)

I destroyed them [*šāmad*—Hiphil] *from before you* [**total kill**], and you took possession of their land. . . . I sent the hornet ahead of you, which *drove them out* [*gāraš*—Piel; **drive out**] before you. (Josh 24:8, 12)[3]

Several observations from these texts undermine the multiple-source proposal. First, the combination of drive-out language (*gāraš* and its synonyms) and total-kill language (*ḥāram* and its synonyms) is found in both Deuteronomic and non-Deuteronomic sources. Second, the pattern set out by Schwartz for how Israel would come to dispossess the Canaanites in Deuteronomic literature (total kill-terror-drive out) varies, as seen in the Deuteronomy passages above. For example, Deuteronomy 7:1-2 reverses Schwartz's order, indicating that Yahweh would first drive out the Canaanites before handing them over to Israel for complete destruction. Third, a number of passages in Deuteronomy describe driving out the Canaanites without using any total-kill language (Deut 4:38; 11:23; 18:12). These exceptions to Schwartz's pattern of "total kill, terror, drive out" suggest that the driving out of the Canaanites in Deuteronomic literature could happen independently, without annihilation (more on this below also). Fourth, Ralph Hawkins notes that while the term *ḥērem* (a total-kill term) plays a large role in Deuteronomy's discussion of the fate of the Canaanites, Numbers 18:14 indicates that

---

[3]The two texts from Joshua are not Pentateuchal, but they illustrate the continuation of the phenomenon.

its use is not restricted to Deuteronomic passages.[4] Therefore, the drive-out
and total-kill language of the Pentateuch cannot be restricted to only certain
sources, and so Schwartz's attempt to link total-kill language exclusively with
Deuteronomic sources and drive-out language (no total kill used) with non-
Deuteronomic sources fails to provide an adequate explanation of the relationship between total-kill and drive-out language.

LITERAL MEANS: DRIVE OUT BY (LITERAL) TOTAL KILL

Taking total-kill language in a literal (not hyperbolic) sense, Gregory Beale
proposes that the two sets of war instructions against the Canaanites ought
to be understood as a relationship of means: *drive out by (means of) literal
total kill.* He contends: "The way that Israel was to 'drive out' and 'dispossess'
[drive out] the Canaanites was *by* annihilating them [total kill]."[5] Consequently, some Canaanites may have fled before Israel's attacks and escaped,
probably going into exile in other lands, though this does not seem to be the
norm.[6] He also allows for the possibility that some Canaanite cities may have
initiated peace talks (and so avoided being wiped out). If any Canaanites then
remained in the land, it was due to Israel's disobedience in failing to destroy
any hiding Canaanites when they found them.[7]

This thesis that the driving out is to be by means of total killing takes into
account *some* but not *all* of the available evidence, and so it ultimately falls
short. The numerous passages cited above containing both total-kill and
drive-out language clearly show that both driving out and total killing are to

---

[4]Ralph K. Hawkins, *Joshua*, Evangelical Exegetical Commentary (Bellingham, WA: Lexham,
forthcoming). The focus of the term in Num 18:14 is not on the total destruction of the
Canaanites but on giving the Levites items that are *ḥērem*. In addition, the blessing of Moses
(Deut 33:27) uses the Hebrew word *grš* ("drive out"), a term that Schwartz identifies with
non-Deuteronomic sources. It is sometimes argued that Deut 33 is an older source ap-
pended to Deuteronomy (e.g., Moshe Weinfeld, *Deuteronomy 1–11*, AB [New York: Doubleday, 1991], 9-10). If so, the later Deuteronomic editor apparently felt comfortable using the
expression in constructing the message of the book.

[5]G. K. Beale, *The Morality of God in the Old Testament*, Christian Answers to Hard Questions (Philipsburg, NJ: P&R, 2013), 41 (italics added).

[6]Beale notes that this may have happened more often than Joshua records (*Morality of God*,
41). For further discussion see below on hear-fear-flee sequences.

[7]Beale, *Morality of God*, 41. Paul Copan and Matthew Flannagan draw a different conclusion,
arguing that the expulsion of the Canaanites was the primary objective of Israel's battles
(*Did God Really Command Genocide? Coming to Terms with the Justice of God* [Grand
Rapids: Baker, 2014], 80-81).

be elements of Israel's war with the Canaanites. The question remains: What is the relationship between drive-out and total-kill instructions? The evidence shows no consistent drive-out-by-total-kill sequence in the Pentateuchal passages or in the Joshua-Judges texts where total-kill and drive-out actions are described together. Instead, we find variation in how driving out and total killing are to be accomplished. This variation prevents "drive out by (literal) total kill" from being the best description of how these actions relate to each other. We also see that the recounting of particular incidents does not establish that the rumor or fear of total-kill warfare drives the Canaanites out of the land. Finally, numerous passages show how the driving out of Canaanites could be described *independently* of any total-kill actions. These lines of evidence demonstrate that a thesis that the driving out is to be by means of total killing takes cannot be sustained. Let's examine each line of evidence in turn.

No consistent drive-out-by-total-kill sequence in the Pentateuch or in Joshua-Judges. The theory that driving out was to be by literal total killing has it that hearing rumors of literal total-kill battles induces fear among the Canaanites, causing them to flee from the land in terror. A hear-fear-flee pattern drives them out of the land. But the Pentateuchal passages do not convey any set order in which driving out or total killing would happen. A passage such as Exodus 23:23-33 contains the needed sequence. But the order of drive-out and total-kill actions varies in other Pentateuchal passages. For example, Deuteronomy 7:1-2 reverses the order, with its sequence of temporal clauses listing the things that Yahweh will do to facilitate Israel's taking of the land: "When [1] the LORD your God brings you into the land you are entering to possess and [2] *drives out before you* many nations . . . and when [3] the LORD your God has delivered them over to you and [4] you have defeated them, [5] *then you must destroy them totally.* Make no treaty with them, and show them no mercy." In response to what Yahweh has already done (the first three actions, including driving out), and after Israel's defeat of the Canaanites (the fourth action), Israel is commanded in Deuteronomy 7:2 then to kill all the Canaanites (the fifth action).[8]

---

[8]Gordon J. McConville, *Deuteronomy*, AOTC (Downers Grove, IL; InterVarsity Press, 2002), 151-52; see also Daniel I. Block, *Deuteronomy*, NIVAC (Grand Rapids: Zondervan, 2012),

Thus, in Deuteronomy 7:1-2 driving out the Canaanites is not the result of total-kill warfare but is another component of Israel's coming to possess the land. The passages in the Pentateuch that use both drive-out and total-kill language do not provide any consistent sequential pattern for how these actions are to be accomplished. Consequentially, we cannot draw firm conclusions about a sequential relationship between drive-out and total-kill actions from Pentateuchal descriptions.

Likewise, clear evidence for a drive-out-by-total-kill pattern is absent from Joshua-Judges passages that combine drive-out and total-kill language. A plausible candidate for a drive-out-by-total-kill sequence may be in Joshua 24, where Joshua rehearses Israel's conquest up to that point:

▶ Joshua 24:8 indicates that Yahweh destroys (šāmad—Hiphil) the Amorites living east of the Jordan (total kill).

▶ Then after crossing the Jordan, Yahweh sends "the hornet," which drives out the Canaanites (Josh 24:11-12).[9]

▶ The people later affirm that Yahweh did indeed drive the nations out before them (Josh 24:18).

This sequence would *seem* to follow a drive-out-by-total-kill pattern. However, such a progression is complicated because in Joshua 24 Yahweh does not explicitly link the actions of the hornet that drives out the Canaanites to any literal total-kill actions on Israel's part. In fact, Israel's swords and bows have nothing to do with the driving out in this case. Yahweh makes this clear, saying, "You did not do it [driving out the Canaanites] with your own sword and bow" (Josh 24:12). The problem with using this text as a reference to terror resulting from Israel's (literal) total-kill actions is that all the passages in Joshua describing total kill of the Canaanites involve Israel in martial activities (i.e., using sword and bow) against the Canaanites (Josh 6:21; 8:24; 10:28, 30, 32, 35, 37, 39; 11:10-11, 12, 14; 13:22; 19:47). The total-kill

---

207. Compare Deut 33:27, where Yahweh's driving out Israel's enemies either precedes or is concurrent with wiping out (total kill) the Canaanites.

[9]The "hornet" (ṣir'â), when taken literally, refers to a plague of hornets/wasps, or when taken figuratively, to divinely induced fear/terror (possibly in response to a report of Yahweh's total-kill actions). Robert L. Hubbard Jr., *Joshua*, NIVAC (Grand Rapids: Zondervan, 2009), 553; Eugene Carpenter and Michael A. Grisanti, "צִרְעָה," *NIDOTTE* 3:847; see Ex 23:28; Deut 7:20.

passages in Joshua emphasize the importance of *both* Yahweh's decisive role and Israel's actions. But in Joshua 24:12 the actions of the hornet are linked to Yahweh alone. As a result, the reference to the hornet in Joshua 24:12 does not refer to terror produced by news of a literal total-kill destruction of other cities (which then drove out any remaining, fearful Canaanites). A more likely referent is divinely induced terror or confusion that functions *independently* of total-kill actions, as is the case in Joshua 10.[10]

Joshua 23 may also at first appear to follow a drive-out-by-total-kill sequence, for there Israel is reminded of "everything the LORD your God has done to all these nations for your sake; it was the LORD your God who fought for you" (Josh 23:3). Joshua then reminds Israel of how Yahweh will drive the Canaanites out of the land (Josh 23:5).[11] However, the actions referenced in Joshua 23:3 are not specified, so that when Joshua speaks of "everything the LORD your God has done to all these nations," total-kill actions are only one possible referent. The sentence could also refer to Yahweh's drive-out actions or to Israel's participation in non–total kill battles, making this an ambiguous case of "drive out by total kill" at best. Thus, we do not find any clear evidence for an explicit drive-out-by-total-kill sequence in any passage in Joshua-Judges.[12]

No hear-fear-flee sequences. While we do not find decisive evidence for a text that combines drive-out and total-kill language in a drive-out-by-total-kill sequence, we might look for evidence of such a pattern within the larger narrative and specific accounts. As noted above, the drive-out-by-total-kill

---

[10]Exodus 23:27-28 parallels the terror and confusion Yahweh will send against Israel's enemies, which will cause them to flee (Ex 23:27), with the hornet that would drive out the Canaanites of the land (Ex 23:28). "I will send my *terror* [*ʾêmâ*] ahead of you and *throw into confusion* [*hāmam*—Qal] every nation you encounter. I will *make all your enemies turn their backs and run*. I will send *the hornet* [*ṣirʿâ*] ahead of you to *drive the Hivites, Canaanites and Hittites out* of your way" (Ex 23:27-28).

In this passage, when understood figuratively, the hornet may refer to *either* divinely induced terror or confusion. Joshua 10:10 indicates that it is divine confusion (*hāmam*—Qal) that causes the Canaanites in the battle at Gibeon to flee before Israel. Only *after* this divinely sent confusion does Israel engage in total-kill actions (Josh 10:28, 35, 37, 39, 40). In this case, divinely sent confusion functions in the same manner as the hornet in Ex 23:27-28, *separate from* any previous total-kill actions.

[11]Joshua 23:9 indicates that Yahweh has already driven out nations before Israel, and Josh 23:12-13 warns Israel that Yahweh's continued work in driving the Canaanites out of the land is contingent on their avoidance of intermarriage with the Canaanites.

[12]E.g., Josh 14:6-15 tells how Caleb is able to drive out the Anakites still living in Judean hill country with Yahweh's help (Josh 14:12).

thesis implies that (1) enemies will *hear* news of Israel's literal total-kill actions against Canaanite cities, which (2) will induce *fear* within the Canaanites, and (3) will cause them to *flee* the land. Yet when we examine the evidence for a Canaanite hear-fear-flee pattern, we do not find clear support for such a sequence narrated in the books of Joshua and Judges either. In fact, we find other miracles and partial-kill (not total-kill) factors that produce fear—Israel crossing the Red Sea on dry land; the defeat of the Egyptian army (not killing all Egyptians); the defeat of kings Sihon, Og, and their armies (not killing all their people); the dry crossing of the Jordan—but never Israel's reputation as a literal total-kill war machine.[13]

The expectation of a hear-fear-flee pattern in Joshua and Judges is set for readers by Pentateuchal passages announcing how Yahweh will send fear and terror before the Israelites, which will make the people of Canaan flee before them: "I will send my terror ahead of you and throw into confusion every nation you encounter. I will make all your enemies turn their backs and run" (Ex 23:27; see also Deut 2:4, 24-25; 7:20-22; 11:22-25). The words of Rahab and the report of Joshua's spies confirm the fear of the citizens of Jericho at the news of Israel's dry crossing of the Red Sea and Israel's battles against two Amorite kings:

> I know that the LORD has given you this land and that *a great fear of you has fallen on us*, so that all who live in this country are melting in fear because of you. We have heard how the LORD dried up the water of the Red Sea for you when you came out of Egypt, and what you did to Sihon and Og, the two kings of the Amorites east of the Jordan, *whom you completely destroyed*. When we heard of it, *our hearts melted in fear and everyone's courage failed* because of you, for the LORD your God is God in heaven above and on the earth below. (Josh 2:9-11; see also Josh 2:24)

Similarly, Joshua 5:1 says, "Now when *all the Amorite kings* west of the Jordan and all the Canaanite kings along the coast heard how the LORD had dried up the Jordan before the Israelites until they had crossed over, *their hearts melted in fear* and they *no longer had the courage to face the Israelites*."

---

[13]Joshua 2:10 refers solely to the defeat/destruction of kings Sihon and Og but includes an obviously understood extension to their armies. This does not, however, include the killing of their entire population base. See chapter ten on hyperbole in Deut 2:34; 3:6; 20:10-18.

Yet no descriptions of flight follow these hear-fear sequences. Moreover, when the people of Gibeon hear about what Israel has done to Jericho and Ai (Josh 9:3), they use a deceptive ploy to wrangle a peace treaty out of Joshua, but they do not flee. The Gibeonites explain, "Your servants have come from a very distant country because of the fame of the LORD your God. For *we have heard reports of him*: all that he did in Egypt, and *all that he did to the two kings of the Amorites east of the Jordan*—Sihon king of Heshbon, and Og king of Bashan, who reigned in Ashtaroth" (Josh 9:9-10). These passages illustrate a hear-fear sequence among the Canaanites because of Israel's previous battles against the Amorites east of the Jordan, yet it appears that no Canaanites flee as a result. What we are told is that they deal with the fear through building coalition armies (Josh 10:1-5; 11:1-5).[14]

The drive-out-by-total-kill thesis falls short for lack of two elements. First, even though Israel's victories are part of the fear factor, no clear evidence shows that these past battles involved literal total kill. If it was Israel's *literal* total-kill warfare that struck fear into the hearts of the Canaanites and caused them to flee the land, one would think it a perfect opportunity for the narrator to explain how Israel's total-kill language meant something *different* from ANE total-kill language. For example, the narrator could have said, "Unlike the foreign nations Israel's total-kill warfare was a literal reality, not rhetorical overstatement. Thus, the nations were struck with fear because Israel's type of warfare was far more destructive." But, this clarity about Israel's supposed total-kill war actions (and literalness as the fear factor) is missing in the biblical explanation. This missed explanation would have been compelling since neighboring ANE peoples used the same total-kill language as hyperbole. Second, and even more decisive, the drive-out-by-total-kill thesis also needs to find evidence of the final component of the hear-fear-flee sequence, namely, that this news *actually* drives the Canaanites out of the land. What we do find is quite to the contrary.

As we saw above, Rahab tells Joshua's spies that the people of Jericho are terrified of the Israelites because of hearing what Yahweh has done in Egypt

---

[14]One has to be careful to distinguish between prebattle flight, which we are describing here, and mid- or postbattle flight when either the king is captured/killed or defeat seems immanent (e.g., Josh 10:11).

and in Israel's battles against Sihon and Og. Like Rahab, some occupants of Canaan cooperate or make peace with the Israelites, but we are not told that any of the people of Jericho, for example, flee as a result of hearing/fearing. Instead, they attempt to capture Joshua's spies (Josh 2:2-7) and then endure a seven-day siege before succumbing to Joshua and the Israelites (Josh 6). Meanwhile, though Joshua 5:1 reports that *all* (*kol*) the Amorite kings west of the Jordan and *all* (*kol*) the Canaanite kings along the coast are so afraid that they "no longer had the courage to face the Israelites," this is (once again) most likely hyperbole. After all, the Amorites in the city of Ai do not flee from Israel; they fight and win the first battle of Ai (Josh 7:7). Rather than fleeing the land in fear, other Amorites also wage war and initiate battles against Israel: "When all the kings west of the Jordan heard about these things—the kings in the hill country, in the western foothills, and along the entire coast of the Mediterranean Sea as far as Lebanon (the kings of the Hittites, Amorites, Canaanites, Perizzites, Hivites and Jebusites)—*they came together to wage war* against Joshua and Israel" (Josh 9:1-2).

Similarly, when Adoni-Zedek hears "that Joshua had taken Ai and totally destroyed [*ḥāram*—Hiphil] it, doing to Ai and its king as he had done to Jericho and its king" (Josh 10:1), he gathers a coalition of five Amorite kings to attack Gibeon and do battle with the Israelites. Likewise, when Jabin, king of Hazor, hears of Israel's total-kill victory over the kings of southern Canaan, he responds by gathering a coalition (including Amorites) into "a huge army, as numerous as the sand on the seashore" (Josh 11:4), which fights against Israel. These Canaanites hear of Israel's total-kill battles, but rather than flee in fear, they fight against Israel. Joshua 6–12 gives no examples of Canaanites who flee based on hearing frightening rumors. Instead, fear prompts them to form stronger coalition armies to fight against the Israelites. If anything, we have a hear-fear-*fight* sequence described in Joshua 6–12.

That none of the Canaanites described in Joshua 6–12 attempt to flee or make a peace treaty (other than the Gibeonites) may be explained by a comment in Joshua 11:20, "It was the LORD himself who hardened their hearts to wage war against Israel, so that he might destroy them totally, exterminating them without mercy, as the LORD had commanded Moses." While this may provide a story-line explanation for the absence of descriptions of driving out the Canaanites by fear, the fact remains that there is no drive-out-by-total-kill language sequence and no hear-fear-flee action sequence described in Joshua 6–12. This does not mean that no Canaanites could have been driven off the land because of their fear of Israel's battles, but we are not told of this anywhere in Joshua. As a result, the above passages cannot be used to support the drive-out-by-total-kill sequence advocated by Beale.

With the absence of drive-out-by-total-kill sequences or hear-fear-flee progressions in the narratives of Joshua comes mention of the continuing presence of the Canaanites in the second half of the book of Joshua and in Judges. In Joshua 13–19, readers learn that Yahweh will drive the Sidonians out of the land (Josh 13:6), but:

- ▶ The Israelites do not drive out the people of Geshur and Maakah (Josh 13:13).

- ▶ Caleb needs to drive the Anakites out of the hill country (Josh 14:12).

- ▶ Judah cannot dislodge the Jebusites (Josh 15:63).

- ▶ Ephraim does not dislodge the Canaanites living in Gezer (Josh 16:10).

- ▶ Manasseh does not drive (the Canaanites) out completely (Josh 17:13).

- ▶ Ephraim/Manasseh cannot drive out Canaanites because of their iron chariots (Josh 17:18).

These examples involve ample time for news of the battles of Joshua 6–12 to reach and drive off the Canaanites, yet these groups resolutely remain in the land. The (at times attempted) driving out of the Canaanites in these chapters happens independently of any total-kill notices.[15] Similarly, as Israel continues its battles against the Canaanites after Joshua's death and engages in a total-kill battle (Judg 1:17), this does not induce drive-out panic and flight. The references to Israel's battles in Judges are described exclusively in terms of Israel's success or failure to drive out (not totally kill) the Canaanites.

---

[15]Joshua 3:10 is a drive-out notice, and no total-kill language has appeared thus far in the narrative. Here the advance of the presence of Yahweh into the Promised Land via the ark of the covenant will serve as proof that Yahweh will drive out the Canaanites. This statement is not tied to total-kill language, and it emphasizes that it is the *presence of Yahweh* (and not the news of Israel's battles) that will drive out the Canaanites.

Before moving to the next point, let us summarize our findings thus far. We have seen that numerous texts in the Pentateuch (and some in Joshua-Judges) use both total-kill terminology and drive-out language to describe Israel's battles against the Canaanites. However, the Pentateuchal passages do not provide a consistent order for how driving out and total killing will occur. Nor do we find clear evidence for a drive-out-by-total-kill pattern in the texts of Joshua that combine drive-out and total-kill language. The drive-out-by-total-kill thesis assumes a hear-fear-flee progression, where Canaanites will hear word of Israel's total-kill battles, prompting great fear among them and causing them to flee the land (a nonmanual driving off). But when we look for such a Canaanite reaction to Israel's total-kill battles within the larger narrative structure of Joshua and Judges, we find no examples reported.

At this point we introduce a fourth and final argument against the drive-out-by-total-kill thesis where we find a singular focus on driving out. This leads to considering a different type of relationship between the Old Testament's drive-out and total-kill language.

Driving out without total killing. Numerous passages present driving the Canaanites out of the land as a legitimate war action *without* any mention of killing them. (1) In some passages God himself drives out Israel's enemies, indicating that the expulsion of the Canaanites can be thought of as independent of total-kill actions (Ex 34:11-17, 24; Lev 18:24; 20:23; Num 32:21; Deut 4:37-38; 6:19; 11:23; 18:12; Josh 3:10; 13:6; see also Judg 2:3, 23). (2) At other times, the Israelites receive explicit instructions to drive out the Canaanites with no mention of killing them.[16] (3) Furthermore, reports after the fact of what happened in the battles frequently speak of Israel driving the Canaanites out of the land without any mention of killing (Num 32:39; Josh 15:14; Judg 6:9; 11:23; 1 Kings 14:24; 21:26; 2 Kings 16:3; 17:8, 11; 21:2; 1 Chron 17:21; 2 Chron 20:7; 28:3; 33:2; Ps 44:2; 78:55; 80:8). (4) Finally, forward-looking, mid-conquest reports of what Israel still needs to do focus exclusively on driving the Canaanites out of the land (no mention of killing;

---

[16]Given episodic parameters (not merely a few verses' separation), see Num 33:51-55; Deut 6:18-19; 18:13-14 (compare Caleb's driving out the Anakim in Josh 14:12 in response to God's command).

Josh 13:6; see also Judg 2:3, 23). Of course, some degree of killing may (or may not) have happened alongside driving out the Canaanites; the point here is that the biblical text often places the primary and exclusive focus on driving the Canaanites out of the land. Driving out was a legitimate/acceptable war method by itself at times and also in conjunction with killing. Within the biblical material drive-out methods of war do not play second fiddle to total-kill methods.[17]

In short, the proposal that the total-kill language and the drive-out language of the Pentateuch stem from different sources does not adequately explain why these two aspects of Israel's battles with the Canaanites appear together in the same contexts. Similarly, the drive-out-by-total-kill option does not mesh with the evidence in the Pentateuch or in Joshua-Judges and also does not account for the times when drive-out language appears independently of any total-kill language. Rather, the evidence most likely indicates that total-kill language and drive-out language refer to tactics that relate to each other as two different *means* of achieving a larger *goal*: the establishment of Yahweh's people on Yahweh's land free from idolatry.

SHARED-GOAL EQUIVALENCY: TOTAL KILL (HYPERBOLE) AND/OR DRIVE OUT

This third option understands that total killing and driving out have an and/or relationship. Israel is instructed to do either or both—because the goal, not the means, is of primary importance. Either of these options (and other strategies

---

[17]One further (fifth) argument against the drive-out-by-total-kill thesis involves the *physicality* of driving people out of a land in ANE warfare and in the biblical accounts. Beale's sequence requires only one physical action on Israel's part, namely, the literal total kill of any Canaanites they meet. Then the *nonphysical* fear factor of spreading rumors (based on Israel's literal total kill) was to drive the remaining Canaanites out of the land before Israel arrived. However, the drive-out language of Scripture and the ancient world often includes an understood physical "push out" or "chase out" component that is attached to warfare or even to the absence of killing. For example, the Egyptians physically drive Israel out of Egypt (with no killing objective). Had the Israelites been captured by the Egyptian army, they would have been physically driven back to Egypt through the prodding of whip or sword or threat of death. Though not explicit, it is likely (see evidence presented in chapter three) that the first literary Canaanites—Adam and Eve—were physically driven out of the garden by the sword-wielding angel who afterward stands guard at the entrance to Eden. Also, the northern and southern kingdoms are physically driven out of the land and into exile without killing everyone.

as well) in a cumulative effort could accomplish the goal of achieving a new Eden and sacred space with the exclusive worship of Yahweh.[18] Key to understanding the relationship between texts that call for the annihilation of the Canaanites and texts that call for their expulsion from the land is recognizing that these directives are not mutually exclusive in the biblical text. We have already looked at evidence in the Pentateuch and Joshua-Judges showing how language about total destruction of the Canaanites appears side by side with descriptions of driving out the Canaanites (Ex 23:23, 27-28; Deut 7:1-2, 22-24; 12:29-30; 33:27; Josh 24:8, 12). This already suggests that total-kill actions and drive-out actions are related to a larger goal, namely, that Israel will take possession of the land as sacred space for Yahweh worship.

Furthermore, the prophets view expulsion from the land as achieving the same goals as total destruction for both Israel and Israel's enemies. Jeremiah 48 records an extended oracle prophesying the ways in which Moab will be ruined. The oracle makes clear that the destruction of Moab will include both the slaughter of its inhabitants (Jer 48:2, 8-10, 15) and their exile/flight from the land (Jer 48:6-7, 28, 43-45). Toward the end of the oracle, Jeremiah says, "Moab will be destroyed [*šāmad*—Niphal] as a nation because she defied the LORD" (Jer 48:42; see also Jer 48:2). The verses that precede and follow make it clear that Jeremiah has in mind destruction by warfare. A similar assessment just a few verses later pronounces Moab's fate but specifies, "Woe to you, Moab! The people of Chemosh *are destroyed*; your sons are taken *into exile* and your daughters *into captivity*" (Jer 48:46).[19] In this case, the destruction (*ʾābad*) of the people of Moab (total killing) stands parallel to the exile (driving out) of Moabite young people. In Yahweh's pronouncement of judgment, exile accomplishes the same end as the destruction of the Moabite people.

---

[18]Other strategies include avoiding mixed marriages, killing the royal family (and army), and destroying pagan high places and idols.

[19]Chemosh was the main god of the Moabites. Jeremiah's quote here is adapted from Num 21:27-30, which is a taunt song celebrating the defeat of the Moabites by Sihon, king of the Amorites (one of the Canaanite kings in the Transjordan area), who was in turn defeated by the Israelites. Though the song speaks of the destruction of the Moabite people, Sihon did not completely destroy Moab, for Israel passes along its borders and Balak, the king of Moab, attempts to hire Balaam to curse Israel. This taunt song expresses the defeat of Moab in terms of both destruction and exile (or driving the Moabites from occupying the land), showing that the twin goals of driving out and destroying have ancient roots.

Elsewhere Jeremiah describes Yahweh's judgment of Israel due to idolatry (Jer 9:12-15). This judgment culminates (Jer 9:16) with Jeremiah saying, "I will *scatter* [drive out] them among nations that neither they nor their ancestors have known, and I will pursue them with the sword until *I have made an end of them* [total kill]." Here also, Yahweh's dual punishments (scattering/exile and destruction by the sword) serve as two means of accomplishing the same goal—judgment for persistent idolatry. These texts and others like them (Is 27:8; Jer 43:4; 49:36-37; Lam 1:15-18; 4:6-16; Ezek 5:2, 12; 6:6-10; 11:1-21; 12:14-16; 17:21; 29:8-12; 39:23) underscore how Israel's prophets understood the expulsion of a people group as accomplishing the same purposes as their destruction by the sword.

There is also evidence that the Egyptians viewed the expulsion and/or the annihilation of the enemy as accomplishing the same purpose. An Egyptian ritual text (The Repulsing of the Dragon and the Creation) describes driving Apophis (the dragon) away from the ship of the sun god Re as it sails through the dangers of the night sky. The enemy is both obliterated and driven off, allowing Re's ship to pass safely through the heavens.

> See thou, O Re! Hear thou, O Re! Behold, *I have driven away thy enemy; I have wiped him out with my feet*; I have spat upon him. Re is triumphant over thee [variant reading: over his every fallen enemy]. . . . *Drive thou away, consume thou, burn up every enemy* of pharaoh—life, prosperity, health!—whether dead or living. . . . [Thus] thou shalt be in thy shrine, thou shalt journey in the evening-barque, thou shalt rest in the morning-barque, thou shalt cross thy two heavens in peace, thou shalt be powerful, thou shalt live, thou shalt be healthy, thou shalt make thy states of glory to endure, *thou shalt drive away thy every enemy* by thy command; for these have done evil against pharaoh—life, prosperity, health!—with all evil words: all men, all folk, all people, all humanity, and so on, the easterners of every desert, and every enemy of pharaoh—life, prosperity, health!—whether dead or living, *whom I have driven away and annihilated.* Thou dissolvest fallen, Apophis. Re is triumphant over thee, Apophis.[20]

An inscription from the temple of Pharaoh Ramses III at Medinet Habu introduces the pharaoh by saying, "Under the majesty of Horus: mighty Bull,

---

[20]*ANET*, 7 (italics added).

valiant Lion, strong-armed, lord of might, capturing the Asiatics; Favorite of the Two Goddesses: Mighty in Strength, like his father, Montu, *destroying the Nine Bows, driving [them] from their land.*"[21] In this case, Ramses is said both to destroy Egypt's enemies and to drive them away, thereby securing Egypt from foreign threat. These Egyptian examples provide further evidence that driving the enemy off the land functioned in the same way as killing them—both were legitimate means of securing the land.

We can go further. Note the relationship of the actions listed in the following passages: Exodus 23:23, 27-28 indicates that Yahweh will "wipe out" the Canaanites, yet just a few verses later he indicates that he will "make all your enemies turn their backs and run," and he will send the "hornet," which will drive out the Canaanites.[22] Similarly, Deuteronomy 9:3 says, "He will destroy them; he will subdue them before you. And you will drive them out [*yāraš*—Hiphil] and annihilate them [*'ābad*—Hiphil] quickly, as the LORD has promised you." In addition, note "when the LORD your God has destroyed [*kārat*—Hiphil] the nations whose land he is giving you, and when you have driven them out [*yāraš*] and settled in their towns and houses" (Deut 19:1). In all three texts, driving the Canaanites out is unnecessary if they have already been literally exterminated, unless the total-kill language is hyperbolic. Yet if the language of total destruction is indeed hyperbolic (as we argue it is), then the commands to drive out and destroy the Canaanites are two different means to the same end. In fact, driving out in the minds of ancients was just as good as and thus a functional equivalent to total killing.

As we have already seen, numerous Pentateuchal texts reference the driving out of the Canaanites without any total-kill mention (Ex 33:2; 34:11; Lev 18:24-25, 28; Num 33:51-56; Deut 4:37-38; 6:18-19; 11:22-23; 18:13-14; see also Josh 24:8, 11-12, 18). These passages indicate that the total-kill destruction of the Canaanites was not always linked to their geographical expulsion from the land and that driving out the Canaanites could serve

---

[21]*ARE* 4:62. The Nine Bows is a designation for the traditional enemies of the Egyptians.

[22]The word "wipe out" (*kāḥad*) includes the destruction of the identity of the original inhabitants of Canaan (see Ps 83:4[5], where Israel's enemies say, "let us *destroy them* [*kāḥad*—Hiphil] as a nation, so that Israel's name is remembered no more"); see John H. Walton and J. Harvey Walton, *The Lost World of the Israelite Conquest* (Downers Grove, IL: InterVarsity Press, 2017), 214-16.

independently as an end in itself. Conversely, texts such as Numbers 21:1-3; Deuteronomy 2:34; 3:6; 20:16-17, which describe the complete destruction (ḥērem) of the Canaanites without referencing their expulsion, also indicate that the total-kill destruction and territorial expulsion of the Canaanites could function independently of each other as alternative ways of establishing Yahweh's people in the land of Canaan.[23] That total-destruction language and expulsion language can occur together in the same passage and stand separately indicates that literal annihilation of the Canaanites is not the ultimate goal. Rather, the expulsion and/or the total-kill destruction of the Canaanites (thus curbing their military power and influence) are two means to achieving the same goal.

One final and/or functional equivalency example comes from Judges 1. The book of Judges uses total-kill language only once—in relation to Israel's actions against Zephath (or Hormah) in Judges 1:17.[24] However, two verses later, in Judges 1:19, drive-out language takes center stage. The narrator summarizes Judah's activities positively, saying that "the LORD was with the men of Judah," yet they are unable to *drive out* (*yāraš*—Hiphil) the inhabitants of the valley, because they have iron chariots. Similarly, Judges 1:20 notes that Caleb is able to *drive off* the Anakites, but in the next verse, the Benjaminites are *unable to drive out* the Jebusites (Judg 1:21).

In Judges 1, both methods (total killing and driving out) are used by Judah. The rest of the tribes in Judges 1 fail to expel the Canaanites from their allotted tribal areas (Judg 1:27, 28, 29, 30, 31, 32, 33). Instead, they allow the Canaanites to settle among them (though eventually putting them to forced labor; Judg 1:28, 30, 33). Significantly, when the messenger of Yahweh addresses the tribes, the problem is *not* that Israel failed to engage in total-kill warfare or even that they only attempted to drive out the Canaanites. The

---

[23]Note the use of other total-kill terms without reference to driving out: *šāmad* = Deut 31:3-4; Josh 9:24; 11:14, 20; 2 Kings 21:9; 1 Chron 5:25; 2 Chron 29; Ps 106:34; *kālâ* (Piel) = Josh 8:24; *kārat* (Hiphil) = Josh 11:21; Judg 4:24; *nākâ* (Hiphil) = Num 21:24, 35; 25:17; Deut 1:4; 2:33; 3:3; 4:46; Josh 8:21-22; 10:10, 20, 26, 28, 30, 32, 33, 35, 37, 39, 40, 41; 11:8, 10-12, 14, 17; 12:1, 6-7; 13:12, 21; 15:16; 19:47; 20:13; 29:7; Judg 1:4-5, 8, 10, 12, 17, 25; 3:29, 31; 6:16; 8:11; 11:21, 33; *ʾābad* (Hiphil) = Deut 8:20.

[24]The only other use of *ḥāram* in Judges comes when Israel vows to "fix" the near-annihilation of the Benjaminites by calling for the total destruction of Jabesh-Gilead in Judg 21:11 because it failed to appear in a national-tribal war against the Benjaminites.

problem is that Israel failed to exercise *either option*, allowing the Canaanites and their gods to become traps and snares for the Israelites (Judg 2:3-4; 3:4-6) and a test of Israel's loyalty (Judg 2:21-23).[25]

In sum, the Pentateuch, Joshua-Judges, and the broader ANE world seems to have understood total-kill (hyperbole) language and drive-out language in an either-or or both-and sense of *functional equivalency* as a means of legitimate warfare.

THE GOAL: EXCLUSIVE WORSHIP OF YAHWEH ON *TERRA SANCTA* SOIL IN A NEW EDEN

The overarching goal of Yahweh war adds further clarity about the relationship between the means (total killing [hyperbole] *and* driving out) used to accomplish the goal. One's ultimate goal affects the meaning of the component actions that flow into it. We will develop the last section of this chapter on the goal of Yahweh's holy war in three expanding parts:

- the goal, part 1: the exclusive worship of Yahweh

- the goal, part 2: . . . on *terra sancta* soil

- the goal, part 3: . . . in a new Eden

The goal, part 1: The exclusive worship of Yahweh. The top-shelf or ultimate goal of Yahweh war—*the exclusive worship of Yahweh*—must inform the meaning of all the subordinate parts and pieces (specific wording and instructions) that are instrumental to accomplishing this goal. When total-destruction language and the language of expulsion describe two means (seemingly contradictory), they do so in relationship to a unifying goal. These two means for *how* Israel is to take the Promised Land are linked by a key theological perspective explaining *why* Israel is to battle the Canaanites. The ultimate theological goal of Israel's wars with the Canaanites is the sanctification of land to promote the exclusive worship of Yahweh.

Deuteronomy 20:16-18 instructs Israel to "not leave alive anything that breathes" and "completely destroy" the Canaanites. The theological reason

---

[25]A third acceptable alternative to killing and/or driving out during the time of the Kings once they already had possession of the land was simply to destroy the high places and idols (2 Kings 18:4-5; 23:5, 8, 13, 15, 19-20; 2 Chron 14:3; 17:6; 32:12; 34:3).

for these drastic actions is that the Canaanites "will teach you to follow all the detestable things they do in worshipping their gods, and you will sin against the Lord your God" (Deut 20:18). Yahweh's command here reflects the rationale of other total-kill passages (Deut 8:18-20; 12:28-31). The same concern with idolatrous worship is true of passages that use expulsion language exclusively (Ex 34:11-17; Num 33:51-56; Deut 6:13-14, 18-19; 11:16, 22-23, 28) and of texts that combine total-kill and expulsion language (Ex 23:23, 30-32; Deut 7:1-4, 16-26; 12:28-31; Josh 23:4-13; 24:8, 11-23).

This confluence of total-kill language, drive-out language, and demolishing Canaanite forms of worship may be illustrated in Deuteronomy 12, where Israel is told to destroy Canaanite places of worship (Deut 12:1-4) so that it can focus exclusively on the worship of Yahweh (Deut 12:5-7). At the end of this chapter, Yahweh emphasizes how Israel is to treat not only Canaanite worship installations but the Canaanites themselves, using both total-kill and drive-out language (Deut 12:29). The rationale for these severe measures is laid out in Deuteronomy 12:30-31: "Be careful not to be ensnared by inquiring about their gods, saying, 'How do these nations serve their gods? We will do the same.' You must not worship the Lord your God in their way, because in worshiping their gods, they do all kinds of detestable things the Lord hates. They even burn their sons and daughters in the fire as sacrifices to their gods." In Deuteronomy 12, the real threat is not the Canaanites themselves—the real peril lies in the enticement of their forms and gods of worship.

That the primary concern behind Israel's battles with the Canaanites lies in Canaanite worship forms and the gods they worship can also be seen in the warnings given to Israel. If Israel engages in Canaanite-style worship, they themselves will be liable to total-kill and drive-out warfare (see appendix C for a development of this topic). In Numbers 33:55-56 Yahweh warns, "If you do not drive out the inhabitants of the land, those you allow to remain will become barbs in your eyes and thorns in your sides. They will give you trouble in the land where you will live. And then *I will do to you what I plan to do to them.*" Similarly, Deuteronomy 11:16-17 relates the same type of warning but uses the language of complete destruction: "Be careful, or you will be enticed to turn away and worship other gods and bow down to them. Then the LORD's anger will burn against you, and he will shut up the heavens so that it will not rain and the ground will yield no produce, and *you will soon perish from the good land the LORD is giving you*." Deuteronomy 8:19-20 likewise warns, "If you ever forget the LORD your God and follow other gods and worship and bow down to them, I testify against you today that *you will surely be destroyed.* Like the nations the LORD destroyed before you, so *you will be destroyed* for not obeying the LORD your God." When Israel worships like the Canaanites, it can expect the same fate as the Canaanites.[26] By announcing that Israel is also susceptible to losing the land because of idolatrous worship, these warnings reveal that the issue is not the Canaanites per se, but proper life and worship on Yahweh's land.

These same concerns are evident even in the book that describes Israel's wars with the Canaanites. Joshua 23 recounts how Yahweh has both destroyed (Josh 23:4) the Canaanites and driven them off (Josh 23:5, 9; see also Josh 23:13), and it then concludes, "If you violate the covenant of the LORD your God, which he commanded you, and go and serve other gods and bow down to them, the LORD's anger will burn against you, and you will quickly perish from the good land he has given you" (Josh 23:16). Joshua 24 also describes how Yahweh destroys the Canaanites (Josh 24:8) and drives them off (Josh 24:18), and it then goes on to warn Israel: "If you forsake the LORD and serve foreign gods, he will turn and bring disaster on you and make an end of you, after he has been good to you" (Josh 24:20).

These cases illustrate that while the destruction and expulsion of the Canaanites are not mutually exclusive, neither are they ends in themselves. Rather, they are two methods by which to achieve the same goal. There was an element of judgment that justified Israel's wars in the understanding of the ancient audience.[27] Nevertheless, the key concern is the establishment

---

[26]Israel is also told that the Canaanites are to be destroyed because of their wickedness (Deut 9:3-5). Israel's past flirtation with idolatry then (Deut 9:12, 16) serves as a warning that if they engage in the same behaviors in the land, they too will be destroyed.

[27]While this chapter does not explore the judgment element at length, we would argue that similar implications follow from total-kill and drive-out language for the Canaanites as for Israel in reverse holy war. The functional equivalency of total killing and/or driving out applies to the shared goal of establishing a new Eden but also to the shared element of judgment. Walton and Walton's proposed blunting of the judgment element against the Canaanites is intriguing but problematic. They argue that phrases such as "I will do to you what I plan to do to them" (e.g., Num 33:56) acknowledge that the actions experienced by

of conditions in which Yahweh will be the exclusive focal point of Israel's worship. That the same fate—expulsion and/or destruction—awaits an unfaithful Israel if it engages in the same practices as the Canaanites shows that the ultimate goal of Israel's conquest activities is not, strictly speaking, the elimination of the Canaanites. It is the establishment of conditions leading to the exclusive worship of Yahweh on Yahweh's sacred land.

Goal, part two: Exclusive worship on* terra sancta *soil. Israel's battles with the Canaanites cannot be fully appreciated unless we also recognize that for the biblical authors the land already belongs to Yahweh, so he can direct its tenancy, and that Yahweh's land is sacred space, so it needs to be treated as holy. Failure to do so will result in destruction and/or expulsion from the land.[28]

Both the Pentateuch and the Deuteronomistic History assume Yahweh's ownership of the land and, consequently, his right to determine the conditions of occupancy for the land. Deuteronomy and Joshua both emphasize that the Israelites' right to the land stems primarily from the fact that it has been given to them by Yahweh.[29]

In a sense the land of Canaan is not conquered land in Deuteronomy; it belonged to Yahweh all along. The gift of Yahweh's land to the Israelites stems from an understanding of Yahweh as the supreme king who rules over not only Israel but all heaven and earth (Deut 4:39; 10:14, 17). The Song of

---

the Israelites in reverse holy war will be similar to those experienced by the Canaanites, but they will take place for different reasons. Israel is bound to Yahweh in a covenant, while the Canaanites are not (Walton and Walton, *Lost World of the Israelite Conquest*, 118-33). However, in our view the covenantal distinction does not override the theme of shared judgment. The Eden analogy (later in this chapter), the emerging Israelite understanding of Yahweh's sovereignty over all nations (e.g., Deut 32:8; Ps 22:27-28), the divine judgment of other nations outside the covenant (e.g., Jon 1:2; 3:2-4; Nah 1:7-11; Dan 4:24-32; 5:18-28), and the analogical element of judgment in reverse holy war (appendix C) point to the likelihood of an element of Yahweh's judgment as at least *one* component of the rationale for Israel's actions against the Canaanites.

[28]A clear example of this can be seen in Josh 6–7. Joshua 6 describes the battle at the Canaanite city of Jericho using total-destruction language. Rahab and her family escape destruction because she recognizes Yahweh's supremacy (Josh 2:9-11; 6:22-25). By contrast, Joshua 7 relates the story of Achan's failure to abide by instructions about items from the city devoted to Yahweh. As a result, Achan and his family receive the same treatment as the Canaanites—they are liable to total destruction (Josh 7:11-12, 25-26).

[29]Deut 1:8, 21, 25, 35-36, 39; 2:29; 3:18, 20; 4:1, 21, 38, 40; 5:16, 31; 6:10, 23; 7:13; 8:1, 10; 9:6, 23; 10:11; 11:8-9, 17, 21, 31; 12:1, 10; 15:4, 7; 16:20; 17:14; 18:9; 19:1-3, 8, 10, 14; 21:1, 23; 24:4; 25:15, 19; 26:1-3, 15; 27:2-3; 28:8, 11, 52; 30:20; 31:7; 32:49, 52; 34:4; Josh 1:2, 6, 11, 13, 15; 2:9, 14, 24; 5:6; 9:24; 18:3; 21:43; 22:4; 23:13, 15-16.

Moses assumes Yahweh's kingship over Israel and the whole earth: "When the Most High gave the nations their inheritance, when he divided all mankind, he set up boundaries for the peoples according to the number of the sons of [God]. For the LORD's portion is his people, Jacob his allotted inheritance" (Deut 32:8-9).[30] Yahweh, as supreme ruler, sets out responsibility for the various nations, along with their borders, among the members of his heavenly court. But for his own responsibility and care, Yahweh chooses the people of Israel as well as the land with its borders. Norman Habel notes, "The image promoted in Deuteronomy is that of a universal monarch who controls vast domains, of which Canaan happens to be one."[31] It is Yahweh's land, granted to Israel to possess.

*Yahweh's land as sacred space (*terra sancta*) in the Pentateuch.* Meanwhile, the land given to the people of Israel is not any old patch of dirt. It is sacred space. Habel, like Gerhard von Rad before him, notes that Israel conceived of the land not only as the Promised Land but also as Yahweh's sanctuary land.[32] Habel points out that the concept of a deity owning the lands connected to

---

[30]The NIV reads "the number of the sons of Israel" instead of "the number of the sons of God," but the LXX reads "the number of the angels of God," and the Dead Sea Scroll 4Q37 (also called 4QDeut[j)] reads "the sons of God," a reference to the court of Yahweh; compare ESV, NRSV. For an explanation of the reading "sons of God," see Daniel I. Block, *The Gods of the Nations: Studies in Ancient Near Eastern National Theology*, 2nd ed. (Grand Rapids: Baker, 1988, 2000), 25-32.

[31]Norman C. Habel, *The Land Is Mine: Six Biblical Land Ideologies*, OBT (Minneapolis: Fortress, 1995), 37. Habel's comments here stem from his examination of Deut 4–11, but they may be extended to cover the perspective of the entire book. This image is reinforced by the resemblances between Babylonian land-grant (*kudurru*) documents and Deut 27. Andrew Hill shows that Deut 27 served as a type of kingly land-grant ceremony set within the larger covenant-like structure of Deuteronomy, though the Deut 27 ceremony is clearly a Hebrew adaptation of a covenant of grant. Thus, the land of Canaan is Yahweh's land, granted to Israel to possess before the conquest has even begun (Hill, "The Ebal Ceremony as Hebrew Land Grant?," *JETS* 31 [1988]: 399-406; see also Block, *Deuteronomy*, 623-24).

[32]Gerhard von Rad, "The Promised Land and Yahweh's Land in the Hexateuch," in *The Problem of the Hexateuch and Other Essays*, trans. E. W. Trueman Dicken (New York: McGraw-Hill, 1968), 85-88; Habel, *Land Is Mine*, 97-113. Habel discusses the land as Yahweh's sanctuary land primarily in relation to Lev 25–27. Von Rad distinguishes between two different conceptions of land: the Promised Land and Yahweh's land. Christopher J. H. Wright observes, however, that these issues are two sides of the same coin, for Yahweh's ability to grant the land assumes his ownership (*God's People in God's Land: Family, Land, and Property in the Old Testament* [Grand Rapids: Eerdmans, 1990], 10). Habel discerns six different land ideologies in the biblical record. However, at least five of Habel's ideologies (land as source of wealth, land as conditional grant, land as family lots, land as YHWH's personal *nahalah*, and land as Sabbath bound) stem from the concept of Yahweh's ownership of the land.

his or her sanctuary was well known throughout the ANE. But even beyond the central sanctuary, entire lands, regions, or nations could be claimed by a deity, so that the whole land could be viewed as an extended sanctuary.[33] Practically speaking, the lands controlled by a deity could be enlarged by sending the king out to expand the deity's territory. Conquered plunder, slaves, and land would then be given for the sustenance and service of the sanctuary and its patron deity. Evidence suggests that Egyptian temples in the twelfth century BC owned one-third of all arable land and that by the eleventh century BC, most lands were owned by temples.[34] Jan Assmann says, "It was possible to conceive of Egypt as a single huge temple, 'the temple of the entire world.'"[35] The same was likely true for early Sumerian cities.[36]

The ancient Israelites also thought of the entire land as sacred space. This brought additional requirements for holy living. The accounts of the patriarchal practice of building altars throughout the land promised to Abraham may in part stem from their nomadism, but they also imply that the land was sacred space where Yahweh could be worshiped, well before the selection of the place for Yahweh's dwelling (Deut 12:5).[37] In the Song of the Sea Moses says that Yahweh will bring Israel "to your holy dwelling" and "bring them in and plant them on the mountain of your inheritance—the place, LORD, you made for your dwelling, the sanctuary, Lord, your hands established" (Ex 15:13, 17). These verses suggest that the place where Yahweh will plant his people is not just a building but the entire land surrounding a (new) mountain—Mount Zion—in which all of Yahweh's rescued people can dwell. Likewise, Naaman's request to transport some soil (*'ădāmâ*) back to his country in order to build an altar to Yahweh there (2 Kings 5:17) implies a level of sanctity for Israelite ground.[38] Moreover, the absence of the temple

---

[33]Habel, *Land Is Mine*, 100-101.

[34]David O'Connor, "The Social and Economic Organization of Ancient Egyptian Temples," *CANE*, 320.

[35]Jan Assmann, *The Search for God in Egypt* (Ithaca, NY: Cornell University Press, 2001), 27.

[36]John F. Robertson, "The Social and Economic Organization of Ancient Mesopotamian Temples," *CANE*, 444-45.

[37]The patriarchs built altars across the land at Shechem (Gen 12:7; 33:18-20), Bethel (Gen 12:8; 13:4; 35:1), Hebron (Gen 13:18), the mountains of Moriah or Jerusalem (Gen 22:9; see also 2 Chron 3:1), and Beersheba (Gen 26:25).

[38]Noted by Menahem Haran, *Temples and Temple-Service in Ancient Israel* (Oxford: Clarendon, 1978; repr., Winona Lake, IN: Eisenbrauns, 1985), 39.

does not imply the absence of sacred space (e.g., the Garden of Eden, Mount Sinai).[39] Sandra Richter points out that in Jeremiah 7:7, the place of Yahweh's choosing is both the temple and "the land I gave to your forefathers forever and ever." In Chronicles (2 Chron 3:1), the place is specified as Jerusalem, but in Ezra 6:12 it is likely the Persian province of Yehud, and in Nehemiah 1:9 it is the entire land, not just the temple. Psalm 114:1-2 identifies the entire land of Judah with Yahweh's sanctuary, saying, "When Israel came out of Egypt, Jacob from a people of foreign tongue, Judah became God's sanctuary, Israel his dominion" (see also Ezek 21:2). This interchange between holy temple, holy mountain, holy city, and holy land was common in the ANE, Richter writes, so that the relationship between them

> may be expressed with synecdoche—the part stands for the whole and the whole for the part. Hence, it is possible to speak of the deity's entire land-holdings by means of speaking of the critical center of them, the temple. . . . Hence, for the Deuteronomist and his later colleagues to identify *the place*, which was first identified with the promised land, with the central sanctuary and with the regal-ritual capital city in which it is housed is perfectly consistent with the worldview of the biblical text.[40]

Yahweh's ownership of the land means that he can set the rules for tenancy within the land.[41] A failure to keep Yahweh's tenancy requirements results in the loss of the land: "But if your heart turns away and you are not obedient, and if you are drawn away to bow down to other gods and worship them, I declare to you this day that you will certainly be destroyed. You will not live long in the land you are crossing the Jordan to enter and possess" (Deut 30:17-18). Similarly, Deuteronomy 4:25-26 says,

> After you have had children and grandchildren and have lived in the land a long time—if you then become corrupt and make any kind of idol, doing evil in the eyes of the Lord your God and arousing his anger, I call the

---

[39]John M. Lundquist, "What Is a Temple? A Preliminary Typology," in *The Quest for the Kingdom of God: Studies in Honor of George E. Mendenhall*, ed. H. B. Huffmon, F. A. Spina, and A. R. W. Green (Winona Lake, IN: Eisenbrauns, 1983), 208.

[40]Sandra L. Richter, *The Deuteronomistic History and the Name Theology: lᵉ šakkēn šᵉmô šām*, BZAW 318 (Berlin: de Gruyter, 2002), 55.

[41]See the repeated instructions in Deuteronomy governing life in the land (e.g., Deut 4:5, 14, 40; 5:33; 6:1; 11:8-9; 12:1; 19:14; 30:16).

heavens and the earth as witnesses against you this day that *you will quickly perish from the land* that you are crossing the Jordan to possess. You will not live there long but will certainly be destroyed. (see also Deut 11:16-17; 28:45-46, 63-64; Josh 23:16)

The land is Yahweh's *terra sancta*. Failure to maintain the rules set out for sacred space in Yahweh's lands results in either expulsion or death. In this way of looking at sacred space, Yahweh may then choose to expel and/or destroy the occupants of that land, whether they be Israelites or Canaanites.

Yahweh's land as sacred space in the book of Joshua. While several texts draw attention to the land as sacred space, this view of the land is particularly evident in passages that describe Israel's battles with the Canaanites. Admittedly, the book of Joshua does not explicitly call the Promised Land sacred space, but many elements in the book evoke a sense of the sacredness of the land. For example, Joshua instructs the people before they cross over the Jordan River to consecrate themselves (Josh 3:5), bringing to mind similar preparations for Yahweh's presence at the sacred mountain of Mount Sinai (Ex 19:22; see also Ex 19:10). Joshua's circumcision of the Israelite men of war just before attacking the Canaanites (Josh 5:4, 6) is tactically suspect, because it incapacitates Israel's army in case of a surprise attack. Its purpose, however, is ritual, bringing Israel's soldiers back into full covenant compliance as they embark on the upcoming military expedition within the Promised Land. Circumcision was not observed while wandering outside the land, but occupation of the land required a heightened level of consecration to Yahweh for the Israelites. Similarly, the celebration of the Passover marks the close of Israel's wilderness wanderings and takes on a heightened poignancy when celebrated for the first time in the Promised Land. Passover sacrifices are to occur only at "the place [Yahweh] will choose as the dwelling for his Name" (Deut 16:5-6). That the temple (the eventual dwelling place for Yahweh's name) had not yet been built and that this ceremony takes place at Gilgal, not Jerusalem, suggests that the land is perhaps already considered Yahweh's sacred space at some level. More directly evocative of the land as sacred space is Joshua's encounter with the commander of the army of Yahweh (Josh 5:13-15). The passage parallels Moses' first contact with Yahweh by the burning bush at the sacred mountain (Ex 3:1-6). During the encounter,

Joshua is told, "Take off your sandals, for the place [*māqôm*] where you are standing is holy [*qōdeš*]" (Josh 5:15). Sarah Lebhar Hall notes,

> The only times in the Hebrew Bible where both *māqôm* and *qōdeš* appear in the same sentence are in passages which describe (1) the places where Moses and Joshua have these encounters, and (2) the courts, rooms, and chambers of the tabernacle and temple. Outside Moses' and Joshua's experiences, this association of words is always used in connection with the sanctuary.[42]

Considering these observations, we may surmise that Yahweh's presence signals that Joshua is standing on Yahweh's "temple lands" as he is about to begin the conquest of Canaan.

Setting Israel's battle at Jericho within the context of warfare on Yahweh's sacred land also helps explain the tactics in Israel's seven-day siege of Jericho. Lebhar Hall observes that Yahweh's instructions (Josh 6:1-5) and the subsequent battle at Jericho should be read as a continuation of Joshua's encounter with the commander of Yahweh's armies.[43] Israel's seven-day circumambulation of Jericho in Joshua 6 does not follow any known battle tactics. Instead, Israel's actions resemble a worship ritual or ceremony.[44] Viewing the land as Yahweh's sacred space makes a worship procession as part of Israel's first battle in the land more understandable.

Grasping the horns of the altar in the tabernacle seems to have functioned as a sort of temporary asylum (1 Kings 1:50-53; 2:28-34). The dispersion of cities of refuge around the country to serve as asylum cities in cases of an inadvertent death (Josh 20) extends the role of the central sanctuary to these six towns.[45] These mini-sanctuaries scattered throughout Yahweh's temple

---

[42]Sarah Lebhar Hall, *Conquering Character: The Characterization of Joshua in Joshua 1–11*, LHBOTS 512 (New York: T&T Clark, 2010), 87. This purposed reading of Joshua standing on holy ground (i.e., sacred space) is not mutually exclusive with other purposes, such as portraying Joshua as the new Moses.

[43]Lebhar Hall, *Conquering Character*, 82-88. Lebhar Hall argues for literary continuity between Josh 5:13-15; 6:1-5 based on links with the call of Moses in Ex 3, comparison with other ANE military literature, and the identity of the speaker in Josh 5:13; 6:1-5 as Yahweh.

[44]Daniel E. Fleming highlights several biblical and ANE parallels to the seven-day siege in Josh 6, noting that the story of Jericho's siege need not imply the presence of a shrine or religious festival, as warfare and religious practice were often deeply intertwined ("The Seven-Day Siege of Jericho in Holy War," in *Ki Baruch Hu: Ancient Near Eastern, Biblical, and Judaic Studies in Honor of Baruch A. Levine*, ed. R. Chazan, W. W. Hallo, and L. H. Schiffman [Winona Lake, IN: Eisenbrauns, 1999], 211-28).

[45]See Richard Nelson, *Joshua*, OTL (Louisville, KY: Westminster John Knox 1997), 228.

lands could serve in much the same way as the altar horns in the tabernacle/ temple, thereby extending the sanctuary into the land.

When the Transjordan tribes built an altar on the east bank of the Jordan, a civil war almost broke out (Josh 22:33). The perspective of the tribes on the western side of the Jordan was that the Transjordanian tribes built an altar in contravention to the sanctuary law (Deut 12:8-12), and they advise their kinfolk, "If the land you possess is defiled, *come over to the LORD's land*, where the LORD's tabernacle stands, and share the land with us. But do not rebel against the LORD or against us by building an altar for yourselves, other than the altar of the LORD our God" (Josh 22:19). Clearly, they consider the land on the west bank of the Jordan *terra sancta*. Robert Hubbard explains,

> [Their] comment . . . assumes—perhaps hyperbolically for the sake of argument —that Transjordan is not "the LORD's land" but land belonging to some other deity. It voices the Cisjordanian perspective that east-bank land is not "holy" as Canaan is. It implies that the distance of the Transjordanians from Yahweh's center of gravity leaves them vulnerable to the gravitational pull of local defiling forces.[46]

The conflict is resolved when the Transjordanian tribes submit that the purpose of the altar is not for offering sacrifices (and thereby not in contravention of the central sanctuary law of Deut 12); it is to give witness to the unity between the two groups.

Thus, not only do Pentateuchal texts provide an understanding of Yahweh's land as sacred space, but so also does the book of Joshua. In this context, descriptions of destruction or expulsion of the Canaanites in the book fall under the auspices of an ancient rationale for the actions of the Israelites, in which Israel's battles are a means by which the land can be sanctified, preparing for the exclusive worship of Yahweh at his sanctuary within his sanctuary lands.

The goal, part three: Exclusive worship on* terra sancta *soil as a new Eden. Now for the third part of the goal: the exclusive worship of Yahweh is to take place on *terra sancta* soil conceptually framed *as a new Eden*. A theological analogy drawing on the portrayal of the land as Yahweh's sacred

---

[46]Robert L. Hubbard Jr., *Joshua*, NIVAC (Grand Rapids: Zondervan, 2009), 489; see also Richard S. Hess, *Joshua*, TOTC (Downers Grove, IL: InterVarsity Press, 1996), 321.

space in the book of Joshua sets the destruction and expulsion language used to describe the fate of the Canaanites into the larger biblical story line. As with the last two parts of the goal discussion, this third part, on the new Eden, should break any stalemates over exactly how to understand the relationship between destruction language and expulsion language.

A growing body of evidence suggests that the Garden of Eden in Genesis is portrayed using vocabulary and imagery that evokes the tabernacle/temple.[47] In Genesis 2:16-17, Yahweh places the man that he formed in the garden and gives him free access to all its trees, except the tree of the knowledge of good and evil, for "when you eat from it you will certainly die." The man and the woman enjoy a wonderful state of harmony and fellowship with Yahweh in his garden sanctuary. But when both the man and woman disobey God, they must be expelled from Yahweh's garden. To prevent the man from stretching out (*šālaḥ*—Qal) his hand to take from the tree of life (Gen 3:22), "The LORD God banished him [*šālaḥ*—Piel] from the Garden of Eden to work the ground from which he had been taken" (Gen 3:23). The use of the verb *šālaḥ* (Piel) can have the sense of "drive out" and acts as a synonym for other drive out terms such as *gāraš* (Piel), "drive out"; *nāšal* (Qal), "drive away, expel"; and *yāraš* (Qal and Hiphil), "possess, dispossess."[48] In this situation, certain death is to accompany rebellion against Yahweh's command (Gen 2:17). But physical death does not immediately follow the man and woman's disobedience (see Gen 5:1-5), and instead, they are expelled from the garden to make a new life for themselves elsewhere, outside Yahweh's sanctuary lands.

---

[47]G. K. Beale, *The Temple and the Church's Mission: A Biblical Theology of the Dwelling Place of God*, NSBT (Downers Grove, IL: InterVarsity Press, 2004); Beale, "Eden, the Temple, and the Church's Mission in the New Creation," *JETS* 48 (2005): 5-33; Jon D. Levenson, *Creation and the Persistence of Evil: The Jewish Drama of Divine Omnipotence* (San Francisco: Harper & Row, 1988); Gordon Wenham, "Sanctuary Symbolism in the Garden of Eden Story," in *Proceedings of the 9th World Congress of Jewish Studies, Jerusalem, August, 1985* (Jerusalem: World Union of Jewish Studies, 1986), 19-25; repr. in *I Studied Inscriptions from Before the Flood*, ed. Richard S. Hess and David T. Tsumura (Winona Lake, IN: Eisenbrauns, 1994), 399-404. Block argues that the tabernacle reflects Eden imagery (versus Eden reflecting tabernacle imagery) but fundamentally supports the link between the Garden of Eden and the tabernacle (Daniel I. Block, "Eden: A Temple? A Reassessment of the Biblical Evidence," in *From Creation to New Creation: Biblical Theology and Exegesis*, ed. Daniel M. Gurtner and Benjamin L. Gladd [Peabody, MA: Hendrickson, 2013], 3-29).

[48]See the scapegoat that is driven out of the camp (Lev 16:10), Judah's expulsion from Jerusalem into exile (Jer 24:5; 29:20), and Yahweh's threat to expel Hananiah from the land and his imminent death within a year of expulsion (Jer 28:16-17), all of which also use *šālaḥ* (Piel).

The expulsion (*šālaḥ*—Piel) of the man and the woman from the garden sanctuary is analogous to the expulsion of the indigenous inhabitants of the Promised Land as described in Leviticus. After a long list of prohibited sexual relationships in Leviticus 18, Israel is told, "Do not defile yourselves in any of these ways, because this is how the nations that I am going to drive out [*šālaḥ*—Piel] before you became defiled" (Lev 18:24). After a similar list in Leviticus 20, Yahweh says, "You must not live according to the customs of the nations I am going to drive out [*šālaḥ*—Piel] before you. Because they did all these things, I abhorred them" (Lev 20:23). The fate of the man and the woman in being expelled from Yahweh's garden sanctuary is similar to the rationale for the fate of the Canaanites, who are to be expelled from God's sanctuary lands.[49]

The Eden narrative also uses the verb *gāraš* (Piel) to describe the eviction of the man and woman from the garden, saying, "After he drove the man out [*gāraš*], he placed on the east side of the Garden of Eden cherubim and a flaming sword flashing back and forth to guard the way to the tree of life" (Gen 3:24). This is the same word that is used elsewhere to describe Israel's expulsion of the Canaanites (Ex 23:28-31; 33:2; Deut 33:27; Josh 24:12, 18; Judg 2:3; 1 Chron 17:21; Ps 78:55; 80:8). The military overtones of this expulsion are heightened when we note that Yahweh sets cherubim along with a *flaming sword* that goes back and forth—a particularly deadly martial image—to guard the entrance to the garden.[50] Cherubim, serving as guardians to God's presence, are embroidered not only on the curtains guarding access to the tent of meeting (Ex 26:1; 36:8) but also on the curtain guarding access to the holy of holies (Ex 26:31-33; see also 1 Kings 6:32). Two cherubim stand with wings outstretched to symbolically cover and protect

---

[49]Again, components of Walton and Walton's analysis appear problematic (see note above) because of the strong and widespread analogies between Israel's expulsion from the land and the expulsion of the Canaanites. At a rhetorical level, it seems that the analogy "I will drive you out as I drove them out" requires an understanding of *some* form of God's judgment on the Canaanites in order for the corresponding threat against Israel to have any teeth.

[50]Gordon Wenham notes that with the revolving flaming sword, "The idea is clear: a revolving or zigzagging sword, especially one wielded by angels, is one that is sure to hit and bring death" (Wenham, *Genesis 1–15*, WBC [Waco, TX: Word Books, 1987], 86). Note also the frequent association between the sword and fire in military contexts: Josh 11:11; Judg 1:8; 18:27; 20:48; 2 Kings 8:12; Is 66:16; Ezek 5:2; Nah 3:15; Dan 11:33.

the atonement cover of the ark, which sits between the cherubim (Ex 26:18-22; 37:7-9; Num 7:89; see also 1 Kings 6:23-28). These angelic warriors wield a deadly weapon as they guard access to Yahweh's sanctuary.

The threat of death for disobedience coupled with humanity's expulsion from Yahweh's first garden sanctuary (Gen 2:17; 3:23) forms a theological analogy for Yahweh's command to destroy the Canaanites. The same holds true for Israel if it fails to keep Yahweh's commands (see appendix C). In light of the Promised Land in Joshua being *terra sancta*, along with the concern over idolatry and the worship of other deities in both Pentateuchal literature and the final speeches of Joshua, the *expulsion* and/or the *destruction* of the Canaanites echoes the Eden narratives.

This second half of this chapter, focusing on the exclusive worship of Yahweh on his sanctuary lands, confirms that the goal of an action often determines the meaning of subordinate instrumentality taken to achieve said goal. The *goal* of Yahweh's holy war tells us what to think about the relationship between *killing Canaanites* and *driving Canaanites out of the land*. If the goal of holy war in Scripture is the exclusive worship of Yahweh on *terra sancta* soil as a new Eden, then killing and driving out are simply two means that function in an and/or relationship toward achieving the same unifying goal.

CONCLUSION

We have seen that the Pentateuch and Joshua-Judges use the language of both destruction and expulsion when describing the fate of the Canaanites. At times conquest texts use drive-out language, and at other times the language of total killing. Sometimes these two ideas are located in the same texts. We have argued that the evidence best aligns with understanding the expulsion of the Canaanites from the Promised Land and the destruction of the Canaanites as two alternative (not mutually exclusive [contradictory] or causally stacked [the one *by* the other]) options for how Israel could come to possess the land of Canaan. Moreover, we have presented evidence from the book of Joshua and elsewhere that suggests that the land of Canaan was viewed by the ancient Israelites as *terra sancta*—that is, as sacred (temple) space. Consequently, the destruction and/or the expulsion of the Canaanites were seen as a way of sanctifying sacred space. This overarching goal explains why the language of total destruction and expulsion is often found in connection with language calling for the destruction of Canaanite forms of worship—Yahweh will not allow the worship of other deities within his own sanctuary lands, as Israel's kings later learned the hard way. Yahweh will not share his sanctuary with any other gods (see 2 Kings 22:1–23:30; Ezek 8:1–10:22; 11:22-25).

In this light, the goal of Israel's battles within the land of Canaan, from an ancient Israelite perspective, is not the destruction of the Canaanites per se, or genocide. Rather, the focus is on (re)claiming Yahweh's sanctuary lands and creating conditions for the exclusive worship of Yahweh on that land. Israel is threatened with the same fate if they defile the land by engaging in Canaanite-like practices (see appendix C). Whether we are talking about literary Canaanites (Adam and Eve, the northern kingdom, the southern kingdom) or ethnic Canaanites, both means—removal from sacred space *or* death—accomplish the same goal. If total-kill and drive-out instructions are both acceptable options for achieving the primary goal of restoring *terra sancta* (as we have argued), then this chapter provides yet another good piece of evidence for understanding the total-kill language in a hyperbolic (not literal) sense.

If biblical authors understood Yahweh's sacred space as the overriding goal, and driving out was an acceptable alternative to killing (both achieved the same goal), then the total-kill language ought to be understood as hyperbole. If one says, "Kill *all* of them!" and in the same breath, "Oh, yes, kick them out of the land; that is fine too!" it seems reasonable to infer that the "all" in the kill command is not literal.

13

ANCIENT WAR ATROCITIES

THIS CHAPTER IS NOT AN EASY READ. War atrocities in the ANE were almost limitless in variety and destructiveness, and the darkly twisted cruelty of ancient warfare is well preserved in annals and artistry. They provide something of a war museum through which to quietly walk and ponder a collection of extremely disturbing portraits. Though these grotesque war images are difficult to gaze at, the experience is nonetheless necessary. Contemporary readers who have not contemplated the war atrocities of an ancient world can easily miss the redemptive side of biblical war texts. This chapter is by no means exhaustive, but the range of atrocities covered below provides a sufficient sampling of the social context of unrestrained military violence within which Scripture ought to be read. After a prolonged viewing of ancient war atrocities, we can view with greater comprehension the war scenes in biblical texts that depict Israel's military actions.

PORTRAITS OF ANCIENT NEAR EASTERN WAR ATROCITIES

ANE people preserved war stories in stone and metal artistic displays and in written documents—inscriptions, war annals, and the like. The title of a recent work, *Extreme Violence in the Visuals and Texts of Antiquity*, indicates the nature of these sources.[1] Paleo-forensic investigation, while comparatively sparse, provides additional data for reconstructing ancient war atrocities.[2]

---

[1] This is an English translation of the German title of Martin Zimmermann, ed., *Extreme Formen von Gewalt in Bild und Text des Altertums*, Münchner Studien zur Alten Welt (Munich: Herbert Utz Verlag, 2009), 350-51.

[2] H. Cohen, V. Slon, A. Barash, H. May, B. Medlej, and I. Hershkovitz, "Assyrian Attitude Towards Captive Enemies: A 2700-Year-Old Paleo-forensic Study," *International Journal of Osteoarchaeology* 25 (2015): 265-80.

Captives stripped naked—genitals exposed and sometimes shaved.
Imagine taking a hundred prisoners from the recent war(s) against terrorism, shipping them to the White House, Parliament Hill, or 10 Downing Street in the UK—any location of governmental power—and parading them across the lawn in front of cheering crowds. Media cameras would highlight with zoomed-in shots that these war captives had been stripped of all their clothing and were being paraded completely naked in front of a gathering of jeering and taunting victors. As the spectators saw the exposed genitals of the war captives, they would also notice that some (perhaps many) prisoners have had their pubic hair shaved off to make their genitals even more visible to onlookers.

Public humiliation of this extreme sort was so common and significant in the ancient war context that depictions of naked captives are numerous.[3] Binding prisoners with ropes or shackles dealt with the threat of concealed weapons, so removing a captive's clothing was not a defensive action by captors to guard against retaliation. Rather, the primary reason for stripping captives completely naked and in some cases shaving their pubic hair was to expose their genitals; it ritualized to an extreme the public shaming of defeated captives.[4] Given an ancient-world emphasis on public modesty and on the use of clothing to conceal (in contrast to many modern contexts), this exposure would have been far more demeaning than modern readers might immediately sense.

Within the biblical text the notion of stripping captives naked and exposing their genitals—an extreme act of prisoner humiliation by foreign nations—is viewed with horror and disdain. This was not an acceptable or Yahweh-approved practice for Israelite warriors to use against their enemies. The action within Scripture is always seen as deplorable. That Yahweh would use this heinous war act in punishing Israel and other nations does not make

---

[3]The practice of stripping captives naked was common in Egyptian and Assyrian iconography. See Mark D. Janzen, "The Iconography of Humiliation: The Depiction and Treatment of Bound Foreigners in New Kingdom Egypt" (PhD diss., University of Memphis, 2013), 113-14, 265, 273, 278, 282, 286. See also Zainab Bahrani, *Rituals of War: The Body and Violence in Mesopotamia* (New York: Zone Books, 2008), 150.

[4]On stripping naked war captives and forcibly shaving their pubic hair, see Saul M. Olyan, "Ritual Inversion in Biblical Representations of Punitive Rites," in *Worship, Women and War: Essays in Honor of Susan Niditch*, ed. John J. Collins, T. M. Lemos, and Saul M. Olyan, BJS (Providence, RI: Brown University Press, 2015), 139-41.

it less deplorable or make it acceptable for use by Israelite soldiers. Rather, war-punishment texts employ a type of truncated-causation language (see appendix G). This combines Yahweh's sovereignty over all nations with the fact that he brings about a measure of this-world, contextualized justice that involves using foreign war practices. The nations would experience a taste of their own just deserts. Biblical texts of this kind—about stripping naked and exposing genitals and buttocks—provide warnings of humiliating war actions by foreign nations against Egypt and Cush (Is 20:1-6) and against Israel itself (Lam 4:21; Ezek 16:36-39; 23:9-10; Hos 2:3) but are never enacted by Israel as part of its war actions.[5]

Ancient texts that talk about stripping *dead* war victims belong in a different category from stripping captives naked for the purpose of public humiliation. The armies of Israel at times stripped dead enemies of armor and valuables, but the context emphasizes taking valuable loot and not stripping enemies completely naked as a part of genital display and public humiliation (2 Sam 2:21; 23:10). Often language referring to stripping the dead means the removal of the outer garments and/or armor as part of battlefield looting. All ancient armies collected postbattle valuables that they could use or sell. This was the case whether it was the Philistines stripping dead Israelite warriors (1 Sam 31:8-9; 1 Chron 10:8-9) or vice versa.[6] Ancient texts and iconography that include the total stripping of dead bodies for severe shaming generally accentuate the nakedness of the victims.

According to the biblical records, the parading of captives completely naked for genital and buttock display was never part of Israel's military practices and would not have been viewed as a Yahweh-approved military action. Israel's aversion to parading nude captives in the war practices of foreign nations, its own broader social customs concerning clothing and modesty, and its more restrained (often better) treatment of war prisoners in general (see below) suggest a likely disapproval of this sort of extreme war-prisoner shaming.

---

[5]See the Ammonite half-body (buttocks) exposure and half shaving off of Israel's envoy's beards—an action aimed at humiliating King David (2 Sam 10:4; 1 Chron 19:4).

[6]While Samson killed and stripped thirty Philistine men from Ashkelon (Judg 14:19), it was probably a stripping of their outer, festive clothing (similar to Joseph's brothers stripping him of his ornate robe). The outer, expensive clothing thus became valuable in Samson's riddle trade.

Binding prisoners in painful, torturous positions. Prisoners in the ANE were typically shown bound with their arms hanging in a somewhat natural position. Their wrists were tied at waist level behind their back. By ancient standards this was the least painful form of binding captives; it would be comparable to modern-day handcuffing procedures.

Egyptian iconography, however, portrays many defeated captives bound in severely painful and contorted positions. Some captives were bound with the left arm brutally bent so far behind their heads that their (left) hand fell limp in front of their face. Mark Janzen's study of Egyptian war captives points out that for most people this position is virtually impossible to be in without dislocating the shoulder, tearing the ligament at the elbow, straining neck muscles, and restricting blood flow to the bent-down head.[7] Some captives are shown with their arms bent behind their backs and their wrists pulled so high and tight that they reached the armpit level of the same arm. Other captives are displayed with their arms behind their backs in an X-shaped position; their elbows meet and are bound together at the spine. This binding would have totally dislocated the shoulders and in some cases shattered the elbows.[8] Janzen notes that X-shape binding was "one of the most humiliating and brutal of all . . . but also one of the most common [of the pain-inflicting type]."[9] Often metal or wooden manacles were added to the use of rope bindings and offered yet further variations on the same theme. Egyptian artwork proudly displays over a dozen different contortions that would have inflicted pain on their victims to an utterly excruciating—out of one's mind—degree.[10] The Egyptian armies were masters at inflicting pain—severe and torturous agony—simply by the way in which they secured their

---

[7]Janzen, "Iconography of Humiliation," 60.

[8]In a hospital emergency room, for someone who has dislocated a shoulder (perhaps due to a sports injury), each second seems like an eternity. The pain is so intense that, even if they do not scream, tears stream down their face from the pain, and morphine is needed to relax the muscles enough for the doctor to snap the joint back into place. Just imagine experiencing the dislocation of two shoulder joints at the same time and possibly the added dislocation or shattering of the elbows.

[9]Janzen, "Iconography of Humiliation," 61.

[10]This paragraph reports on Egyptian artwork showing rope (and manacles) torture; the Assyrians also, to a lesser extent, included forced bodily contortions and binding as part of their war artistry. See Janzen, "Iconography of Humiliation," 151. For the extensive variety of painful bindings see Janzen, "Iconography of Humiliation," 68, 64, 92, 103, 111-12, 143, 162-219.

nude captives. Janzen summarizes the result: "The enemies of Egypt are not simply defeated; they are humiliated, tortured, and broken."[11]

As far as we know, this type of body-binding torture was not a part of Israel's war conduct. Given explicit restrictions on slave mutilation and other forms of painful torture (see below), such binding/torture actions would have, by inference, been far beyond the bounds of Yahweh-approved war measures.

Whole communities captured and sold as slaves. Ancient war almost always included enslavement. It was the prerogative of victors to take and distribute people and property as they saw fit. Enslavement of the defeated king's household and his ruling elite was a norm—a given—of ANE warfare. This practice had the pragmatic advantage of destabilizing the enemy, making it less likely for them to rebel. Also, as with the seizing of valuable property, captives were selected for their personal value—knowledge, beauty, skills. However, at times entire populations from defeated cities were taken and sold off at trade-route depots and seaports as slaves.

The biblical prophets viewed the taking of entire communities and selling them for economic profit as a highly disturbing war atrocity. Enslavement of a whole community for crass financial gain was hardly considered a just punishment of an insubordinate vassal. The biblical prophets cried out against this type of extreme exploitation of vulnerable populations for profit. One could argue that all wars—ancient and modern—to some degree contain economic motivations, even if they are secondary. Economic tainting is hard to eradicate even in reasonably just wars. However, what awakened the prophetic voices in Israel was the unrestrained war machines of the ancient world, driven by drunken greed.

Capturing and selling off entire communities was especially profitable along trade routes close to Israel. The prophetic blasts against enslaving and selling entire communities are closely connected to routes that fed the north-south axis (Mesopotamia and Egypt) and the entire eastern Mediterranean world through the seaports of Gaza and Tyre.[12] The prophet Amos's oracles scream

---

[11]Janzen, "Iconography of Humiliation," 26.
[12]Jeremy M. Hutton, "Amos 1:3–2:8 and the International Economy of Iron Age II Israel," *HTR* 107, no. 1 (2014): 81-113.

with outrage against Gaza/Philistia, Tyre, and Edom (Amos 1:6-12). Joel and Ezekiel similarly bring scathing indictments against Tyre, Sidon, and the regions of Philistia for kidnapping and human trafficking.[13] Obviously, war-induced human trafficking was not limited to these identified cities or regions. War raids that captured and then sold captives (seemingly without any treaty violation) were widely practiced in the ANE and were a highly profitable byproduct of war for military victors.[14] Amos decries this monstrous war act in his day: the violent mass kidnapping of entire populations with the intent to sell them into slavery. The horror of such violence is that legitimate reasons for war (at least when viewed within that world) are lacking and replaced by unrestrained greed and economic exploitation. Entire kinship groups would be fragmented as they were sold off in piecemeal lots on the various trade routes.

Enslavement of some portion of conquered populations in the process of creating or enforcing suzerain-vassal treaties was viewed as a normal part of ancient-world warfare. In that context suzerain-vassal treaties provided a somewhat civilized way to facilitate monetary payment (tribute) in exchange for alliance, group protection, and some stability within a larger empire. For the biblical prophets, the war violence of raiding and selling entire populations on trade routes for immediate economic benefit (war for pure profit that leaves no population base and provides no treaty benefits) amounted to a blatantly greedy version of war violence. As Nili Wazana has argued, this

---

[13]Joel 3:4-8; Ezek 27:13 (see some allusions to a war context in Ezek 27:10-11, 14); see also Rev 18:13. The blunt turnaround in Joel 3:7-8, with Yahweh bringing the same horrid action back against the perpetrators, is obviously problematic. It represents an element of justice, yes, but it is justice forged on the anvil of a fallen world, justice that retaliates in like measure despite how heinous the original act itself was. Nevertheless, the Yahweh-initiated enslavement action envisioned by Joel differs in two ways from the original action: (1) it changes the motive from unbridled greed to equally measured (though far from perfect-world or even best fallen-world) justice, and (2) it uses multiple levels of causation and/or truncated causation wherein the Israelites themselves are not going to enact this ugly, partially unjust justice against these regions. The retaliatory enslavement/selling of humans would come at the hands of others—Babylon, Alexander the Great, and Antiochus IV. If other texts can be invoked here (e.g., the reverse holy war of the Assyrians against Israel), Yahweh would hold these pay-back-in-like-measure enslavers also accountable for the wrongness of their military actions even though they served his big-picture, *lex talionis* purposes.

[14]I. Mendelsohn, *Slavery in the Ancient Near East: A Comparative Study on Slavery in Babyslonia, Assyria, Syria, and Palestine from the Middle of the Third Millennium to the End of the First Millennium* (New York: Oxford University Press, 1949), 1-4, 92-94, 121. See also William J. Hamblin, *Warfare in the Ancient Near East to 1600 BC: Holy Warriors at the Dawn of History* (New York: Routledge, 2006), 156, 205-7.

unbridled, inhumane practice clashes with Amos's more restrained war ideology, and thus he cries out to his world: "You have gone too far!"[15]

Digging up graves, scattering bones, and forced grinding of ancestral bones. For the most part, Western culture does not value keeping the bones of ancestors close by in a family burial cave. Current Western traditions accept cremation—turning bones to powder and spreading the ashes across a field or lake—as a perfectly honorable treatment of dead family members. Alternatively, we simply bury either the cremated ashes or the full body in a cemetery grave with no intention of reburial. All of these options are acceptable and viewed simply as a preferential choice to honor the wishes of the deceased or, if those are unknown, the preferences of the family members.

But the ancient world handled their dead quite differently. Immediately upon death, the corpse was typically buried temporarily or stored in a safe location where the flesh could decompose. The family would later remove the bones for cleaning, drying, and storing in a cave or some secure location. This ancestral bone collection would be kept near the family even when the family was forced to move or the ancestor died away from the family plot of land.[16]

---

[15]Nili Wazana, "'War Crimes' in Amos's Oracles Against the Nations (Amos 1:3–2:3)," in *Literature as Politics, Politics as Literature*, ed. David S. Vanderhooft and Abraham Winitzer (Winona Lake, IN: Eisenbrauns, 2013), 501. Wazana makes a masterful contribution to understanding Amos's war oracles—her case for *extremity* (war acts that go too far) as a major part of the Amos's war-crime condemnations is well developed. However, her downplaying (1) the *nature* of the crime and (2) other underlying *motivational* factors is not as convincing across *all* cases in Amos 1:3–2:3. For example, this chapter will handle the ripping open of pregnant women and its narrative occurrence not as an acceptable war practice but as the biblical author does (1 Kings 15:16) when he highlights Menahem's use of excessive action and cruelty—it paints the dark and sinister side of this king's character. The narrator of Kings laments excessive war cruelty as Amos does. Furthermore, those familiar with Hutton's "Amos 1:3–2:8 and the International Economy" will appreciate his excellent contribution on the underlying economic framework in Amos 1:3–2:8, which addresses troubling motives, especially economic exploitation and greed. In this chapter, we use a blended approach to Amos's war oracles that includes three aspects: *extremity*, *motive*, and the *nature* of the war act itself (in certain cases). In the particular case of capturing and selling entire communities, one should probably add a fourth component, namely, the contrastive backdrop of *broader military norms*. Exchange of wealth/tribute in ancient warfare (involving to some extent economic greed) played a key motivational role in standard suzerain-vassal relationships, but it did so most of the time by enacting only a partial enslavement of populations and granting a stability benefit and protection within the empire. Compared with this norm of ancient warfare, the exploitive greed of simply taking and selling whole populations is far starker.

[16]See Saul M. Olyan, "Unnoticed Resonances of Tomb Opening and Transportation of the Remains of the Dead in Ezekiel 37:12-14," *JBL* 128 (2009): 496-99. In rare cases where

The careful treatment of ancestral bones in the ancient world was part of how families honored their dead. Preservation and care for ancestors' bones expressed the highest level of respect for the deceased themselves, and it protected their participation in the afterlife, even if for some that simply meant a peaceful, resting state for eternity. Of course, today we know that literally millions of living microorganisms enjoy their own unseen world within every square foot of soil and that, given enough time, our molecular structure eventually becomes part of microbes, insects, plants, and animals. While some of us might prefer burial over cremation, it matters little to our eventual molecular redistribution around the planet. But viewed through the lens of ancient burial practices, digging up and scattering or destroying the beloved ancestral bones would have been the epitome of disrespect for the dead and a torturous experience for family members.

Digging up graves and scattering ancestral bones. Ancient warriors at times dug up the graves of defeated royal families and other ruling elites, spreading their bones in distant locations and so making it impossible to retrieve them. The punitive goal of this activity was to humiliate and distress living survivors and seemingly to affect negatively the afterlife of the dead.[17] The razor-sharp pain inflicted by this practice would have cut deep into the psyche of the defeated people group in at least five ways. First, the *spreading* of ancestral bones by enemy soldiers functioned as a ritual reversal of the normal caring act of *gathering* the bones.[18] It completely undid the family's careful burial rites and replaced them with the opposite—cruel and utter disdain for their

---

bones were moved (e.g., Joseph, Saul, Jonathan), it was always to reestablish family unity between the living and the dead. See Gen 50:25; Ex 13:19; Josh 24:32; 1 Sam 31:13; 2 Sam 21:12-14.

[17]For how this ruthless action functioned as a ritualized reversal of burial norms, see Olyan, "Ritual Inversion in Biblical Representations of Punitive Rites," 135-46. For biblical examples of hostile exhumation, exposure, and scattering of Israelite bones by foreign invading armies, see Jer 8:1-2; Is 14:19. See also Saul M. Olyan, "Was the 'King of Babylon' Buried Before His Corpse Was Exposed? Some Thoughts on Isa 14, 19," *ZAW* 118 (2006): 423-26.

[18]Many biblical texts emphasize the "gathering" of the dead (their bones) to their people. For example, Gen 25:8, "Abraham breathed his last . . . and he was *gathered* to his people." Contemporary readers often do not realize that this gathering literally meant collecting their bones and making them part of the family bone collection. In short, it was a gathering together (not scattering) of the dead family members. See also Ishmael (Gen 25:17), Isaac (Gen 35:29), Jacob (Gen 49:29, 33), and others.

dead family members. The scattering inflicted a sense of separation from loved ones that gathering had countered. Second, the exposure of bones to the sun gave these ancestors (in addition to random, distant scattering) no burial at all. Again, the complete reversal of burial customs is at play. Exposure to the elements undid the caring actions of loved ones.

Third, digging up enemy graves and scattering the bones would have cruelly reawakened the grief and pain that family members experienced over the deceased's original passing. It metaphorically ripped off any bandage and traumatically reopened the wound. On a psychological level families were forced to relive the death of their loved ones. Fourth, in the ancient mindset the scattering of enemy bones seems to have affected their afterlife state in two ways: (1) it upset their ability to find peace and rest in the afterlife, and (2) at the very least it placed in question the deceased's participation in future life activities, when that was part of a culture's afterlife beliefs. Finally, this military action typically happened *after* the battle was concluded. After the victory was secure, the soldiers would then spend time digging up graves and scattering the enemies' ancestral bones. The postbattle treatment of captured survivors (and their families) in this manner clearly speaks to the intentional cruelty of further deepening the victims' grief and loss far beyond the recent battle loss.

Forced grinding of ancestral bones. Digging up, exposing to the sun, and randomly spreading the enemies' ancestral bones after a victory held a possible further element of traumatic pain. Some ancient armies increased the horror by forcing their captives to grind up their ancestors' bones with their own hands. Ashurbanipal's battle reliefs provide a graphic picture of captives kneeling and grinding up the bones of dead family members.[19] Assyrian soldiers stand over and behind each captive, holding their necks in a shackle brace while raising a mace over their heads that threatened to crush their skulls. The written version can be found in Assyrian treaty threats: "May the grain for grinding disappear from you; instead of grain may your sons and daughters grind your bones."[20]

---

[19]Simo Parpola and Kazuko Watanabe, *Neo-Assyrian Treaties and Loyalty Oaths*, SAA 2 (Helsinki: Helsinki University Press, 1988), 47 [fig. 14; BM 124801].

[20]Parpola and Watanabe, *Neo-Assyrian Treaties and Loyalty Oaths*, 46 (Esarhaddon's succession treaty, §40, lines 445-46). The bones of the governor of Nippur were carried back

It is one thing to watch an invading army abuse your loved ones; it is yet another to be forced to be the agents of that abuse. Of course, if the bones were turned to powder, they were easier for soldiers to disperse. No longer did they have to haul the bones some distance and then spread them. They could torment their captives as they watched (or perhaps were forced to participate in) their loved ones' remains being thrown to the wind. Compared with scattering bones randomly at a distance, grinding bones to powder totally dashed any hopes of even a partial recovery by future generations. The increased torment in the forced grinding and likely direct witness of dispersing their ancestors' bone powder would have made this act of war torture profoundly traumatic.

Scattering bodies of the war dead. Not surprisingly, dishonoring their enemies' ancestral bones matched how ancient armies treated recently fallen dead soldiers on the battlefield. War victims were sometimes subject to gross acts of dismemberment after the battle; their mutilated corpses were left for the pleasure of animals and birds of prey.[21] Assyrian soldiers dismembered the bodies of an enemy palace household and fed the pieces "to the dogs, swine, wolves and eagles, to the birds of the heaven, and the fish of the deep."[22] As with the ritual act of scattering ancestral bones, the war dead were at times scattered or dumped into rivers and oceans to carry them off to other locations, thereby distributing their body parts over a wide region.[23] For heightened cruelty in the scattering ritual, victorious armies at times carried the bodies (or bones) of dead kings long distances to entirely different countries.[24]

---

to Nineveh for punitive grinding, most likely as part of a victory celebration. See Seth F. C. Richardson, "Death and Dismemberment in Mesopotamia: Discorporation Between the Body and Body Politic," in *Performing Death: Social Analyses of Funerary Traditions in the Ancient Near East and Mediterranean*, ed. Nicola Laneri, OIS 3 (Chicago: Oriental Institute of the University of Chicago, 2007), 197-98.

[21]It appears that Israel sometimes left its war-dead enemies unburied (perhaps temporarily or just as a taunt). David chides the Philistines along these lines (1 Sam 17:44, 46). However, it seems unlikely that Israelite warriors participated in extensive postbattle mutilation rituals and scattering of dead enemies' body parts or bones from ancestral graves. We have no evidence of such scattering by Israelite armies and, more importantly, such desecration of dead was not practiced in the treatment of their greatest foe, namely, the enemy king. See discussion below on impalement.

[22]As cited by Richardson, "Death and Dismemberment in Mesopotamia," 197.

[23]Richardson, "Death and Dismemberment in Mesopotamia," 200.

[24]Ashurbanipal recounts his treatment of the dead kings of Elam: "I took their bones to the land of Assyria, imposing restlessness upon their ghosts. I deprived them of ancestral

Foreign, non-Israelite armies performed these heinous bone-scattering actions as part of their postbattle rituals and then proudly recorded them in their annals and iconic art. They considered these war actions as positive displays of bravado and military strength, not as morally decrepit and shameful actions. By contrast, Israel's treatment of its captives and of the dead moves in a dramatically different direction. We have no evidence that Israelite warriors dug up non-Israelite graves and scattered enemy bones, whether in whole or powdered form.[25] In fact, the weight of evidence makes this unlikely. First, Israel was not permitted to abuse the bodies of domestic criminals in this scattered-bones manner (Deut 21:22-23), and in the case of war, this domestic restriction seems to have been carried over to the dead bodies of foreign kings. The slain body of the defeated king—greatest of all their foes—was to be kept intact and buried by sunset. Thus, the war treatment of dead bodies (even those of the enemy elites) reflects how Israel

---

offerings (and) libations of water." Cited and translated by Saul M. Olyan, "Ritual Inversion in Biblical Representations of Punitive Rites," 138n13.

[25]The one biblical case of Josiah exhuming the bones of Israel's priests and burning them on the altar (2 Kings 23:16, 19-20; see also 1 Kings 12:25–13:2) is the only evidence of this practice by Israelites within the Hebrew Bible. While Josiah may well have been mimicking foreign war practices, this one exception text cannot be used to establish that the practice was normative within either Israel's judicial system or its military scene. Several lines of evidence suggest this exhuming and bone-burning action was a highly unusual one-time act designed to make a statement in the context of Josiah's reforms—one encouraging the people to move away from pagan fertility gods and their hideous practices (temple prostitution, sacrificing children, etc.) and return to worshiping Yahweh. First, the context clearly describes a ritualized action taken against Israel's own priests; it is not a story of Israel's warriors exhuming bodies of dead enemies after a battle. There is no hostile war action against a foreign military foe, even if the text might be rhetorically dressed in similar clothes. Second, the explicit purpose for burning the dead priests' bones on the altar is to defile it: "Josiah . . . had the bones removed from them [the priests' graves] and burned on the altar *to defile it*" (2 Kings 23:16). The defiling action is intended to stop any further worship of the false gods and thereby turn Judah's hearts back to Yahweh. So it holds both a restorative and a punitive function. Third, the act of Josiah is an ironic and profound statement about Yahweh not wanting human sacrifice (unlike the worship of Molech and child sacrifice, which the narrator highlights in the immediate context—2 Kings 23:10). The point is this: if these Israelite priests want to worship the fertility gods and burn children to Molech, their own bones will be burned on an altar and turned to ash. The talionic action ties the burning of priests' bones on the altar to (the same priests?) offering young children as sacrifices. Fourth, Josiah grinds up an Asherah pole and sprinkled its dust on the graves of the common people; he does not exhume their bodies. Nor does he burn or scatter their bones. This suggests a purposeful step down, away from any broad-based punitive action (unlike what happened at times in the unbridled version of foreign bone-scattering practices); it shifts the focus from any static sense of a grave-related rituals to levels of responsibility for idolatry.

was instructed to treat its own criminal dead. For further discussion, see the section below on impaling.

Second, Amos's scathing blasts against the heinous war crimes of foreign nations repudiate the dishonoring destruction of the dead. Amos considers this to be war hatred taken too far; he condemns Moab for having "burned to ashes the bones of Edom's king" (Amos 2:1). Not only does Amos's "you've gone too far" rebuke match what we know of the restrained actions of Israel's armies toward dead enemies, but also it makes little sense for the prophet to decry this foreign military action if it were considered a Yahweh-approved action for Israel's military.

Extensive bodily mutilations and counting of heads, hands, and phalli.
Ancient war portraits of bodily mutilations from (living and dead) captives include the cutting off of every human extremity imaginable—entire legs, feet, ears, noses, tongues, lips, arms, hands, genitals, and so on. The blinding of prisoners is also frequently displayed in these grisly scenes. Pictures of such war actions are readily available through museum-based and archaeological websites.[26] The scribal version in written annals confirms grisly mutilations as an integral part of ancient war for controlling foreign vassal populations. Ashurbanipal, an Assyrian king, proudly declares, "I chopped up their [my enemies'] flesh and let it be displayed in all other countries."[27] His son and royal heir liked to "slice open the bellies [of his opponents]" as though they were young rams "so that their intestines might wrap around their feet."[28] The bodies of hated enemy captives became a canvas for displaying a public message. Darius the Median ruler describes what he did to one of his rebel enemies: "I cut off his nose, his ears, and his tongue, and I

---

[26]For various sites (e.g., the British Historical Museum) see E. Bleibtreu, "Grisly Assyrian Record of Torture and Death," *BARev* 17, no. 1 (1991): 52-61; see also R. D. Barnett, E. Bleibtreu, and G. Turner, *Sculptures from the Southwest Palace of Sennacherib at Nineveh* (London: British Museum Press, 1998).

[27]See Andreas Fuchs, "Waren die Assyrer grausam?," in *Extreme Formen von Gewalt*, 107-8 (our English translation).

[28]Fuchs, "Waren die Assyrer grausam?," 106 (our English translation). Slicing the belly and pulling out the intestines may well have been performed on live, standing captives, who were bound or held by their arms (as well as on dead captives). On cutting off the hands and feet of war captives (along with blinding them) in Esarhaddon's succession treaty, see Parpola and Watanabe, *Neo-Assyrian Treaties*, 57 (§95, lines 626-31). On cutting off body parts and slicing open internal organs in ancient warfare, see Fabrice De Backer, "Cruelty and Military Refinements," *Res Antiquae* 6 (2009): 13-50.

put out one of his eyes. He was held bound at my gate. All the people saw him. Then I impaled him."[29]

War mutilations often focused on certain body parts—heads, hands, and penises—for counting purposes. While the Assyrians liked to stack and count human heads, the Egyptians were famous for cutting off hands and phalli.[30] Stacking hundreds of enemy heads outside the gates of a defeated city left a horrible monument that would demoralize and dishearten the vassal; it also warned other cities of the price of rebellion. Piling up heads provided the victors a pragmatic means of measuring the dead—a mountain of dead. Similarly, the collection of hands and penises pronounced a sobering decree of death and defeat. Along with helping to count the slain, the victory piles of hands and penises seem to have symbolized an end to their enemy's ability to conduct war (hands) and to enjoy offspring and sexual pleasure (penises).[31]

Israelite war actions at times included body mutilations. Warriors from the tribe of Judah cut off the thumbs and big toes of the ruler Adoni-Bezek, seemingly as an act of talionic justice for his having performed such mutilations against enemy kings. David severed Goliath's head as a victory display (1 Sam 17:46), and he cut off two hundred enemy foreskins to give to Saul for his daughter's hand in marriage (1 Sam 18:25-27).[32] These war mutilations in the Bible

---

[29]As cited by Bruce Lincoln, "An Ancient Case of Interrogation and Torture," *Social Analysis: The International Journal of Social and Cultural Practice* 53, no. 1 (2009): 159.

[30]Dominik Bonatz, "Ashurbanipal's Headhunt: An Anthropological Perspective," *Iraq* 66, no. 1 (2004): 93-101; Janzen, "Iconography of Humiliation," 202, 212, 230, 261, 285.

[31]Cutting off and collecting the penises of the slain enemy warriors would have reinforced the right of victors to the sexual conquest of the defeated army's wives and daughters. It functioned as a ritualized corollary to war rape. A pile of captured penises and their attached scrotum sacks (like the trophy piling of heads or hands) is proudly displayed in the artwork on the mortuary temple of Ramses III at Medinet Habu.

[32]Cutting off the head of a warrior in ancient warfare, especially if he wore heavy armor, could be a merciful act if he had been mortally wounded and was slowly dying. The break in armor between the head and chest gear offered a spot for quickly killing one's foe.

Other mutilation examples are instructive but clearly part of ad hoc domestic punishments. In 2 Sam 4:1-12 David cuts off the hands and feet of two Israelites who presumptuously (without his directive or approval) assassinated one of Saul's children. They had run to David with the "good news." David has them both killed and their hands and feet cut off as ironic measure of justice—the hands that assassinated Ish-Bosheth and the feet that carried the news to David. This domestic judicial action by David is intended to stop any further killing of Saul's children, including the lame son of Jonathan (Mephibosheth), whose case is highlighted in the same chapter (see 2 Sam 16:9-13; 20:13-22).

rightly repulse modern readers. By Geneva/Hague standards, Israelite warfare was clearly barbaric. Nevertheless, such mutilations by Israelite warriors—as disgusting as they are to us—were few and ad hoc compared to the excessive and almost systemic use of bodily mutilation within the ancient world of war. Yahweh warriors did not produce massive piles of human heads as war monuments to mark a victory; they did not mutilate captive bodies beyond recognition.[33]

Within the framework of the ancient world, Israel's war practices were considerably restrained, though we would certainly disapprove of them today. This characteristic of war restraint by Israel was not happenstance. It appears to be rooted in the more humane treatment of people that was part Israel's broader handling of crime and punishment. Just as Israelites were restricted from mutilating slaves as a form of punishment (or they went free; Ex 21:26-27), they were also significantly restricted in what they could do in handling domestic criminals compared to the excessive brutality of the ancient world. Bodily mutilations for domestic crimes among the Israelites themselves were extremely rare. On the other hand, bodily mutilation for domestic crimes among the Hittites, Egyptians, Assyrians, and Babylonians were extensive—almost nauseatingly so. We will return to this mirrored universe at the close of this chapter.

Ripping open pregnant women. Ripping open the wombs of pregnant women takes ancient war atrocities to a heightened extreme. The cruel nature of this act was so unbearable for ancients they could hardly cast their eyes on it.[34] An invading soldier grabbed a pregnant woman and used a knife, sword, or his sharp spear to slice open her protruding stomach in order to kill the unborn infant. The Hebrew Bible uniformly views ripping open pregnant women as a detestable war action. The dark casting by the biblical narrator in 2 Kings provides an understanding that Yahweh condemns the savage actions of Menahem, who sacks the city of Tiphsah and "ripped open all the pregnant women" (2 Kings 15:16) for not opening their city gates. Similarly, the prophet

---

[33]Moreover, Israel's prescribed temple iconography (pomegranates, palm trees, flowers, cherubim) contrasts starkly with the gruesome war scenes of bodily mutilations found on many ANE temples.

[34]One Neo-Babylonian lament captures this heart-wrenching sentiment: "My eyes cannot look on . . . the ripping of the mother's wombs." Cited by Shalom M. Paul, *Amos*, Hermeneia (Minneapolis: Fortress, 1991), 68.

Amos indicts the Ammonites because they "ripped open the pregnant women of Gilead in order to enlarge [Ammon's] borders" (Amos 1:13).[35] The biblical authors viewed ripping open the womb as utterly repugnant—"a brutal act of savage and unforgiveable cruelty committed against defenseless human beings."[36] Israelite armies were never authorized to act in this manner.

By way of dramatic contrast, outside Israel the ancient war act of slicing open pregnant women was often seen as a badge of heroic conquest and honor. An Assyrian hymn praises the war exploits of Tiglath-pileser I: "He slits the wombs of pregnant women, he blinds the infants, he cuts the throats of their strong ones."[37] With similar military applause a stone relief from Ashurbanipal's palace depicts the ripping open of pregnant Arab women. The multiple war scenes portray Assyrian soldiers using the sharp end of a spear to cut open a pregnant Arab woman (from the lower part of her extended belly upwards) and then removing the fetus.[38]

Impaling live captives on stakes. Impaling or staking involved the victorious soldiers pushing a long, rounded wooden pole into the victim's anus.[39] The stake was slowly pushed through the human body so that it avoided hitting the vital organs (hoping not to damage them); it either exited the body through the captive's mouth or simply remained inside the chest cavity. Once the stake with the body was mounted in the ground, it offered a grisly scene of live torture for a prolonged time.[40] A properly skewered captive could live in this position of extreme agony for several days before finally succumbing to death.

---

[35]See the ripping open of pregnant women as a horrifying potential war consequence within the prophetic voices of Elisha (2 Kings 8:12) and Hosea (Hos 14:1).

[36]Paul, *Amos*, 68.

[37]Mordechai Cogan, "'Ripping Open Pregnant Women' in Light of an Assyrian Analogue," *JAOS* 103, no. 4 (1983): 756.

[38]Peter Dubovsky, "Ripping Open Pregnant Arab Women: Reliefs in Room L of Ashurbanipal's North Palace," *Orientalia* 78, no. 3 (2009): 394-419.

[39]While the anus (vagina for women) was often used, other torn/lacerated openings in the stomach, chest, or chin were used for variation.

[40]The whole point of impaling *alive* was to maximize the excruciating pain of the victims and make a display for other captives, who were sometimes forced to watch. Assyrian king Tiglath-pileser records his impaling live leaders: "I impaled alive his chief ministers; and I made his country behold (them)" (COS 2:117A, 286). As other examples in this section will attest, sometimes the display of impaled-*alive* leaders or soldiers was for the psychological subjugation of the vassal residents within the conquered city.

What makes the impaling of enemies even more hideous is that it was sometimes done after chopping off body parts—the hands and legs. War reliefs show soldiers cutting off the legs and arms of live captives and then (in the next scene) impaling the same captives on staked display with shortened stubs. Historians surmise that wounded legs and arms were cauterized to stop the impaled person from bleeding to death.[41] The sexual overtones of anal (or vaginal) penetration by thrusting a pole up into the body communicated sexual conquest for the victor—not unlike vaginal penetration in battlefield rape of females.[42] Eventually vultures and other birds would begin eating the flesh off the bodies of the impaled captives.

Ancient war scenes often depict captives outside city walls impaled alive on posts. Depending on the stone relief or metal etching, the artist displays one, two, three, or even six humans on stakes outside the conquered city. But this creative version of impaling is merely representative and limited by the medium of art. The war annals show that the reality was far worse than a handful of impaled people. In taking one city, the Assyrian king Ashurnasirpal II killed six hundred enemy troops but managed to capture four hundred soldiers alive. In front of the city gates he piled the heads of the dead soldiers. The living soldiers were less fortunate. He impaled alive the four hundred captured soldiers around the city—an act of mass torture and psychological warfare. After a prolonged set of battles, Darius the Median ruler defeated and captured his enemy Fravarti. Darius cut off Fravarti's nose, ears, and tongue and put out one of his eyes. He then bound him at the city gates for all the people to see. As the final and climatic act of war triumph, Darius had Fravarti impaled alive along with his foremost followers.[43] While impaling is far more common in Assyrian accounts, Egyptian records similarly reveal postbattle impaling (or sometimes burning live captives) as a way of demonstrating the pharaoh's harsh dealings with his enemies.[44]

---

[41]De Backer, "Cruelty and Military Refinements," 30.

[42]Adultery and abortion were at times punished in the ANE world—Sumer, Babylonia, and Assyria—by impaling the woman involved. One of the cruelest forms of death, such penetration of the female body was "highly symbolic of the sexual control of women by men." Elisabeth Meier Tetlow, *Women, Crime, and Punishment in Ancient Law and Society*, The Ancient Near East 1 (New York: Continuum, 2004), 34, 68, 138, 261n73.

[43]Lincoln, "Ancient Case of Interrogation and Torture," 159.

[44]Akhenaten impaled 225 Kushite captives; Mernptah impaled Libyans who were left alive.

At this point we can understand the Bible within its brutal context. Modern readers of the biblical war texts can now see a marked difference in the practice and values of Israelite warriors. The differences are as follows:

- ▶ Only *dead* captives were hung on a pole for display (no torture of live captives).

- ▶ No widespread impaling (primarily limited to the king).

- ▶ Display of the dead body lasted for several hours, rather than for days.

- ▶ The body was taken down and buried before sunset.

Perhaps the most dramatic difference is the absence of physical torture and a measure of dignity for the dead body. Israel's purpose for hanging a dead enemy (a king) on a pole was to signal the taking of the city. With the death of the king, the city had fallen and been subdued. Pole hangings within the biblical war texts were not used to inflict prolonged torture on live captives for days, followed by the prospect of their bodies being eaten by vultures. Several lines of biblical evidence support understanding Israel's pole-hanging practice as only for *already-dead* (not living) enemy kings. First, the most explicit text, Joshua 10:26, uses two verbs for killing/ending of life before mentioning the hanging of the body for display:

> And afterward Joshua *smote them*, and *slew them*, and hanged them [the five kings] on five trees: and they were hanging upon the trees until the evening. (KJV)

> Afterward Joshua *struck them down* and *put them to death*, and he hung them [the five kings] on five trees. And they hung on the trees until evening. (NRSV)

> Then Joshua *put the kings to death* [the NIV combines the two Hebrew verbs] and exposed their bodies on five poles, and they were left hanging on the poles until evening. (NIV)

This death-then-hanging sequence likely reflects what happened in the other, less explicit cases of the conquest narratives because of the linked treatment of all the enemy kings, with accounts stating repeatedly that the treatment of one king matched that of other kings (Josh 8:2; 10:1, 28, 30). Second, Nili Wazana has shown that the war actions against the kings in the conquest

---

See Janzen, "Iconography of Humiliation," 253-56.

passages deliberately echo the instructions of Deuteronomy 21:22-23, which limits the duration of hanging of Israel's executed criminals on poles. Criminals were not to be left hanging overnight but buried on the same day. This literary connection between the Joshua war texts and Deuteronomy strengthens the likelihood that the death of an enemy king, like the death of an Israelite criminal, happened *before* the body was placed on a pole for display.[45] Third, if the purpose of Israel's impaling had been to inflict as much pain as possible on live victims, it seems counterproductive to end this ritualized torture by sunset. In the ancient world impaling live captives provided a means of prolonged torture for days. Had Israelite soldiers impaled enemy kings alive in order to torture them, then in the case of an afternoon battle they would have just started torturing their victims when it would abruptly have to stop. Ending the hanging of the body by sunset (a few hours after capture) instead of several days suggests that Israel's purpose was symbolic declaration of defeat, and only after death, rather than inflicting torture through live impaling.

Fourth, the emphasis on removal from the tree, burial, and keeping the body intact—not allowing it to be eaten by vultures if left on a pole for days—clashes with the dismemberment that accompanied some ANE impalings. Israel's comparatively humane and respectful treatment of the human body upon death seems logically incongruent with the use of torture to bring about a slow and painful death. Finally, whenever the biblical text provides a stated means of death for conquered enemy kings, it is always with the sword—"He [Joshua] put the city and its king *to the sword*" (Josh 10:28; see Josh 10:30, 37; 11:10; see also Deut 20:13; Josh 6:21, 24; 8:24; 10:32, 35, 37, 39; 11:11-12, 14; Judg 1:25). Israel did not capture and keep enemy kings (or other captives) alive for the purpose of torture and slow death through impaling.[46]

---

[45]Nili Wazana, "'For an Impaled Body Is a Curse of God' (Deut 21:23): Impaled Bodies in Biblical Law and Conquest Narratives," in *Law and Narrative in the Bible and Neighbouring Ancient Cultures*, ed. Klaus-Peter Adam, Friedrich Avemarie, and Nili Wazana, FAT 2, Reihe 54 (New York: Mohr Siebeck, 2012), 67-98. Wazana argues that Israel's more humane form of no-torture impaling and more respectful treatment of the body through burial before sunset (with criminal law [Deuteronomy] affecting war actions [Joshua]) should be seen as intentional branding: the horrid and bragged-about impaling customs of the Assyrians are cast as "the opposite of the Israelite norm" (p. 96).

[46]Even in 1 Sam 15:8, where King Agag is wrongly kept alive by Saul, the enemy king is eventually killed by the sword (1 Sam 15:33) and not by prolonged horrifying death from impaling, flaying, or other forms of torture.

Flaying the skin from live captives. Flaying live captives was another ghastly and painful means of torture. Perhaps the best-known flaying scene is that of Ashurbanipal, king of Assyria, who proudly displayed several enemy captives (probably from ruling families) staked to the ground. The details of the stone relief are graphic. The naked male captives are lying facedown with their arms and legs spread open and tied separately to one of four stakes; a wooden spacer bar is attached to the ankles with lashed ropes to limit their resisting movements. Assyrian soldiers used knives to peel the skin off these live captives.[47] Should death not ensue immediately, the skinned captives were left to die from bleeding, exposure to the sun, and/or being eaten by wild animals and birds.

But the horror of flaying does not stop there. Once the human skin was removed from the captive, it then became a valuable item for further war propaganda. The human skin, like that taken from an animal, became a ritualized war trophy. Sometimes the human skin was draped for display at the city gates of the defeated city or used to make furniture that would adorn the victor's palaces. Either way, flaying the enemy—even if only the leaders—functioned as a powerful and fearful reminder of the lengths to which ancient rulers would go to secure control over their vassal regions.

The display of human skin as war trophies in strategic city locations and in the stone portraits of flayed captives is matched by the bold statements of the war annals. Far from being ashamed of such inhumane actions, Ashurnasirpal II proudly records the war punishment of insubordinate rebels: "I flayed as many nobles as had rebelled against me [and] draped their skins over the pile [of corpses]; some I spread out within the pile, some I erected on stakes upon the pile. . . . I flayed as many right through my land [and] draped their skins over the walls."[48]

The flaying of live captives in ancient warfare has always bothered me (Bill here). When I came to realize that our contemporary expression "So

---

[47]The Ashurbanipal iconography and its related literary references combine two horrific actions—tearing out a captive's tongue and flaying. See Theodore J. Lewis, "'You Have Heard What the Kings of Assyria Have Done': Disarmament Passages Vis-à-vis Assyrian Rhetoric of Intimidation," in *Isaiah's Vision of Peace in Biblical and Modern International Relations: Swords into Plowshares*, ed. Raymond Cohen and Raymond Westbrook (New York: Palgrave Macmillan, 2008), 83-85.

[48]As cited by Bleibtreu, "Grisly Assyrian Record of Torture and Death," 55.

and so is going to skin you alive!" had its historical roots in the actual skinning of live persons, a shudder ran down my spine. Perhaps my aversion goes deeper because as a young boy I learned to trap, kill, and skin animals (we lived in the north, where it was a way of life). So I know exactly what it is like to peel the skin off a dead animal.[49] My mind transfers this picture far too easily from the animal to the human domain. In fact, the experience for me is so graphic that even pondering this horrific act of war for any length of time makes me physically nauseous. Yet, this visceral reaction is precisely what the ancient kings wanted to produce in their intended audience. Since many (perhaps most) people in the ancient world had firsthand experience peeling the skin from animals, the flaying of humans would evoke deep and lasting chills among those who either saw these human skins, gazed on the artistic version, or heard the stories of what happened.

This chapter is hardly exhaustive. We could easily have doubled its length and included many other examples of heinous actions in ancient warfare. But this is sufficient to make the point. Against the backdrop of ancient war atrocities, the Israelite practice of killing the enemy king, his key leaders, and captured soldiers shows restraint and far less cruelty, a redemptive movement.

A MIRRORING SCENARIO: DOMESTIC CRIME AND PUNISHMENT

The conclusion of this chapter on war atrocities—that Israel's war actions were at least incrementally redemptive within their day—is further established through what might be described as a mirroring connection between domestic (courtroom judgments) and foreign (war) punishment scenes. When the biblical (rod and whip) crime and punishment texts are read within their larger ancient social context, one discovers similar incrementally redemptive findings in Israel's *domestic* crime and punishment.

Setting aside smaller, local battles, most ANE wars were fought within a highly structured suzerain-vassal framework where treaties warned of

---

[49]My revulsion to the ancient practice of flaying recently took on even greater aversion when I learned that Nazi soldiers in the Auschwitz war camps, based on survivor testimony and other evidence, *may have* used human skin to make lampshades and/or other tattooed-skin trophies.

the kinds of punishment that would befall an insubordinate rebel state or vassal who "sinned" or rebelled against the suzerain. As a result, ancient war involved a mentality of crime and punishment. Within this ancient horizon, war was viewed as the king of an empire punishing rebel kings and their countries for the "crime" of rebellion.

Aside from the overlapping framework of crime and punishment that ties together the foreign (war) and domestic punishments (beatings), some of the specific punishments themselves leave a telltale calling card about the overlap. Most importantly for this book, however, is the point of the mirrored findings: on the whole *the far more egregious war punishments by Egypt, Babylon, or Assyria (compared with Israel) parallel the far more egregious domestic punishments by other nations (compared with Israel).* This finding is hardly coincidental. In a world that legitimized war within a classic framework of crime and punishment, the domestic realm of justice would have naturally influenced and shaped the international war realm.[50] Simply put, for many ancient nations outside Israel, the utterly horrendous punishments in their domestic courts probably influenced the egregious nature of their war actions (and vice versa). Similarly, the restricted nature of Israel's domestic/court-approved punishments likely influenced its (comparatively) restrained military actions. Here are a few samples of domestic judicial punishments from Egypt, Assyria, Babylon, and Persia:

▶ Corporal beatings: There was no limit on beatings with the rod or whip; some crimes required a punishment of two hundred lashes and five open wounds.

▶ Corporal mutilation: Many crimes were punished by cutting off body parts—noses, eyes, ears, tongues, hands, genitals, breasts, and others.

▶ Torture leading to death: Torture was a part of the ANE spectrum of punishments. Women in certain cases of adultery were impaled alive as a punishment (a very graphic and sexually symbolic statement).

---

[50]Lincoln makes the case that the excessive mutilations in war at times paralleled similar mutilations in civil/domestic crime and punishment situations in order to make social statements about "criminal" war enemies ("Ancient Case of Interrogation and Torture," 157-72). An overlapping or shared communicational coding transferred meaning easily between the two realms.

▶ No proper burial: Domestic criminals were at times denied proper burial as part of their punishment.

Compared with these highly egregious samples of ancient justice, Israel's punishment for domestic crimes (no more than forty lashes; only one case of mutilation) were highly restrained and incrementally redemptive as they sought to live out justice within their real-world context.[51]

CONCLUSION

Over the years we have collected many ancient portraits and inscriptions of war atrocities for use in educational settings. The emotive impact is greater when one sees these war atrocities preserved in graphic visual renderings combined with verbal commentary. Contemplating the artistic renderings of what happened in the list of ANE war atrocities is unforgettably jarring. Many ancient battles included a range of the following inhumane and grotesque actions:

▶ stripping captives naked and parading them with shaved genitals

▶ excruciatingly painful rope bindings that dislocated and shattered joints

▶ mutilating (often live) captives—cutting off the tongue, toes, noses, genitals, hands, feet, legs, head, and more

▶ blinding prisoners

▶ displaying body parts—stacking piles of heads at the city gate or piling up hands and penises

▶ capturing whole communities and selling them on the slave market

▶ no burial of the dead

▶ digging up ancestral graves and scattering the bones

▶ forcing captives to grind up ancestral bones

▶ raping women and young girls as part of the battle conquest

---

[51]We invite readers who want to explore incrementally redemptive findings in the domestic realm of corporal punishment to read William J. Webb, *Corporal Punishment in the Bible: A Redemptive-Movement Hermeneutic for Troubling Texts* (Downers Grove, IL: Inter-Varsity Press, 2011), especially chapters three through five.

- slicing open pregnant women and killing the unborn

- impaling live victims on stakes pushed through their bodies

- flaying alive—cutting/peeling the skin from live captives staked to the ground

While unpleasant to reflect on, an accurate picture of the grisly nature of ancient war is important for reading the biblical war texts. The war atrocities listed above are either explicitly or implicitly denounced within the biblical text. Unlike the praise and glory given these acts of extreme violence by foreign gods, artwork, and annals, such war crimes were not considered Yahweh-approved war actions for Israel.

So here is how this chapter fits within the argument of this book. If the biblical or Yahweh-approved war actions by Israelite soldiers did *not* include either (1) the above list of ANE war atrocities or (2) the total-kill elimination of the Canaanites, as argued in several previous chapters, then Israel's war measures would have been considered mild or comparatively moderate within its larger ancient context. Repugnant as the biblical war texts are for modern readers (we cannot escape our ingrained Hague/Geneva horizon), they were markedly restrained in their day. To put it another way, the clear movement away from well-known war atrocities of the ancient world betrays significant incremental movement in a good, redemptive direction. Unlike many in the ancient world, the biblical writers viewed the above war atrocities as a list of shameful war actions and not something to be proud of. This incrementally redemptive war ideology within Scripture, as read within the social context of its day, advances a greater respect and dignity even for one's enemies on the battlefield.

As another contribution to the book, this chapter on war atrocities further supports our square-pegs, round-holes thesis about the traditional answers to the ethics of total-kill human slaughter that we find in biblical holy war (sure *seems* like genocide): God commanded it, God is holy and just, and the Canaanites were excessively sinful/evil. We have argued that these traditional answers relate well to the broader story-line questions of the Bible that plagued the original audience. They answer why God drove the Canaanites from the land—similar to why he expelled other

Canaanite-*like* players (Adam and Eve, Israel, Judah, and others) from the sacred space of Eden or the new Eden.[52] But the traditional answers do not address (chapter two), and in fact were never intended to address, our modern ethical questions about ancient military conduct. They do not address our modern questions about genocide and war rape that we see in the Bible. The corollary for this square-pegs, round holes thesis is provided by this chapter: *it is unlikely that the original audience would have seen the ethical issues of their genocide rhetoric and postbattlefield, marital (war) rape that we now see*. Given the extreme nature of ancient war violence catalogued in this chapter, the biblical authors would have understood their own war ethic as embracing a kinder, gentler, and more humane treatment of their enemies. What troubled the original readers were the ultrainhumane acts of war violence in their world; the prophet Amos addresses some of these, and they align well with the contents of this chapter. The original authors and audience were not writing or reading the biblical text from the horizon of Hague and Geneva, as we are today. In sum, ethical questions about the concrete-specific military actions of Israel's army within the pages of Scripture (specifically how they functioned in warfare) were simply not on the radar of the original readers. Rather, the authors of the biblical text were already pushing toward a Geneva/Hague–*like* journey of their own making—one contextually rooted in their own time.

One final comment—Israel's kinder and more humane treatment of its enemies in war, relative to the war atrocities of this chapter, is not wishful thinking inspired by Jewish or Christian vested interests. There is a whole second universe of parallel evidence—a mirroring framework of crime and punishment found within the domestic realm that supports the incrementally redemptive war thesis of this book. If one studies domestic cases of crime and punishment for the citizens of various ANE countries (crimes requiring two hundred strokes with the rod and five open wounds,

---

[52]The original readers' ethical issues were not with how Israelite warriors conducted their military actions during the period of the conquest, judges, or later kings but with the larger question at the level of the story line about the legitimacy of removing various (literary) Canaanite groups from sacred space throughout the biblical metanarrative. See chapter three.

impaling women for certain acts of adultery, cutting off body parts, prolonged torture) and Israel's highly curtailed version of corporal punishment, the war story falls into place. It reflects a similar pattern. Within the ancient-world context, Israel's comparatively restricted war actions duplicated its restraint and pursuit of greater human dignity that occurred in its corporal-punishment actions.

14

YAHWEH AS UNEASY WAR GOD

The Subversive War Texts

SINCE MANY BIBLICAL WAR TEXTS DEPICT Yahweh's participation with Israel in warfare in a seemingly positive light, readers can easily conclude that Yahweh accepts Israel's warfare without reservation, commends it, and is perhaps even fond of its bloody battles, much like other ANE gods. But that is not the case. A collection of antiwar or subversive war texts in Scripture tells a dramatically different story. These biblical texts expose our faulty perceptions of Yahweh because they present Yahweh as *an uneasy/highly reluctant war God*.[1] Over the seven years that we have been working together on this book, these texts have challenged us to rethink our traditional understanding of how Yahweh functions in Israel's warfare.

AN EASY ONE TO OVERLOOK

The portrait of Yahweh as an *uneasy/highly reluctant war God* is an easy one to miss, however, for several reasons. First, most readers are predisposed toward not seeing Yahweh's negative assessments of war, because the same God issues those war instructions and commands. We automatically assume that God's involvement in delivering war directives to his people expresses the furthest extent of his desire for them and is without any real ethical issues simply because of the source. However, this is a flawed perspective, as we have discussed earlier (see chapter three on God as source and his use of an

---

[1]When we base our understanding of Yahweh solely on texts that (seemingly) endorse Israel's battles without reservation, we end up with an incomplete and therefore faulty concept of God. Old Testament texts that depict Yahweh as an uneasy war God provide us with a fuller and more accurate portrait of Yahweh's stance toward warfare.

incrementally redemptive ethic). Second, many Christians—just as we did—grew up in church settings where David and other war heroes were viewed *only* positively when it came to military matters. They were our celebrated heroes. Sure, they had their shortcomings (David's adultery with Bathsheba, for example), but not in the area of war practices. Somehow those were overlooked. Third, many biblical texts *seem* to present Yahweh as willingly (not reluctantly) going along with Israel's war plans. In other words, a negative assessment suggesting accommodation on Yahweh's part simply is not raised in each and every war text.[2] Such accommodation qualifiers would make the story line cumbersome and mitigate against applauding some of the good things, though achieved with an ethically flawed means, that Israel was attempting to do.[3]

Moreover, many biblical texts show Yahweh's war involvement. For example, the Hebrew Bible shares with contemporaneous ANE cultures a description of Yahweh as warrior.[4] Many texts that reflect so-called Zion theology portray God's warlike actions at the expense of Israel's enemies (e.g., Ps 46:8; 48:4-7; 76:6-7).[5] Other passages depict God fighting on Israel's behalf and describe him as combatant par excellence: "The LORD is a warrior; the LORD is his name" (Ex 15:3; see also Is 42:13; Jer 20:11; Zeph 3:17). This description is certainly a prominent picture of God in the Old Testament, and it often appears without stating his dissatisfaction with the situation.

Nevertheless, if we rely exclusively on these passages that voice no counterpoint to construct our theological portrait of God's values and priorities, it will result in an incomplete view of God. Thankfully, the Old Testament also

---

[2]It would be awkward to raise accommodation issues in every war text. Furthermore, there is a Catch-22 at an incentive level, where Yahweh is torn between applauding some of Israel's good intentions—(getting rid of idolatry) or making incremental moves in the right direction (no sadistic treatment of enemy kings when captured)—while saddened by violent war methods. Yet this is precisely the tension of living with an incremental ethic, where we wish to encourage the good without always pointing out the bad.

[3]Most parents can relate to applauding their children's efforts while at the same time desiring that they go further. Like Yahweh in the war texts, we as parents do not voice our fullest desires or hopes at each and every turn.

[4]Manfred Weippert, "'Heiliger Krieg' in Israel und Assyrien: Kritische Anmerkungen zu Gerhard von Rads Konzept des 'Heiligen Krieges in alten Israel,'" *ZAW* 84 (1972): 460-93.

[5]See John H. Hayes, "The Tradition of Zion's Inviolability," *JBL* 82 (1963): 419-26; Ben C. Ollenburger, *Zion, the City of the Great King: A Theological Symbol of the Jerusalem Cult*, JSOTSup 41 (Sheffield: JSOT Press, 1987).

contains numerous seedbed and breakout passages that help us to see another portrait of God, as an uneasy war God who does not revel in battle or destruction and who grieves the mayhem that warfare inflicts on his creation.[6]

SUBVERSIVE WAR TEXTS

An investigation into Yahweh as an uneasy/highly reluctant war God reveals a gap and tension between what happens in Israel's war practices and what God would have truly hoped for. Yahweh's involvement in Israel's warfare requires that he leave his lofty untainted home, so to speak, and stoop low, very low, when working with his people. Yahweh accommodates his desired plan-A actions for his people to something closer to the norms and ethics of fallen human beings—yes, even in practices as dreadful as warfare—in order to walk with his people in a broken, sin-stained world, move them gently and incrementally toward something better (partial steps of redemption even in their war practices), and strategically unfold new chapters in the canonical journey to a final Eden (full redemption).[7]

Not all the subversive war texts speak the same way. Some are loud and dramatic. They shout Yahweh's negative assessment of Israel's war practices from the rooftops. They tell us that Yahweh is not really happy as a war God. These dramatic portraits show Yahweh as a tearful war God; they show the unwillingness of Yahweh to have his name and reputation tarnished by David's bloody warrior hands. Preventing David from building the temple provides an "I am not David!" portrait of Yahweh and a pattern counter to the norms of temple building in the ANE world. Instead Yahweh establishes a dwelling place for his name and reputation with a shalom identity, without the war scenes common to ANE temples. Equally dramatic are the hamstringing of captured war horses and the burning of chariots, the instructions banning kings from purchasing warhorses,

---

[6]Seedbed ideas slightly modify existing cultural norms, while breakout ideas overturn cultural norms. See William J. Webb, *Slaves, Women and Homosexuals: Exploring the Hermeneutics of Cultural Analysis* (Downers Grove, IL: InterVarsity Press, 2001), 83-105.

[7]Throughout Scripture we see God giving commands or instructions to his people, and though the instructions come from an untainted, pristine, holy God, they hardly reflect justice or love at a concrete-specific level in their best or highest ethical expression. For examples, see chapter three. The same is true of the war texts. It is as if God says in them, "Have it your way to this extent."

warnings against having a king in the first place—an action explicitly tied to war issues—and so forth.

However, other subversive war texts are more quiet and subtle. They provide smaller or implicitly negative assessments of war and Israel's participation in war. They are important but far too plentiful to handle within this chapter. We list a number of these in appendix G. Still other subversive texts are invisible to contemporary readers without the backdrop of an ancient world. Our first example comes from this invisible category—the nonviolent, spoken-word means by which Yahweh brings about creation.

The God who creates without conflict. Origin stories significantly affect our view of the fundamental design and purpose of the world, as well as our views of the designer, and one place where we glimpse the reluctant war God is in the very first chapter of the Bible. This is particularly so when we compare Genesis 1 with the Enuma Elish, a contemporary ANE creation account. The Enuma Elish is a Mesopotamian epic that was read at the Festival of the New Year to commemorate the god Marduk's ascension to the head of the Babylonian pantheon.

The Enuma Elish, like Genesis 1, begins in primordial time and sets out the creation of the habitable world. However, in the Enuma Elish a massive battle ensues between Marduk, the champion of the gods, and Tiamat together with her consort Qingu. Marduk engages in single combat with Tiamat, decisively defeating her. The Enuma Elish describes the pitched battle:

> They strove in single combat, locked in battle.
> The lord spread out his net to enfold her,
> The Evil Wind, which followed behind, he let loose in her face.
> When Tiamat opened her mouth to consume him,
> He drove in the Evil Wind that she close not her lips.
> As the fierce winds charged her belly,
> Her body was distended and her mouth was wide open.
> He released the arrow, it tore her belly,
> It cut through her insides, splitting the heart.[8]

Marduk then splits Tiamat's carcass into two parts, using half of her body to fashion the sky and the other half to make the earth. Similarly, Qingu, Tiamat's

---

[8]*ANET*, 67.

consort and the leader of her forces, suffers the fate typical of human leaders who support a rebellious monarch (see appendix A) when he is handed over to the god Ea for punishment. After putting Qingu to death, Ea uses the desecrated remains of Qingu's body to create humanity.

> "It was Kingu who contrived the uprising,
> And made Tiamat rebel, and joined battle."
> They bound him, holding him before Ea.
> They imposed on him his guilt and severed his blood (vessels).
> Out of his blood they fashioned mankind.[9]

The biblical creation narrative in Genesis 1 has many similarities (and significant differences) with the Enuma Elish, and scholars have debated the extent of its influence on the biblical creation account.[10] In this case, however, it is important to note a key difference between the two creation stories and the portraits of divinity they contain. The Enuma Elish relies heavily on war and warfare imagery to highlight Marduk's mastery of the created order.[11] Creation in Genesis 1, on the other hand, proceeds without any hint of battle or conflict as God creates effortlessly by the power of his spoken word. Evidence for an underlying conflict motif (or *chaoskampf*) in Genesis 1 has not held up under scrutiny, though the chapter likely functioned as a polemical response to ANE martial concepts of creation.[12] Consequently, *the Genesis 1 portrait of God's use of nonviolent methods of creation presents a strong contrast with Mesopotamian conflict-based portraits of creation by the gods.* Because origin stories point toward larger conceptions of reality, the positioning of this nonviolent creation narrative at the beginning of Israel's account of origins signals the marginalization of warfare

---

[9]*ANET*, 68.

[10]For a brief summary see Bernard F. Batto, *In the Beginning: Essays on Creation Motifs in the Ancient Near East and the Bible* (Winona Lake, IN: Eisenbrauns, 2013), 119-21.

[11]See Carly L. Crouch, *War and Ethics in the Ancient Near East*, BZAW 407 (Berlin: de Gruyter, 2009), 23-24. Marduk brings order to creation using the traditional weapons of warfare and the forces of nature, linking kingship, warfare, and the establishment of order out of chaos.

[12]On *chasokampf* in Genesis 1, see Richard J. Clifford, *Creation Accounts in the Ancient Near East and in the Bible*, CBQMS 26 (Washington, DC: Catholic Biblical Association of America, 1994), 140-41; David Tsumura, *Creation and Destruction: A Reappraisal of the Chaoskampf Theory in the Old Testament* (Winona Lake, IN: Eisenbrauns, 2005), 9-140.

to the periphery of how a good cosmos functions.[13] Order is instead established and maintained by the power of God's word. Israel's God does not need to fight in order to establish order in his world, in contrast to the Mesopotamian view, which understood warfare as integral to the founding and preservation of order.

The God who grieves war violence. In addition to the nonviolent creation of the world in Genesis 1, a frequently overlooked aspect of God's character is his grief at the results of war. Israel often uttered its own grief, sorrow, and pain at the devastating results of war, as in the book of Lamentations:

> Our skin is hot as an oven,
>> feverish from hunger.
> Women have been violated in Zion,
>> and virgins in the towns of Judah.
> Princes have been hung up by their hands;
>> elders are shown no respect.
> Young men toil at the millstones;
>> boys stagger under loads of wood.
> The elders are gone from the city gate;
>> the young men have stopped their music.
> Joy is gone from our hearts;
>> our dancing has turned to mourning. (Lam 5:10-15; see also Neh 2:3;
>>> Ps 44:8-16; Lam 1:3)

God himself also grieves for the suffering of his people as a result of war. Terrence Fretheim has collected several passages in the Hebrew Bible that highlight the pathos of God. Fretheim points out that in such passages, "Generally speaking, the language is not that of lament and accusation; it is the language of mourning and compassion."[14] Through his prophets, God expresses grief and sorrow at the war-induced suffering of his people. Oracles against Israel are described as "words of lament and mourning and woe" (Ezek 2:10; see Amos 5:1-2), and Yahweh laments over the coming suffering

---

[13]One biblical passage contains battle motifs related to creation (Ps 74:12-17), while other divine-battle passages refer to the defeat of chaotic waters and beasts in the establishment (Ps 104:6-9; Job 38:8-11) or maintenance of cosmic order (Is 51:9-10; Job 26:7-14; 41:1-5). The presence of divine-battle language in passages such as Ps 74 does not reduce the importance of the conflict-less account of creation in Gen 1; it highlights Gen 1 as a breakout passage.

[14]Terrence E. Fretheim, *The Suffering of God* (Philadelphia: Fortress, 1984), 130.

of Israel's princes (Ezek 19:1, 14) and his people (Jer 9:10-11). Yahweh even places himself among the sufferers in Jeremiah 9:17-18: "This is what the LORD Almighty says: 'Consider now! Call for the wailing women to come; send for the most skillful of them. Let them come quickly and wail over us till our eyes overflow with tears and water streams from our eyelids.'"

Yahweh's grief, though, is not reserved only for his own people. Ezekiel's oracles against the foreign nations are lamentations expressing grief about the coming of judgment (Ezek 27:2; 28:12; 32:2, 16; see also Ezek 30:2; 31:18). More poignantly, Isaiah's oracles against the Moabites repeatedly describe the Moabites' cry, wail, and lament over the devastation that will soon consume their land. But the prophet, speaking for Yahweh, also cries for Moab:

> So I weep, as Jazer weeps,
>   for the vines of Sibmah.
> Heshbon and Elealeh,
>   I drench you with tears! (Is 16:9; see also Is 15:5)

> My heart laments for Moab like a harp,
>   my inmost being for Kir Hareseth. (Is 16:11)

Jeremiah contains a similar set of oracles with similar indications of divine mourning:

> "I know her insolence but it is futile,"
>   declares the LORD,
>   "and her boasts accomplish nothing.
> Therefore I wail over Moab,
>   for all Moab I cry out,
>   I moan for the people of Kir Hareseth.
> I weep for you, as Jazer weeps,
>   you vines of Sibmah.
> Your branches spread as far as the sea;
>   they reached as far as Jazer.
> The destroyer has fallen
>   on your ripened fruit and grapes." (Jer 48:30-32)

> "In Moab I will put an end
>   to those who make offerings on the high places
>   and burn incense to their gods,"
>   declares the LORD.

"So my heart laments for Moab like the music of a pipe;
>   it laments like a pipe for the people of Kir Hareseth.
>   The wealth they acquired is gone." (Jer 48:35-36)

These passages portray a God who does not take pleasure in the devastation brought by war. Yahweh cries a river of tears not only for his own people but also (remarkably so) for his *enemies* when they are destroyed by war. Fretheim summarizes the implications of these passages well when he says, "That God is represented as mourning over the fate of non-Israelite peoples as well as Israelites demonstrates the breadth of God's care and concern for the sufferers of the world, whoever they might be. Israel has no monopoly on God's empathy."[15]

Killing with kindness (2 Kings 6:8-23; see also 2 Chronicles 28:9-15). The Elisha narratives give us another snapshot of a reluctant war God, via a situation in which the typical conventions of war are turned on their head in order to avoid the needless slaughter of an enemy. Second Kings 6:8-23 begins with the Arameans at war with the Israelites. The Arameans' attempts to waylay the king of Israel are repeatedly frustrated when the prophet Elisha tips off the king of Israel about the locations of the ambushes (2 Kings 6:8-12). As a result, the king of Aram sends out horses, chariots, and a strong force (2 Kings 6:14) to capture Elisha in the city of Dothan. The Aramean forces are no cause for fear, however, because Yahweh's horses and chariots of fire fill the surrounding hills (2 Kings 6:16-17). Yahweh's forces have the high ground and the ability to crush the Arameans *but do not.*

Since Elisha's servant fears the Aramean force, the prophet comforts him with words from a typical prebattle war oracle, "Don't be afraid" (2 Kings 6:16; see Deut 1:21; 3:2; 20:3; Josh 8:1; 11:6; 10:8; 2 Kings 19:6; Is 7:4). Elisha asks Yahweh to strike the Arameans, and he does (2 Kings 6:18). The Hebrew verb translated "strike," *nākâ*, commonly refers to the killing of enemy soldiers, which is what the audience would expect when hearing Elisha ask that Yahweh strike (*nākâ*) the Arameans (2 Kings 6:18).[16] But Elisha instead asks Yahweh to strike them with a (nonlethal) bright light or blindness.[17] Whether

---

[15]Fretheim, *Suffering of God*, 137.

[16]On *nākâ*, see *HALOT*, "נכה," 697-98.

[17]The Hebrew *sanwērîm*, "bright light," occurs only here and in Gen 19:11. Rachelle Gilmour ably argues that the bright light is the means by which the Arameans are struck and that temporary blindness is the result. Moreover, the Arameans can navigate the twelve miles

blindness or a bright light, the weapon of Yahweh is not a normal physical weapon, since it inflicts no permanent damage.

Moreover, when Elisha leads the blind and bedazzled Arameans right into the heart of downtown Samaria, the Israelite king eagerly anticipates an opportunity to strike down (*nākâ*) his Aramean enemies (2 Kings 6:21).[18] But Elisha prohibits him from slaying the defenseless POWs: "'Do not kill [*nākâ*] them,' he answered. 'Would you kill [*nākâ*] those you have captured with your own sword or bow?'" (2 Kings 6:22). Elisha ensures the safety of the Aramean force, and he also invokes the traditions of hospitality, whereby guests are granted temporary family status, receiving protection, food, and even lodging. Mario Liverani notes that when hospitality has been granted, "The guest, who is in some way assimilated with members of the host household, cannot be injured, and certainly cannot be killed."[19] At the same time, the protocols of hospitality prohibit guests from harming their host. The Arameans are thereby transformed from mortal enemies into honored guests while simultaneously ensuring the safety of the Israelites.

Captured combatants in the ANE were sometimes killed, but the vast majority were turned into slaves.[20] The offer of food and water, along with the provision of a feast for enemy POWs before sending them home, however, is stroke of genius.[21] The invocation of the code of hospitality is so powerful that the Aramean soldiers cannot attack their hosts, resulting in the cessation of hostilities. As such, this peaceful inversion of typical warfare

---

from Dothan to Samaria, which suggests a temporary or partial occlusion of vision rather than full blindness ("A Note on the Horses and Chariots of Fire at Dothan," *ZAW* 125 [2013]: 310-11; see also Mordechai Cogan and Hayim Tadmor, *II Kings*, AB [New York: Doubleday, 1988], 74).

[18]Emphasized by repetition of the Hebrew root *nākâ (ha'akkeh 'akkeh*—"shall I kill, I will kill").

[19]Mario Liverani, "Adapa, Guest of the Gods," in *Myth and Politics in Ancient Near Eastern Historiography*, ed. Zainab Bahrani and Marc Van De Mieroop (London: Equinox, 2004), 16.

[20]For an example of where captives are killed, see *ARE* 3:113. For examples of turning captives into slaves, see *ANET*, 261; T. R. Hobbs, *2 Kings*, WBC (Waco, TX: Word Books, 1985), 78.

[21]Ronnie Goldstein notes two examples from the reign of Assyrian king Ashurbanipal of the provision of food and water for captives to suggest that such a gesture is an overture of peace and is part of a complex process of political wrangling and one-upmanship whereby the side that offers peace is the side with the greater status and honor. The repeated avoidance of bloodshed (of both the Israelite king and the Aramean force), however, indicates that in this case, the key issue is not political wrangling for status and honor but the prevention of violence. See Goldstein, "The Provision of Food to the Aramean Captives in II Reg 6,22-23," *ZAW* 126 (2014): 104.

practices, particularly in light of the intimation of the superiority of Yahweh's horses and chariots (2 Kings 6:17), serves as a breakout from typical
biblical and ANE warfare practices and represents a highly significant redemptive approach to warfare hostilities. Yahweh's enemies are turned into
guests, and hostilities are quelled by the use of creative, nonviolent tactics.

David's bloody hands (1 Chronicles 22:6-10; 28:3). One common theme
in the description of ancient warfare involves the connection between
victory in battle and the building (or restoration) of temples. In short, the
ANE world followed a standard three-step pattern: *battle*, *build*, and *boast*.
A king who had fought a victorious battle would then build a temple for his
god, in which the king would boast about his triumph by commissioning
artists to memorialize it. In contrast to ANE norms of temple building, the
Old Testament distances sanctuary construction and restoration from military success, particularly for some of its most notable warriors. The association between sanctuary construction (or renovation) and military success
can be found across the ANE, as the following examples show, while providing a context for understanding David's bloody hands in a new light.

Egypt. The boasts of Wahenekh Intef I of Egypt include his building of
temples for the gods, followed by a description of his military campaigns
on the northern frontiers.[22] Pharaoh Amenhotep II describes himself on
the Amada Stele as "raging like a panther, when he courses through the
battlefield; there is none fighting before him; an archer mighty in smiting;
a wall protecting Egypt; firm of heart . . . trampling down those who rebel
against him; instantly prevailing against all the barbarians with people
and horses, when they came with myriads of men." Several lines later,
readers are told, "He is a king with heart favorable to the buildings of all
gods, being one who builds their temples [and] fashions their statues."[23]
On the Gebel Barkal Stele from the temple of Thutmose III, the pharaoh
claims to have made an eternal dwelling for Amon, while also portraying
himself as a fearsome warrior.[24] Ramses II, after the battle of Qadesh,
inscribes in the temple of his patron, "Have I not made for you monuments

---

[22]*ARE* 1:421-23.
[23]*ARE* 2:792-93.
[24]*COS* 2:2B, 14.

in great multitude, filled your temple with my booty, built for you my Mansion of Millions-of-Years."[25]

Egyptian temple iconography includes warfare scenes ranging from the benign, such as a triumphal relief in the Karnak temple showing Amun-Re receiving the list of cities and villages conquered by Shoshenk I, to more graphically violent depictions. The ritual portrayal of the pharaoh smiting his enemies was common from the fourth millennium BC to the second century AD in Egyptian contexts, but the mortuary temple of Ramses III at Medinet Habu is an extraordinary example of this topos, with variations of this motif occurring in almost every room.[26] For example, the tower entrance to the temple includes a gigantic depiction of Ramses smiting captives with his mace while holding them up by the hair as the god Amun watches. The northern outer walls of the temple show piles of severed right hands and penises, totaling three thousand of each, according to the accompanying inscription.[27]

Mesopotamia. Victory in battle also leads to building cities and temples in Mesopotamian literature. In the divine realm, Marduk establishes his house (his temple) in the Enuma Elish on the heels of his victory over Tiamat and Qingu:

> Above the Apsu where you have resided,
> The counterpart of Esharra which I have built over you,
> Below I have hardened the ground for a building site,
> I will build a house, it will be my luxurious abode.
> I will found therein its temple.[28]

As in the divine realm, temple building by warrior kings takes place on the human level. Ninurta-kudurrī-uṣur, governor of the land of Suḫu and the land of Mari, recounts a battle in which he slayed 1,616 enemy troops. Shortly thereafter, he builds the city of Kār-Apla-Adad and the temple of Apla-Adad.[29] After defeating an enemy coalition, Iahdun-Lim, king of Mari, inscribed on

---

[25]*AEL* 2:65.

[26]See José das Candeias Sales, "'The Smiting of the Enemies' Scenes in the Mortuary Temple of Ramses III at Medinet Habu," *Oriental Studies: Journal of Oriental and Ancient History* 1 (2012): 79-116.

[27]*ARE* 4:52.

[28]*ANET*, 502.

[29]*COS* 2:115B, 281.

the temple of Shamash how he "heaped up their dead bodies" before going on to build the temple of his god Shamash.[30] The Cylinder Inscription of Sargon II boasts about his rule as having "no prince equal to him . . . who has smashed all lands like pots" before listing the lands he has conquered.[31] After this lengthy conquest boast, Sargon relates building the temple of Shamash.[32] Nebuchadnezzar II, the Babylonian king who famously conquered and destroyed Jerusalem, fought the Egyptian army at the Battle of Carchemesh and boasted on clay cylinders found in the ruins of the ziggurat of Borsippa that he "defeated and destroyed it until it was completely annihilated."[33] However, he is also remembered for his renovation of Esagil (the temple of Enlil and the gods), the restoration of Ezida (the temple of Nabû), E-temen-anki (the ziggurat of Babylon), and E-urimin-ankia (the ziggurat of Borsippa).[34]

Hittites. Evidence for the association between sanctuary construction and battle victory in Hittite literature is scarcer than the Egyptian and Mesopotamian evidence. However, in a fragmentary prayer, the Hittite king Tudhaliya IV vows to build a temple to the sun goddess in Arinna and to offer sacrifices on Mount Tagurka at the defeat of his enemy.[35]

The Levant/Phoenicia. One section of the Ugaritic Baal Cycle describes the god Baal's battle and defeat of the sea-god (Yamm), while a second, related episode describes his successful procurement of permission from El, the head of the pantheon, to build a house (temple) for himself, illustrating how victory in battle in the divine realm at Canaanite Ugarit was linked to temple construction.[36] In the Aramaic Zakkur Inscription, Zakkur king of Hamath and Lu'ash recounts how he defeated a coalition of seventeen Syrian kings before embarking on a building program that included fortifying cities and building shrines and temples.[37] The Moabite king Mesha waged total-kill (*ḥērem*) warfare against the Israelite town of Ataroth and

---

[30]*COS* 2:111, 260.

[31]*ARAB* 2, §118.

[32]*ARAB* 2, §119.

[33]Jean-Jacques Glassner, *Mesopotamian Chronicles*, ed. Benjamin R. Foster, SBLWAW (Atlanta: Society of Biblical Literature, 2004), 19:227.

[34]*COS* 2:122B, 310.

[35]Itamar Singer and Harry A. Hoffner, *Hittite Prayers*, SBLWAW (Atlanta: Society of Biblical Literature, 2002), 11:108-9.

[36]*COS* 1:86.

[37]*COS* 2:35.

then built a sanctuary to his god Kemosh, where he erected a stele com-
memorating his victory and building projects.[38] The Phoenician king Aza-
tiwada, in recounting the accomplishments of his reign, combines military
success with temple building, saying:

> And I smashed the rebels;
> And I crushed all evil which was in the land.
> And I established the house of my lord in goodness.[39]

Similarly, a mid-fifth-century BC sarcophagus inscription by ʾEshmunʿazor,
king of Sidon, recounts how he rebuilt the houses of the gods ʿAshtart,
ʾEshmun, Baal, and ʿAshtart-Name-of-Baʿl (the consort of Baal) and conquered Dor, Joppa, and the Plain of Sharon.[40]

David the great warrior king as temple builder? This ANE backdrop of
temple building by warrior kings helps us understand the character of
Yahweh in the story of David's bloody hands. The typical ANE pattern was
for a king to go to war for his god(s), build the god a temple, and boast about
victories with warfare imagery engraved on the temple walls. By way of
striking contrast, however, this theme is largely absent from the biblical
text.[41] Moreover, the iconography of the tabernacle/temple is completely
devoid of the portraits of violence so often seen on ANE temples.[42] Solomon,

---

[38]*COS* 2:23, 137–38. Mesha builds a *bmt*, "high place," which is not a temple but does serve
as a religious sanctuary.

[39]*COS* 2:31, 149.

[40]*COS* 2:57, 183.

[41]The one exception might be the construction of the tabernacle after the defeat of the Egyptians in Ex 15 and the Amalekites in Ex 17. However, Moses is certainly no warrior-king,
which breaks from the typical form of the motif linking battle success with the same individual who builds/renovates the temple. In addition, at the defeat celebrated in Ex 15, Moses
and the Israelites are spectators, and in defeating the Amalekites, they respond to an attack
and fight a defensive battle.

[42]The adornments are floral (e.g., palm trees—1 Kings 6:29, 32; flowers—1 Kings 6:29, 32;
pomegranates—1 Kings 7:18, 20; lilies—1 Kings 7:22; gourds—1 Kings 7:24), and faunal
patterns (the bulls of the bronze sea—1 Kings 7:25, 29; 2 Chron 4:3; lions—1 Kings 7:29),
cherubim (1 Kings 7:29), and geometric shapes (chains—2 Chron 3:5, 16). The symbolism
of the flowers and animals, along with the numerous depictions of cherubim used to deco-
rate the temple, evokes the initial place of Yahweh's presence, the Garden of Eden. Temples
were frequently thought of as microcosms of the world in the ANE. The absence of war
language and imagery from the biblical temple, when coupled with the absence of battle
and war imagery in the account of the creation of the cosmic temple in Gen 1–2 (see above),
reinforces the idea that warfare is not an innate, valued, or healthy part of the functioning
of Yahweh's universe.

the man of peace (1 Chron 22:9) and the builder of Israel's first temple, significantly strengthens the capabilities of the military (1 Kings 4:26; 10:26, 29 // 2 Chron 1:14, 17; 9:25) and fortified cities (1 Kings 9:15-19; 11:27; 2 Chron 8:4-6), yet the only mention of his military victories is one line saying, "Solomon then went to Hamath Zobah and captured it" (2 Chron 8:3). Joash, Jotham, Ahaz, and Josiah are the only Judahite kings who renovate the Jerusalem temple. Of these four, only Jotham is credited with any military success (2 Chron 27:5), but the extent of his temple renovations consists of building the Upper Gate in order to provide access to the temple (2 Kings 15:35 // 2 Chron 27:4).[43]

The rejection of David, Israel's greatest warrior king, as builder of the temple (2 Sam 7:5-7; 1 Chron 17:4-6) is a highly significant break with the common ANE theme of victorious war king as temple builder. Victor Hurowitz's survey of temple building in the Bible and Mesopotamia shows that "it was considered important and even essential that a temple should be built only with explicit divine consent."[44] The warrior kings who fought their gods' battles naturally won the honor to build their temples. Not so with David. Despite Yahweh's sanction of Israel's battles, David's plan to build Yahweh's temple is rejected in favor of his son Solomon (2 Sam 7:12-13), the man of peace.[45] The Chronicler specifies that it is the "much blood" spilled and "many/great wars" fought that lie behind Yahweh's rejection of David as temple builder:[46]

---

[43]See André Lemaire, "The Evolution of the 8th-Century B.C.E. Jerusalem Temple," in *The Fire Signals of Lachish: Studies in the Archaeology and History of Israel in the Late Bronze Age, Iron Age, and Persian Period in Honor of David Ussishkin*, ed. Israel Finkelstein and Nadav Na'aman (Winona Lake, IN: Eisenbrauns, 2011), 195-202.

[44]Victor Hurowitz, *I Have Built You an Exalted House: Temple Building in the Bible in Light of Mesopotamian and North-West Semitic Writings*, JSOTSup 105 (Sheffield: JSOT Press, 1992), 163.

[45]On Yahweh's sanction, see, e.g., "The LORD gave David victory wherever he went" (1 Sam 23:1-2, 4; 30:8; 2 Sam 5:12, 19, 23-25; 8:6, 14; 22:1; 1 Chron 11:10, 14; 14:10; 18:6, 13).

[46]NIV: "many wars"; NASV, NRSV: "great wars." Various reasons for David's rejection are found in the Hebrew Bible: Yahweh's mobility among his people (2 Sam 7:6-8), David's preoccupation with battling his enemies (1 Kings 5:3), and the choice of Solomon as builder (1 Kings 8:18-19). The charge of shedding blood is not usually connected with the killing involved in warfare. However, the Chronicler seems to extend the principle of Num 33:35 to David, so that his shedding of blood in war pollutes the land (see 1 Chron 22:8) and thereby potentially excludes Yahweh's dwelling on the land. Warriors could ritually cleanse themselves over a seven-day period (Num 31:19-24). David, however, remained culpable in Yahweh's eyes and so was disqualified as temple builder. See the discussion in Donald F.

David said to Solomon: "My son, I had it in my heart to build a house for the Name of the LORD my God. But this word of the LORD came to me: 'You have shed *much blood* and have fought *many [great] wars*. You are not to build a house for my Name, because you have shed *much blood* on the earth in my sight.'" (1 Chron 22:7-8)

But God said to me [David], "You are not to build a house for my Name, because you are a *warrior and have shed blood.*" (1 Chron 28:3)

While infrequent, some ANE texts do mention the rejection of temple-building bids. Horowitz points out, "The biblical accounts are unique, however, in being the only ones which venture to explain why the deity responded negatively to the request of a king who is otherwise viewed in a positive light."[47] Yahweh's astonishing rejection of David is heightened when we consider the otherwise very positive portrait of David in Chronicles. That Israel's warrior-king par excellence is not allowed to build the temple for Yahweh due to the blood on his hands breaks away from the typical ANE celebrations of warfare success and the accompanying status boost that kings received for their military prowess when they did major work on their patron deity's temple.

This negative portrait of David in war tells of Yahweh's concern that his name and reputation not be tarnished by the reputation of Israel's most successful warrior king. Unlike the gods of the ANE, Yahweh does *not* reward David's slaughterhouse war actions by not allowing him to build the temple. These biblical texts speak with displeasure about Israel's acts of war—especially within an ancient world where David should have been the one to build Yahweh's temple. Not allowing David to build the temple was a dramatic move.

Ultimately, Yahweh wants his name and reputation that resides in his temple to be definitively separate from David's much-blood, great-wars reputation, and (conversely) more closely aligned with an understanding of Yahweh's character as profoundly tilted toward peace. The fourfold repetition of

---

Murray, "Under YHWH's Veto: David as Shedder of Blood in Chronicles," *Biblica* 82 (2001): 457-76; Gary N. Knoppers, *1 Chronicles 10–29*, AB (New York: Doubleday, 2004), 772-75. Note, however, the perspective in Brian E. Kelly, "David's Disqualification in 1 Chronicles 22:8: A Response to Piet B. Dirksen," *JSOT* (1998): 53-61.

[47]Hurowitz, *I Have Built You an Exalted House*, 165.

the word *name* and the twofold play on *name* and *peace* emphasize shalom (not war) as at the core of Yahweh's being:

> David said to Solomon: "My son, I had it in my heart to build a house for the *Name* of the LORD my God. But this word of the LORD came to me: 'You have shed *much blood* and have fought *many [great] wars*. You are not to build a house for my *Name*, because you have shed *much blood* on the earth in my sight. But you will have a son who will be a man of peace and rest, and I will give him rest from all his enemies on every side. His *name* will be *Solomon* [root = shalom], and I will grant Israel *peace* [shalom] and quiet during his reign. He is the one who will build a house for my *Name*. He will be my son, and I will be his father. And I will establish the throne of his kingdom over Israel forever.'" (1 Chron 22:7-10)

This enshrined detachment from David's warrior reputation creates theological sacred space that *separates* who Yahweh is at the very core of his character (name) with significant *distance*—a sense of holy distance—from this fallen world and its standards of war (even among his own people). In short, the choice of Solomon (peace) over David (war) for temple building portrays Yahweh's uneasy relationship with warfare; Israel's bloody wars are Yahweh's less-than-preferred, accommodated means of accomplishing his earthly purposes.

All the king's horses (Deuteronomy 17:14-20). Another place where we catch a glimpse of Yahweh as the reluctant warrior God is in Deuteronomy 17. When it comes to the way that Israel thought about and understood the role of its kings, Israel's royal ideology was largely like that of its ANE neighbors. However, this similarity also brings into sharp focus important differences in outlook. Bernard Levinson notes, "Precisely because of the extent to which the royal ideology of ancient Israel is identical to that of the ancient Near East, the points of divergence are the more remarkable."[48] One of the key areas of difference lies in the parameters placed around the king's power by Yahweh. While other ANE kings sought to expand and develop their armed forces by acquiring war horses and chariots, the "law of the king" (Deut 17:14-20) seeks to limit the king's ability to build a powerful army by accumulating war horses and thus, at the very least, curbs aggressive warfare.

---

[48]Bernard M. Levinson, "The Reconceptualization of Kingship in Deuteronomy and the Deuteronomistic History's Transformation of Torah," *VT* 51, no. 4 (2001): 511.

Today's weapons of mass destruction are multikiloton nuclear warheads. In the ancient world the weapons of mass destruction were horses and chariots. They were the most desired (and feared) weapons of war because of their quick-strike capability and the increased payload of multiple warriors with multiple weapons. Before the advent of chariots, archers might engage the enemy from a distance (with marginal accuracy), but horses and chariots allowed archers the mobility to attack from multiple angles before wheeling away to safety. Close-range archers were deadly accurate, and a second or third person in the chariot wielding a curved sword had a height advantage over warriors on the ground.

Kings throughout the ANE during the period of Israel's monarchy sought to expand the reach of their power by acquiring horses because hundreds if not thousands of horses were necessary to conduct a chariot battle that lasted more than an hour.[49] Warhorses were so desirable that "the warhorse became the ultimate symbol of power in literature, art, and reality."[50]

Captured horses were valuable due to their previous training and battle experience, allowing kings to forgo the costs of the typical six-month training period for new chariot horses.[51] The desirability of accumulating horses for ANE kings becomes evident when we examine ancient booty lists. These lists enumerate the people, animals, and objects armies captured in battle and provide insight into what was considered a valuable prize of war. For example, Egyptian pharaoh Thutmose III boasts of capturing 3,400 prisoners and 2,041 horses after a battle at Megiddo.[52] Assyrian king Sargon II says, "I besieged and conquered Samaria. I took as booty 27,290 people who lived there. I gathered 50 chariots from them."[53]

Israel was not immune to the temptation of securing large numbers of horses (and chariots). First Kings 4:26 indicates that Solomon built 4,000

---

[49]Deborah O'Daniel Cantrell, *The Horsemen of Israel: Houses and Chariotry in Monarchic Israel (Ninth-Eighth Centuries B.C.E.)*, HACL 1 (Winona Lake, IN: Eisenbrauns, 2011), 74. Exhaustion and/or death required the frequent replacement of horses throughout a battle.

[50]Deborah O'Daniel Cantrell, "'Some Trust in Horses': Horses as Symbols of Power in Rhetoric and Reality," in *Warfare, Ritual, and Symbol in Biblical and Modern Contexts*, ed. Brad E. Kelle, Frank Ritchel Ames, and Jacob L. Wright, AIL 18 (Atlanta: SBL Press, 2014), 131.

[51]Cantrell, *Horsemen of Israel*, 34, 41.

[52]*COS* 2:2A, 12; compare Ramses III (*ARE* 4 §111, 66); Amenhotep II (*ANET*, 246).

[53]*COS* 2:118E, 296; compare Tiglath-pileser (*COS* 2:117A, 286); Shalmaneser III (*ANET*, 277); Sennacherib (*ANET*, 288).

chariot stalls and kept 12,000 horses, some of them imported at a cost of 150 shekels apiece (1 Kings 10:28), while Isaiah 2:7 indicates that the land was filled with horses. In support of these numbers, the Kurkh Monolith attributes 2,000 chariots (4,000 to 6,000 horses) to King Ahab.[54]

It is precisely in this context that we need to read the "law of the king" in Deuteronomy 17:14-20. While Israel's earthly kings serve as commander in chief of the army, they are not to rely on their military prowess or the strength of their chariot forces for their ultimate defense: "The king, moreover, must not acquire great numbers of horses for himself or make the people return to Egypt to get more of them, for the LORD has told you, 'You are not to go back that way again'" (Deut 17:16). This prohibition contrasts with the practice of ANE kings, who did all they could to stockpile these ancient weapons of mass destruction. It also counters the tendency of Israelite kings to find security in the typical instruments of warfare and instead insists that the king's primary focus is learning Torah (Deut 17:18-20). Yahweh Sabaoth, the Lord of heaven's armies, is Israel's true defender (Ps 46:7; 48:8; Is 37:16-20).

Yahweh's desire that war leaders not build up their capabilities for weapons of mass destruction is already at play in the conquest narratives. In Joshua 11, after defeating a coalition of Canaanite kings, Yahweh instructs Joshua, "Hamstring their horses and burn their chariots" (Josh 11:6). David similarly hamstrings all but one hundred of the captured chariot horses of the army of Zobah (2 Sam 8:4 // 1 Chron 18:4). We might immediately cringe at the maiming of these animals. However, cutting the *flexor metatarsus* allowed horses to continue to stand but not trot or canter until the cut healed. They could still be used for breeding stock or domestic purposes.[55] Like the law of the king above, these instances of hamstringing depart from the typical ANE ideology of accumulating as many warhorses as possible with which to wage war on a large scale and pursue expansionistic and imperialistic aspirations. Yahweh wanted his people to be owners of cattle in a land flowing with milk and honey, not a people whose land was full of warhorses and chariots—the instruments of human oppression and domination.[56]

---

[54]*COS* 2:113A, 264.

[55]O'Daniel Cantrell, *Horsemen of Israel*, 42-43.

[56]Walter Brueggemann, *Divine Presence amid Violence: Contextualizing the Book of Joshua* (Eugene, OR: Cascade Books, 2009), 33-41.

If we put this picture of no horses and chariots together with the portrait of a God who does not like David's war killings and weeps at the destruction of his enemies, we see good evidence that the issue on the table in Scripture is not just about trusting God. It is also about the destructive power of warfare and about care for human beings—even one's enemies. It is about *trusting God with less violent means* to achieve peace and security in the land.

Kings will feed the war machine (1 Samuel 8). After the death of Moses and Joshua, Israel is led by a series of charismatic judges who direct their battles against foreign oppressors. However, the Israelites eventually ask Samuel to appoint a king. They explain, "Then we will be like all the other nations, with a king to lead us and *to go out before us and fight our battles*" (1 Sam 8:20). Israel already has a divine warrior who is to lead them into battle (see Judg 8:22-23), and so both Yahweh and Samuel see this request as a rejection of Yahweh's leadership (or at least exclusive leadership). Yahweh accommodates the people's demand but spells out its implications:

- ▶ The king will make their sons fight (and die) in his army (1 Sam 8:11).

- ▶ The king will draft their sons and daughters into the development, sustenance, and administration of the king's war machine (1 Sam 8:12-13).

- ▶ The king will appropriate the people's fields to give to his own faithful servants (1 Sam 8:14; see 1 Kings 21).

- ▶ He will tax the people's labors (1 Sam 8:15-17) and use the income to sustain his servants and officials (*sārîsîm*), many of whom will serve him as military leaders (see 1 Kings 22:9; 2 Kings 25:19).

- ▶ The people will then cry out for relief from their chosen king, but Yahweh will refuse to listen (1 Sam 8:18).

Ironically, though the people ask for a king to fight their battles, they will end up fighting the king's battles. Moreover, Samuel is clear that the installation of a king as war leader is a divine accommodation and not Yahweh's ultimate desire (1 Sam 8:9, 18). The gulf between Israel's chosen war path and Yahweh's desire to have no king affects the war scene in subversive ways and with an antiwar sentiment:

▶ *High(er) internal casualties*: Samuel's words point to the ongoing high price that the people will pay in terms of the many internal casualties of war. Conscription for the king's wars means that families will lose fathers and sons in battle.

▶ *Fighting unsanctioned battles*: The lack of Yahweh's full support raises cautions about the legitimacy of the king's future battles. Without Yahweh's explicit sanction, victory in battle will prove impossible. However, Israel's kings are prone to the seduction of fighting unsanctioned battles that waste the lives of Israel's young men (2 Sam 17:1-14; 2 Kings 14:7-13; compare Judg 9). By concentrating responsibility for battle leadership in the hands of a human king, that king can initiate a war on a whim or personal grudge.

▶ *The habit of warfare*: In contrast to the judges, who are temporary war leaders raised up by Yahweh to deliver Israel from specific oppressors, kings habitually make war. In fact, the regularity of the kings' wars is proverbial, with springtime known as "the time when kings go off to war" (2 Sam 11:1 // 1 Chron 20:1). Kings are more easily drawn into fighting wars because that is what kings do (it is a part of the culture of kingship). First Samuel 8 attempts to deter Israel from developing a culture of warfare that accompanies kingship.

▶ *The high cost of readiness for war*: Samuel's warning about the material cost of supporting the king's war machine (1 Sam 8:12-13, 15-17) finds validation during Solomon's reign in the form of high taxes (1 Kings 12:4) to support the infrastructure needed to build and maintain a standing army (1 Kings 4:27-28) and chariot forces.

▶ *The corruption of pride*: Samuel does not directly refer to the temptation of pride and its impact, but later biblical texts illustrate how the seduction of pride often led to expansionistic war policies, resulting in kings overextending their abilities and bringing destruction on themselves and their people (2 Chron 25:17-22; Ezek 28:5-8, 17; 31:1-14; Dan 4:1-28).

Samuel's and, more importantly, Yahweh's objection to the institution of kingship is deeply rooted in the *profoundly negative war-related consequences* kings will have for the life of God's people. Chief among them is that the choice for kingship is a choice for war. A king will promote a culture of warfare and violence. The biblical objections to the demand for a king emphasize that Yahweh's preference is to avoid warfare and the institutions that foster warfare.

The loving and forgiving God (Exodus 34; see also Jonah). Over the years both of us (Gord and Bill) have journeyed in our understanding of God as revealed in Scripture. Our thinking has migrated through three distinct phases, as illustrated in figure 14.1.

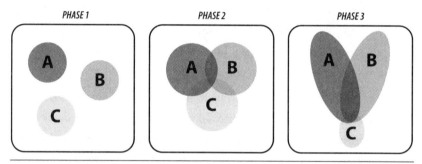

Figure 14.1. An unevenly weighted loving God

As young Christians, we thought about God's attributes like the picture in phase one. God's characteristics or attributes were distinct and separate. Like a grocery list that names different items, God was holy, just, loving, and so on. While in seminary one of the great things we learned was that God's attributes were all intersecting, as in the Venn diagram of phase two. This meant that God's attributes were all hyphenated, not bifurcated. They were adjectivally influential: God was lovingly just and justly loving. In the years of study that have followed—we could call it phase three—we have come to understand more fully the disproportional or unevenly weighted relationship of God's attributes. Not all of God's attributes are equally weighted; some are far more dominant than others. This change in our thinking resulted in no small part due to the influence of texts such as Exodus 34 (see also Jonah).

The portrait of God as markedly weighted toward love and forgiveness (far more so than toward justice or punishment) in Exodus 34 offers Christians tremendous insight into Yahweh as a reluctant war God. In two ways

Yahweh's character and disposition (his glory) lean significantly in one direction compared to another. The first sense of disproportionate weighting can be seen in the declaration of Yahweh's name and reputation being composed of an unequal grouping of attributes (fig. 14.2). Within the sevenfold description of Yahweh, *six* attributes are contrasted with *one* attribute (Ex 34:6-7).

The ratio of clustered attributes is a lopsided six to one.[57] However, the imbalanced weight of God's character or attributes

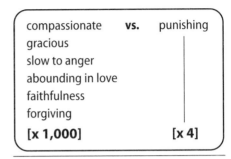

Figure 14.2. The lopsided character of God

becomes far more disproportional once we catch another contrasting feature within this Exodus text—Yahweh is predisposed toward the sixfold cluster on the left "to the thousandth [generation]" compared with only "the third or fourth generation" on the right column.[58] It is not our objective here to address the specific intergenerational aspects of this text. Rather, our point is that, whatever the intergenerational meaning, the one-thousand-to-four ratio (like the six-to-one ratio) clearly conveys a sense of Yahweh's greater *disposition* toward the sixfold attributes compared with enacting punishment.[59] One could say that Yahweh is *predisposed toward love and forgiveness in lavish proportions compared with his very restricted desire to enact justice/punishment*. Yahweh is a profoundly gracious God.

---

[57]Almost all language used to capture the disproportionate idea is inadequate because such English words (uneven, disproportionate, unequal, etc.) often contain a sense of imperfection. For instance, our term *lopsided* captures the imbalance in Ex 34 nicely, but the word itself frequently (though not always) implies imperfection. Perhaps the use of any of these terms requires qualification: God's character is *lopsided* in a perfect sense. In fact, it is our *evenly* distributed ideas about God's character that betray human imperfection.

[58]While there is an ellipsis in the Hebrew text after the word *thousand*, the most probable understanding is that the contrast supplies the referent, namely, "generations." Elsewhere Yahweh's attributes (love, etc.) are tied to a *thousand*, and the word *generations* is explicit (Deut 7:9; 1 Chron 16:15; Ps 105:8).

[59]We should not understand the one-thousand-to-four with literal crassness or mathematical precision (e.g., 250:1), since one thousand in the Hebrew Bible often means far greater—Yahweh owns the cattle on a thousand hills (Ps 50:10). The numbers themselves are not as important as the gigantic difference between them and what that emphasizes. The point of contrastive disproportion then becomes even more pronounced.

So what does the Exodus 34 portrait of Yahweh have to do with holy war? After Israel has rebelled against God with the golden-calf incident, Yahweh is prepared to wipe them out. That threatened action by Yahweh is known as *reverse holy war* (see appendix C). Yahweh is ready to "destroy them" and "wipe them off the face of the earth" (Ex 32:10, 12); he uses the total-kill language of holy war.[60] Moses pleads with Yahweh to not destroy the entire Israelite people based on two reasons: (1) the broader *political* impact—what Egypt would think—and (2) the *promise* to Abraham about producing a great people. His brokenhearted entreaty moves Yahweh to show mercy: "Then the LORD relented and did not bring on his people the disaster he had threatened" (Ex 32:14). This act of mercy anticipates God's fuller disclosure of his compassion, love, and forgiveness in Exodus 34. Contextually Exodus 32–33 provides the literary staging for the self-revelation of God's unevenly weighted character in Exodus 34.[61]

When Moses reaches the bottom of the mountain and encounters the idolatry and (related) sexual play, a partial reverse holy war judgment ensues with swords and a plague, but in a very restricted sense (not wiping out the entire people; Ex 32:26-35).[62] With this reduced reverse holy war in the background, Yahweh reveals his glory—that is, what is remarkable and important and praiseworthy about his character—so that Moses can be assured, despite the golden-calf rebellion, that Yahweh will still go with them (Ex 33:14-23). The portrait of Exodus 34—a God who is far more disposed toward love and forgiveness—is a direct commentary on the (reverse) holy war actions of Yahweh in Exodus 32. Beyond Moses's two reasons mentioned

---

[60]The theme of (reverse) holy war continues beyond Ex 32:10-12 into the next chapter (Ex 33:3, 5).

[61]Several elements in Ex 32–33 foreshadow the revelation of Yahweh's character as lopsidedly loving: Yahweh relents (*nāḥām*)—he changes course out of a disposition of mercy—anticipating his lopsided love (Ex 32:12, 13); Yahweh knows Moses' name and character (Ex 33:17), but Moses does not (yet) fully know the character of Yahweh; Yahweh drops hints of his sixfold forgiving nature by promising to reveal his name, adding, "I will have mercy on whom I will have mercy, and I will have compassion on whom I will have compassion" (Ex 33:19). The threat of destruction also anticipates Yahweh's just discipline (Ex 34:7).

[62]Israel's "play" is most likely sexual, drunken orgies combined with the worship of false gods. Here at Sinai, as at Baal Peor just before entering the land, Israel participates in sacred-sex idolatry in a similar manner to the fertility rites of Canaanite worship. See Richard M. Davidson, *Flame of Yahweh: Sexuality in the Old Testament* (Peabody, MA: Hendrickson, 2007), 97-102.

above, the mountain experience reveals to Moses (3) *the deepest reason* for why Yahweh can relent and forgive sin and rebellion. Yahweh's profoundly weighted disposition toward love and forgiveness (compared with punishment) explains his holy war actions at the very core of who this God so unlike other ANE gods was/is. Yahweh's compassionate and forgiving character (relenting from calamity) affects not only his treatment of Israel but also the treatment of Israel's enemies, like Assyria, much to the displeasure of punishment seekers such as Jonah (Jonah 3:9; 4:2).

The mountain portrait of Yahweh as a relenting war God—far more weighted in his character and disposition toward tender compassion, love, and forgiveness (rather than punishment)—converges well with the earlier portrait of Yahweh as a tearful war God. Compared with the depictions of callous and war-drunk ANE gods, this disproportionately gentle picture of Yahweh is particularly striking.[63]

Faith in armor and the armor of faith (1 Samuel 17). A final passage that subverts ancient Israel's warfare practices describes an episode in the life of Israel's most celebrated warrior, David, in an account that at first seems to applaud the violence of warfare. Typical ANE (and some biblical) battle accounts tend to emphasize the bravery and heroism of the protagonist. The account of David and Goliath (1 Sam 17) participates in this practice while at the same time subverting typical battle accounts in two ways. The first is in its depiction of "trash talking," which was a common form of ancient psychological warfare and permeates the chapter.[64] Goliath taunts the Israelites, repeatedly challenging them to send him a worthy opponent for single combat (1 Sam 17:10, 25). David's response recognizes that the ultimate target of Goliath's insult is not human but divine (1 Sam 17:26, 36). Significantly, when they meet on the field of battle, both combatants mock the weapons used by the other, and the contrast is striking. Goliath does not consider David a worthy challenger because of his age and his choice of

---

[63]The pictures of war violence on ANE temples tell the story of their gods' thirst for war (see the above discussion of David's bloody hands and the peaceful imagery in Yahweh's temple). See also the opening discussion about Marduk's love for war violence.

[64]See David T. Lamb, "'I Will Strike You Down and Cut Off Your Head' (1 Sam 17:46): Trash Talking, Derogatory Rhetoric, and Psychological Warfare in Ancient Israel," in *Warfare, Ritual, and Symbol in Biblical and Modern Contexts*, ed. Brad E. Kelle, Frank Ritchel Ames, and Jacob L. Wright, AIL 18 (Atlanta: SBL Press, 2014), 111-30.

sticks and stones for weapons (1 Sam 17:43). David, on the other hand, mocks Goliath for thinking that his sword, spear, and javelin—typical battle weapons—will prove effective (1 Sam 17:45). But more significantly, David moves the focus away from weapons altogether by pointing to the real source of his victory, "*You come against me* with sword and spear and javelin, *but I come against you* in the name of the LORD Almighty, the God of the armies of Israel, whom you have defied" (1 Sam 17:45). The outcome of the battle shows that the decisive weapon is faith in Yahweh.

Closely related to the emphasis on reliance on Yahweh is the way in which the narrative also undermines reliance on weapons and a wrongheaded sense of invulnerability. First Samuel 17:5-7 highlights Goliath's fearsomeness by its description of his height and especially with its catalog of his weapons: "He had a bronze helmet on his head and wore a coat of scale armor of bronze weighing five thousand shekels; on his legs he wore bronze greaves, and a bronze javelin was slung on his back. His spear shaft was like a weaver's rod, and its iron point weighed six hundred shekels. His shield bearer went ahead of him" (1 Sam 17:5-7). Goliath is basically a well-armored tank. J. P. Fokkelman observes, "The Philistine embodies belief in armaments, the ideology of reliance on military force, the desire for invulnerability."[65] Saul buys into this belief when he attempts to equip David with his own armor (1 Sam 17:38), but David dismisses it, as he does Goliath's armor (1 Sam 17:45), as unhelpful and unnecessary. In fact, Goliath's impressive armor becomes his greatest liability when he is felled by David's stone, for its weight hinders his ability to rise, and David dispatches Goliath with, ironically, his own sword (1 Sam 17:51).

Gregory Wong shows how 1 Samuel 17 emphasizes the futility of military armament through its enumeration of weapons.[66] The narrator systematically dismisses each piece of armament in a diminishing, five-four-three-two-one pattern. The sequencing starts with an initial catalog of Goliath's *five* pieces of armor (helmet, mail coat, greaves, javelin, and spear, 1 Sam 17:5-7). Saul clothes David (1 Sam 17:38-39) with his own *four* pieces of

---

[65]Jan P. Fokkelman, *Narrative Art and Poetry in the Books of Samuel* (Assen: Van Gorcum, 1986), 2:148.

[66]Gregory T. K. Wong, "A Farewell to Arms: Goliath's Death as Rhetoric Against Faith in Arms," *BBR* 23 (2013): 43-55; see also Fokkelman, *Narrative Art*, 2:187.

armor (helmet, mail coat, sword, and tunic), which are rejected by David and replaced with four shepherd's tools (staff, five stones, bag, and sling, 1 Sam 17:40). Later, Goliath's *three* weapons (sword, spear, and javelin, 1 Sam 17:45) cannot hold up, nor can *two* prevail (sword and spear, 1 Sam 17:47). Instead, David's unconventional weapon (a shepherd's sling) overcomes Goliath's remaining *one* weapon—his sword (1 Sam 17:50-51), illustrating how reliance on military armament proves futile for decisive victory.[67] Faith in a warrior's weapons is a misplaced faith; a shepherd's tools prove more than sufficient to defeat the arms of the most feared warrior when combined with faith in Yahweh.

As in the story of David and Goliath, Yahweh often acts in concert with Israel in warfare through atypical, *weaker* war methods—reducing the number of troops (Gideon), getting rid of chariots and horses (the strongest weapons; see Deut 17:16; Josh 11:4-6), fighting with a shepherd's staff and raised hands (Moses; Ex 4:4; 7:19-20; 8:5, 16; 9:23; 10:13; 17:9-13), walking around a city (Josh 6:1-15), an ox goad (Shamgar; Judg 3:31), a well-timed rain (Deborah; Judg 5:19-22), a tent peg (Jael; Judg 5:24-27), a donkey's jaw bone (Samson; Judg 15:14-16), temporary blinding and a feast (2 Kings 6:8-23), and so forth.[68] There can be no doubt that Yahweh is attempting to teach Israel to place their trust in him (their God) and not in their weapons of war. On this we should all agree.

But can we carry the argument further? These war accounts involving inferior weapons and fewer soldiers do not automatically, in isolation from everything else, move toward a "less violence is better" understanding of Yahweh. We need to acknowledge that. However, they do collectively highlight that Yahweh could win battles with *whatever* means he wished to support. That is a lesson Israel refuses to learn; they go instead with a king and are inclined toward greater-kill methods (such as the accumulation of war horses and other ANE weapons of mass destruction). Beyond this point,

---

[67]Wong, "Farewell to Arms," 45, 52-53, following Ariella Deem, who convincingly argues that David's slingstone sank between Goliath's greaves (*miṣḥâ*) rather than his forehead (causing him to topple), so that every piece of Goliath's armor is rhetorically written off. Even Goliath's greaves are rejected because of their malfunction ("'... And the Stone Sank into His Forehead': A Note on 1 Samuel XVII 49," *VT* 28 [1978]: 349-51).

[68]In Judg 7–8 Yahweh has Gideon reduce the number of Israel's warriors from 32,000 to 10,000 and eventually to 300.

however, we must think *logically and theologically* based on the other portraits above. In other words, we need to combine the David and Goliath story with the other portraits we have just seen: Yahweh can disarm an entire Aramean army through acts of kindness and hospitality (kindness is his preference over the Israelite king's twice-repeated call for killing the enemy soldiers); Yahweh cries tears over the war destruction of his enemies; Yahweh overturns cultural expectations about warrior kings building temples and paints David's bloody war actions in a dreadfully negative light; Yahweh is profoundly inclined toward love and forgiveness as a war God; and so on.

Now we return to David and Goliath. If Yahweh can use whatever means he wishes to win battles, these other subversive texts tell us (logically and theologically) that he would have preferred means that were *far less violent* and perhaps *as nonviolent as possible*, given that he was a peaceful, nonviolent creator, tearful, kind, not happy with David's bloodied hands, and has shalom at the very core of his character. Do we know exactly what Yahweh's plan A was for Israel before accommodating to their war paths? Do we know what Yahweh's preferred fighting strategy, with faith as a weapon, would have looked like for his covenant people if Yahweh could have had his druthers? No. We do not.[69] Nor do we need to know this plan A in complete detail in order to move forward in our thinking about Yahweh. Here is what we can discern with a fair bit of certainty (and it is enough): *an accommodation gap existed between Israel's war practices and what Yahweh truly wanted to develop in the lives of his redeemed people.*

It is hard to imagine that Yahweh's point in calling for Israel's faith is for them to watch him become a massive killing machine on their behalf through preposterously weak and unlikely instruments of war. Such would contradict the nature of Yahweh as revealed in other subversive war texts. At the height of David's war career, Yahweh slams the door shut on that option when he identifies his core characteristic (his name and reputation) not as a *warrior-king* God but as a *shalom-king* God. That and the other subversive portraits above provide enough insight into plan A (Yahweh's preferred will for Israel) to surmise that it would include something far more redemptive than what we encounter within Israel's war actions.

---

[69]For further reflection on plan A, see appendix F.

CONCLUSION

These subversive war passages and others like them (see appendix H) do not directly overturn the war ethos of the ANE or ancient Israel. However, they do push us to ask, Why does Yahweh shed tears at the destruction of Israel's enemies? Why is he a weeping war God? Why does he not want a king for his people, and why does he counter with various war liabilities as reasons? Why does Yahweh strictly forbid acquiring ancient-world weapons of mass destruction—horses and chariots—when every other ANE power was trying to acquire them? Why does Yahweh require his people to destroy these highly destructive weapons when they capture them? Why does Yahweh refuse to have the greatest Israelite warrior build him a temple? Why does Yahweh take such ritualized pains to separate his name and reputation from Israel's prized warrior and instead connect his character with shalom? What ANE god in their right mind would have acted like Yahweh? The subversive war texts in this chapter present a portrait of Yahweh as a highly reluctant war God who is not exactly eager to participate with Israel in its wars. These Old Testament texts inform us of a God who unexpectedly subverts the practice of war among his people.

When taken together, this collection of portraits presents a hopeful and redemptive picture of Yahweh and his attitude toward warfare. We see that war is not endemic to the healthy workings of creation. We see a tender-hearted God who grieves the effects of war not only on his own people but even on Israel's enemies. Moreover, Yahweh does not revel in warriors' prowess, so often trumpeted in ANE writings, but instead seeks to restrict his leaders' ability to wage aggressive and highly destructive wars. At times Yahweh even circumvents the devastation of battle through peaceful hospitality and other nonviolent means.

Perhaps the most profound and striking statement about Yahweh's attitude toward war is made when David's bloody hands are not allowed to build the temple, showing how strongly Yahweh is tilted toward peace, while the ANE celebrated and valorized war in their temple building. The distancing of Yahweh's name and reputation from the war-king David and instead the aligning of his name and reputation with shalom makes for a stunning repudiation of ANE temple-building norms. It creates temple distance—a gap of holy proportions—between (1) how Yahweh truly wants his redeemed people to act and (2) what he is willing at an accommodation level to do with them. Yahweh bears mostly in silence the divine humiliation of wearing hip waders (stoop-low accommodation) during Israel's wars. But not always. We have reviewed some intriguing exceptions. In these passages, we see hints of the coming day when the brokenhearted, reluctant warrior God will set up his kingdom of shalom, which will do away with war altogether.

Maranatha.

15

THE CROSS, RESURRECTION, AND ASCENSION OF JESUS

The Battle Already Won

THIS CHAPTER EXPLORES THE IMPACT of the ministry of Jesus—his life, death, resurrection, and ascension—on the troubling ethics of Old Testament holy war. How could the cross, resurrection, and ascension play any role in untangling the military ethics that we encounter way back in Israel's conquest narratives? Those Old Testament war texts seem far removed. The connections may not appear obvious or explicit. Nevertheless, the objective of this chapter is to highlight several ways—substantial and necessary ways—that Jesus' life, his death on the cross, his resurrection, and his enthronement in the heavens ease the ethical tensions created by biblical holy war.

THE CROSS AS AN ETHICAL LOOKING GLASS

Before presenting our positive case, allow us to explain where our journey within the war texts has *not* taken us. In short, we have not been persuaded by Greg Boyd's looking-glass approach to reading the Old Testament conquest narratives (and other violent texts) through the lens of Jesus' death on the cross.[1] Boyd proposes that all the war violence of the Old Testament should be read through the "looking-glass lens" of God's sacrificial love demonstrated on the cross. When Christians do so, they will see the level of painful-but-loving accommodation to which God

---

[1]Gregory A. Boyd, *The Crucifixion of the Warrior God*, 2 vols. (Minneapolis: Fortress, 2017); Boyd, *Cross Vision: How the Crucifixion of Jesus Makes Sense of Old Testament Violence* (Minneapolis: Fortress, 2017).

stoops as he reluctantly goes along with certain violent actions in the biblical war texts.

Much within Boyd's approach is helpful. We obviously share an accommodation perspective on God's participation in Old Testament holy war. While we understand the *extent* of that accommodation as considerably less than Boyd does, and we provide what seems to us a more *balanced* approach through an emphasis on (incremental) redemptive movement, we applaud Boyd's efforts to pinpoint the ways in which biblical war texts stand at odds with Jesus' love ethic.[2] We do not take exception to Boyd framing a cross-like, sacrificial love ethic as one among several possible litmus tests for evaluating what is potentially within the accommodation picture. For us, the Spirit's role in enacting Jesus' new law of love and its manifestation though the fruits of the Spirit (as opposed to the deeds of the flesh) offers an equally credible basis for this task.

However, we are not inclined to accept Boyd's requirement that God's love always be nonviolent and noncoercive.[3] These features seem largely imported into the biblical text. First, there is the matter of *nonviolence*. Our approach departs from Boyd dramatically because we include within divine reluctance some (unspecified) amount of violence as a *legitimate part* of the outworking of God's loving actions.[4] In the realm of human ethics, numerous examples of the most loving action include at least some degree of potential for or engagement in violent force. For example, an emergency SWAT team that takes out shooters in a terrorist attack protects vulnerable lives; the drug

---

[2]Boyd uses accommodation extensively to explain any appearance of divine violence; we by comparison limit the extent of accommodation and use a more mixed portrait (some divine-violence accommodation, some not accommodation). Also, the basis for our accommodation argument is tied much more closely to evidence within the war texts themselves.

[3]We have restricted our critique of Boyd's view of the cross as a looking glass to certain key issues. For a fuller evaluation of Boyd's perspective, see the review by Paul Copan, "Greg Boyd's Misunderstandings of the 'Warrior God,'" The Gospel Coalition, January 26, 2018, www.thegospelcoalition.org/reviews/crucifixion-warrior-god-greg-boyd/. While we differ with Copan on certain details and would want to nuance some of his critiques, we nonetheless share the bulk of his concerns.

[4]We do not pretend to know all the mitigating circumstances or factors (stated and unstated, seen and unseen) involved in each use of divine violence as a loving divine action in a fallen world. Our approach does not attempt to be rid of divine violence completely (like Boyd) but instead, where possible, to understand it better. Sometimes we embrace accommodation when the evidence leads that direction, but other approaches (not simply accommodation) are possible and used throughout this book.

bust that turns violent sometimes requires police to use lethal force to preserve their own lives and subdue the drug traffickers. It seems artificial within a sinful, fallen world to completely remove violent force in the expression of reluctant but also most loving actions. The potential and sometimes actual use of violence is not always antithetical to love.

The same can be said for *noncoercive* force. Boyd wishes to remove from God's loving actions anything that smacks of coercion. Once again, in the realm of human ethics we see coercion (action that violates another's person's will) as sometimes required to accomplish the most loving action. Examples of coercive force that may fall within the parameters of loving actions include parents who place screaming children in car seats against their will and governments that impose martial law or a neighborhood lockdown to prevent the violence of extremist groups or opportunistic looters. When it comes to the biblical war texts, Boyd's favorable appeal to Israel and/or God driving out Canaanites from the land hardly squares with his own definition of love being completely noncoercive.[5] Any land-resettlement program of people groups (no matter how kind and gentle) may involve some degree of coercion. Even if enticed by overwhelmingly positive incentives (contra the "hornet" plan; Ex 23:27-30; Deut 7:20; see also Josh 24:12), some Canaanite residents would probably still not have wanted to leave their homes.[6]

In short, Boyd's approach is cleaner and more comprehensive than ours. It fixes everything and in the here and now. Fair enough—those are nice features. Yet, our less-imposing accommodation approach, which includes some amount of violence (though it is messy), seems to align better with how ethics work in a fallen world and also with the portrait of divine love in the biblical text. As will be seen, our less-tidy approach leaves the final resolution of the justice dilemma to the unfinished or not-yet aspects of Christ's return and administration of justice in the new heavens and new earth (see chapter sixteen and conclusion).

---

[5]Boyd, *Crucifixion of the Warrior God*, 1:303, 404; 2:964-74.

[6]In our view, hell (a place devoid of God's holy temple-like presence) is the most loving option for those who do not want to leave behind this old (literary) Canaanite-like world and move to the new heavens and new earth.

Concerning hornets: Whatever the meaning of God sending hornets to drive out the inhabitants of the land, it does not appear to be a positive incentive. The negative motivation of stinging hornets (whether literal or metaphorical of some other reality) would hardly be classified as noncoercive.

If we cannot follow Boyd's looking-glass approach, how then do we see the cross, resurrection, and ascension as helpful in understanding the troubling ethics of Old Testament holy war? Our response has several parts but one unifying theme: *These inseparably linked first-advent events move the justice story (as a component of biblical holy war) forward toward its climax and resolution.* The life, death, resurrection, and ascension of Jesus provide unlimited divine power and resources to bring an ultimate resolution to the embedded injustices of holy war in the biblical story line.

THEMATIC CONTINUITY: WAR LANGUAGE AND JESUS

Like it or not, war language pervades the portrait of Jesus in the New Testament. Biblical writers paint the canvas of Christian lives and the extension of Jesus' mission with similarly warlike colors. The seminal work *God Is a Warrior*, by Tremper Longman III and Daniel G. Reid, draws attention to this frequent use of war language throughout Scripture.[7] Since their book is split in half between its focus on the Old Testament and on the New Testament, it illustrates well how the continued use of the war theme connects the early Christian story with the holy war themes of the Old Testament. Even a brief sample of war language within the New Testament illustrates its dominance in framing a theology of Jesus and his followers:[8]

▶ The call to "prepare the way [highway] . . . in the wilderness" paints Jesus' mission as a divine warrior's triumphal procession to his holy mount (Mk 1:2-3; Lk 1:3, 76; 3:4; see Is 40:3-4; 57:14; 62:10), a new exodus.

▶ When driving out demons, Jesus "wages war" against Beelzebub, the prince of demons, who is viewed as a strongman and fierce warrior

---

[7]Tremper Longman III and Daniel G. Reid, *God Is a Warrior*, SOTBT (Grand Rapids: Zondervan, 1995), 1-204.

[8]For an excellent overview of biblical war language that connects both Testaments, see Daniel G. Reid and Tremper Longman III, "When God Declares War," *Christianity Today*, October 28, 1996. See also the essays of Merrill and Longman in C. S. Cowles, Eugene H. Merrill, Daniel L. Gard, and Tremper Longman III, *Show Them No Mercy: Four Views on God and Canaanite Genocide*, ed. Stanley N. Gundry (Grand Rapids: Zondervan, 2003), 88-93, 179-87. For more reflection on warfare themes in the New Testament, see Gregory A. Boyd, *God at War: The Bible and Spiritual Conflict* (Downers Grove, IL: InterVarsity Press, 1997), 169-293. Beyond these introductory sources, the literature is massive. For further bibliography on spiritual warfare and holy war themes within the New Testament, see Boyd, *Crucifixion of the Warrior God*, 2:1305-10, 1311-12.

within another opposing kingdom that fights against Jesus (Lk 11:17-23 [esp. Lk 11:22]; Mk 3:23-26; see Is 49:24-26), a new conquest.

▶ Though a cruel instrument of Roman execution, the cross itself is transformed into a triumphant military procession in which Jesus leads captive the defeated evil principalities and powers of this age (Col 2:14-15).

▶ Christians in this cosmic military battle are captured by Jesus from the domain of Satan, become part of his grand procession of war captives, and form a new temple building (Eph 4:7-13; see Ps 68:18). Along the victory highway of second exodus, God leads Christians in "triumphal procession" in Christ, spreading the fragrance of Christ's gospel (2 Cor 2:14-17).

▶ The death and resurrection of Jesus are viewed with vivid war language as a battle that defeats the "last enemy" of sin (assumed) and death (1 Cor 15:25-26).

▶ As to a victorious warrior king, all things are now subjected under the feet of the risen and ascended/enthroned Christ (Eph 1:22; see Ps 8:6).

This sampling of New Testament war language could be multiplied several hundred times over.[9]

Readers of Scripture with strong pacifist convictions, soft pacifist leanings, or even leanings toward reduced and least-possible violence (such as both of us) struggle to varying degrees with this war language. Many Christians have restricted their use of war-theology language in the public forum and church worship particularly after 9/11.[10] Such changes are understandable. But we cannot run from it entirely, nor should we. Much within Scripture

---

[9]The process of gathering war-language expressions in the New Testament is relatively easy. First take a lexicon that is domain based (not alphabetical) and look up various domains related to war, conflict, military, and the like. Then do a word search on those Greek terms in the New Testament. For a domain-based lexicon, see Johannes P. Louw and Eugene A. Nida, eds., *Greek-English Lexicon of the New Testament Based on Semantic Domains*, 2nd ed. (New York: United Bible Society, 1988), 55.1–55.25 (see also 20.1-88; 37.1-138; 39.1-61; 76.1-26). One will find long lists of New Testament texts where the biblical authors employ a range of military terms to describe Jesus and Christian mission.

[10]Note the silencing of Christian hymns such as "Onward Christian Soldiers [Marching on to War]," or the name change of a major campus ministry, dropping "Crusade" language.

embraces the categories of our fallen world to talk about theology. That is because of the *analogical* nature of human language. War language in the Bible raises the mere tip of a (mammoth) iceberg in terms of Wittgenstein-type questions about how human language works within theology. With analogical language we must wisely and humbly discern between *things that carry over in the analogy* and *things that do not carry over*. We might invoke the ending of the Serenity Prayer, about knowing the difference between things we can and cannot change: "God grant us the wisdom to discern the difference."[11] That prayer is equally needed, perhaps more so, in the daunting task of discerning the difference between things that carry over and things that do not in the fallen-world analogical language that shapes much of theology.[12] So we proceed with caution, humility, and some unavoidable discomfort. And proceed we must.

One of the strongest ties between Jesus and Old Testament holy war comes at the level of war-language continuity. While war language as a way of describing Jesus is quite different in its referential meaning (see below), its carryover affords readers of the New Testament an opportunity to say, "Hey, the Old Testament story line continues!" It also enables New Testament readers to see overlap with their own lives and experiences. Warlike battles framing Jesus' life and our lives (though very different from battles in the Old Testament) extend the biblical story line and provide a valuable way of fusing our promise or covenant connection with the past. Presenting Christian lives and the life of Jesus through war and battle language intentionally roots our *present* existential reality in the Old Testament conquest battles of the *past*.

Nevertheless, we need to ask what within this continuity and pervasive New Testament/Jesus use of (analogical) war language provides "better answers" for wrestling with the troubling ethics of Old Testament holy war. The next points reach into this war-language pool to make the ethical case.

---

[11]The Serenity Prayer is popularly attributed to Protestant theologian Reinhold Niebuhr.
[12]For a treatment of the atonement in cross theology that astutely handles the analogical nature of the language with the notion of *parable-like* portraits see Fleming Rutledge, *The Crucifixion: Understanding the Death of Jesus Christ* (Grand Rapids: Eerdmans, 2017), 1-669.

CANONICAL DEVELOPMENT: A DIFFERENT
KIND OF (SPIRITUAL) BATTLE

A canonical bump of seismic proportion takes place at the advent of Jesus. Something stark and abrupt happens to holy war as we follow the biblical story: *Jesus forever changes the nature of the battle to a spiritual one.* Within the canonical story line, holy war battles move away from the domain of physical warfare with horses and chariots (Old Testament) into a spiritual or metaphysical domain of conflict with sin, evil forces, and death (New Testament). Jesus does not seem interested in conquering geographically or ethnically defined kingdoms in this world by using invading human armies. He does not raise a group of followers to rebel against Roman rule and rid the Promised Land of land-defiling heathen. Instead, Jesus drives out demons from human beings (Mt 7:22; 8:16, 31; 12:27-28; Mk 1:34; 3:23; 7:26; 16:17; Lk 9:1; 11:18-20) and heals the sick from all people groups.[13] Ironically, he welcomes into his kingdom literary Canaanites and ethnic Canaanites, along with other despised foreigners, while rejecting self-righteous ethnic Israelites.[14] These are good indicators that the topography of the battlefield has changed and changed dramatically. The new boundaries involve allegiance to Christ and following him, not allegiance to national, geopolitical divisions defined by this world.

This canonical development within the story line of holy war—the radical change in the kind of battle that dawns with Jesus—offers us one of the better answers. No longer is the struggle for securing a kingdom achieved by humans fighting against other humans, as with military battles like those in Joshua, Judges, Samuel, or Kings. This answer does not fix everything; it stops the bleeding at a particular point in history. The war damages have stopped recurring due to a strategic advancement in the canonical story line. It limits the liabilities of holy war to a specific precross time and place. In that respect, the days of *literal* holy war come to an end with the death of

---

[13]Mt 4:23-24; 8:7-13 (healed a Roman centurion's servant; see also Lk 7:3-7); Mt 12:15 ("all who were ill" in a large crowd; see also Mt 14:14); Mt 14:35 (in the countryside people brought "all their sick" for healing); Mt 15:28 (a Canaanite woman's daughter); Mt 15:30 (great crowds came and brought their sick); Mk 5:23 (a synagogue leader's daughter; see also Lk 8:50); Lk 4:40 (healed "all who had various kinds of sickness"); Lk 6:17-19 (healed sick people from Tyre and Sidon); Lk 22:51 (the high priest's servant's ear).

[14]See the discussion of reversal in Jesus' kingdom in chapter three.

Jesus, much like literal animal sacrifice comes to an end with the cross.[15] Only the *metaphorical* (or spiritual) sense of both holy war and animal sacrifice continue after the death of Christ, and into the eschaton.

Of course, this better answer (one that puts an end to the recurring collateral damage prevalent in literal holy war) has weight only if the canonical change in warfare is a permanent one and does not shift back in some future epoch to the literal wielding of military weapons. The next chapter will argue, despite the literal readings of some interpreters, that the second coming of Jesus retains this new and changed canonical focus on a spiritual and cosmic battle. Jesus does not revert to human battle objectives along the lines of Joshua's day. While this change may not seem like much, the shift in the kind of battle in the biblical story line is an important one. It removes the need to wage war with the old physical weapons—swords, chariots, and so forth. Correspondingly, the ethical liabilities of such old-world battles are no longer present.[16] With the introduction of Jesus to the story line, holy war will never (with legitimate biblical sanction) include God's people (Christians) in a literal holy war killing other human beings to further the kingdom of Jesus.[17]

EXTREME CRUELTY AND INJUSTICE OF THE CROSS

Jesus' horrific suffering on the cross provides yet another better answer to the injustice of Old Testament holy war texts. The crucifixion of civilian criminals—particularly those who were viewed as a threat to the Roman empire—mirrored the torturous deaths of foreign war enemies. The Roman soldiers stationed at Jerusalem who crucified Jesus as a criminal may themselves have

---

[15]If this "ends with the cross" analogy between literal holy war and literal animal sacrifice holds true, then at least *some* of the why for God's accommodating use of holy war (as with animal sacrifice) may be related to the orientation of ancient cultures to such methods of connecting with deity and the land/nation/territory-based understanding of their deities.

[16]Going forward in the story line, the ethical benefits of this better answer should be apparent. The ethical damage of holy war within the biblical story line remains an isolated component that is primarily in the past.

[17]Obviously, the Crusades do not fall within the purview of legitimate biblical sanction. However, we are *not* saying that God will never use human warfare in the present or future to achieve his purposes. If God is sovereign, he can achieve good outcomes (nothing will thwart his redemptive goals) even through the convoluted route of evil agency. But this divine use of literal human warfare reflects truncated causation and is very different from and not as ethically problematic as the direct agency of the Joshua conquest battles. See appendixes C and G.

impaled or crucified captured war enemies at other locations and times. The Roman army had the gruesome reputation of crucifying hundreds of fleeing enemies as part of keeping a military grip on their empire.[18]

On the cross Jesus experienced the extreme cruelty of a war-related execution, and the false charges against him place his death in the category of total (not partial) injustice. Few ancient war atrocities (see chapter thirteen) could outdo the degree of pain and suffering of crucifixion. Few torturous spectacles viewed by throngs of gathered onlookers could exceed the prolonged public humiliation of death on a cross. And since Jesus was innocent, no war atrocities in the history of humanity could outweigh the total injustice that was part of such a bloody, brutal, and barbaric death as his on Calvary. What Jesus experienced with crucifixion was not simply a component of injustice embedded within fallen-world justice. Rather, he bore on himself a punishment that was totally (not partially) unjust.

This experience of torturous pain and total injustice infuses within Jesus the kind of hard-bought character qualities needed to adequately listen to and rightly address the injustice that others have experienced. Picture victims of injustice standing before Jesus at the judgment at the great white throne. If they suffered unjustly because of war (even within the unfolding drama of biblical holy war), they would be less likely to shout in complaint over painful war experiences. They would know from the cross what Jesus had experienced; Jesus would know about their suffering. There is something about standing in the presence of someone with a shared-atrocities horizon that quiets the conversation.

Yet there is a flip side to this justice encounter. While the shared horizons of extreme violence make for deep and profound interpersonal understanding, they also give Jesus the compassion to listen and the credibility to speak profound justice into their cases. A lawyer who has experienced something of the injustice of her client can make a more powerful case in representing that client. In the final courtroom scene (Rev 20:11-15) Jesus

---

[18]Robert L. Webb, "The Roman Examination and Crucifixion of Jesus: Their Historicity and Implications," in *Key Events in the Life of the Historical Jesus*, ed. Darrell L. Bock and Robert L. Webb, WUNT 247 (Tübingen: Mohr Siebeck, 2009), 695-700. Section 2.2, "Crucifixion in the Ancient Mediterranean World," gives detailed evidence for the extreme cruelty of Roman crucifixion as well as its prevalence.

functions as judge, jury, crown attorney, and legal-aid lawyer. His finalized justice in untangling the wrongs of the past will be filtered through the reservoirs of his shared experiences. Having experienced extreme violence and injustice himself, Jesus is uniquely qualified to sort through the mess of fallen-world injustices.

THE CROSS REDEEMS PEOPLE WITHIN *ALL* NATIONS

The cross of Jesus and the atonement cuts across all geographic, ethnic, and national boundaries. While the crucifixion on Calvary was a local event, the redeeming impact of Jesus' death and the offer of salvation was overtly extended to all nations and to all people groups within those nations. This cross-all-nations (yes, a double meaning intended for *cross*) offer, begun with the first advent of Jesus, continues with its spreading force to the very point of Jesus' return. The corollary language of no boundaries describes both the *death* of Jesus and the encompassing *gospel* message:

Concerning Jesus' death for *all* people groups:

- ▶ "You were slain, and with your blood you purchased for God persons *from every tribe and language and people and nation*" (Rev 5:9).

- ▶ The cross will draw "all people" to Jesus (Jn 12:32).

- ▶ Jesus dies for "all [people]" (2 Cor 5:15).

- ▶ The death of Jesus brings righteousness, justification, and life to "all people" (Rom 5:12, 18; 1 Cor 15:22).

- ▶ Jesus gives himself as a ransom for "all people" (1 Tim 2:6; see also 1 Tim 2:4; 4:10).

- ▶ Salvation is offered to "all people" (Titus 2:11); God accepts people from "every nation" who fear him (Acts 10:35).

The gospel of Jesus—his death, resurrection, and ascension—proclaimed for *all* people:

- ▶ The disciples are commanded to go into "all the world" (Mk 16:15) and preach the gospel to/in "all nations" (Mt 24:14; Mk 13:10; Lk 24:47), to "all creation" (Mk 16:15; Col 1:23), and "to the ends of the world" (Rom 10:18).

- ▸ The disciples are to make disciples of "all nations" (Mt 28:19; Mk 13:10; Rev 14:6).

- ▸ Through the preaching of the gospel "all peoples on earth" will be blessed (Acts 3:25; Gal 3:8).

- ▸ Paul's ministry is one of calling "all the Gentiles" to obedience (Rom 1:5; 16:26; see also 2 Tim 4:17).

Here is the point of the all-nations message and reception of the cross. Jesus' death on the cross and the spread of the gospel (conveying the good news of the cross, resurrection, and ascension) was a death inclusive of all peoples. The cross was not ethnically or geographically tagged. There were and are Jesus followers in every nation, people, and language group. The Gospels and Epistles support a Christology and cross theology that anticipate where we ought to go with our thinking about the eschaton. The cross cannot be reversed, set aside, or ignored.

When we ponder possible scenarios of a future holy war in the book of Revelation, we must not forget about the no-boundaries or cross-all-nations extension of Jesus' death and the gospel. We need to read John's Apocalypse and set our expectations of what will happen in the eschaton alongside what we know for sure about the *uninterrupted extension of the gospel to all nations*. Even during the time of the seals, trumpets, and bowls in the book of Revelation, an angel is charged with proclaiming the eternal gospel "to those who live on the earth—to every nation, tribe, language and people" (Rev 14:6; see also Rev 5:9). Christ's kingdom extends uninterrupted to all nations, resulting in believers all around the world living within the boundaries of every geopolitical entity.

At the return of Jesus many believers will thus be physically embedded in each of the nations. Believers will live beside nonbelievers in every region of the world. This perspective is further confirmed beyond the cross theology (above) by the parable of the sheep and goats (Mt 25:31-46; see also the wheat and tares, Mt 13:24-34), which speaks of Jesus as eschatological judge. At the final judgment "all the nations" will be gathered before Jesus, and at that point he will separate believer from nonbeliever. Such a separation at the final judgment implies that believers will live among the nations until the end of this age.

If Jesus' followers are spread across the world living within all nations, certain future holy war scenarios seem improbable. For instance, it makes little sense to posit a final battle where Jesus sides with one nation or several nations (and their literal human armies) to fight the great apocalyptic war against other nations (and their literal human armies). In fact, any kind of normative or literal human battle violates the blood of Christ being shed for all nations. The universal nature of the gospel—bringing salvation benefits from the cross into all nations—makes it problematic for Jesus and his followers to some future day align themselves with one or more earthly nations and fight in a literal military battle against another group of earthly nations. Such a future scenario would seemingly require the physical destruction of brothers and sisters in Jesus within other nations.

Maybe we should permit the death of Jesus for all nations to adjust our expectations of the future. Perhaps the days of *literal* holy war fighting are done. Possibly the cross of Calvary and the gospel of the kingdom drive a deathly spike into any christological notion of geo-ethno-national holy war ideology. At the very least we should be open to such a conclusion. This cross-all-nations theology of Jesus' death anticipates where we are headed in the next chapter.

THE PASSION OF JESUS AND HEAVEN'S TEARS

My own (Bill here) theological journey to the cross as the ultimate place of God's tears for a broken world began in earnest as I watched my oldest son, Jon, slowly go downhill from a degenerative brain disease. It was a long and painful death. Some days it was nothing short of torturous for Marilyn and me to watch our beloved boy from age thirteen to twenty-six slowly slip away—from a healthy young man, to a walker, to a wheelchair, to a bedridden quadriplegic, to someone racked with pain relieved only by doses of morphine every four hours. I could not help this theological reflection. It was simply too easy to think about a heavenly father watching his son die on the cross or about Jesus' earthly mother, Mary, sobbing at the cross. This is the mystery of the cross. What father, if he had any control over these matters, would ever permit his son to endure such a horrid death?

I came to realize that Jesus' painful and tear-filled crucifixion *on earth* fused ever so tightly with the portrait of a crying and suffering God *in heaven*. God is broken by the brokenness of our world. Heaven's tears over the carnage of our world converge at Calvary. As I muddled my way through numerous readings on this topic, I was particularly drawn to Jürgen Moltmann's work *The Crucified God*. Countering the traditional view that God cannot suffer, Moltmann argues that the church fathers got it wrong. They made the mistake of seeing only two alternatives: "either essential incapacity for suffering, or a fateful subjection to suffering." Either God cannot suffer or, if he can, he must be subject to it. But there is "a third form of suffering," Moltmann proposes, "a voluntary laying oneself open to another and allowing oneself to be intimately affected by him; that is to say, *the suffering of passionate love*."[19]

Moltmann rightly points out that love makes us vulnerable to pain. You and I could read the obituaries of the newspaper every day without shedding a tear. But if you have ever *loved* someone who is dying . . . there is potential for untold pain. So it is with God, the so-called war God. As developed in chapter fourteen, Yahweh cries a river of tears over wars that he brings both against Israel (reverse holy war) *and* against his enemies (holy war). Heaven's tears over Calvary and the death of his son converge with these wetted or, better put, drenched war texts, where we discover Yahweh crying, broken and despondent. To my surprise, it is within these war texts that we find the most explicit expression of a God crying over the brokenness of the world.

Where was God when Jesus struggled for hours in a torturous death on the cross? Or where was God when our son Jon went through a hellish, morphine-mediated death? Frankly, I do not know. On my bad days I am tempted to think that God delights in morbidity. That he is a sick and twisted deity. But, if God is crying and broken with pain because of the pain of our world, then I am faced with the mystery of the cross. If God (a good God) suffers with

---

[19]Jürgen Moltmann, *The Crucified God: The Cross of Christ as the Foundation and Criticism of Christian Theology* (Minneapolis: Fortress, 1993), 230 (italics added); Moltmann, *The Trinity and the Kingdom* (Minneapolis: Fortress, 1993), 23. See also Moltmann, "The Passion of Christ and the Suffering of God," *Asbury Theological Journal* 48, no. 1 (1993): 19-28; Richard Bauckham, *The Theology of Jürgen Moltmann* (New York: T&T Clark, 1995), 59.

us in our suffering, then we are faced with the most enigmatic of all questions: Why should he suffer? In the quietness of my mind comes only one answer . . . because he loves. Because he loves infinitely, one could speculate that he suffers infinitely.

This realization begins to melt my bitterness. It begins to heal my wizened and gnarled soul. *For I cannot stay angry at someone who suffers with me in my suffering.* Try as I may, I cannot stay angry. Dietrich Bonhoeffer came to a similar conclusion in the quiet of his Nazi prison cell days before his execution: "Only the suffering God can help [my suffering]."[20] Divine tears offer no easy fix for understanding the troubling ethics of Old Testament war texts. It is not an objective answer crafted with syllogisms. But it does hold out the offer of mystery or the unexplainedness of God—the mystery of the cross, of the brokenhearted God, of the passionate love of God. Mystery draws us deep into the divine unknown. In God's tears one can find solace and potentially renewed trust in the unfolding mystery of God.

THE CROSS, TORN CURTAIN, AND NEW TEMPLE

This fifth answer comes at the very moment when Jesus takes his last breath: the curtain in the holy of holies of the Jerusalem temple is torn from top to bottom (Mt 27:51; Mk 15:38; Lk 23:45). If one were to go back to chapter twelve and reread it through the lens of a new-temple theology of the cross, one would quickly figure out the nature of this better answer in relation to holy war ethics. The Jesus story at the exact moment of his death on the cross forever changes the meaning of temple. The old temple in Jerusalem ceases to be a dwelling place for Yahweh. Come Pentecost, God's new temple dwelling is resident within people (individuals and communities), not a place. God's dwelling is no longer in one geographical location, tied to a specific nation with defined borders. The new temple of the crucified and resurrected Jesus forever ends physical holy war (in any literal military engagement) like that of the former epoch, which was inextricably tied to land-and-nation ideas about temple. Jesus breaks with Israel's temple norms and with temple theology in the ancient world.

---

[20]Dietrich Bonhoeffer, *Letters and Papers from Prison* (London: SCM Press, 1967), 361.

THE SPIRIT'S PRESENCE IN NEW-TEMPLE COMMUNITIES

A sixth way in which Jesus' death, resurrection, and ascension puts an abrupt end to any literal (human armies) holy war in the canonical story line is through the presence of the Sprit. The leaving of Jesus and the coming of the Spirit (Jn 14–16; Acts 1–2) signals a whole new era of God's extension of the kingdom to the ends of the earth. The Spirit is the new-temple presence of God in the ongoing gathering of Jesus' followers. This further reiterates the point above about a new kind of temple that is no longer rooted in a physical location, land, or territory. That change affects Old Testament holy war in monumental ways (see chapter twelve).

But there is another concept that develops with the filling of the Spirit and the new-temple dwelling of believers, namely, the potential for a kind of inner transformation well beyond what was achieved under Moses. The fruit of the Spirit (versus the deeds of the flesh), the writing of the law on human hearts (not on stone), and the law of love as the rule of community all emerge with the coming of the Spirit and living out this new borderless sense of Jesus' theology. Just maybe, with this new-temple Spirit-filled influence, the words of the new Moses (Jesus) on the new mountain (Matthew's sermon on the mount) will be fulfilled. Believers in Jesus who live with the indwelling Spirit are called on to no longer return punch for punch, to love their enemies, and to go the second mile. Whether these measures of magnanimous love require total absence from any violence is a matter for debate. But these new-mountain words of Jesus must mean something! At the very least, we must see our lives taking the incremental developments in the war ethic that we find within the Old Testament and moving those scrimmage markers further downfield. As with the slavery texts and the movement toward abolitionism, Christians today should champion the redemptive spirit/Spirit already within the biblical war texts and take that spirit further to something well beyond Hague and Geneva conventions.

THE CROSS CARRIES THE STORY LINE FORWARD

A closing better answer is that the cross *carries the story line forward* to the point of final justice. The cross, resurrection, and ascension provide the divine power to transform the blood-soaked narrative of salvation history with life and bring about the possibility of making all things right. Like lined-up dominoes, the death, resurrection, and ascension collectively advance the story line with what is absolutely required to achieve the final steps of (in)justice resolution.

Think about the story line backward. Put the events in reverse order, and then the impact of the cross can be seen more clearly. Start with the end of the story: the new heavens and a new earth of Revelation 21. The old earth has passed away or, more likely, has been so profoundly renewed by the concentrated throne-room presence of God and Jesus come down that it is *like* the old earth no longer exists. Either way, a new heavens and new earth have replaced the old. The last judgment is conjoined with the renewed earth, already in place. The final judgment (Rev 20:11) and the new heavens and new earth (Rev 21:1) begin together with the removal of the old heavens and old earth.[21] In other words, the final judgment does *not* take place in the old, fallen world. It happens in the new world. The very first scene in this perfect, sinless world is the resurrection of dead human beings and their judgment by Christ.

So let's work backward. How did we get to this new-earth judgment scene at the end of the biblical story line? Of course, the picture of the enthroned Jesus come down from heaven to judge the whole of humanity in the new world (Rev 20:11; 5:6; 22:1) draws on the earlier postresurrection *ascension* of Jesus into the heavens. Ascension to the heavens (Acts 1:9-11) in the story line and within biblical theology depicts Jesus as the ascended and enthroned Lord.[22] He judges in the final scene from the center of the throne as the exalted one who long ago in his ascension became the inaugurated King of

---

[21]Based on Rev 20:11 (the removal of the old, sin-tainted earth and sky), commentators note well that the great-white-throne judgment takes place in the new, pristine world (Grant R. Osborne, *Revelation*, BECNT [Grand Rapids: Baker Academic, 2002], 719; G. K. Beale, *The Book of Revelation*, NIGTC [Grand Rapids: Eerdmans, 1999], 1039). With God's throne room (in the heavens) coming down to earth, creation morphs into an entirely new earth and new heavens, and the old, sin-polluted earth flees.

[22]The ascension of Jesus (Acts 1:9-11) brings Jesus to God's side ("the right hand of God," Acts 2:33) and thus provides the narrative basis for a Lukan theology of exaltation and enthronement (Acts 2:33-36). See other New Testament texts that describe Jesus' ascension in more general terms as exalted to the side of God (Eph 1:19-22; 1 Tim 3:16; Heb 1:3; 4:14; 6:19-20; 9:24; 1 Pet 3:21-22). See also Darrell L. Bock, *Acts*, BECNT (Grand Rapids: Baker, 2007), 69, and Craig S. Keener, *Acts: An Exegetical Commentary*, vol. 1, *Introduction and 1:1–2:47* (Grand Rapids: Baker Academic, 2012), 712, 720-21, 725-31.

kings and Lord of lords. But what about the dead human beings who are raised to life (Rev 20:12-15)? Here the resurrection of all human beings—great and small, the righteous and the unrighteous—reminds us that the power for such human resurrection resides in the historic *resurrection* of Jesus, which broke the bonds of death. Finally, what about this heavenly cubed city that descends to earth? The image of the cubed holy of holies and heavenly throne room (free of any sin contamination) coming down to earth and the fleeing of the sin-stained old world (no place for the old earth and sky) picture the direct impact of the *death of Jesus*, which washes away the sins of the world.

In short, the interconnected nature of Jesus' death, resurrection, and ascension provide for what is needed not only for his present inaugurated ministry as high priest and king but also his future role as returning king and judge on the (new) earth. The cross, resurrection, and ascension carry the story line (both chronologically and functionally) to the point where final justice awaits.

CONCLUSION

This chapter discusses how the cross, resurrection, and ascension of Jesus play a crucial role in addressing the thorny issues of Old Testament holy war ethics. We have offered several ideas to get the conversation started.[23] First, the cross marks a unique change or advancement in the canonical story line that stops the recurring ethical damage from literal holy war ever happening again (not unlike the end of literal animal sacrifice). It does so by moving holy war (fighting between human armies) from the literal to the spiritual/metaphorical domain. Second, the extreme cruelty and injustice experienced by Jesus in his warlike crucifixion by Roman soldiers (the horizon of shared ancient-world atrocities) makes him uniquely qualified to hear, judge, and

---

[23]This chapter would look much different if written by two Christian theologians and not, as it was, by two textually rooted professors of biblical studies. Theologians can move gracefully from abstracted ideas (above) down to the topic at hand; professors rooted in biblical texts (such as ourselves) rummage around for clues within texts and move from them upward, hoping to meet the theologians somewhere in the middle. We would love to see theologians who take our ethical approach to the war texts address a theology of the cross and its outworking of reconciliation with regard to the question of ethical injustices in Old Testament holy war.

untangle the ethical mess of those who experienced embedded (in)justice in ancient biblical holy war. Third, the cross-all-nations extension of the death of Jesus and his gospel should make us at least open to, if not inclined to, seeing the final eschatological battle in a metaphorical (not literal) light.

Fourth, the portrait of a suffering and crying God both in the cross of Jesus and in the holy war texts takes us deep into the mystery of divine love and vulnerability. While this does not directly fix the ethical problem, it surely helps us realize where God is in all this suffering. It is hard to remain angry at someone who suffers with us in a suffering world. Fifth, the torn temple curtain at the death of Jesus and emerging new-temple ideas completely reconfigure the temple-land-nation ideology of the Old Testament and ancient world. Any land-tied, nation-based literal warfare becomes obsolete and nonsensical for Jesus' followers, who worship in a new, people-based temple. Sixth, the coming of the Spirit confirms new-temple theology but also affords the opportunity for taking the ethics of biblical warfare (its laws) with its incremental redemptive movement to new levels of fulfillment well beyond Hague and Geneva. On a personal level we are called to be less retaliatory (no longer punch for punch) and more giving (go the extra mile).

Finally, Jesus' death and empty tomb carry the redemptive story line forward to the point of final justice. The unfolding implications of crucifixion, resurrection, and ascension lie deep within the spiritual substrata of what it takes to make the next thing happen. These first-advent Jesus events create the theological impetus that makes it possible for the story line to move forward toward a much-awaited moment in the eschaton—the ultimate resolution of all past injustices with the coming of the final and complete justice that Jesus brings to the new heavens and new earth.

16

JESUS AS APOCALYPTIC WARRIOR

One Word Will Fell Them

THIS CHAPTER LOOKS AT JESUS as an apocalyptic warrior. It argues that Jesus as a *spoken-word* apocalyptic warrior fights in a metaphorical (not literal) battle in the book of Revelation with a kind of holy war different from what we encounter in the Old Testament. With this metaphorical (not literal) understanding of Jesus as apocalyptic warrior and with other canonical developments in hand, chapters fourteen, fifteen, and sixteen unite the Yahweh-and-Jesus God portraits of Scripture—Old and New Testament—in a way that connects well with the core of Christian theology found in the Gospels and Paul.

The portraits of Yahweh and Jesus across the canonical story line of Scripture are like a jigsaw puzzle with three pieces—first, middle, and last:

Old Testament: Yahweh as a *past* warrior

Gospels and Paul: Jesus and the Spirit as leading/indwelling a peaceful, non-violent movement

Revelation: Jesus as a *future* apocalyptic warrior

The *traditional* view joins pieces (1) and (3) in a nice pairing with a highly literal understanding of both. However, piece (2), the core element of Christianity, remains largely dislocated from the other two pieces. The *antitraditional* view connects the middle piece with the last piece. Yet it has a significant (almost Marcion-like) dislocation from the Yahweh piece of the puzzle. This book's *realigned-traditional* view offers a more unifying solution—one that links together all three pieces of the canonical story with a sense of each piece belonging with the others. We argue that *when envisioned through the lens of the Old Testament subversive war texts*, the portrait of Yahweh as warrior converges well with the Jesus of the Gospels and the Spirit in Paul, and with Jesus as an apocalyptic warrior who fights in a *metaphorical sense* (one spoken word) and whose *justice expands* beyond the final battle into the great-white-throne enactment of pristine justice.

Christians generally do not debate this central or middle piece of the canonical puzzle: *Jesus of the Gospels and the Spirit in Paul as a peaceful, nonviolent religious movement.* At its core Christianity represented by Jesus and the Spirit is a peace-loving religious movement that does not advocate violence or lead/disciple with violence.[1] A brief summary of the second piece of the puzzle—Jesus of the Gospels and Paul—as it fits within the biblical holy war story line can be found in the introduction and chapter three (see also chapter fifteen).

Advocates of the traditional position may point out that in the Gospels a very small portion of *apocalyptic* Jesus material places war imagery within the second piece of the puzzle (Mt 24:3-31; Mk 13:3-27; Lk 21:5-28). Two brief responses. First, the apocalyptic material in the Gospels is talking about the future return of Jesus, so it does not change what we are saying about the first-century Jesus and the core of Christian theology being peaceful. Second and more importantly, the apocalyptic Jesus material in the Gospels in its final fulfillment should probably be interpreted the same way as the apocalyptic Jesus portrait within the book of Revelation.[2] We

---

[1]Some may object by appealing to certain cases of *alleged* violence (e.g., Jesus overturning tables in the temple). Yet, such forceful and dramatic actions functioned as pedagogical warnings against impending consequences without Jesus using physical violence toward those one might consider his enemies. See the recent contributions of David J. Neville, *The Vehement Jesus: Grappling with Troubling Gospel Texts* (Eugene, OR: Cascade Books, 2017); Mark L. Strauss, *Jesus Behaving Badly: The Puzzling Paradoxes of the Man from Galilee* (Downers Grove, IL: InterVarsity Press, 2015).

[2]That there is a partial fulfillment of the apocalyptic Jesus material in the Gospels in the fall of Jerusalem by Rome's military conquest in AD 70 certainly demonstrates that literal warfare is *plausible* in the eschaton. But the historical sacking of Jerusalem by the Romans was *not* directly accomplished by God's people or by Jesus himself; it was what we have labeled as indirect or truncated-causation warfare (see appendix G). This hardly squares with the directly fought battle in Revelation, led by Jesus. Thus, the battle-theme correlation between the fall of Jerusalem and Jesus' final return functions at an *abstracted* thematic level and not in the minute details. Furthermore, pattern fulfillment with multiple stages does not require a literal battle for the ultimate realization of Jesus' coming to

hope this chapter on Jesus as apocalyptic warrior in Revelation makes a persuasive case for a metaphorical (not literal) interpretation of the final eschatological battle that ushers in Jesus' return.

John's Apocalypse looms especially large in putting together the entire canonical portrait of holy war because some Christian scholars defend the complete rightness, goodness, and ethical purity of Old Testament holy war (the traditional view) by casting a spotlight on the apocalyptic Jesus. The argument could be framed like this: we need to accept Yahweh's war actions because Jesus as the apocalyptic warrior wields the sword just like the God of the Old Testament. Along these lines Tremper Longman portrays Jesus as "just as violent" as the Yahweh warrior of the Old Testament:

> Jesus in the New Testament is no less violent than the revelation of God in the Old Testament. . . . [Christians who separate Jesus from the wars of Yahweh wrongly avoid] the judgment and divine warrior passages of the book of Revelation or any of the New Testament apocalyptic passages. . . . [The book of Revelation and apocalyptic holy war are] just as violent and bloody as— actually, probably more [violent and bloody] than—the Old Testament.[3]

The implied logic of this argument seems strained.[4] Should Christians accept the grievous ethical problems of Old Testament holy war because Jesus' apocalyptic war has equal or greater ethical problems? Or is it acceptable for God in the Old Testament to act in an ethically deficient manner because Jesus behaves equally badly, if not worse, in the New Testament? Such ethical reasoning is not persuasive.[5] However, it is not our intent to

---

advance the pattern and fulfillment. As this chapter will show, the final eschatological battle is uniquely different from all past human battles. On interpreting Jesus' apocalyptic discourses, see David J. Neville, *A Peaceable Hope: Contesting Violent Eschatology in the New Testament Narratives* (Grand Rapids: Baker, 2013), 17-216.

[3]Tremper Longman III, "A Response to C. S. Cowles," in *Show Them No Mercy: Four Views on God and Canaanite Genocide*, ed. Stanley N. Gundry (Grand Rapids: Zondervan, 2003), 58-60 (compare 109). For similar continuity alignments between Jesus war and Yahweh war in terms of an ethical assessment, see Eugene H. Merrill, "A Response to C. S. Cowles," in *Show Them No Mercy*, 49 [compare 88-90], and Daniel L. Gard, "The Case for Eschatological Continuity," in *Show Them No Mercy*, 132.

[4]Though in their context the arguments of Longman, Merrill, and Gard's "violent Jesus" intend to counter the Marcion-like view of Cowles, the implied logic is that Christians ought to accept the violence of Yahweh's holy war because the Jesus they follow is just as violent.

[5]The argument fails on the basis of logic alone. One cannot absolve the Old Testament of ethical problems in its holy war texts by finding equal (or greater) problems in the New Testament. That merely compounds the problem rather than solving it.

dwell on the logic of such reasoning. Instead, we wish to examine the thematic connections between the Testaments and unearth the interpretive assumptions about the apocalyptic Jesus that lead to this kind of argument.

Thematic continuity between Yahweh war and apocalyptic-Jesus war has blinded Christians to redemptive elements in the relationship. Somehow we have missed what is markedly different about Jesus' apocalyptic holy war in both its rhetoric and its reality. This difference offers a far better answer for Christians wrestling with holy war problems within the Bible (certainly a better answer than one that compounds the problem). Accordingly, this chapter compares Yahweh's Old Testament holy war with Jesus' apocalyptic holy war by asking three questions: (1) What are the similarities? (2) What are the differences? (3) What ethical implications arise from these similarities and differences?

THE SIMILARITIES

What similarities does Jesus' apocalyptic holy war in the book of Revelation share with Yahweh's holy war in the Old Testament? The similarities or thematic connections involve war language, Old Testament source traditions, and objectives related to idolatry.

Similarity one: War language. The most graphic depiction of war comes in Revelation 19, where John describes what he sees in an apocalyptic vision:

> I saw heaven standing open and there before me was a white horse, whose rider is called Faithful and True. With justice he judges and makes war. His eyes are like blazing fire, and on his head are many crowns. He has a name written on him that no one knows but he himself. He is dressed in a robe dipped in blood, and his name is the Word of God. The armies of heaven were following him, riding on white horses and dressed in fine linen, white and clean. Coming out of his mouth is a sharp sword with which to strike down the nations. He will rule them with an iron scepter. He treads the winepress of the fury of the wrath of God Almighty. On his robe and on his thigh he has this name written:
> KING OF KING AND LORD OF LORDS.
>
> And I saw an angel standing in the sun, who cried in a loud voice to all the birds flying in midair, "Come, gather together for the great supper of God, so that you may eat the flesh of kings, generals, and the mighty, of horses and their riders, and the flesh of all people, free and slave, small and great."

Then I saw the beast and the kings of the earth and their armies gathered together to make war against the rider on the horse and his army. But the beast was captured, and with him the false prophet who had performed the miraculous signs on its behalf. With these signs he had deluded those who had received the mark of the beast and worshiped its image. The two of them were thrown alive into the fiery lake of burning sulfur. The rest [of the kings of the earth and their armies] were killed with the sword coming out of the mouth of the rider on the horse, and all the birds gorged themselves on their flesh. (Rev 19:11-21)

Through the language of ancient warfare one can appreciate at least a thematic connection between John's Apocalypse and the scenes of Old Testament war. John envisions the armies of the kings of the earth gathered together to fight against an opposing army. Jesus rides into battle on a white horse, wields a sword, and brings justice through making war. Blood spills in the battle, and with stains like those from grapes in a winepress, the messianic warrior fights with blood-soaked clothes. The kings of the earth and their armies are entirely slaughtered with the sword, and their bodies lie strewn across the battlefield—the dead become food for the birds of the air.

Along with this gritty and even grotesque battle scene in Revelation 19, the reader encounters war themes elsewhere in the book. War rhetoric increases from Revelation 12 onward—anticipating the battle scene of Revelation 19—with war conflict on two levels, namely, (1) Satan/the dragon fighting against the angels in heaven and (2) the dragon and his two beasts fighting against the saints on earth. Here are the pertinent passages:[6]

Then *war broke out in heaven*. Michael and his angels fought against the dragon, and the dragon and his angels fought back. But he was not strong enough, and they lost their place in heaven. The great dragon was hurled down—that ancient serpent called the devil, or Satan, who leads the whole world astray. He was hurled to the earth, and his angels with him. (Rev 12:7-9)

Then the dragon was enraged at the woman and went off *to make war against the rest of her offspring*—those who obey God's commandments and hold fast their testimony about Jesus. (Rev 12:17)

---

[6]For one of the most thorough treatments of warfare language in the book of Revelation, see Benjamin Steen Stubblefield, "The Function of the Church in Warfare in the Book of Revelation" (PhD diss., Southern Baptist Theological Seminary, 2012).

People worshiped the dragon because he had given authority to the beast, and they also worshiped the beast and asked, "Who is like the beast? Who can wage war against it?"

The beast was given a mouth to utter proud words and blasphemies and to exercise its authority for forty-two months. It opened its mouth to blaspheme God, and to slander his name and his dwelling place and those who live in heaven. It was given power to wage war against God's holy people and to conquer them. And it was given authority over every tribe, people, language and nation. All inhabitants of the earth will worship the beast—all whose names have not been written in the Lamb's book of life, the Lamb who was slain from the creation of the world.

Whoever has ears, let them hear.
"If anyone is to go into captivity,
    into captivity they will go.
If anyone is to be killed with the sword,
    with the sword they will be killed."

This calls for patient endurance and faithfulness on the part of God's people. (Rev 13:4-10)

The ten horns you saw are ten kings who have not yet received a kingdom, but who for one hour will receive authority as kings along with the beast. They have one purpose and will give their power and authority to the beast. *They will make war against the Lamb*, but the Lamb will overcome them because he is Lord of lords and King of kings—and with him will be his called, chosen and faithful followers. (Rev 17:12-14)

Beyond these dominant war texts, one encounters the language of holy war scattered throughout the book. Jesus is viewed as the sword-wielding messianic warrior (Rev 1:16; 2:12, 16). The saints who follow Jesus are repeatedly encouraged to fight in the apocalyptic battle so as to be "conquerors." The military aspect of this *nikaō* language is easily missed by English readers (the NRSV translation, "conquers," better conveys the military sense than "overcomes"). Christ as the ultimate victor or conqueror hands out the spoils of battle to his faithful army of followers. Note the close connection between conquering and the promises: "To him who conquers [*nikaō*] . . . I will give . . . ." In other words, the spoils of victory go to those who conquer in battle by following Jesus (Rev 2:7, 11, 26; 3:5, 12).

Similarity two: Holy war source traditions. The source traditions for war material in Revelation draw it even closer to Old Testament holy war. For instance, the saints in Revelation fight in a battle against Babylon, a well-known warmonger and paradigmatic enemy of the past. While the actual referent is Rome or perhaps an escalated Rome-like enemy of the future, the important point is that these enemies of first-century Christians were painted with the brushstrokes of historic battle enemies of Israel. Within this war context the messianic warrior (depicting Jesus) connects well with Old Testament holy war traditions from Isaiah because they view him as the leader of a renewed and finally successful quest for the land (Is 63:1-6). The new Promised Land in Revelation, of course, is no longer Canaan; it is the entire earth. Jesus will bring his people into the land of a new Eden, realized in the new heavens and the new earth. The 144,000 of Revelation 7—the universal church or people of God (not literal, ethnic Jewish males)—should probably be understood as an army or militia marching in battle configuration as Israel once did in the desert, a new Israel now moving toward conquest of the land like an army numbered for battle.[7]

Even in the interim stages of holy war (before the final battle of Rev 19) Jesus fights with his sword against those within the Asia Minor congregations whose members are following the Jezebel-like or Balaam-like prophets of their day. This kind of reverse holy war is similar to what happens when Yahweh fights against his own people. Of course, the Gog

---

[7]Revelation 7:4-8 is a census or counting of the tribes of Israel (new Israel in the theology of Revelation). As noted by Richard Bauckham (*The Theology of the Book of Revelation*, NTT [Cambridge: Cambridge University Press, 1993], 77), the census within Israel was "always a reckoning of the military strength of the nation, in which only males of military age were counted." See Ex 30:1-11; Num 1:1-43; 2:1-34; 26:1-51; Is 11:11-16. Aside from military counting 12,000 from each tribe, the 144,000 are viewed as males who did "not defile themselves with women" (Rev 14:4). The purity of the male 144,000 likely indicates at a thematic allusion level the notion of war preparations (see Deut 23:9-14), as when David's troops abstain from all sexual relations while on campaign (1 Sam 21:5; 2 Sam 11:9-13; see also Is 31:4-5; 24:23; Ps 149:2). See Craig S. Keener, *Revelation*, NIVAC (Grand Rapids: Zondervan, 2000), 371; Grant R. Osborne, *Revelation*, BECNT (Grand Rapids: Baker Academic, 2002), 529. The background war allusions are then carried into John's present-day reality, namely, the sexual abstinence from Jezebel and the false cults (both idolatry and banned sexuality in the pagan temples; Rev 2:14; see also Rev 2:20) within the seven letters.

and Magog traditions from Ezekiel also serve as a basis for the final battle of Revelation 19–20 (whether a battle fought in two parts or one single battle).[8]

Similarity three: Holy war and idolatry objectives. The objective of eliminating idolatry—at the heart of Old Testament holy war—is also found at the core of the war material in Revelation. That solidifies the connection. There should be no doubt about the intentional ties. Jesus fights with his holy war sword against those who "hold to the teaching of Balaam, who taught Balak to entice the Israelites so that they ate food sacrificed to idols and committed sexual immorality" (Rev 2:14; see also Rev 2:20). Similarly, the saints are seen as fighting in a holy war against the beast; they must not be seduced into false worship of the beast and his image, an expression of idolatry (Rev 13:8, 12, 15; 14:11; 16:2; 19:20; 20:4). In sum, John clearly sees the warlike battle of the saints and Jesus in line with the holy war battles of old, intent on keeping God's people away from idolatry.[9]

Not surprisingly, then, we agree with scholars who see war in the book of Revelation as thematically connected to Yahweh's holy war within the Old Testament. Jesus functions as the ultimate apocalyptic warrior who carries the story line forward with the conquest of the entire earth as a new Eden, a land undefiled by the pollution of idolatry. Furthermore, we readily acknowledge that the war portrait of the book of Revelation, at least in terms of its rhetoric (an important qualification), *seems* just as violent and grotesque as the Old Testament war passages.

That is where our agreement ends. We do not agree that Jesus as apocalyptic warrior somehow legitimizes the ethics of Old Testament holy war. Rather, we would suggest that the continuity between Old Testament holy war and New Testament apocalyptic battle themes lies primarily at an abstracted level (conflict, defeat, triumph, etc.) while moving the story line toward an ultimate resolution and climax. Yet, that ultimate pattern or thematic fulfillment is achieved through a strikingly different kind of warfare—

---

[8]Whether Rev 19:11-21; 20:7-10 are viewed as two battles with one thousand intervening years between them (premillennial) or as one single battle (amillennial), both of John's texts have source material that is derived from Ezekiel's Magog battle.

[9]For a helpful overview of idolatry in Roman Asia Minor see David A. deSilva, *Unholy Allegiances: Heeding Revelation's Warning* (Peabody, MA: Hendrickson, 2013), 11-34; J. Nelson Kraybill, *Apocalypse and Allegiance: Worship, Politics, and Devotion in the Book of Revelation* (Grand Rapids: Brazos, 2010), 53-70.

not with literal bloodshed or literal weapons. In short, citing Jesus' apocalyptic battle as grounds for approving all that is ethically problematic within Old Testament holy war fails to see the transformative nature of the rhetoric and reality in Revelation. This ethical insight becomes clear as one explores the differences between Old Testament and New Testament holy war.

THE DIFFERENCES

What distinguishes Jesus' apocalyptic holy war in the book of Revelation from Yahweh's holy war in the Old Testament? Here are seven differences to explore.

Difference one: No indiscriminate slaughter of noncombatants. First, unlike Old Testament holy war that included the indiscriminate killing of noncombatants—the elderly, women, children, and babies (at least at a rhetorical level in the text)—there is no comparably indiscriminate war slaughter in the book of Revelation. In fact, holy war in the Apocalypse is always seen as a matter of choice either to follow the beast (by taking his mark) or to follow the Lamb (by taking his mark; Rev 13:14-17; 16:2; 19:20; 20:4; see also Rev 14:9-11). None of the war scenes in Revelation suggest the killing of infants or babies. The language places the warriors in the category of adults who are fighting holy war by choice. In the final apocalyptic battle it is the dragon, the two beasts, the kings of the earth, and their armies (all adult language and that of military combatants) who have gathered to make war against the rider on the white horse and his army.[10]

Difference two: No ethnic annihilation/genocide. A second difference in the holy war described in the book of Revelation is the absence of any ethnic annihilation rhetoric, since the eschatological battle crosses ethnic and national boundaries. There is not even the hint of genocide within the New

---

[10]In Rev 2:16 Jesus the apocalyptic warrior proclaims: "I will soon come to you [plural; whole congregation] and will fight against them [subgroup of Balaam/Jezebel-like people] with the sword of my mouth." As with the final apocalyptic battle, this usage of Jesus' sword is also not literal, does not involve indiscriminate total killing of the whole group, and depicts a reality that has multiple levels of causation. Revelation 2:12, 16 carries the Old Testament holy war theme along the lines of reverse holy war (Isaiah and Jeremiah), where Yahweh attacks his own people (here Jesus attacks part of the church). But unlike Old Testament holy war, in this apocalyptic holy war battle within the church there are no indiscriminate mass graves (attacking the whole community) or virgins granted as incentives for participants on the good side.

Testament text. Unlike Old Testament holy war rhetoric, which seems at times to include helpless victims caught in the tragedy of ethnicity and geography—born to the wrong parents, in the wrong place, and at the wrong time—any overtones of such ethnic slaughter are absent from apocalyptic holy war. In fact, the reverse is true. The armies in the final apocalyptic battle are drawn from "all the kings of the earth"—every nation, tribe, and tongue. This is similar to the complete ethnic diversity found among those who follow the Lamb and are a part of his armies. On neither side of the battle are the armies defined by ethnic labels.[11]

If one ponders these first two dissimilarities together, a markedly different war portrait emerges in the Apocalypse compared to the ethnically and geo-graphically focused killing of Canaanites. The diverse ethnicity of the war-riors on both sides of the apocalyptic battle—every nation, tribe, and tongue—maximizes the factor of choice. The choice is not forced or mired by racial connections or land ties. Their fate in war is not sealed simply due to factors over which they have no control. Ethnicity and geography in apoc-alyptic war do not create an added dimension of entangled mess that plays out so prominently in Old Testament holy war.

Difference three: No reward of good-looking virgins. One of the more problematic features of Old Testament holy war is that male warriors are granted the option of taking attractive females from the spoils of battle. In the Jesus war texts, however, there is a transformation in both rhetoric and reality, so that a third difference in apocalyptic holy war is that it involves no promise or enshrined right for males to obtain good-looking virgins from among the captive women. Continuity lies in the fact that Jesus also promises rewards to the overcomers (better translated "conquerors"): "To him who overcomes/conquers I will give [these promises]." The victory promises that the Lamb later distributes to his army include eating from the tree of life (Rev 2:7), not being hurt by the second death (Rev 2:11), enjoying the eschato-logical banquet (Rev 2:17), reigning over the nations (Rev 2:26), dressing in

---

[11] The 144,000 from Israel should not be understood as an ethnic or limited people-group identity; John makes clear that figure (note the transition from hearing to seeing) with the reality of a great multitude from every nation and tongue. The two groups—144,000 and the great multitude—are the same in Rev 7 and part of John's transformative language. See further discussion below.

white (Rev 3:5), being made a pillar in the new temple (Rev 3:12), and even sitting with Christ on the throne (Rev 3:21).[12]

None of these promised rewards has a male-dominated perspective or outcome. The conquerors are not defined by gender, and rewards are equally shared by male and female followers of Jesus. More importantly, no offer or promise of female virgins—eternally ready for sensual service—becomes an incentive for male warriors. Instead, the war ideology of the Old Testament is transformed within the New Testament into a different and far better eschatological reality. All followers of the Lamb—both male and female—in a collective sense are seen as a virgin and bride of Christ, and that by choice, not by coercion or force.[13]

Difference four: The final battle is really no battle at all. A fourth difference—and this is a big one—is that the greatest battle of apocalyptic holy war is no literal battle whatsoever. The meaning is metaphorical. A number of clues suggest that John never intended the apocalyptic battle to be read literally.

First clue: Only one "little" weapon.[14] The entire battle of Revelation 19 is fought with only one weapon—one little sword. Jesus brings no chariots of war, nor any of the monstrous military equipment known to Roman armies of John's day. He brings only a sword onto the battlefield against the amassed weapons of all the kings of the earth and their armies. This is a David-and-Goliath encounter if there ever was one. Jesus is severely outgunned, or shall we say outsworded, in this showdown. If we carry the eschatological battle forward into today's context, then all of this world's most powerful weapons are pitted against one little sword. The imbalance is absurd and points to a nonliteral or metaphorical understanding of the final battle.

Second clue: Only one warrior fights with the one sword. While vast armies follow Jesus into the final battle, it appears that only the warrior-king

---

[12]In fact, the whole of the new Jerusalem and the new heavens and earth are given to the Lamb's followers (his conquerors) for ruling with Christ in a democratized or shared Davidic covenant: "He who triumphs/conquers [*nikaō* language] will inherit all this, and I will be his God and he will be my son" (Rev 21:7).

[13]See the 144,000. Taken literally they are 144,000 (12,000 from each of the twelve tribes of Israel) males who "did not defile themselves with women." Yet this is a portrait of the entire church from every ethnicity and gender, since the figure is made clear and transformed with its reality in the second half of Rev 7.

[14]Note the citation of Martin Luther's hymn later for the inclusion of "little" here. Our primary point at this juncture is that the weaponry on Jesus' side includes only *one* weapon.

himself does the killing. John writes that after the beast and the false prophet are captured, "The rest [i.e., the kings of the earth and their armies mentioned earlier; Rev 19:19] were killed with the sword coming out of the mouth of the rider on the horse" (Rev 19:21).[15] The kings of the earth and their armies are killed in battle by only one horse rider with only one weapon. This is indeed unusual, if taken literally, since it does not conform to the way normal battles are fought. Imagine a Roman general leading a massive army and being the only one to swing a sword; his armies simply watch for the duration of the battle. This departure from normal military practice suggests that John is purposefully transforming the rhetoric to engage his readers with a different, nonliteral reality.[16]

Third clue: A sword in the mouth, not in the hand. Twice in the final battle story the sword that Jesus uses to strike down the foe is said to come from his mouth (Rev 19:15, 21). The sword is not held in the rider's hand or tucked away safely in its sheath. This additional departure from standard military practice offers yet another clue about how John is transforming the language.[17] Obviously, the sword in the mouth is not literal any more than the battle itself is literal. Rather, the location of the sword in Jesus' mouth (the place where one speaks) aligns nicely with the name Jesus is given in this war context; he is called "the Word of God" (Rev 19:13).[18] The final apocalyptic battle is not fought by normal weapons such as swords and spears (Rev 19:13).[19] No, it is fought with the word of Christ. As Martin Luther's hymn puts it, "One little word shall fell them."[20]

---

[15]"The rest" in Rev 19:21 refers back to Rev 19:19 and those who were left after the capture of the beast and the false prophet. From Rev 19:19 the clearest referent would be "the kings of the earth and their armies."

[16]The clue of Jesus alone fighting (not the saints) in the final battle converges with the call of Revelation for saints to be faithful witnesses and, if need be, martyrs. See Stephen Pattermore, *The People of God in the Apocalypse: Discourse, Structure and Exegesis* (Cambridge: Cambridge University Press, 2004), 195.

[17]One is tempted to wonder what Mary (Jesus' mother) would say if she saw her son riding along with a sword in his mouth. Would he accidentally swallow it? Would the steel break his teeth? Would the galloping motion of the horse make it hard to hold and swing?

[18]David L. Barr, "Doing Violence: Moral Issues in Reading John's Apocalypse," in *Reading the Book of Revelation: A Resource for Students*, ed. David L. Barr (Atlanta: Society of Biblical Literature, 2003), 97-108.

[19]Compare 4 Ezra [Esdras] 13:9, "[He]neither lifted his hand nor held a spear or any weapon of war."

[20]"A Mighty Fortress Is Our God" was composed by Martin Luther between 1527 and 1529

Original creation is spoken into existence by God, and now with one word Christ ushers in the new creation.

Fourth clue: All of humanity is united (not divided) in war against God. The apocalyptic war of Revelation 19, in featuring united forces, is unlike battles normally fought by humans and thus radically unlike the battles fought by Israel in holy war. In normal human battles, the kings of the earth are split into rival factions; one group of kings and countries battles against another group. However, in the book of Revelation the final battle has nothing to do with a split between opposing human armies, that is, some countries perhaps aligned with Israel fighting against other countries who seek to wipe out Israel. No, such popular ideas have no basis in the book of Revelation. Rather, the apocalyptic battle is a completely unusual battle in that *all* the kings of the earth and their people are aligned together to fight against God (Rev 19:19; see Rev 16:12-16 [Rev 16:14: "the kings of the whole world"]; Rev 20:7-8).[21] That the final battle unites all earthly rulers to fight against God provides yet another clue about how John wants us to understand this holy war.

In sum, these several clues from apocalyptic holy war confront us with the probability that no literal battle actually happens. Jesus speaks one word, and the "battle" instantaneously comes to its conclusion. The great apocalyptic battle, for all of its war-rhetoric staging, invites the reader to understand its fulfillment in simply one word spoken by Christ. A metaphorical understanding still means that it is real—very real. Jesus' metaphorical sword brings justice by forever ending the injustice of this world (the final battle shuts the doors on Babylon-like powers inflicting any further pain and suffering), and thus it answers the prayers of the souls under the altar who cry out for justice (Rev 6:9-10). Jesus fights for justice as an apocalyptic warrior in a *metaphorical sense* (one word will fell them) by ending the reign of every evil power on the earth and in the cosmos. Furthermore, we will see below

---

with obvious allusions to the book of Revelation and the military fortress envisioned in Ps 46.

[21] Steven J. Friesen comments, "This conflict between the churches and those who worship the Beast dominates the latter half of the book. This is not two equal communities facing off; John portrays it as a small network of faithful witnesses against everyone else" (*Imperial Cults and the Apocalypse of John: Reading Revelation in the Ruins* [Oxford: Oxford University Press, 2001], 192).

that justice expands from the final battle into a second phase with a great-white-throne encounter with Christ that enacts perfectly just justice.

Difference five: No eternal driving out of all "Canaanites" from the new Eden. A fifth difference of holy war in Revelation is an even greater emphasis on and opportunity for transforming the enemy. In Old Testament conquests one encounters minor exceptions to the rule of total kill or its functional equivalent, "Drive them out of the land." For example, the Gibeonites are not driven out or killed because they trick the Israelites into making a covenant with them. Rahab and her family are welcomed into the Israelite fold because they fight subversively (they hide Israel's spies) against their own people. Yet, other than these occasional exceptions (even if paradigmatic of other occurrences), the standard rule is to make no covenants with the Canaanite people of the land. At least at a rhetorical level, all rebel Canaanites within the land have to be killed or expelled.

Trace the theme of the hostile nations and kings of the earth throughout the book of Revelation, however, and we discover an unexpected twist in the story line. In the Old Testament the foreign nations living in Canaan had to be moved out. But what is remarkably different about apocalyptic holy war is that we find *some* of the formerly hostile kings of the earth and the nations (the greatest enemies in the final apocalyptic battle) participating in the new heavens and the new earth.[22] What a surprise! It is unlikely that this transformation of the most ardent war enemies into followers of Jesus teaches universalism. No, the final judgment themes within the book are far too dominant to suggest otherwise. But it does say *something*.[23] It suggests that

---

[22]Revelation 21:24, "the nations and . . . the kings of the earth will bring their splendor into it"; Rev 21:26; 22:2. See Allan J. McNicol, *The Conversion of the Nations in Revelation*, LNTS 438 (London: T&T Clark, 2011), 75-82.

[23]Osborne writes, "What is surprising is that it is the 'kings of the earth' who enter the New Jerusalem. Earlier they aligned themselves with the beast (17:2, 18; 18:3, 9), led the armies at Armageddon (16:16; 19:19), and therefore were destroyed with those armies (19:21). In Isa 60:3 it is 'kings,' so John has deliberately stressed 'the kings of the earth.' He evidently wishes to emphasize how God's mercy ultimately triumphs over evil and has redeemed some even from among 'the kings of the earth'" (Osborne, *Revelation*, 763). See also Stubblefield ("Function of the Church in Warfare," 202), who similarly writes, "The most frequent usage of the phrase 'the kings of the earth' indicates rebellious leaders in league with Babylon (e.g., 6:15; 17:2, 18). This is exactly what makes 21:24-26 such a stunning reversal for the fate of the nations in the created order." Like Osborne, Stubblefield presents this view of wider hope of redemption in Revelation without adopting a universalist position or

at least *some* of those enemies who die in the final battle participate as the redeemed in the new heavens and earth. Not all of the eschatological Canaanites, if you will, are forever banned from the eternal Promised Land. Unexpectedly, some of them find their way into the eternal holy land and bring their glory into the new Jerusalem.[24]

Perhaps this greater emphasis on and potential for enemy transformation (compared with Old Testament holy war) is related to yet another factor—the sixth difference.

Difference six: No more one-size-fits-all justice. The justice and judgment of Old Testament holy war is in a sense brutally impersonal. Everyone is either killed or driven out of the land; the justice could be described as one size fits all, at least in its rhetoric. But this type of monolithic justice is not the case in apocalyptic holy war.

Compared with the impersonal and ill-fitted justice of Old Testament holy war, one discovers a far better justice in apocalyptic theology, since John ties together the great-white-throne judgment (Rev 20) and the white-horse battle (Rev 19). The great white throne is not a separate, disconnected event from apocalyptic holy war; it is the aftermath of the battle, where the victorious king decides what to do with the captives. It functions as the concluding phase—the finalized justice—of the apocalyptic battle. Since there is no literal battle in the book of Revelation, the reality of John's transformed war rhetoric lies in a spoken word that ushers in Christ as king and judge of the earth. The battle announcement describing the rider on the white horse as one who "with justice . . . judges and wages war" (Rev 19:11) thus anticipates the post-battle judgment phase. John's war rhetoric must be understood not only as a spoken word (it is finished), which carries us into a new world, but also as the great-white-throne event (word and act) that immediately follows.

---

attempting to quantify the outcome. See also David Matthewson, "The Nations in Revelation," *TynBul* 53 (2002): 121-42.

[24]A similar story of apocalyptic grace and repentance with a surprise twist is found in Rev 11:13 (see 1 Kings 19:18). The apocalyptic text echoes 1 Kings 19:18 but with the reversal. Instead of the typical *one-tenth* survival rate (only 7,000 live), in the earthquake collapse of the great city *nine-tenths* survive (only 7,000 die), and it appears, given the weight of evidence, that the survivors have a genuine change of heart and find redemption. These strange turns of grace within the story (war enemies switching sides to follow the Lamb) happen either at the last glimpse of light in the old creation order or, in the case of the kings of the earth, even after the final battle word of Christ—"it is finished"—is spoken.

Hopefully we can now see the better justice that apocalyptic holy war offers compared with its Old Testament antecedents. War justice comes ultimately at the throne-room judgment scene in Revelation 20. At that final judgment the focus is on what each individual has done. The repeated emphasis in twenty or so biblical judgment texts is on the works/deeds of each person; there is no group assessment or collective judgment.[25] God weighs the actions and heart of every single individual. All human beings give an account of their lives. We would suggest that it is here—at the final judgment (the continued-justice stage of the holy war battle)—that God takes into account all of the fallen-world injustices that have affected human lives, and he separates the finally unrepentant from the repentant. If God embodies ultimate justice in a profound and absolutely pristine way (and we believe he does), then he will use this opportunity to undo the injustices of all of human history, even the injustices created within Old Testament holy war. After all, Old Testament holy war represents divine justice, but of an accommodated, fallen-world sort—justice shaped by a rugged, tattered, and torn world.

Difference seven: The saints fight with weapons of virtue (not violence). A seventh and final difference with apocalyptic war is that the saints fight only with their virtue, not with physical violence. As one reads Revelation, the saints are pictured as fighting in an ongoing apocalyptic battle with weapons of virtue and character. Instead of swords and spears, their weapons are faithfulness, truth, martyrdom, the word of God, the testimony of Jesus, and the blood of the Lamb. Revelation 12:9-11 highlights these conquering weapons even if, ironically, military triumph for Christians comes through their own death:[26]

---

[25]Job 34:11, 25; Ps 62:12; Prov 24:12; Eccles 12:14; Jer 17:10; 32:19; Ezek 33:20; Hos 4:7-9; 12:2; Mt 12:34-36; 16:27; 25:31-46; Jn 3:20; 5:28-29; Rom 2:5-8; 14:10-12; 2 Cor 5:10; Rev 2:23; 22:11-12. For a recent development of the subject, see Alan P. Stanley, ed., *Four Views on the Role of Works at the Final Judgment* (Grand Rapids: Zondervan, 2013).

[26]Michael's war and his victory are inseparable from the war and victory of the saints. Believers defeat the dragon through the blood of the Lamb *and* their own faithfulness unto death. See Bauckham, *Theology of the Book of Revelation*, 75; see also G. K. Beale, *The Book of Revelation*, NIGTC (Grand Rapids: Eerdmans, 1999), 269. In Rev 15:2, as in Rev 5:5, those who are victorious have conquered by remaining faithful through death. Roy R. Millhouse captures the irony well: "For the people of God in the book of Revelation, conquering is not killing; it is remaining faithful to their testimony, even if it meant their being killed." See Millhouse, "Re-Imaging the Warrior: Divine Warrior Imagery in the Book of Revelation" (PhD diss., Baylor University, 2012), 386. For the connection between faithful witness and the resultant death of Christians in Revelation as part of the war theme, see Antoninus King

The great dragon was hurled down—that ancient serpent called the devil, or
Satan, who leads the whole world astray. He was hurled to the earth, and his
angels with him.

Then I heard a loud voice in heaven say:

"Now have come the salvation and the power
    and the kingdom of our God,
    and the authority of his Christ.
For the accuser of our brothers,
    who accuses them before our God day and night,
    has been hurled down.
They [the saints] triumphed over [nikaō] him
    by the blood of the Lamb
    and by the word of their testimony;
they did not love their lives so much
    as to shrink from death." (Rev 12:9-11)

I, John, your brother and companion in the suffering and kingdom and patient
endurance that are ours in Jesus, was on the island of Patmos *because of the*
word of God and the testimony of Jesus. (Rev 1:9)

When he opened the fifth seal, I saw under the altar the souls of *those who had*
been slain because of the word of God and the testimony they had maintained.
(Rev 6:9)

And I saw the souls of those who had been beheaded *because of their testimony*
about Jesus and because of the word of God. They had not worshiped the beast
or its image and had not received its mark on their foreheads or their hands.
(Rev 20:4)

The same irony and transformation of war triumph for Christians is mirrored
in the Christology of the book. The military triumph of the Lion is achieved
through his death as a Lamb, not through physical violence and killing.[27] In
Revelation 5:5-6 the contextual referent of *nikaō* (triumph) is Christ's death
on the cross as that which establishes his right to open the seals:

Wai Siew, *The War Between the Two Beasts and the Two Witnesses*, LNTS 283 (Edinburgh:
T&T Clark, 2005), 272-77; Stubblefield, "Function of the Church in Warfare," 185-92.

[27]War victory is seen earlier in Rev 3:21 as *already* accomplished in the death of Christ (and
in the death of his followers), since the victory occurs before Christ is seated on the throne:
"To him who is victorious [*nikaō*], I will give the right to sit with me on my throne, just as
I was victorious [*nikaō*], and sat down with my Father on his throne."

> Then one of the elders said to me, "Do not weep! *See, the Lion of the tribe of Judah, the Root of David, has triumphed* [*nikaō*]. He is able to open the scroll and its seven seals."
>
> *Then I saw* [not a Lion but] *a Lamb, looking as if it had been slain*, standing in the center of the throne, encircled by the four living creatures and the elders. The Lamb had seven horns and seven eyes, which are the seven spirits of God sent out into all the earth. (Rev 5:5-6)

The classic transition in John's apocalypse between first *hearing* an announcement and then *seeing* something strangely different should cause us to stop and ponder.[28] John hears about one thing (a Lion) but then sees something quite different (a Lamb, looking slain). The most powerful of images—a lion—is transformed by the image of a lamb. The power of the lion imagery is not eliminated, since the slain Lamb hardly lacks might: the Lamb stands in the center of God's throne—the most powerful place in the universe—and the Lamb has seven horns. But the slain Lamb imagery suggests that the methods of Jesus' power and rule differ from those of this world.

Richard Hays captures the imagery transformation well: "The shock of this reversal discloses the central mystery of the apocalypse: God overcomes the world not through a show of [violent military] force but through the suffering and death of Jesus, 'The faithful witness.'"[29] The imagery of standing at the center of the throne and seven horns clearly retains the image of power (true of the Lion), but ironically power is now seen as accomplished and enacted by the slain Lamb.[30] Victory and power within

---

[28]As in Rev 5:5-6, a transition and surprising juxtaposition between hearing and seeing comes in Rev 7. Rev 6 anticipates a number for those who will be slain before God brings justice. The number is then announced in Rev 7, and John hears that number: 144,000. Then he sees the content of the number in a transformed way: the 144,000 are in fact the great multitude! One component of this hearing-then-seeing transition in Rev 7 is to understand the church as those who function as the new/true Israel (in contrast to ethnic Israel/Jews who are not seen as true Israel; see Rev 2:9; 3:9).

[29]Richard B. Hays, *The Moral Vision of the New Testament: Community, Cross, New Creation: A Contemporary Introduction to New Testament Ethics* (New York: HarperSanFrancisco, 1996), 175; see also David L. Barr, "The Lamb Who Looks like a Dragon: Characterizing Jesus in John's Apocalypse," in *The Reality of Apocalypse: Rhetoric and Politics in the Book of Revelation*, ed. David L. Barr (Atlanta: Society of Biblical Literature, 2006), 209.

[30]The lamb does not remove or replace the lion; the two images should be taken together. However, the dominant usage of Lamb Christology (twenty-eight times) compared with Lion Christology (only once in Rev 5:5 and perhaps a second time in Rev 10:3), along with

Revelation come through being faithful unto death, sacrificial death.[31]

When compared with Old Testament holy war, where military conquest was achieved through slaughtering one's enemies with weapons of bronze and iron, this ironic and highly transformed language about achieving victory through being faithful even unto death places apocalyptic holy war into a far more noble and virtuous category. We may not want to hear it (for it sounds strange to the ear), but a theology of the slain lamb (Rev 5:5-6) along with the slain saints (Rev 6:9-10) is what empowers victory in the eschatological battle.[32]

CONCLUSION

Given the weight of evidence, the portrait of Jesus as an apocalyptic warrior should be interpreted in a metaphorical (not literal) sense. With one word he will fell the enemy and usher in the new heavens and new earth. A portrait of Yahweh as an uneasy/reluctant warrior God derived from the subversive war texts of the Old Testament (chapter fourteen) merges well with the one-spoken-word portrait of Jesus as apocalyptic warrior (chapter sixteen). This is especially true if one considers that the apocalyptic Jesus portrait is the end of the story within canonical development and unencumbered by the weight of Israel's war practices departing from Yahweh's desired path.

Significant ethical implications flow from examining the similarities and differences between the Testaments. First, the understanding of Jesus as equal or more violent in the book of Revelation distorts the meaning of John's Apocalypse and wrongly uses continuity at a thematic level to legitimize the problematic ethics of Old Testament holy war. Yes, continuity

---

the surprise hearing-seeing transition of the lion image in Rev 5:5-6, strongly argues that the norms of power have been reshaped and redefined by Christ's sacrificial death.

[31]In contrast to the exploitive power of Babylon/Rome (power used for its own drunken and gluttonous consumption), Jesus derives and uses his power in a strikingly different manner, namely, for the sacrificial benefit of others. Millhouse states, "In the book of Revelation, the Messianic Divine Warrior always conquers in a manner antithetical to the way the present-day order conquers. The text not only guides John's audience to this conclusion, it sets forth the same challenge to the audience. Roman power—or any other power in this order—exploits for victory; divine power sacrifices itself. The rider on the white horse is the Lamb standing as slain, even as the Lamb standing as slain is the Lion of the Judah who conquered" ("Re-Imaging the Warrior," 342).

[32]For an excellent development of slain-Lamb theology and its relationship to the army of martyrs in Revelation see Bauckham, *Theology of the Book of Revelation*, 73-80.

plays an important part of the story line of Scripture as we head toward a new Eden. God's sacred space now covers the entire earth (not just Palestine), and idolatry must be banished so that the whole of humanity can live in harmony and intimacy with God. But the apocalyptic portrait of Jesus fighting in the final battle neither minimizes nor magically justifies the atrocities of Old Testament holy war. That sort of reasoning should be recognized and rejected as faulty.

Instead, Christians need to discover in the Apocalypse of John a far more positive and inspiring way of untangling the ethics of biblical holy war. The apocalyptic ending to the Bible's redemptive story brings to us an exciting and hopeful picture. It unfolds a vision of God's unaccommodated ethical actions finally bringing the enactment of justice without embedded injustices; Jesus as the apocalyptic warrior transforms Old Testament war traditions. The apocalyptic battle of Revelation engages the reader with ethical development at a rhetorical and even more so a reality level. In apocalyptic holy war there will be:

- ▶ no indiscriminate slaughter of women and children

- ▶ no ethnically focused annihilation or genocide

- ▶ no taking virgin females as a reward for male warriors

- ▶ no military battle at all—just one word (*metaphorical* meaning) from the mouth of Christ

- ▶ a greater chance for even the most ardent of enemies to end up among the redeemed

- ▶ a more personalized and authentic-encounter form of justice (not one size fits all)

- ▶ a battle won with a different set of weapons: faithfulness, the word of God, and, ironically, martyrdom of saints (depicted as an army of martyrs) who mirror the death of Christ

Yes, the apocalyptic version of holy war thematically continues the Old Testament story line, but its use of holy war ideology markedly differs from the Old Testament, and it contains in those differences significant ethical development. This redemptive development within the canonical story line offers a climactic and hopeful finish. The greatest hope of the apocalyptic ending is found in the war theme once its *rhetoric* (the figure of speech of the "final battle") is cleared away and aligned inseparably with the judgment scene that follows. The final *reality* carries us into the pristine beauty of God's well-measured, individually based dealings with humanity in ways that are no longer diluted or tainted by this fallen world.[33]

Even so, come Lord Jesus.

---

[33]For readers with lingering questions about violence in John's Apocalypse, see appendix I.

CONCLUSION

The Unfinished Justice Story

IN THESE CLOSING PAGES we unpack our final better answer. We have saved this answer—the very best of the better answers—to the end because this answer carries forward the redemptive elements that we have already discovered into God's ultimate justice. This concluding focus merges well with the ethical insights we have gathered from the study of biblical war texts within their ANE setting. But most of all, this last answer reminds us of still more to come in God's unfinished justice story.

A GAP REMAINS

At the close of this book on holy war ethics, we recognize that a significant ethical gap remains. We have not solved everything. Our reading of the biblical war texts continues to trouble us, and we still consider them to be bloody, brutal, and barbaric. That much has not changed. Furthermore, it is not likely to change in this lifetime, given our deeply ingrained Hague-and-Geneva war horizons.

Yet something good has happened. We do not want to minimize the positive part of the experience. Our hearts are not nearly as heavy nor our minds as perplexed as when we first started this project. We have come to read both the total-kill and war-rape texts far differently from when we started this book fourteen years ago. While not knowing exactly where the evidence would take us, we are profoundly thankful for new ways of reading and understanding these war passages. Our journey of rethinking the biblical war texts has permitted us to look through an ancient-world window and appreciate what shines strikingly redemptively in the ethical darkness. We have cataloged, chapter by chapter, a series of what we believe are better answers—better than the traditional answers that we formerly held—regarding the ethics of holy war in Scripture.

Nevertheless, an ethical gap remains between (1) the better answers we have discovered and discussed in this book and (2) our belief in a God who is pristine in his justice and ethics in a fully (not just partially) realized and enacted sense. On the one hand, this book has helped us close the gap with various small, medium, and even dramatically large elements of redemptive movement within the biblical war texts, especially when paired with the subversive war portraits of Yahweh (and Jesus) as reluctant participants in the violence that plagues our broken world. It has permitted us to sense God at work in even the ugliest of war scenes. On the other hand, we encounter many elements of unresolved justice or embedded unfairness in instances of fallen-world justice within the biblical war texts.

Ultimately, our final better answer to the ethics of biblical warfare looks to the future, when God can and will, based on his revealed character, resolve *all* (no hyperbole here) temporal injustice questions through an eternal turning of the tables. Helping to close the ethical gap is a final better answer derived from Pauline theology (and elsewhere), namely, the eternal weight of glory.

CLOSING THE GAP: THE ETERNAL WEIGHT OF GLORY

Our final better answer to troubling war ethics in Scripture is what the apostle Paul identifies as "the eternal weight of glory" (2 Cor 4:17 NASB). Paul calls his considerable present-world suffering "momentary, light affliction" *compared with* the eternal weight of glory. With many biblical authors, Paul envisions a compensatory or turning-of-the-tables element that will mark the greatness and grandeur of our future life in the presence of God.

Just to be clear, Paul's present-day suffering was *not* light or momentary—anything but. In fact, 2 Corinthians contains three lengthy catalogs (2 Cor 4:8-12; 6:4-10; 11:23-29) that describe in detail the pain and injustice Paul experienced in ministry. Nevertheless, Paul can say that in a *comparative* sense the eternal weight of glory is so unimaginably wonderful that from the perspective of the eschaton looking back—when we've been there ten thousand years—even the harshest pains and injustices of this life will by comparison seem merely momentary, light afflictions.

This theme of eschatological reversal is common in Scripture. John in his apocalyptic vision encourages his readers to persevere through suffering because someday they will reign with Christ. Readers are repeatedly alerted to their eschatological destiny as kings and priests (Rev 1:6; 5:10; 20:4-6; 22:3-4); the Davidic covenant is rewritten with fulfillment extending now to the entire community (Rev 21:7). Coregency with Christ entails a destiny of ruling in some way over the new heavens and new earth (Rev 21:7). C. S. Lewis captured the imagination and wonder of these biblical texts with his four thrones of Cair Paravel for the sons of Adam and the daughters of Eve.[1]

The prophets similarly speak about a future day for God's people when the brokenness and pain of this world—its river of tears—will be replaced with laughter, joy, and dancing (Is 25:8; 35:10; 51:11; Jer 31:12-13; see Rev 7:17; 21:4). Even God's own tears (Is 16:9; Jer 9:1) over his reluctant, heart-wrenching participation in human warfare will come to an end when the swords of this world are beaten into plowshares (Is 2:4; Mic 4:3).[2] The joy of the eschaton will be of such a magnitude and duration that present-world tears, sorrow, and brokenness will be transformed into a far deeper and more meaningful experience of eternal bliss.

Thus, the final better answer is simply this: *someday God will make everything right*. He will right all wrongs at the great white throne of justice. He is at heart a profoundly compensatory, table-turning God. He is a God of perfect justice and love. That being so, he will correct every drop of injustice within the culturally rooted and seemingly ill-fitting justice that we encounter in the biblical war texts and in all of our personal experiences. Another chapter of the justice story takes place in the next world and for all of eternity—that's a long time. Not everything is resolved in this lifetime. The authors of Scripture beckon us to wait expectantly for a future day and trust that God's justice story is still unfolding. At present, we are called to believe in an *unfinished* justice story.

Someone might ask, "What about nonbelievers? How does this turning-the-tables theme affect them?" It is one thing to see how the eternal weight

---

[1]In the Chronicles of Narnia, the four thrones for Peter, Lucy, Edmund, and Susan are representative of broader human destiny.

[2]See the discussion of Yahweh as a crying war God in chapter fourteen.

of glory compensates believers for injustices and hardships experienced within the brutalities of this world (even as collateral damage from reluctant but divinely directed war actions). However, how does this future recompense answer apply to nonbelievers? Here we must consider (1) the individually based nature of the great-white-throne judgment alongside (2) the God who turns the tables on injustices in the eschaton. If God's character does not change based on the person he is addressing (believer or nonbeliever), then God's "I will fix injustice" nature will inform everything that is part of the eternal treatment of believers and nonbelievers. Since the final judgment is individually based (no "one size fits all"; Rev 20:11-15), the complexities of each human life can be weighed and given a fair assessment.[3] God's compensatory, righting-all-wrongs character does not change when addressing nonbelievers.

So this is our final better answer: *the justice story is not yet finished*. Ethical deficiencies of this present world are not to be swept under the carpet. Many unresolved or embedded elements of injustice within fallen-world enactments of justice will be corrected on a future day. The biblical story line encourages us to believe in a God of complete and profoundly pristine justice who will someday right all wrongs. He will do so in the case of believers and nonbelievers, for his character does not change.

THIS WAR BOOK WITHIN A SPECTRUM OF VIEWS

This book reflects our fourteen-year journey in rethinking the biblical war texts and wrestling with their troubling ethics. Like many Christians now, we struggle with the ethics of seeming genocide (total kill, including women and children) and war rape (forcibly taking female captives as wives) in Scripture. The intersection between violence and religion in our contemporary media—almost a daily occurrence—pushes us to ask serious ethical questions about how we understand holy war within the biblical story line.

This book unfolds our findings about the ethics of holy war texts within a larger spectrum of competing views. We can present our findings in several thesis statements:

---

[3]See chapter sixteen and how the pristine, untainted, individualized (no "one size fits all") justice helps as a better answer.

Thesis one: Square pegs, round holes. The traditional answers to the ethics of holy war (God's holiness, the evil of the Canaanites, etc.) are good answers, but not for our contemporary ethical questions about genocide and war rape. The traditional answers fit well when aligned with the ethical and justice questions of the original readers—questions all the way through Scripture but especially crystallized in the eyes of the exilic and postexilic community. Their questions were more about the justice of God in driving out various literary Canaanites (the Israelites themselves included) in creating sacred space and a new Eden. The original readers would not have been troubled by the ethical problems that we have addressed—total-kill rhetoric and the domestic version of war rape included within Scripture. These issues, understood within the extremes of ancient war violence, would not likely have been on their radar.

Thesis two: Total-kill rhetoric as hyperbole. We have argued that the biblical authors used total-kill language in a hyperbolic (not literal) fashion. Understanding the biblical war texts within the war genre of the ancient world aids our ethical assessment by creating a zero marking on the ethical baseline. The biblical authors, like other ANE writers, used hyperbolic total-kill rhetoric to describe the reality of a sound defeat (along with communicating an emotive element). Despite good intentions, the traditional position creates its own ethical problem (genocide, the killing of babies, etc.) by holding literally to the total-kill language. The evidence for hyperbole presented in five chapters and three appendixes far outweighs any grounds for literalism.

Thesis three: Divine accommodation. This book makes a case throughout for recognizing ways in which God has accommodated his actions to the ethics of ancient warfare. Scripture does not present a detached vision of God. Rather, we find a God who is willing to engage our messy world. Yahweh puts on hip waders as he walks within the ethical sewer water of this fallen world; his actions taken via humans (whether his holy warriors are Israel or Assyria or Babylon) do not automatically cast what he does into a pristine ethical category. Like many aspects of the temporal, fallen-world justice of Scripture, God stoops down (way down) in our world as he seeks to bring about his redemptive story.

Thesis four: An incremental, redemptive-movement ethic. Some of the most exciting findings of this book come from learning to read the biblical war texts within the broader context of ANE warfare. When we do so, we see that, despite accommodation, God is moving his people with incremental steps in a good and redemptive direction amid the ugliness of ancient-world warfare. The chapters on hyperbole remove a major ethical obstacle—a millstone around the neck that the traditional position urgently needs to rid itself of. Hyperbole, in addition, establishes an ethical baseline with the surrounding war culture. With that ethical baseline, we can begin to see redemptive elements more clearly. The chapters on war rape and other ancient war atrocities make an important point: compared with the larger ANE context, Israel's actions in warfare and the treatment of their captives are more humane and far less cruel. Similarly, the restraint in Israel's violence (against the grain of cultural norms) is nothing short of astonishing when it comes to the treatment of a captured king, his ruling elite, and common soldiers.

Thesis five: Converging God portraits, bringing Yahweh and Jesus together. By drawing attention to numerous lesser-known subversive war texts in the Old Testament, a picture of Yahweh as a crying, brokenhearted war God emerges. As a reluctant participant in war, Yahweh is unique and highly out of place next to ANE gods who gladly rejoiced to see their victorious warriors build them temples and express graphic war scenes on their sacred walls. Not so with Yahweh. The subversive war texts of the Old Testament help us configure our understanding of Yahweh in a way that converges with Jesus of the Gospels and with Jesus as apocalyptic warrior when that image, once again, is properly understood in a real but nonliteral sense.

Our realigned traditional view is situated in the middle of the spectrum of five views, as shown in figure C.1.

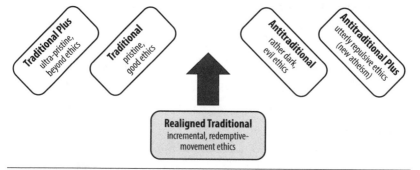

Figure C.1. The spectrum of holy war ethics

At least in some measure, our book attempts to address five competing views across the ethical spectrum (see figure 0.1 in the introduction). First, the realigned traditional label is our way of saying that the traditional answers to the ethics of biblical holy war need to be realigned with a different set of questions. The traditional answers simply do not help us answer questions about the ethics of genocide or war rape in the biblical text. They align better with another set of questions. Second, our realigned-traditional view challenges (1) those who do not want to acknowledge any real ethical issues in the holy war traditions of Scripture and (2) those who seem to see only deplorable ethical elements in the biblical texts without exploring and finding that which is ethically redemptive. Viewing Scripture through the lens of an incremental ethic permits Christians to acknowledge real ethical problems while also affirming remarkable redemptive elements. Third, the extensive chapters arguing for hyperbole are directed toward both the traditional and the antitraditional sides in their (ironically) shared literal understanding of total-kill rhetoric. Fourth, the evidence for hyperbole and incremental ethics should result in muting some of new atheism's disdain, and it should move traditionalists toward reconsidering ancient cultural aspects of biblical war texts. Finally, the painful discontinuity of Yahweh and Jesus portraits by both traditionalists (Yahweh colors/redefines Jesus) and antitraditionalists (Jesus colors/redefines Yahweh) has an opportunity for revised reflection in the Yahweh-Jesus convergence that we propose.

BIBLICAL WAR ETHICS: OUR FINDINGS IN A NUTSHELL

One topic in this book was war rape. Ethical problems with the treatment of female captives in Israel's war texts make it difficult for modern readers to appreciate anything redemptive in them. Nevertheless, if we journey back into an ancient-world horizon (markedly different from ours), we have an opportunity to see the redemptive side of the biblical text even in this domain. That journey takes us to a gruesome and violent war context where warriors routinely ravaged women as part of their victory rituals, spoke about female captives in terms of their sexual body parts, and displayed rape scenes in their nationally sponsored war art—corresponding to literary bravado about war rape. This backdrop of pervasive sexual violence in war is needed to appreciate the biblical perspective. Israel's war story pushes redemptively at the margins of a rape-crazed war world:

- ▶ no battlefield rape permitted

- ▶ no artwork or literary counterpart that glorifies war rape

- ▶ no perpetual rape of temple-slave prostitutes (war captives as a source)

- ▶ reduced likelihood of domestically owned slave prostitutes (war captives as a source)

- ▶ various restrictive measures placed on Israelite warriors attracted to beautiful captive women

When sex and violence in war collide within Scripture, we discover the real and sometimes even bold actions of an incremental ethic that embodies its underlying redemptive spirit. When read within the horizon of an ancient world, the heavy darkness of war rape texts such as Deuteronomy 21 and Numbers 31 is pierced by numerous shafts of bright, redemptive light—meaning easily missed from our present-day horizon.

A second topic in this book was genocide. This book argues extensively for understanding total-kill language in a hyperbolic (not literal) sense. The weight of evidence strongly favors a hyperbolic approach, which has important implications for the ethics of the biblical conquest accounts. The use of hyperbole in describing Israel's battles against the Canaanites reduces the severity of Israel's actions so that, while lives were undoubtedly lost, not everyone was killed and genocide did not take place. Genocide did not take place in the biblical accounts any more than it did in the rest of ANE warfare. Israel fought its wars in much the same way as did other ancient armies. Making a solid case for total-kill language as hyperbole thus provides an ethical baseline (a starting point) within the ancient war horizon from which we can view either minor or major increments of redemptive movement.

While difficult for readers to journey through (as it was for us to research and write), students of Scripture will never fully understand the biblical war texts until they have also spent time pondering the utterly debased treatment of the enemy in ANE warfare. This book offers what might be described as a walk through an ancient-world war museum where readers can contemplate, should they choose to do so, the graphic details of grotesque ancient war actions:

- ▶ stripping captives naked and parading them with shaved genitals

- ▶ excruciatingly painful rope bindings that dislocated and shattered joints

- ▶ mutilating (often live) captives—cutting off tongue, toes, nose, genitals, hands, feet, legs, head, etc.

- ▶ blinding prisoners

- ▶ public displays of body parts—stacking piles of heads at the city gate or piling up hands and penises

- ▶ capturing whole communities and selling them on the slave market

- ▶ no burial of the dead

- ▶ digging up ancestral graves and scattering the bones

- ▶ forcing captives to grind up ancestors' bones

- ▶ raping women and young girls as part of battle conquest

- ▶ slicing open pregnant women and killing their unborn babies

- ▶ impaling live victims on stakes pushed through their bodies

- ▶ flaying alive—peeling the skin from live captives staked to the ground

While not pleasant to reflect on, an accurate picture of the grisly nature of ancient war is important for reading the biblical war texts. The war atrocities listed above are either explicitly or implicitly denounced within the biblical text. Unlike the praise and glory given these acts of extreme violence by foreign gods, royal art reliefs, and royal annals, such war crimes were not considered Yahweh-approved war actions for Israel.

If the biblical or Yahweh-approved war conduct by Israelite soldiers did *not* include either the above list of ANE war atrocities or the literal total-kill elimination of the Canaanites, then Israel's war measures would have been considered mild or comparatively moderate within the larger context.[4] Repugnant

---

[4]We have argued the hyperbole thesis extensively in chapters eight through twelve and appendixes A through C.

as the biblical war texts are for modern readers (we cannot escape our in-grained Hague/Geneva horizon), they were markedly restrained for their day. To put it another way, the clear movement away from well-known, expected war atrocities marks significant movement in a good, redemptive direction. Unlike many in the ancient world, the biblical writers viewed the above war atrocities as a list of shameful war actions, not something to be proud of. This incrementally redemptive war ideology within Scripture, as read within the social context of its day, advances a greater respect and dignity even for one's enemies on the battlefield.

These findings are not wishful thinking inspired by Jewish or Christian vested interests. A whole second universe of parallel evidence—a mirrored crime-and-punishment framework found within the domestic realm—supports the incrementally redemptive war thesis of this book.[5] In short, the more egregious *war* punishments by Egypt, Babylon, and Assyria (compared with Israel) parallel the more egregious *domestic* punishments by other na-tions (compared with Israel). If one studies domestic crime-and-punishment cases for the citizens of various ANE countries (some crimes requiring beatings with two hundred blows of the rod and five open wounds, impaling women for certain acts of adultery, cutting off all kinds of body parts, pro-longed torture, etc.) and comparatively sees Israel's highly curtailed version of corporal punishment, the war story falls better into place. It reflects a similar pattern. Within the ancient-world context, Israel's comparatively re-stricted war actions duplicated its restraint and pursuit of greater human dignity that occurred in its corporal-punishment actions.

A FINAL WORD

We end by coming back to the *best* of the better answers. The initial re-demptive steps that we have discovered within the biblical war texts find their telos in God's ultimate justice story. At the close of this age, when all of humanity sits on the front porch of a new heaven and new earth, God will

---

[5]In a world that legitimized war within a crime-and-punishment framework, the domestic realm of justice would naturally have influenced and shaped expectations and actions in the international war realm. Simply put, for many ancient nations the utterly horrendous pun-ishments in their domestic courts probably influenced the egregious nature of their war actions and vice versa.

continue to write the presently unfinished justice story. Scripture's theme of eschatological hope (the eternal weight of glory that offsets or compensates for present-day suffering and injustice) closes any remaining ethical gap. Christians are called on to believe in a God of unfathomable goodness and consistent character—someday this God will make *all* things right.

LIST OF ONLINE APPENDIXES

Download these appendixes at
ivpress.com/bloody-brutal-and-barbaric.

BIBLIOGRAPHY

Ackerman, Susan. *Warrior, Dancer, Seductress, Queen: Women in Judges and Biblical Israel.* New York: Doubleday, 1998.

Aharoni, Yohanan. *The Land of the Bible: A Historical Geography.* Rev. ed. Translated by Anson Rainey. Philadelphia: Westminster, 1979.

Allen, James P. *The Ancient Egyptian Pyramid Texts.* Edited by Peter Der Manuelian. SBLWAW 23. Atlanta: Society of Biblical Literature, 2005.

Alter, Robert. *The World of Biblical Literature.* New York: Basic Books, 1992.

Anderson, Francis I. "Israelite Kinship Terminology and Social Structure." *BT* 20 (1969): 29-39.

Anderson, Gary A. *A Time to Mourn, a Time to Dance: The Expressions of Grief and Joy in Israelite Religion.* University Park: Pennsylvania State University Press, 1991.

Arnold, Bill T. *1 & 2 Samuel.* NIVAC. Grand Rapids: Zondervan, 2003.

Assante, Julia. "From Whores to Hierodules: The Historiographic Invention of Mesopotamian Female Sex Professionals." In *Ancient Art and Its Historiography*, edited by A. A. Donohue and Mark D. Fullerton, 13-47. Cambridge: Cambridge University Press, 2003.

———. "The Kar.kid/harimtu, Prostitute or Single Woman? A Re-consideration of the Evidence." *UF* 30 (1993): 5-96.

Assis, Ellie. "The Choice to Serve God and Assist His People: Rahab and Yael." *Biblica* 85 (2004): 82-90.

Assmann, Jan. *The Search for God in Egypt.* Ithaca, NY: Cornell University Press, 2001.

Aune, David E. *Revelation 17–22.* WBC. Nashville: Thomas Nelson, 1998.

"The Avalon Project at Yale Law School: The Laws of War." http://avalon.law.yale.edu /subject_menus/lawwar.asp. Accessed March 7, 2019.

Baadsgaard, Aubrey. "Trends, Traditions, and Transformations: Fashion in Dress in Early Dynastic Mesopotamia." PhD diss., University of Pennsylvania, 2008.

Bahrani, Zainab. *Rituals of War: The Body and Violence in Mesopotamia.* New York: Zone Books, 2008.

Barr, David L. "Doing Violence: Moral Issues in Reading John's Apocalypse." In *Reading the Book of Revelation: A Resource for Students*, edited by David L. Barr, 97-108. Atlanta: Society of Biblical Literature, 2003.

———. "The Lamb Who Looks Like a Dragon: Characterizing Jesus in John's Apocalypse." In *The Reality of Apocalypse: Rhetoric and Politics in the Book of Revelation*, edited by David L. Barr, 205-20. Atlanta: Society of Biblical Literature, 2006.

Barnett, R. D., E. Bleibtreu, and G. Turner. *Sculptures from the Southwest Palace of Sennacherib at Nineveh.* London: British Museum Press, 1998.

Barrett, Lois. *The Way God Fights.* Peace and Justice Series 1. Waterloo, ON: Herald, 1987.

Batto, Bernard F. *In the Beginning: Essays on Creation Motifs in the Ancient Near East and the Bible.* Winona Lake, IN: Eisenbrauns, 2013.

Bauckham, Richard. *The Theology of Jürgen Moltmann.* New York: T&T Clark, 1995.

———. *The Theology of the Book of Revelation.* NTT. Cambridge: Cambridge University Press, 1993.

Beale, G. K. *The Book of Revelation.* NIGTC. Grand Rapids: Eerdmans, 1999.

———. "Eden, the Temple, and the Church's Mission in the New Creation." *JETS* 48, no. 1 (2005): 5-31.

———. *The Morality of God in the Old Testament*. Christian Answers to Hard Questions. Phillipsburg, NJ: P&R, 2013.

———. *The Temple and the Church's Mission: A Biblical Theology of the Dwelling Place of God*. NSBT 17. Downers Grove, IL: InterVarsity Press, 2008.

———. *We Become What We Worship: A Biblical Theology of Idolatry*. Downers Grove, IL: InterVarsity Press, 2004.

Beale, G. K., and Mitchell Kim. *God Dwells Among Us: Expanding Eden to the Ends of the Earth*. Downers Grove, IL: InterVarsity Press, 2014.

Bendor, Shunya. *The Social Structure of Ancient Israel: The Institution of the Family (Beit 'Ab) from the Settlement to the End of the Monarchy*. Jerusalem Biblical Studies 7. Jerusalem: Simor, 1996.

Bleibtreu, Erika. "Grisly Assyrian Record of Torture and Death." *BARev* 17, no. 1 (1991): 52-61, 75.

Block, Daniel I. *Deuteronomy*. NIVAC. Grand Rapids: Zondervan, 2012.

———. "Eden: A Temple? A Reassessment of the Biblical Evidence." In *From Creation to New Creation: Biblical Theology and Exegesis*, edited by Daniel M. Gurtner and Benjamin L. Gladd, 3-29. Peabody, MA: Hendrickson, 2013.

———. *The Gods of the Nations: Studies in Ancient Near Eastern National Theology*. 2nd ed. ETS Studies 2. Grand Rapids: Baker, 2000.

———. *Judges, Ruth*. NAC 6. Nashville: Broadman & Holman, 1999.

———. "The Period of the Judges: Religious Disintegration Under Tribal Rule." In *Israel's Apostasy and Restoration: Essays in Honor of Roland K. Harrison*, edited by A. Gileadi, 41-57. Grand Rapids: Baker, 1988.

Bock, Darrell L. *Acts*. BECNT. Grand Rapids: Baker, 2007.

Bodner, Keith. *1 Samuel: A Narrative Commentary*. Sheffield: Sheffield Phoenix, 2009.

Bonatz, Dominik. "Ashurbanipal's Headhunt: An Anthropological Perspective." *Iraq* 66, no. 1 (2004): 93-101.

Bonhoeffer, Dietrich. *Letters and Papers from Prison*. London: SCM Press, 1967.

Boxall, Ian. *The Revelation of Saint John*. BNTC. London: Continuum, 2006.

Boyd, Gregory A. *Cross Vision: How the Crucifixion of Jesus Makes Sense of Old Testament Violence*. Minneapolis: Fortress, 2017.

———. *The Crucifixion of the Warrior God*. 2 vols. Minneapolis: Fortress, 2017.

———. *God at War: The Bible and Spiritual Conflict*. Downers Grove, IL: InterVarsity Press, 1997.

Brueggemann, Walter. *Divine Presence amid Violence: Contextualizing the Book of Joshua*. Eugene, OR: Cascade Books, 2009.

Budin, Stephanie Lynn. *The Myth of Sacred Prostitution in Antiquity*. New York: Cambridge University Press, 2008.

Bullinger, E. W. *Figures of Speech Used in the Bible: Explained and Illustrated*. Grand Rapids: Baker, 1968.

Butler, Trent C. *Joshua 1–12*. WBC. 2nd ed. Grand Rapids: Zondervan, 2014.

Cantrell, Deborah O'Daniel. *The Horsemen of Israel: Houses and Chariotry in Monarchic Israel (Ninth-Eighth Centuries B.C.E.)*. HACL 1. Winona Lake, IN: Eisenbrauns, 2011.

———. "'Some Trust in Horses': Horses as Symbols of Power in Rhetoric and Reality." In

Warfare, Ritual, and Symbol in Biblical and Modern Contexts, edited by Brad E. Kelle, Frank Ritchel Ames, and Jacob L. Wright. AIL 18, 131-48. Atlanta: SBL Press, 2014.

Carroll R., M. Daniel, and J. Blair Wilgus, eds. *Wrestling with the Violence of God: Soundings in the Old Testament.* BBRSup 10. Winona Lake, IN: Eisenbrauns, 2015.

Cavanaugh, William T. "Does Religion Cause Violence?" *HDB* 35 (2007): 1-14.

Chapman, Cynthia M. *The Gendered Language of Warfare in the Israelite-Assyrian Encounter.* Winona Lake, IN: Eisenbrauns, 2004.

Chen, Paul Li-Tah. "Familial Guilt and Responsibility in Light of the Biblical Ḥerem with Special Reference to Joshua 5:13–8:29." PhD diss., Trinity Evangelical Divinity School, 2001.

Chisholm, Robert B., Jr. *A Commentary on Judges and Ruth.* Grand Rapids: Kregel Academic, 2013.

Clark, David J. "'Surnames' in the Old Testament? Or: How to be Rude Politely." *BT* 56 (2005): 232-38.

Clifford, Richard J. *Creation Accounts in the Ancient Near East and in the Bible.* CBQMS 26. Washington, DC: Catholic Biblical Association of America, 1994.

Cogan, Mordechai. "'Ripping Open Pregnant Women' in Light of an Assyrian Analogue." *JAOS* 103 (1983): 755-57.

Cogan, Mordechai, and Hayim Tadmor. *II Kings.* AB. New York: Doubleday, 1988.

Cohen, H., V. Slon, A. Barash, H. May, B. Medlej, and I. Hershkovitz. "Assyrian Attitude Towards Captive Enemies: A 2700-Year-Old Paleo-forensic Study." *International Journal of Osteoarchaeology* 25 (2015): 265-80.

Cohen, Ronald. "Legitimacy, Illegitimacy, and State Formation." In *State Formation and Political Legitimacy*, edited by Ronald Cohen and Judith D. Toland, Political Anthropology VI, 69-83. New Brunswick, NJ: Transaction Books, 1988.

Collins, Billie Jean. *The Hittites and their World.* SBLABS 7. Atlanta: Society of Biblical Literature, 2007.

Cooper, Jerrold S. "Female Trouble and Troubled Males: Roiled Seas, Decadent Royals, and Mesopotamian Masculinities in Myth and Practice." In *Being a Man: Negotiating Ancient Constructs of Masculinity*, edited by Ilona Zsolnay, 112-24. New York: Routledge, 2017.

———. "Prostitution." Vol. 11 of *Reallexikon der Assyriologie*, edited by Michael Streck, 12-22. Berlin: de Gruyter, 2006.

Copan, Paul. "Greg Boyd's Misunderstanding of the 'Warrior God.'" Gospel Coalition. January 26, 2018. www.thegospelcoalition.org/reviews/crucifixion-warrior-god-greg-boyd/.

———. *Is God a Moral Monster?: Making Sense of the Old Testament God.* Grand Rapids: Baker, 2011.

Copan, Paul, and Matthew Flannagan. *Did God Really Command Genocide? Coming to Terms with the Justice of God.* Grand Rapids: Baker, 2014.

———. "The Ethics of 'Holy War' for Christian Morality Theology." In *Holy War in the Bible: Christian Morality and an Old Testament Problem*, edited by Heath A. Thomas, Jeremy Evans, and Paul Copan, 201-39. Downers Grove, IL: InterVarsity Press, 2013.

Corson, Richard. *Fashions in Makeup: From Ancient to Modern Times.* London: Peter Owen, 1972.

Cowles, C. S. "The Case for Radical Discontinuity." In *Show Them No Mercy: Four Views on God and Canaanite Genocide*, edited by Stanley N. Gundry, 13-44. Grand Rapids: Zondervan, 2003.

Cross, Frank Moore, and David N. Freedman. *Studies in Ancient Yahwistic Poetry*. SBLDS. Atlanta: Society of Biblical Literature, 1975. Reprint, Grand Rapids: Eerdmans, 1997.

Crouch, Carly L. *War and Ethics in the Ancient Near East*. BZAW 407. Berlin: de Gruyter, 2009.

Davidson, Richard M. *Flame of Yahweh: Sexuality in the Old Testament*. Peabody, MA: Hendrickson, 2007.

Davies, Eryl W. "A Mathematical Conundrum: The Problem of the Large Numbers in Numbers I and XXVI." *VT* 45 (1995): 449-69.

Day, John. "Does the Old Testament Refer to Sacred Prostitution and Did It Actually Exist in Ancient Israel?" In *Biblical and Near Eastern Essays: Studies in Honour of Kevin J. Cathcart*, edited by John F. Healey, Carmel McCarthy, and Kevin J. Cathcart, 2-21. New York: T&T Clark, 2004.

De Backer, Fabrice. "Cruelty and Military Refinements." *Res Antiquae* 6 (2009): 13-50.

De Odorico, Marco. *The Use of Numbers and Quantifications in the Assyrian Royal Inscriptions*. SAAS 3. Helsinki: Neo-Assyrian Text Corpus Project, 1995.

De Prenter, Jannica A. "The Contrastive Polysemous Meaning of חרם in the Book of Joshua: A Cognitive Linguistic Approach." In *The Book of Joshua*, edited by Ed Noort, 473-88. BETL 250. Leuven: Peeters, 2012.

Deem, Ariella. "' . . . And the Stone Sank into his Forehead': A Note on 1 Samuel XVII 49." *VT* 28 (1978): 349-51.

deSilva, David A. *Unholy Allegiances: Heeding Revelation's Warning*. Peabody, MA: Hendrickson, 2013.

Diamond, James A. "The Deuteronomic 'Pretty Woman' Law: Prefiguring Feminism and Freud in Nahmanides." *Jewish Social Studies* 14, no. 2 (2008): 61-85.

Dubovsky, Peter. "Ripping Open Pregnant Arab Women: Reliefs in Room L of Ashurbanipal's North Palace." *Orientalia* 78, no. 3 (2009): 394-419.

Dunn, James D. G. *Jesus Remembered, Christianity in the Making*. Vol. 1. Grand Rapids: Eerdmans, 2003.

Earl, Douglas S. "Holy War and חרם: A Biblical Theology of חרם." In *Holy War in the Bible: Christian Morality and an Old Testament Problem*, edited by Heath A. Thomas, Jeremy Evans, and Paul Copan, 152-75. Downers Grove, IL: InterVarsity Press, 2013.

Edelman, Diana V. "Saul's Battle Against Amaleq (1 Sam. 15)." *JSOT* 35 (1986): 71-84.

Edenburg, Cynthia. "Ideology and Social Context of the Deuteronomic Women's Sex Laws (Deuteronomy 22:13-29)." *JBL* 128 (2009): 43-60.

Ellens, Deborah L. *Women in the Sex Texts of Leviticus and Deuteronomy: A Comparative Conceptual Analysis*. LHBOTS 458. Edinburgh: T&T Clark, 2008.

Ellis, Robert E. "The Theological Boundaries of Inclusion and Exclusion in the Book of Joshua." *RevExp* 95 (1998): 235-50.

Elman, Pearl. "Deuteronomy 21:10-14: The Beautiful Captive Woman." *Women in Judaism* 1 (1997): 1-13.

Esler, Philip F. *Sex, Wives, and Warriors: Reading Biblical Narrative with Its Ancient Audience*. Eugene, OR: Cascade, 2011.

Evans, Paul S. *The Invasion of Sennacherib in the Book of Kings: A Source-Critical and Rhetorical Study of 2 Kings 18–19*. VTSup 125. Leiden: Brill, 2009.

Exum, J. Cheryl. *Plotted, Shot, and Painted: Cultural Representations of Biblical Women*. JSOTSup 215. Sheffield: Sheffield Academic Press, 1996.

Faulkner, Raymond O. *Ancient Egyptian Pyramid Texts.* Oxford: Clarendon Press, 1969.

Feldman, Louis H. "Josephus's View of the Amalekites." *BBR* 12 (2002): 161-86.

Firth, David G. *1 & 2 Samuel.* AOTC. Downers Grove, IL: InterVarsity Press, 2009.

Fischer, John Martin, and Mark Ravizza. *Ethics: Problems and Principles.* New York: Harcourt Brace Jovanovich, 1992.

Flannagan, Matthew. "Did God Command the Genocide of the Canaanites?" In *Come Let Us Reason: New Essays in Christian Apologetics,* edited by Paul Copan and William Lane Craig, 225-49. Nashville: B&H Academic, 2012.

Flannagan, Matthew, and Paul Copan. "Does the Bible Condone Genocide?" In *In Defense of the Bible: A Comprehensive Apologetic for the Authority of Scripture,* edited by Steven B. Cowan and Terry L. Wilder, 297-333. Nashville: B&H Academic, 2013.

Fleming, Daniel E. "The Seven-Day Siege of Jericho in Holy War." In *Ki Baruch Hu: Ancient Near Eastern, Biblical, and Judaic Studies in Honor of Baruch A. Levine,* edited by R. Chazan, W. W. Hallo, and L. H. Schiffman, 211-28. Winona Lake, IN: Eisenbrauns, 1999.

Fokkelman, Jan P. *Narrative Art and Poetry in the Books of Samuel.* Vol. 2. Assen: Van Gorcum, 1986.

Foster, Benjamin R. *Before the Muses: An Anthology of Akkadian Literature.* 3rd ed. Bethesda, MD: CDL Press, 2005.

Fouts, David M. "A Defense of the Hyperbolic Interpretation of Large Numbers in the Old Testament." *JETS* 40 (1997): 377-87.

Frankfort, Henri. *Kingship and the Gods: A Study of Ancient Near Eastern Religion as the Integration of Society and Nature.* Chicago: University of Chicago Press, 1948.

Frayne, Douglas. *Sargonic and Gutian Periods [2334–2113 BC].* RIM.EP 2. Toronto: University of Toronto Press, 1993.

Fretheim, Terrence E. *The Suffering of God.* OBT. Philadelphia: Fortress, 1984.

Friesen, Steven J. *Imperial Cults and the Apocalypse of John: Reading Revelation in the Ruins.* Oxford: Oxford University Press, 2001.

Frymer-Kensky, Tikva. "Virginity in the Bible." In *Gender and Law in the Hebrew Bible and the Ancient Near East,* edited by Victor H. Matthews, Bernard M. Levinson, and Tikva Frymer-Kensky, 79-96. JSOTSup 262. Sheffield: Sheffield Academic Press, 1998.

Fuchs, Andreas. "Waren die Assyrer grausam?" In *Extreme Formen von Gewalt in Bild und Text des Altertums,* edited by Martin Zimmermann, 65-119. MSAW. München: Herbert Utz Verlag, 2009.

Gaca, Kathy L. "Ancient Warfare and the Ravaging Martial Rape of Girls and Women: Evidence from Homeric Epic and Greek Drama." In *Sex in Antiquity: Exploring Gender and Sexuality in the Ancient World,* edited by Mark Masterson, Nancy Sorkin Rabinowitz, and James Robson, 278-97. New York: Routledge, 2015.

———. "Girls, Women and the Significance of Sexual Violence in Ancient Warfare." In *Sexual Violence in Conflict Zones,* edited by E. D. Heineman, 73-88. Philadelphia: University of Pennsylvania Press, 2011.

———. "Telling the Girls from the Boys and Children: Interpreting παῖδες in the Sexual Violence of Populace-Ravaging Ancient Warfare." *Illinois Classical Studies* 35/36 (2012): 85-109.

Gansell, Amy Rebecca. "Women of Ivory as Embodiments of Ideal Feminine Beauty in the Ancient Near East During the First Millennium BCE." PhD diss., Harvard University, 2008.

Gard, Daniel L. "The Case for Eschatological Continuity." In *Show Them No Mercy: Four Views on God and Canaanite Genocide*, edited by Stanley N. Gundry, 113-41. Grand Rapids: Zondervan, 2003.

Geisler, Norman L. *Christian Ethics: Options and Issues*. Grand Rapids: Baker, 1989.

Gensler, Harry J. *Ethics: A Contemporary Introduction*. New York: Routledge, 1998.

Gilmour, Rachelle. "A Note on the Horses and Chariots of Fire at Dothan." *ZAW* 125 (2013): 308-13.

Glassner, Jean-Jacques. *Mesopotamian Chronicles*, edited by Benjamin R. Foster. SBLWAW 19. Atlanta: Society of Biblical Literature, 2004.

Goldstein, Aaron. "Large Census Numbers in Numbers: An Evaluation of Current Proposals." *Presbyterion* 38, no. 2 (2012): 88-108.

Goldstein, Ronnie. "The Provision of Food to the Aramean Captives in II Reg 6,22-23." *ZAW* 126 (2014): 101-5.

Gordon, Pamela, and Harold C. Washington. "Rape as Military Metaphor in the Hebrew Bible." In *A Feminist Companion to the Bible: The Latter Prophets*, edited by Athalya Brenner, 308-25. Sheffield: Sheffield Academic Press, 1995.

Gorman, Michael J. *Reading Revelation Responsibly: Uncivil Worship and Witness; Following the Lamb into the New Creation*. Eugene, OR: Cascade, 2011.

Gottwald, Norman K. *The Tribes of Yahweh: A Sociology of the Religion of Liberated Israel, 1250–1050 BCE*. Sheffield: Sheffield Academic Press, 1999.

Gravett, Sandie. "Reading 'Rape' in the Hebrew Bible: A Consideration of Language." *JSOT* 28, no. 3 (2004): 279-99.

Grayling, A. C. *Wittgenstein: A Very Short Introduction*. Oxford: Oxford University Press, 2001.

Grenz, Stanley J. *The Moral Quest: Foundations of Christian Ethics*. Downers Grove, IL: InterVarsity Press, 1997.

Grossman, Dave. *On Killing: The Psychological Cost of Learning to Kill in War and Society*. Rev. ed. New York: Back Bay Books, 2009.

Habel, Norman C. *The Land Is Mine: Six Biblical Land Ideologies*. OBT. Minneapolis: Fortress, 1995.

Hall, Sarah Lebhar. *Conquering Character: The Characterization of Joshua in Joshua 1–11*. LHBOTS 512. New York: T&T Clark, 2010.

Halpern, Baruch. *David's Secret Demons: Messiah, Murderer, Traitor, King*. Grand Rapids: Eerdmans, 2001.

Hamblin, William J. *Warfare in the Ancient Near East to 1600 BC: Holy Warriors at the Dawn of History*. New York: Routledge, 2006.

Haran, Menahem. *Temples and Temple-Service in Ancient Israel*. Oxford: Clarendon, 1978. Reprint, Winona Lake, IN: Eisenbrauns, 1985.

Hawk, L. Daniel. "The Problem with Pagans." In *Reading Bibles, Writing Bodies: Identity and the Book*. Edited by Timothy K. Beal and David M. Gunn, 153-63. New York: Routledge, 1997.

Hawkins, Ralph K. *Joshua*. Evangelical Exegetical Commentary. Bellingham, WA: Lexham, forthcoming.

Hayes, John H. "The Tradition of Zion's Inviolability." *JBL* 82 (1963): 419-26.

Hays, Richard B. *The Moral Vision of the New Testament: Community, Cross, New Creation; A Contemporary Introduction to New Testament Ethics*. New York: HarperSanFrancisco, 1996.

Heinzerling, Rüdiger. "On the Interpretation of the Census Lists by C.J. Humphreys and G.E. Mendenhall." *VT* 50 (2000): 250-52.

Hess, Richard S. *Joshua*. TOTC. Downers Grove, IL: InterVarsity Press, 1996.

Hill, Andrew. "The Ebal Ceremony as Hebrew Land Grant?" *JETS* 31 (1988): 399-406.

Hobbs, T. R. *2 Kings*. WBC. Waco, TX: Word Books, 1985.

Hoffmeier, James K. *Israel in Egypt: The Evidence for the Authenticity of the Exodus Tradition*. New York: Oxford University Press, 1997.

———. "The Structure of Joshua 1–11 and the Annals of Thutmose III." In *Faith, Tradition, and History: Old Testament Historiography in its Near Eastern Context*, edited by A. R. Millard, James K. Hoffmeier, and David W. Baker, 165-79. Winona Lake, IN: Eisenbrauns, 1994.

Hoffner, Harry A., Jr. "The Treatment and Long-Term Use of Persons Captured in Battle According to the Masat Texts." In *Recent Developments in Hittite Archaeology and History*, edited by K. Aslihan Yener and Harry A. Hoffner Jr, 61-72. Winona Lake, IN: Eisenbrauns, 2002.

Holloway, Steven W. "Use of Assyriology in Chronological Apologetics in *David's Secret Demons*." *SJOT* 17 (2003): 245-67.

Holmes, Arthur F. *Ethics: Approaching Moral Decisions*. Downers Grove, IL: InterVarsity Press, 1984.

Holmes, Robert L. "The Killing of Innocent Persons in Wartime." In *On War and Morality*, 183-213. Princeton, NJ: Princeton University Press, 1989.

Horsley, Richard A. *Revolt of the Scribes: Resistance and Apocalyptic Origin*. Philadelphia: Fortress, 2009.

Howard, David. *Joshua*. NAC. Nashville: Broadman and Holman, 1998.

Hubbard, Robert L., Jr. *Joshua*. NIVAC. Grand Rapids: Zondervan, 2009.

Hughes, Philip E. *Christian Ethics in Secular Society*. Grand Rapids: Baker, 1983.

Humphreys, Colin J. "The Number of People in the Exodus from Egypt: Decoding Mathematically the Very Large Numbers in Numbers I and XXVI." *VT* 48 (1998): 196-213.

———. "The Numbers in the Exodus from Egypt: A Further Appraisal." *VT* 50 (2000): 323-28.

Hurowitz, Victor. *I Have Built You an Exalted House: Temple Building in the Bible in Light of Mesopotamian and North-West Semitic Writings*. JSOTSup 105. Sheffield: JSOT Press, 1992.

Hutton, Jeremy M. "Amos 1:3–2:8 and the International Economy of Iron Age II Israel." *HTR* 107 (2014): 81-113.

Imparati, Fiorella. "Private Life Among the Hittites." In *Civilizations of the Ancient Near East*, 571-86. Edited by J. Sasson. 4 vols. Peabody, MA: Hendrickson, 1995.

Inal, Tuba. *Looting and Rape in Wartime: Law and Change in International Relations*. Philadelphia: University of Pennsylvania Press, 2013.

Jackson, Glenna S. *"Have Mercy on Me": The Story of the Canaanite Woman in Matthew 15:21-28*. JSNTSup 228. New York: Sheffield Academic Press, 2002.

Jacobs, Sandra. "Terms of Endearment? יפת־תאר אשת (The Desirable Female Captive): Her Illicit Acquisition." In *Exodus and Deuteronomy*, edited by Athalya Brenner and Gale A. Yee, 237-57. Texts @ Contexts Series. Minneapolis: Fortress, 2012.

Janzen, Mark D. "The Iconography of Humiliation: The Depiction and Treatment of Bound Foreigners in New Kingdom Egypt." PhD diss., University of Memphis, 2013.

Jas, Remko. *Neo-Assyrian Judicial Procedures*. SAAS 5. Helsinki: Neo-Assyrian Judicial Procedures, 1996.

Jenson, Phillip Peter. *Graded Holiness: A Key to the Priestly Conception of the World*. JSOTSup 106. Sheffield: Sheffield Academic Press, 1992.

Johns, Loren L. *The Lamb Christology of the Apocalypse of John: An Investigation into Its Origins and Rhetorical Force*. WUNT 2/167. Tubingen: Mohr Siebeck, 2003.

Johnstone, Janet M. "Wrapping and Tying Ancient Egyptian New Kingdom Dresses." In *Wrapping and Unwrapping Material Culture: Archaeological and Anthropological Perspectives*, edited by Susanna Harris and Laurence Douny, 59-82. Walnut Creek, CA: Left Coast Press, 2014.

Josberger, Rebekah. "For Your Good Always: Restraining the Rights of the Victor for the Well-Being of the Vulnerable (Deut 21:10-14)." In *For Our Good Always: Studies on the Message and Influence of the Book of Deuteronomy in Honor of Daniel I. Block*, edited by Jason S. DeRouchie, Jason Gile, and Kenneth J. Turner, 165-87. CSHB 3. Winona Lake, IN: Eisenbrauns, 2013.

Kaiser, Walter C., Jr. *Toward Old Testament Ethics*. Grand Rapids: Zondervan, 1983.

Keefe, Alice A. "Rapes of Women/Wars of Men." *Semeia* 61 (1993): 79-97.

Keener, Craig S. *Acts: An Exegetical Commentary*. Vol. 1, *Introduction and 1:1—2:47*. Grand Rapids: Baker Academic, 2012.

———. *Revelation*. NIVAC. Grand Rapids: Zondervan, 2000.

Kelly, Brian E. "David's Disqualification in 1 Chronicles 22:8: A Response to Piet B. Dirksen." *JSOT* (1998): 53-61.

Kern, Paul Bentley. *Ancient Siege Warfare*. Indianapolis: Indiana University Press, 1999.

King, Philip J., and Lawrence Stager. *Life in Biblical Israel*. LAI. Louisville, KY: Westminster John Knox, 2001.

———. "Of Fathers, Kings and the Deity." *BARev* 28, no. 2 (2002): 42-45, 62.

Kitchen, Kenneth A. *On the Reliability of the Old Testament*. Grand Rapids: Eerdmans, 2003.

Kline, Meredith G. *The Structure of Biblical Authority*. Grand Rapids: Eerdmans, 1972. Reprint, Eugene, OR: Wipf & Stock, 1997.

Knoppers, Gary N. *1 Chronicles 10–29*. AB. New York: Doubleday, 2004.

Kraybill, J. Nelson. *Apocalypse and Allegiance: Worship, Politics, and Devotion in the Book of Revelation*. Grand Rapids: Brazos, 2010.

Kruger, Paul A. "Women and War Brutalities in the Minor Prophets: The Case of Rape." *OTE* 27 (2014): 147-76.

Kuhrt, Amélie. *The Ancient Near East: C. 3000–330 B.C.* 2 vols. London: Routledge, 1995.

Kurtz, Donald V. "The Legitimation of the Aztec State." In *The Early State*, edited by Henri J. M. Claessen and Peter Skalník, 169-89. Studies in the Social Sciences 32. New York: Mouton, 1978.

Kurtz, Donald V., with Margaret Showman. "The Legitimation of Early Inchoate States." In *The Study of the State*, edited by Henri J. M. Claessen and Peter Skalník, 177-200. Studies in the Social Sciences 35. New York: Mouton, 1981.

Kwasman, Theodore, and Simo Parpola. *Legal Transactions of the Royal Court of Nineveh, Part 1*. SAA 6. Helsinki: Helsinki University Press, 2000.

Laato, Antti. "Assyrian Propaganda and the Falsification of History in the Royal Inscriptions." *VT* 45 (1995): 198-226.

Lamb, David T. "'I Will Strike You Down and Cut Off Your Head' (1 Sam 17:46): Trash Talking, Derogatory Rhetoric, and Psychological Warfare in Ancient Israel." In *Warfare, Ritual, and Symbol in Biblical and Modern Contexts*, edited by Brad E. Kelle, Frank Ritchel Ames, and Jacob L. Wright, 111-30. AIL 18. Atlanta: Society of Biblical Literature, 2014.

Leiter, David A. *Neglected Voices: Peace in the Old Testament*. Waterloo, ON: Herald, 2007.

Lémaire, André. "The Evolution of the 8th-Century B.C.E. Jerusalem Temple." In *The Fire Signals of Lachish: Studies in the Archaeology and History of Israel in the Late Bronze Age, Iron Age, and Persian Period in Honor of David Ussishkin*, edited by Israel Finkelstein and Nadav Na'aman, 195-202. Winona Lake, IN: Eisenbrauns, 2011.

———. "'House of David' Restored in Moabite Inscription." *BARev* 20, no. 3 (1994): 30-37.

Levenson, Jon D. *Creation and the Persistence of Evil: The Jewish Drama of Divine Omnipotence*. San Francisco: Harper & Row, 1988.

Levinson, Bernard M. "The Reconceptualization of Kingship in Deuteronomy and the Deuteronomistic History's Transformation of Torah." *VT* 51 (2001): 511-34.

Lewis, C. S. *The Great Divorce*. New York: HarperCollins, 2001.

Lewis, Theodore J. "'You Have Heard What the Kings of Assyria Have Done': Disarmament Passages Vis-à-vis Assyrian Rhetoric of Intimidation." In *Isaiah's Vision of Peace in Biblical and Modern International Relations: Swords into Plowshares*, edited by Raymond Cohen and Raymond Westbrook, 75-100. New York: Palgrave Macmillan, 2008.

Lincoln, Bruce. "An Ancient Case of Interrogation and Torture." *Social Analysis: The International Journal of Social and Cultural Practice* 53, no. 1 (2009): 157-72.

Lind, Millard C. *Yahweh is a Warrior: The Theology of Warfare in Ancient Israel*. Kitchener, ON: Herald, 1980.

Lindenberger, James M. *Ancient Aramaic and Hebrew Letters*. 2nd ed. SBLWAW 14. Atlanta: Society of Biblical Literature, 2003.

Lipiński, Edward. "Cult Prostitution and Passage Rites in the Biblical World." *Biblical Annals* 3 (2013): 9-27.

———. "Cult Prostitution in Ancient Israel?" *BARev* 40, no. 1 (2014): 48-56, 70.

Lipshitz, Oded. *The Fall and Rise of Jerusalem: Judah Under Babylonian Rule*. Winona Lake, IN: Eisenbrauns, 2005.

Liverani, Mario. "Adapa, Guest of the Gods." In *Myth and Politics in Ancient Near Eastern Historiography*, edited by Zainab Bahrani and Marc Van De Mieroop, 3-23. London: Equinox, 2004.

Livingstone, Alasdair. *Court Poetry and Literary Miscellanea*. SAA 3. Helsinki: Helsinki University Press, 1989.

Longman, Tremper, III. "The Case for Spiritual Continuity." In *Show Them No Mercy: Four Views on God and Canaanite Genocide*, edited by Stanley N. Gundry, 161-87. Grand Rapids: Zondervan, 2003.

Longman, Tremper, III, and Daniel G. Reid. *God Is a Warrior*. SOTBT. Grand Rapids: Zondervan, 1995.

Loprieno, Antonio. "Slaves." In *The Egyptians*, edited by Sergio Donadoni, 185-220. Chicago: University of Chicago Press, 1997.

Lorton, David. "The Treatment of Criminals in Ancient Egypt." In *The Treatment of Criminals in the Ancient Near East*, edited by J. M. Sasson, 2-64. Leiden, Brill, 1977.

Louw, Johannes P., and Eugene A. Nida, eds. *Greek-English Lexicon of the New Testament Based on Semantic Domains.* 2nd ed. New York: United Bible Society, 1988.

Lundquist, John M. "What Is a Temple? A Preliminary Typology." In *The Quest for the Kingdom of God: Studies in Honor of George E. Mendenhall*, edited by H. B. Huffmon, F. A. Spina, and A. R. W. Green, 205-19. Winona Lake, IN: Eisenbrauns, 1983.

Lutzer, Erwin W. *The Morality Gap: An Evangelical Response to Situation Ethics.* Chicago: Moody, 1972.

Luukko, Mikko, and Freta Van Buylaere, eds. *The Political Correspondence of Esarhaddon.* SAA 16. Helsinki: Helsinki University Press, 2002.

Malamat, Abraham. *History of Biblical Israel: Major Problems and Minor Issues.* Leiden: Brill, 2001.

———. "The Last Kings of Judah and the Fall of Jerusalem." *IEJ* 18, no. 3 (1968): 137-56.

Massey, Preston T. "The Veil and the Voice: A Study of Female Beauty and Male Attraction in Ancient Greece." PhD diss., University of Indiana, 2006.

Matthews, Victor H. *Judges and Ruth.* NCBC. Cambridge: Cambridge University Press, 2004.

Matthewson, David. "The Nations in Revelation." *TynBul* 53 (2002): 121-42.

May, William F. "Virtues in a Professional Setting." In *Readings in Christian Ethics*, vol. 1, *Theory and Method*, edited by David K. Clark and Robert V. Rakestraw, 264-74. Grand Rapids: Baker, 1994.

McCarter, Kyle P. "The Apology of David." *JBL* 99 (1980): 489-504.

McConville, Gordon J. *Deuteronomy.* AOTC. Downers Grove, IL: InterVarsity Press, 2002.

McEntire, Mark. "A Response to Colin J. Humphreys's 'The Number of People in the Exodus from Egypt': Decoding Mathematically the Very Large Numbers in Numbers I and XXVI." *VT* 49 (1999): 262-64.

McFall, Leslie. "The Chronology of Saul and David." *JETS* 53 (2010): 475-533.

McNicol, Allan J. *The Conversion of the Nations in Revelation.* LNTS 438. London: T&T Clark, 2011.

Mendelsohn, Isaac. *Slavery in the Ancient Near East: A Comparative Study on Slavery in Babylonia, Assyria, Syria, and Palestine from the Middle of the Third Millennium to the End of the First Millennium.* New York: Oxford University Press, 1949.

Merrill, Eugene H. "The Case for Moderate Discontinuity." In *Show Them No Mercy: Four Views on God and Canaanite Genocide*, edited by Stanley N. Gundry, 63-101. Grand Rapids: Zondervan, 2003.

Milgrom, Jacob. "On Decoding Very Large Numbers." *VT* 49 (1999): 131-32.

Miller, James E. "A Critical Response to Karin Adam's Reinterpretation of Hosea 4:13-14." *JBL* 128 (2009): 503-6.

Millhouse, Roy R. "Re-Imaging the Warrior: Divine Warrior Imagery in the Book of Revelation." PhD diss., Baylor University, 2012.

Moberly, R. W. L. "Exodus, Book of." In *Dictionary for Theological Interpretation of the Bible*, edited by Kevin J. Vanhoozer, et al, 211-16. Grand Rapids: Baker Academic, 2005.

Moltmann, Jürgen. *The Crucified God: The Cross of Christ as the Foundation and Criticism of Christian Theology.* Minneapolis: Fortress, 1993.

———. "The Passion of Christ and the Suffering of God." *Asbury Theological Journal* 48, no. 1 (1993): 19-28.

———. *The Trinity and the Kingdom.* Minneapolis: Fortress, 1993.

Morriston, Wes. "Did God Command Genocide? A Challenge to the Biblical Inerrantist." *Philosophia Christi* 11 (2009): 7-26.

Murray, Donald F. "Under YHWH's Veto: David as Shedder of Blood in Chronicles." *Biblica* 82 (2001): 457-76.

Muslim Leaders. "Open Letter to His Holiness Pope Benedict XVI." www.catholicculture .org/culture/library/view.cfm?recnum=7910. Accessed March 7, 2019.

Nelson, Richard D. *Deuteronomy: A Commentary.* OTL. Louisville, KY: Westminster John Knox, 2002.

———. *Joshua.* OTL. Philadelphia: Westminster John Knox, 1997.

Neville, David J. *A Peaceable Hope: Contesting Violent Eschatology in the New Testament Narratives.* Grand Rapids: Baker, 2013.

———. *The Vehement Jesus: Grappling with Troubling Gospel Texts.* Eugene, OR: Cascade Books, 2017.

Niditch, Susan. "Eroticism and Death in the Tale of Jael." In *Gender and Difference in Ancient Israel,* edited by Peggy L. Day, 43-57. Minneapolis: Fortress, 1989.

———. *Judges.* OTL. Louisville, KY: Westminster John Knox, 2008.

Niehaus, Jeffrey J. *Ancient Near Eastern Themes in Biblical Theology.* Grand Rapids: Kregel, 2008.

———. "Joshua and Ancient Near Eastern Warfare." *JETS* 31 (1988): 37-50.

The Northern Pikes. "She Ain't Pretty." Music video. Posted September 23, 2008. www .youtube.com/watch?v=LUT4sS0lsss.

Noth, Martin. *The Deuteronomistic History.* Translated by Jane Doull. Revised translation by John Barton. JSOTSup 15. Sheffield: JSOT Press, 1981.

Nugent, John C. *The Politics of Yahweh: John Howard Yoder, the Old Testament, and the People of God.* Eugene, OR: Cascade, 2011.

O'Connor, David. "The Social and Economic Organization of Ancient Egyptian Temples." In *Civilizations of the Ancient Near East,* edited by J. Sasson, 319-29. 4 vols. Peabody, MA: Hendrickson, 1995.

Oded, Bustenay. "History Vis-à-vis Propaganda in the Assyrian Royal Inscriptions." *VT* 48 (1998): 423-25.

Oeste, Gordon K. *Legitimacy, Illegitimacy, and the Right to Rule: Windows on Abimelech's Rise and Demise in Judges 9.* LHBOTS 546. New York: T&T Clark, 2011.

Ollenburger, Ben C. *Zion, the City of the Great King: A Theological Symbol of the Jerusalem Cult.* JSOTSup 41. Sheffield: JSOT Press, 1987.

Olson, Dennis T. "The Book of Judges." In vol. 2 of *The New Interpreter's Bible,* 723-888. 12 Vols. Nashville: Abingdon, 1998.

Olyan, Saul M. *Biblical Mourning: Ritual and Social Dimensions.* New York: Oxford University Press, 2004.

———. "The Biblical Prohibition of the Mourning Rites of Shaving and Laceration: Several Proposals." In *"A Wise and Discerning Mind": Essays in Honor of Burke O. Lang,* edited by Saul M. Olyan and Robert C. Culley, 181-89. BJS 325. Providence, RI: Brown Judaic Studies, 2000.

———. "Ritual Inversion in Biblical Representations of Punitive Rites." In *Worship, Women and War: Essays in Honor of Susan Niditch,* edited by John J. Collins, T. M. Lemos, and Saul M. Olyan, 135-43. BJS 357. Providence, RI: Brown University Press, 2015.

———. "Unnoticed Resonances of Tomb Opening and Transportation of the Remains of the Dead in Ezekiel 37:12-14." *JBL* 128 (2009): 491-501.

———. "Was the 'King of Babylon' Buried Before His Corpse Was Exposed? Some Thoughts on Isa 14,19." *ZAW* 118 (2006): 423-26.

Osborne, Grant R. *Revelation*. BECNT. Grand Rapids: Baker Academic, 2002.

Parpola, Simo. *Correspondence of Sargon II: Part I, Letters from Assyria and the West*. SAA 1. Helsinki: Helsinki University Press, 1987.

Parpola, Simo, and Kazuko Watanabe. *Neo-Assyrian Treaties and Loyalty Oaths*. SAA 2. Helsinki: Helsinki University Press, 1988.

Pattermore, Stephen. *The People of God in the Apocalypse: Discourse, Structure and Exegesis*. Cambridge: Cambridge University Press, 2004.

Paul, Shalom M. *Amos*. Hermeneia. Minneapolis: Fortress, 1991.

Pettit, Philip. "Consequentialism." In *A Companion to Ethics*, edited by Peter Singer, 230-40. Cambridge, MA: Basil Blackwell, 1993.

Pham, Xuan Huong Thi. *Mourning in the Ancient Near East and the Hebrew Bible*. JSOTSup 302. Sheffield: Sheffield Academic Press, 1999.

Pressler, Carolyn. *The View of Women Found in the Deuteronomic Family Laws*. BZAW 216. New York: de Gruyter, 1993.

Provan, Iain, V. Philips Long, and Tremper Longman III. *A Biblical History of Israel*. Louisville, KY: Westminster John Knox, 2003.

Rad, Gerhard von. "The Promised Land and Yahweh's Land in the Hexateuch." In *The Problem of the Hexateuch and Other Essays*, translated by E. W. Trueman Dicken, 79-93. New York: McGraw-Hill, 1968.

Rainey, Anson F. *The Sacred Bridge*. Jerusalem: Carta, 2006.

———. "Who Is a Canaanite? A Review of the Textual Evidence." *BASOR* 304 (1996): 1-15.

Reeder, Caryn A. "Deuteronomy 21.10-14 and/as Wartime Rape." *JSOT* 41, no. 3 (2017): 313-36.

———. "Wives and Daughters: Women, Sex, and Violence in Biblical Tradition." *Ex Auditu* 28 (2013): 122-41.

Reid, Daniel G., and Tremper Longman III. "When God Declares War." *Christianity Today*. October 28, 1996.

Rendsburg, Gary A. "An Additional Note to Two Recent Articles on the Number of People in the Exodus from Egypt and the Large Numbers in Numbers I and XXVI." *VT* 51, no. 3 (2001): 392-96.

Resnick, David. "A Case Study in Jewish Moral Education: (Non-) Rape of the Beautiful Captive." *Journal of Moral Education* 33, no. 3 (2004): 307-19.

Reynolds, Frances. *Babylonian Correspondence of Esarhaddon*. SAA 18. Helsinki: Helsinki University Press, 2003.

Richardson, Seth F. C. "Death and Dismemberment in Mesopotamia: Discorporation Between the Body and Body Politic." In *Performing Death: Social Analyses of Funerary Traditions in the Ancient Near East and Mediterranean*, edited by Nicola Laneri, 189-208. OIS 3. Chicago: Oriental Institute of the University of Chicago, 2007.

Richter, Sandra L. *The Deuteronomistic History and the Name Theology: lᵉ šakkēn šᵉmô šām*. BZAW 318. Berlin: de Gruyter, 2002.

Robertson, John F. "The Social and Economic Organization of Ancient Mesopotamian Temples." In *Civilizations of the Ancient Near East*, edited by J. Sasson, 443-54. 4 vols. Peabody, MA: Hendrickson, 1995.

Ross, Allen P. *Recalling the Hope of Glory: Biblical Worship from the Garden to the New Creation*. Grand Rapids: Kregel, 2006.

Roth, Martha T. *Law Collections from Mesopotamia and Asia Minor*. 2nd ed. SBLWAW 6. Atlanta: Scholars Press, 1997.

———. "Marriage, Divorce and the Prostitute in Ancient Mesopotamia." In *Prostitutes and Courtesans in the Ancient World*, edited by C. A. Faraone and L. K. McClure, 21-39. Madison: University of Wisconsin Press, 2006.

Rutledge, Fleming. *The Crucifixion: Understanding the Death of Jesus Christ*. Grand Rapids: Eerdmans, 2017.

Sales, José das Candeias. "'The Smiting of the Enemies' Scenes in the Mortuary Temple of Ramses III at Medinet Habu." *Oriental Studies: Journal of Oriental and Ancient History* 1 (2012): 79-116.

Sanders, E. P. *The Historical Figure of Jesus*. London: Penguin, 1993.

Schloen, J. David. *The House of the Father as Fact and Symbol: Patrimonialism in Ugarit and the Ancient Near East*. SAHL 2. Winona Lake, IN: Eisenbrauns, 2001.

Schneider, Tammi J. *Judges*. BO. Collegeville, MN: Liturgical Press, 2000.

Scholz, Susanne. "'Back Then It Was Legal': The Epistemological Imbalance in Readings of Biblical and Ancient Near Eastern Rape Legislation." *Bible and Critical Theory* 1, no. 4 (2005): 36.1–36.22.

———. *Sacred Witness: Rape in the Hebrew Bible*. Minneapolis: Fortress, 2010.

Schwartz, Baruch J. "Reexamining the Fate of the 'Canaanites' in the Torah Traditions." In *Sefer Moshe: The Moshe Weinfeld Jubilee Volume*, edited by Chaim Cohen, Avi Hurvitz, and Shalom M. Paul, 151-70. Winona Lake, IN: Eisenbrauns, 2004.

———. *Sacred Witness: Rape in the Hebrew Bible*. Minneapolis: Fortress, 2010.

Seibert, Eric A. *Disturbing Divine Behavior: Troubling Old Testament Images of God*. Minneapolis: Fortress, 2009.

———. *The Violence of Scripture: Overcoming the Old Testament's Troubling Legacy*. Minneapolis: Fortress, 2012.

Seri, Andrea. *The House of Prisoners: Slavery and State in Uruk During the Revolt Against Samsu-Iluna*. SANER 2. Boston: de Gruyter, 2013.

Severs, Boyd. *Warfare in the Old Testament: The Organization, Weapons, and Tactics of Ancient Near Eastern Armies*. Grand Rapids: Kregel, 2013.

Siew, Antoninus King Wai. *The War Between the Two Beasts and the Two Witnesses*. LNTS 283. Edinburgh: T&T Clark, 2005.

Silver, Morris. "Temple/Sacred Prostitution in Ancient Mesopotamia Revisited: Religion in the Economy." *UF* 38 (2008): 631-36.

Simpson, William Kelley, ed., *Literature of Ancient Egypt*. New Haven, CT: Yale University Press, 1972.

Singer, Itamar, and Harry A. Hoffner. *Hittite Prayers*. SBLWAW 11. Atlanta: Society of Biblical Literature, 2002.

Spong, John Shelby. *The Sins of Scripture: Exposing the Bible's Texts of Hate to Reveal the God of Love*. New York: HarperSanFrancisco, 2006.

Stager, Lawrence E. "The Archaeology of the Family." *BASOR* 260 (1985): 1-35.

———. "The Patrimonial Kingdom of Solomon." In *Symbiosis, Symbolism, and the Power of the Past: Canaan, Ancient Israel, and Their Neighbors from the Late Bronze Age Through Roman Palaestina*, edited by William Dever and Seymour Gitin, 63-74. Winona Lake, IN: Eisenbrauns, 2003.

Stanley, Alan P., ed. *Four Views on the Role of Works at the Final Judgment*. Grand Rapids: Zondervan, 2013.

Stern, David. "The Captive Woman: Hellenization, Greco-Roman Erotic Narrative, and Rabbinic Literature." *Poetics Today* 19, no. 1 (1998): 91-127.

Stern, Philip D. *The Biblical Ḥerem: A Window in Israel's Religious Experience*. BJS 211. Atlanta: Scholars Press, 1991.

———. "The Ḥerem in 1 Kgs 20,42 as an Exegetical Problem." *Biblica* 71 (1990): 43-47.

Strauss, Mark L. *Jesus Behaving Badly: The Puzzling Paradoxes of the Man from Galilee*. Downers Grove, IL: InterVarsity Press, 2015.

Stubblefield, Benjamin Steen. "The Function of the Church in Warfare in the Book of Revelation." PhD diss., Southern Baptist Theological Seminary, 2012.

Stuckey, Johanna H. "Sacred Prostitutes." *MatriFocus* 5, no. 1 (2005): 1-7. www.matrifocus .com/SAM05/spotlight.htm.

Swartley, Willard M. *Slavery, Sabbath, War and Women: Case Issues in Biblical Interpretation*. Waterloo, ON: Herald, 1983.

Tacitus. *The Annals of Imperial Rome*. Translated by Michael Grant. Rev. ed. New York: Penguin Books, 1988.

Tatlock, Jason R. "How in Ancient Times They Sacrificed People: Human Immolation in the Western Mediterranean Basin with Special Emphasis upon Ancient Israel and the Near East." PhD diss., University of Michigan, 2006.

Tetlow, Elisabeth Meier. *Women, Crime, and Punishment in Ancient Law and Society*. Vol. 1, *The Ancient Near East*. New York: Continuum, 2004.

Thistlethwaite, Susan Brooks. "'You May Enjoy the Spoils of Your Enemies': Rape as a Biblical Metaphor for War." *Semeia* 61 (1993): 59-75.

Trible, Phyllis. *Texts of Terror*. OBT. Philadelphia: Fortress, 1984.

Tsumura, David T. *Creation and Destruction: A Reappraisal of the Chaoskampf Theory in the Old Testament*. Winona Lake, IN: Eisenbrauns, 2005.

———. *The First Book of Samuel*. NICOT. Grand Rapids: Eerdmans, 2007.

Vanstiphout, H. L. J., trans. *Epics of Sumerian Kings: The Matter of Aratta*. Edited by Jerrold S. Cooper. SBLWAW 20. Atlanta: Society of Biblical Literature, 2003.

Walton, John H., and J. Harvey Walton. *The Lost World of the Israelite Conquest*. Downers Grove, IL: InterVarsity Press, 2017.

Washington, Harold C. "'Lest He Die in Battle and Another Man Take Her': Violence and the Construction of Gender in the Laws of Deuteronomy 20–22." In *Gender and Law in the Hebrew Bible and the Ancient Near East*, edited by Victor H. Matthews, Bernard M. Levinson, and Tikva Frymer-Kensky, 185-215. JSOTSup 262. Sheffield: Sheffield Academic Press, 1998.

———. "Violence and the Construction of Gender in the Hebrew Bible: A New Historicist Approach." *Biblical Interpretation* 5 (1997): 324-63.

Wazana, Nili. "'For an Impaled Body Is a Curse of God' (Deut 21:23): Impaled Bodies in Biblical Law and Conquest Narratives." In *Law and Narrative in the Bible and Neighbouring Ancient Cultures*, edited by Klaus-Peter Adam, Friedrich Avemarie, and Nili Wazana, 67-98. FAT 2, Reihe 54. New York: Mohr Siebeck, 2012.

———. "'War Crimes' in Amos's Oracles Against the Nations (Amos 1:3–2:3)." In *Literature as Politics, Politics as Literature*, edited by David S. Vanderhooft and Abraham Winitzer, 479-501. Winona Lake, IN: Eisenbrauns, 2013.

Webb, Robert L. "The Roman Examination and Crucifixion of Jesus: Their Historicity and Implications." In *Key Events in the Life of the Historical Jesus*, edited by Darrell L. Bock and Robert L. Webb, 669-773. WUNT 247. Tübingen: Mohr Siebeck, 2009.

Webb, William J. "Balancing Paul's Original-Creation and Pro-Creation Arguments: 1 Cor-inthians 11:11-12 in Light of Modern Embryology." *WTJ* 66 (2004): 275-89.

———. *Corporal Punishment in the Bible: A Redemptive-Movement Hermeneutic for Trou-bling Texts*. Downers Grove, IL: InterVarsity Press, 2011.

———. "Gender Equality and Homosexuality." In *Discovering Biblical Equality: Comple-mentarity Without Hierarchy*, edited by Gordon D. Fee, Rebecca M. Groothuis, and Ronald Pierce, 401-13. Downers Grove, IL: InterVarsity Press, 2004.

———. "The Limits of a Redemptive-Movement Hermeneutic: A Focused Response to T. R. Schreiner." *EQ* 75 (October 2003): 327-42.

———. "A Redemptive-Movement Hermeneutic: Encouraging Dialogue Among Four Evan-gelical Views." *JETS* 48 (2005): 331-49.

———. "A Redemptive-Movement Hermeneutic: The Slavery Analogy." In *Discovering Bib-lical Equality: Complementarity Without Hierarchy*, edited by Gordon D. Fee, Rebecca M. Groothuis, and Ronald Pierce, 382-400. Downers Grove, IL: InterVarsity Press, 2004.

———. "A Redemptive-Movement Model." In *Four Views on Moving Beyond the Bible to Theology*, edited by Gary T. Meadors, 215-48. Grand Rapids: Zondervan, 2009.

———. *Returning Home: New Covenant and Second Exodus as the Context for 2 Corinthians 6.14–7.1*. JSNTSup 85. Sheffield: Sheffield Academic Press, 1993.

———. *Slaves, Women & Homosexuals: Exploring the Hermeneutics of Cultural Analysis*. Downers Grove, IL: InterVarsity Press, 2001.

Weinfeld, Moshe. *Deuteronomy 1–11*. AB. New York: Doubleday, 1991.

———. "Divine Intervention in War in Ancient Israel and the Ancient Near East." In *History, Historiography and Interpretation: Studies in Biblical and Cuneiform Literatures*, edited by Hayim Tadmor and Moshe Weinfeld, 121-47. Jerusalem: Magnes, 1984.

———. *The Promise of Land: The Inheritance of the Land of Canaan by the Israelites*. Berkeley: University of California Press, 1993.

Weippert, Manfred. "'Heiliger Krieg' in Israel und Assyrien: Kritische Anmerkungen zu Gerhard von Rads Konzept des 'Heiligen Krieges in alten Israel.'" *ZAW* 84 (1972): 460-93.

Wenham, Gordon J. "The Deuteronomic Theology of the Book of Joshua." *JBL* 90 (1971): 140-48.

———. *Genesis 1–15*. WBC. Waco, TX: Word Books, 1987.

———. "Sanctuary Symbolism in the Garden of Eden Story." In *Proceedings of the 9th World Congress of Jewish Studies, Jerusalem, August, 1985*, 19-25. Jerusalem: World Union of Jewish Studies, 1986. Reprint, In *I Studied Inscriptions from Before the Flood*, edited by Richard S. Hess and David T. Tsumura, 399-404. Winona Lake, IN: Eisenbrauns, 1994.

Wenham, John. "The Large Numbers in the Bible." *JBQ* 21 (1993): 116-20.

Westermann, Claus. *Genesis 1–11: A Commentary*. Translated by J. J. Scullion. Minne-apolis: Augsburg, 1984.

Wilhelm, Gernot. "Marginalien zu Herodot Klio 199." In *Lingering over Words: Studies in Ancient Near Eastern Literature in Honor of William L. Moran*, edited by Tzvi Abush, John Huehnergard, and Piotr Steinkeller, 503-24. HSS 37. Atlanta: Scholars Press, 1990.

Williams, Bernard. "A Critique of Utilitarianism." In *Vice and Virtue in Everyday Life: Introductory Readings in Ethics*, edited by Christina Sommers and Fred Sommers, 123-32. 3rd ed. New York: Harcourt Brace College, 1993.

Wolde, Ellen J. van. "Yael in Judges 4." *ZAW* 107 (1995): 240-46.

Wolterstorff, Nicholas. "Reading Joshua." In *Divine Evil? The Moral Character of the God of Abraham*, edited by Michael Bergmann, Michael J. Murray, and Michael C. Rea, 236-56. Oxford: Oxford University Press, 2011.

Wong, Gregory T. K. "A Farewell to Arms: Goliath's Death as Rhetoric Against Faith in Arms." *BBR* 23 (2013): 43-55.

Wood, Bryant G. "Did the Israelites Conquer Jericho? A New Look at the Archaeological Evidence." *BARev* 16, no. 2 (1990): 44-58.

Wood, John A. *Perspectives on War in the Bible*. Macon, GA: Mercer University Press, 1998.

Wright, Christopher J. H. "Ethics." In *Dictionary of the Old Testament Historical Books*, edited by Bill T. Arnold and H. G. M. Williamson, 259-68. Downers Grove, IL: InterVarsity Press, 2005.

———. *The God I Don't Understand: Reflections on Tough Questions of Faith*. Grand Rapids: Zondervan, 2008.

———. *God's People in God's Land: Family, Land, and Property in the Old Testament*. Grand Rapids: Eerdmans, 1990.

Wrong, Dennis H. *Power: Its Forms, Bases and Uses*. New York: Harper & Row, 1979.

Yee, Gale A. "By the Hand of a Woman: The Metaphor of the Woman Warrior in Judges 4." *Semeia* (1993): 99-132.

Yoder, John Howard. *The Politics of Jesus: Behold the Man! Our Victorious Lamb*. 2nd ed. Grand Rapids: Eerdmans, 1994.

———. *The War of the Lamb: The Ethics of Nonviolence and Peacemaking*. Edited by Glen Stassen, Mark Thiessen Nation, and Matt Hamsher. Grand Rapids: Brazos, 2009.

York, John O. *The Last Shall Be First: The Rhetoric of Reversal in Luke*. JSNTSup 46. Sheffield: Sheffield Academic Press, 1991.

Younger, K. Lawson, Jr. *Ancient Conquest Accounts: A Study in Ancient Near Eastern and Biblical History Writing*. JSOTSup 98. Sheffield: JSOT Press, 1990.

Zehnder, Markus. "The Annihilation of the Canaanites: Reassessing the Brutality of the Biblical Witness." In *Encountering Violence in the Bible*, edited by Markus Zehnder and Hallvard Hagelia, 263-90. The Bible in the Modern World 55. Sheffield: Sheffield Phoenix, 2013.

Zimmermann, Martin, ed. *Extreme Formen von Gewalt in Bild und Text des Altertums*. MSAW. München: Herbert Utz Verlag, 2009.

AUTHOR INDEX

SCRIPTURE INDEX